The Morals of the Market

The Morals of the Market

Human Rights and the Rise of Neoliberalism

Jessica Whyte

VERSO
London • New York

First published by Verso 2019
© Jessica Whyte 2019

1 3 5 7 9 10 8 6 4 2

Verso
UK: 6 Meard Street, London W1F 0EG
US: 20 Jay Street, Suite 1010, Brooklyn, NY 11201
versobooks.com

Verso is the imprint of New Left Books

ISBN-13: 978-1-78663-311-8
ISBN-13: 978-1-78663-346-0 (LIBRARY)
ISBN-13: 978-1-78663-312-5 (UK EBK)
ISBN-13: 978-1-78663-313-2 (US EBK)

British Library Cataloguing in Publication Data
A catalogue record for this book is available from the British Library

Library of Congress Cataloging-in-Publication Data
A catalog record for this book is available from the Library of Congress

Typeset in Minion by Hewer Text UK Ltd
Printed and bound by CPI Group (UK) Ltd, Croydon CR0 4YY

For Ihab

Contents

Introduction: The Morals of the Market

> Any free society presupposes, in particular, a widely accepted moral code. The principles of this moral code should govern collective no less than private action.
>
> *Draft Mont Pèlerin Society Statement of Aims, 1947*

In the wake of 2017's devastating Grenfell fire, the leader of the British Labour Party, Jeremy Corbyn, sparked outrage by calling for the requisitioning of empty investment properties to house survivors of the incinerated apartment block. As the survivors slept out in churches, mosques and local halls, Corbyn's call to appropriate 'land-banked' houses challenged the sanctity of private property. Writing in *The Times* a month later, Conservative Party peer Daniel Finkelstein cited these events as reason to support the Human Rights Act. Comparing Corbyn to the former Venezuelan president, Hugo Chávez, he argued that this was 'exactly the reason we have human rights protection' – so people can 'secure their individual liberty – in this case their right to property – when the popular will is against them'.[1] For this wealthy lord, human rights were not for Grenfell's survivors, among them undocumented migrants who, as Hannah Arendt noted long ago, should have been the exemplary subjects of human rights.[2]

---

1   Daniel Finkelstein, 'Tories Should Embrace the Human Rights Act', *The Times*, 12 July 2017.

2   Hannah Arendt, *The Origins of Totalitarianism* (San Diego: Harcourt Brace, 1976), p. 299.

Rather, human rights were necessary to protect a weak minority, Kensington's absent property-owners, from the passions of the masses.

At least seventy-one people burned to death in Grenfell Tower. For the survivors, its burnt-out remains must be a bitter reminder of loved ones, family members, friends, neighbours. But Grenfell was not only a private catastrophe; it was also a deeply political, public one. Not only does it tell a contemporary 'tale of two cities', as Corbyn put it, referring to the mansions jutting up alongside neglected social-housing towers in the highly unequal borough; it also reveals the racialisation of poverty and vulnerability in a neoliberal period in which racial segmentation occurs as much through the impersonal, 'colour-blind' operation of the market as through direct racial discrimination. The fire was not only a result of what the Grenfell Action Group had previously warned was the dangerous 'ineptitude and incompetence' of the council, which had failed to install a sprinkler system or repair blocked fire-exits. The council's decision to clad the building's façade to improve its appearance when viewed from wealthy surrounding areas – and then to cut costs by opting for cheap, flammable cladding – also played a role, as did the privatisation of fire-safety assessments and cuts to the fire service.[3] Grenfell embodied a 'neoliberal urbanism' characterised by the downgrading of social housing, the flouting of regulations, and the outsourcing of renovations to the lowest bidder, in a context of gentrification and the erosion of the supply of social housing.[4]

Faced with such inequality and neglect, it would be easy to dismiss Finkelstein's invocations of the human rights of investors as pure cynicism. Human rights, it is commonly supposed, embody a concern for human dignity that is deeply at odds with the imperatives of wealth accumulation, and are among the few weapons the most marginalised still have. Indeed, in the wake of the fire, a United Nations envoy announced that the UK might have breached its obligation to provide a human right to housing, and the independent Equality and Human Rights Commission appointed a panel of legal experts to examine whether the government had violated its obligations under the Human Rights Act. One year on, with little affordable housing in the borough,

---

3   Sam Knight, 'The Year the Grenfell Tower Fire Revealed the Lie That Londoners Tell Themselves', *New Yorker*, 27 December 2017.

4   Lisa Tilley and Robbie Shilliam, 'Raced Markets: An Introduction', *New Political Economy* 23: 5 (2018), p. 534.

only 82 of the 203 households who lost their homes in the fire had been permanently re-housed.[5]

However easy it is to dismiss the idea of Kensington's absentee investors as the subjects of human rights, it is more difficult to demarcate a 'true' human rights discourse from cynical appropriations of it. The 'human right to dominate' exists alongside the human rights of the dominated, and human rights have often proved more useful in protecting the wealthy and legitimising the interventions of the most powerful states than in protecting the powerless.[6] Rather than being an isolated instance, Finkelstein's argument for the human rights of property owners has a long lineage among neoliberal politicians and thinkers. When former British prime minister Margaret Thatcher began privatising council housing in the 1980s, she justified it as a way to secure human rights. Evoking a deep connection between liberty and property, Thatcher argued that 'countries which deny private property rights also deny other human rights'.[7] The claim that property rights are an 'essential foundation for other human rights', as the Chicago School economist Milton Friedman put it, provided a political justification for the neoliberal counter-revolution of the late twentieth century.[8]

The language of human rights is notoriously slippery, marked by a 'tactical polyvalence' (in Michel Foucault's words) according to which the effect of identical formulations differs 'according to who is speaking, his position of power [and] the institutional context in which he happens to be speaking'.[9] Nonetheless, to recognise that human rights lack a single meaning – that they are contingent political discourses, not unchangeable, metaphysical attributes of human nature – is not enough to explain the ease with which human rights discourses have been mobilised in defence of wealth and power in the period of neoliberal hegemony. Nor does it explain why it was that a distinctive politics of human

---

5   Robert Booth and Owen Bowcott, 'Where Do We Stand a Year after the Grenfell Tower Fire?', *Guardian*, 14 June 2018.

6   Nicola Perugini and Neve Gordon, *The Human Right to Dominate*, Oxford Studies in Culture and Politics (Oxford/New York: Oxford University Press, 2015).

7   Monica Prasad, *The Politics of Free Markets* (Chicago: University of Chicago Press, 2006), p. 132.

8   Milton Friedman and Rose D. Friedman, 'Appendix B, Chapter 28 (Free to Choose): Documents', in Milton Friedman and Rose D. Friedman, eds, *Two Lucky People: Memoirs* (Chicago: University of Chicago Press, 1998), p. 605.

9   Michel Foucault, *The History of Sexuality Vol. 1* (New York: Pantheon, 1990), p. 100.

rights became prevalent in the period of neoliberal ascendancy and flourished alongside the retrenchment of the welfare state. It does not help us explain why, as the neoliberals instituted a closure of the political imagination by insisting that there was no alternative to endless austerity, human rights defenders disparaged revolutionary politics as totalitarian. For some of their most prominent defenders, the role of human rights was 'not to open the gates of paradise, but to bolt the gates of hell' (in the French 'New Philosopher' André Glucksmann's words).[10]

This book is an investigation of the historical and conceptual relations between human rights and neoliberalism. It has often been noted that the embrace of the language of human rights by leaders of Anglo-American and European states, and by a new generation of international human rights NGOs, took place in the late 1970s, just as governments also began to embrace neoliberalism.[11] Attesting to this convergence, the award of the 1976 Nobel Prize in Economics to the Chicago School's Milton Friedman was followed the next year by Amnesty International's 1977 Nobel Peace Prize. This book seeks to explain why these two revivals and reinventions of liberalism took place at the same time, and why their trajectories have been so intertwined ever since.

In attempting to understand this convergence, I follow the lead of many thinkers who have pointed to convergences and compatibilities between neoliberalism and human rights. Upendra Baxi's pioneering work on 'trade-related market-friendly human rights' traced attempts by major corporations to mobilise the normative force of human rights to defend the rights of capital.[12] Makau Mutua has long argued that the failure of human rights NGOs to pay attention to 'economic powerlessness' has helped to naturalise capitalist markets and subordinated labour relations.[13] Costas Douzinas has similarly argued that negative freedom, which he frames as a euphemism for rejecting state regulation of the economy, has 'dominated the Western conception of human rights and turned them into the perfect companion of

10   André Glucksmann, 'The 2004 TIME 100 – Bernard Kouchner', *Time*, 26 April 2014.

11   See, for instance Samuel Moyn, 'A Powerless Companion: Human Rights in the Age of Neoliberalism', *Law and Contemporary Problems* 77 (2015); Naomi Klein, *The Shock Doctrine: The Rise of Disaster Capitalism* (New York: Picador, 2008).

12   Upendra Baxi, *The Future of Human Rights* (Oxford: Oxford University Press, 2008).

13   Makau Mutua, 'Human Rights and Powerlessness: Pathologies of Choice and Substance Essay Collection: Classcrits: Part I: Thinking through Law's Questions of Class, Economics, and Inequality', *Buffalo Law Review* 56 (2008).

neoliberalism'.[14] For Wendy Brown, the politics of human rights not only 'converges neatly with the requisites of liberal imperialism and global free trade', but also serves to legitimise them.[15] And Susan Marks has suggested that the more recent turn to examining the 'root causes' of human rights violations has in fact shielded the structural context in which violations of human rights are systematically reproduced.[16]

In order to extend these observations, this book returns to another parallel history. Less well noted than the simultaneous rise of neoliberal and human rights in the 1970s is the fact that, in 1947, when, the UN Commission on Human Rights met for the first time at Lake Success to begin drafting an international bill of rights, a group of economists, philosophers and historians were gathered across the Atlantic in the Swiss Alpine village of Mont Pèlerin to consider the principles that could animate a new liberal order. The efforts of the first group resulted in the Universal Declaration of Human Rights (UDHR), which was conceived as 'a common standard of achievement for all peoples and all nations'. The latter grouping founded the Mont Pèlerin Society (MPS), which has been aptly described as the 'neoliberal thought collective'.[17]

While most existing accounts of the relation between human rights and neoliberalism begin in the 1970s, I return to the 1940s to trace the development of neoliberal human rights thinking in the decades prior to the neoliberal ascendancy. In 1947, the divergences between those who drafted the UDHR and the neoliberals of Mont Pèlerin were more significant than their convergences. While both were concerned with threats to human dignity and liberty in the wake of World War II, their solutions differed markedly: the human rights delegates adopted an extensive list of social and economic rights, while the neoliberals depicted state welfare and planning as totalitarian threats to 'Western civilisation'. My focus is on the ways in which neoliberal thinkers viewed the rise of human rights, and then mobilised and developed the language associated with them for their own ends. I suggest that a better

---

14   Costas Douzinas, 'Seven Theses on Human Rights: (3) Neoliberal Capitalism & Voluntary Imperialism', *Critical Legal Thinking* (blog), 23 May 2013, at criticallegalthinking.com.

15   Wendy Brown, '"The Most We Can Hope For . . .": Human Rights and the Politics of Fatalism', *South Atlantic Quarterly* 103: 2 (10 June 2004).

16   Susan Marks, 'Human Rights and Root Causes', *Modern Law Review* 74: 1 (January 2011).

17   Philip Mirowski and Dieter Plehwe, eds, *The Road from Mont Pèlerin: The Making of the Neoliberal Thought Collective* (Cambridge: Harvard University Press, 2009).

understanding of the role of human rights in earlier neoliberal thinking can help us to understand their later convergence.

When a distinctive and powerful version of human rights began to be advocated by NGOs and the US state thirty years after the adoption of the UDHR, earlier attempts to enshrine rights to housing, food, education and medical care were supplanted by a narrow focus on civil and political rights. This version of human rights became hegemonic alongside neoliberal assaults on both the welfare state and postcolonial attempts to restructure the international economy in the interests of global equality. Human rights became the dominant ideology of a period marked by the demise of revolutionary utopias and socialist politics, succinctly encapsulated by Thatcher's insistence that 'there is no alternative'.

The economic transformations of this period were stark, from the rise of austerity and the retrenchment of state welfare provision to the commodification of public services, the deregulation of the finance sector and growing indebtedness. Consequently, critics of neoliberalism have homed in on its economic agenda. Nonetheless, I contend that we cannot understand why human rights and neoliberalism flourished together if we view neoliberalism as an exclusively economic doctrine.

Neoliberalism Against the Economy

Neoliberalism is commonly understood as an amoral economic ideology that subordinates all values to an economic rationality. In a powerful instance of this critique, Wendy Brown argues that neoliberalism's 'economization' of life configures the human 'always, only, and everywhere as *homo economicus*'.[18] Elsewhere she argues that, despite its pragmatic reconciliation with neoconservatism in the United States, neoliberalism is 'expressly amoral at the level of both ends and means'.[19] This form of criticism is not new, and nor is it confined to this neoliberal form of capitalism; it resembles nothing so much as *The Communist Manifesto*'s awe-struck descriptions of the bourgeoisie, which leaves 'no other nexus between man and man than naked self-interest, than callous

---

18 Wendy Brown, *Undoing the Demos: Neoliberalism's Stealth Revolution* (Cambridge, MA: MIT, 2015), p. 31.

19 Wendy Brown, 'American Nightmare: Neoliberalism, Neoconservatism, and De-Democratization', *Political Theory* 34: 6 (2006), p. 692.

"cash payment".[20] Although the argument that capitalism drowns all values in the 'icy water of egotistical calculation' was borrowed from capitalism's earlier conservative critics, Marx and Engels were without nostalgia for feudal bonds cemented by religion and sentimentality. Contemporary critics, while largely agreeing that neoliberalism reduces all values to cash value, have been similarly divided about whether this is cause for celebration or denunciation.

For Michel Foucault, lecturing in 1979, the newly ascendant neoliberalism seemed to offer a refreshing break with the punitive moralism of earlier liberalisms.[21] In the 'purely economic analysis' of the Chicago School's human capital theorist Gary Becker, Foucault saw a fundamentally amoral account of the criminal as a *homo economicus*, who acts expecting a profit and bears the risk of penal sanction. From this perspective, Foucault notes, 'there is no difference between the infraction of the highway code and a premediated murder'.[22] Consequently, a neoliberal penal policy would merely adjust penalties and rules to reduce the supply of crime, while eschewing the attempt to discipline the criminal and cure her of an assumed pathology. Foucault speculated that a neoliberal society would not be a moralising society of normalisation and exclusion, but one in which 'minority individuals and practices are tolerated'.[23] Although he was simultaneously engaged in promoting a new interventionist politics of human rights as a means to open up spaces of freedom for the governed, Foucault seems not to have considered the relation between this new moral politics and the seemingly amoral neoliberalism he so astutely analysed.[24]

20　Karl Marx and Friedrich Engels, *The Communist Manifesto* (London: Pluto, 2008), p. 37.

21　Mitchell Dean, 'Michel Foucault's "Apology" for Neoliberalism', *Journal of Political Power* 7: 3 (2 September 2014).

22　Michel Foucault, *The Birth of Biopolitics: Lectures at the Collège de France 1978–1979*, ed. Michel Senellart, transl. Graham Burchell (New York: Palgrave Macmillan, 2008), pp. 253–4.

23　Ibid., pp. 259–60.

24　For a brilliant account of Foucault's mobilisation of the language of rights, see Ben Golder, *Foucault and the Politics of Rights* (Redwood City, CA: Stanford University Press, 2015). See also Jessica Whyte, 'Human Rights: Confronting Governments? Michel Foucault and the Right to Intervene', in Costas Douzinas, Matthew Stone and Illan Rua Wall, eds, *New Critical Legal Thinking: Law and the Political* (London: Routledge, 2012); and Jessica Whyte, 'Is Revolution Desirable? Michel Foucault on Revolution, Neoliberalism and Rights', in Ben Golder, ed., *Re-Reading Foucault: On Law, Power and Rights* (London: Routledge, 2012).

For Brown, who is more attentive to the impact of neoliberalism on politics, the rise of neoliberal economism is a fundamental threat to democracy and rights.[25] Neoliberalism constitutes subjects who are indifferent to democratic political values and positively antagonistic to egalitarianism, she argues. Consequently, political problems are transformed into individual ones with market solutions, while civil liberties, the rule of law and fair elections are 'wholly desacralized'.[26] Paradoxically, she argues, this provides fertile ground for neoconservative attempts to bolster the foundations of family, religion and state, partly through a civilisational discourse that moralises 'a certain imaginary of the West and its values'.[27]

If neoliberalism is understood in such amoral terms, then international human rights NGOs, with their focus on individual liberty, human dignity, freedom of conscience and bodily integrity, seem an important antidote to the unrelenting economisation of life. Despite her own trenchant criticisms of rights and liberalism in previous works, Brown's indictment of neoliberalism leads her to a surprisingly sympathetic account of the liberal-democratic political model she believes we are losing: 'We are no longer creatures of moral autonomy, freedom, or equality', she writes; 'We no longer choose our own ends or the means to them.'[28] Although Brown provides a compelling account of the economisation of rights in a neoliberal era, the assumption remains that older ideals of dignity, rights and 'even soulfulness' have been sacrificed upon the altar of an unrelentingly economistic dogma.[29]

From the perspective of this book, these accounts of the amoral economism of neoliberalism miss the distinctive morality that was central to its rise. What distinguished the neoliberals of the twentieth century from their nineteenth-century precursors, I argue, was not a narrow understanding of the human as *homo economicus*, but the belief that a functioning competitive market required an adequate moral and legal foundation. As Foucault recognised of the German ordoliberals, neoliberal thinkers aimed to establish (or revive) a set of moral values that would secure social integration in a context of market competition. The founding statement of the Mont Pèlerin Society makes this clear:

25   Brown, *Undoing the Demos*, p. 17.
26   Brown, 'American Nightmare', p. 702.
27   Ibid., p. 709.
28   Brown, *Undoing the Demos*, p. 42.
29   Ibid., p. 111.

diagnosing a civilisational crisis characterised by the disappearance of the conditions for 'human dignity' and threats to freedom of thought and expression, it states that these developments 'have been fostered by the growth of a view of history which denies all absolute moral standards'.[30] Rather than an external supplement, or a pragmatic partner, social conservatism, including explicit appeals to family values, Christianity and 'Western civilisation', was foundational to the consolidation of organised neoliberalism in the mid twentieth century.[31]

Far from reducing all of life to economics, I show that the neoliberals of the mid twentieth century were deeply suspicious of the very idea of the economy. In his polemical 1944 critique of socialist planning, *The Road to Serfdom*, the founder of the Mont Pèlerin Society, Friedrich Hayek, complained about his contemporaries' preoccupation with economic concerns. The values that rank lowest today and are dismissed as nineteenth-century illusions, he argued, are the 'moral values' – 'liberty and independence, truth and intellectual honesty, peace and democracy, and respect for the individual *qua* man instead of merely as the member of an organized group'.[32] Around the same time, the German ordoliberal Wilhelm Röpke criticised the 'economism' that 'judges everything in relation to the economy and in terms of material productivity, making material and economic interests the center of things'.[33]

No doubt there are aspects of neoliberalism that support the charge of economisation. From the Austrian School economist Ludwig von Mises's argument that the market is a permanent election in which each dollar counts as a ballot, to the US public-choice theorist James Buchanan's reconfiguring of politics as a sphere of self-maximising individual competition, to the Chicago School economist Gary Becker's contention that a marriage is a two-person firm and children are household-produced commodities, neoliberalism appears to be the extension of economic rationality to all areas of life.[34] Yet, drawing on

---

30 Statement of Aims, in Dieter Plehwe, 'Introduction', in Mirowski and Plehwe, *Road from Mont Pèlerin*, pp. 24–5.

31 Ibid., p. 5.

32 Friedrich Hayek, *The Road to Serfdom: Text and Documents*, ed. Bruce Caldwell (Chicago: University of Chicago Press, 2007), p. 218.

33 Wilhelm Röpke, *The Social Crisis of Our Time*, transl. Annette Schiffer Jacobsohn and Peter Schiffer Jacobsohn (Chicago: University of Chicago Press, 1950), p. 53.

34 Gary S. Becker, *A Treatise on the Family* (Cambridge: Harvard University Press, 1991); James M. Buchanan, *Theory of Public Choice: Political Applications of Economics* (Ann Arbor: University of Michigan Press, 1972).

the ancient Greek origins of economics in *oikonomia* – the management of a household – the early neoliberals worried that conceiving of the overall market order as an economy licensed the belief that this order was governed by collective solidarity and had a single set of ends that could be managed by Keynesian or social-democratic planners. This, they argued, was the very definition of totalitarianism, and a threat to the individualistic social order of 'the West'. The competitive market they sought to revive was not simply a more efficient means of distributing resources; it was the basic institution of a moral and 'civilised' society, and a necessary support for individual rights.

Friedrich Hayek and the Morals of the Market

In December 1961, Hayek addressed the Congress of American Industry on 'The Moral Elements of Free Enterprise'. The congress, held at New York's Waldorf Astoria hotel, was sponsored by The National Association of Manufacturers, which had a long history of challenging state welfare and organised labour, and attempting to 'sell free enterprise the way Proctor and Gamble sold soap'.[35] Hayek spoke alongside the professor and executive member of the American Meat Institute in Chicago, Herrell DeGraff, and his fellow MPS members and journalists John Davenport and Felix Morley, all of whom addressed questions of morals and values. Hayek's message was that free enterprise required 'not only moral standards but moral standards of a particular kind'.[36] Like the manufacturers he was addressing, Hayek and his MPS companions had long been convinced that a market order required a conducive moral order. From their perspective, the rise of socialism and social democracy was, first of all, a moral problem. No free society would survive, the Austrian economist told this sympathetic business audience, without a moral climate that instils personal responsibility and regards it as just

---

35   Central to this sales pitch was the argument that individual freedom rested on three pillars: representative democracy, civil and religious liberty, and free private enterprise; take away one leg of this 'tripod of freedom', the representatives of business warned, and the whole edifice would crumble. Richard S. Tedlow, 'The National Association of Manufacturers and Public Relations during the New Deal', *Business History Review* 50, no. 1 (1976): p. 33.

36   Friedrich Hayek, 'The Moral Element in Free Enterprise', *Studies in Philosophy, Politics and Economics* (New York: Simon and Schuster, 1967), p. 230.

that people are rewarded materially based on how valuable their services are to their fellows.

Hayek provided a more developed account of the morals of a market society in his late work, *Law, Legislation and Liberty*. Evoking the fall of Rome – and the thesis of its great historian Edward Gibbon, who attributed that fall to a decline in ancient virtue – Hayek warned that, whether or not Gibbon was correct about Rome, 'there can be no doubt that moral and religious beliefs can destroy a civilization'.[37] For Hayek and those he brought together to form the Mont Pèlerin Society, the demise of the morals that sustained a market order threatened their own civilisation with destruction.

'Morals', in this context, referred both to sentiments about right and wrong action and to the system of informal rules of conduct that guide the action of individuals. Hayek distinguished morals from laws by arguing that morals lacked coercive enforcement, but that this did not make them any less crucial to the functioning of a market society. Indeed, Hayek believed that liberalism had taken a significant wrong turn in the nineteenth century, when the British liberal philosopher John Stuart Mill had begun to criticise the 'tyranny of the prevailing morals' thereby encouraging a disregard for moral traditions and a growing 'permissiveness' in society.[38] Although Hayek argued there can be no single, absolute system of rules or morals independent of social organisation, he nonetheless contended that only one system of morals could make possible an open or 'humanistic' society in which individuals are valued as such and are relatively free to pursue their own plans.[39]

According to Hayek, a market society, in which people are guided primarily by expected monetary returns, 'requires somewhat different moral views' than one in which they strive towards shared goals.[40] What Hayek called the 'morals of the market' were a set of individualistic, commercial values that prioritised the pursuit of self-interest above the development of common purposes. A market society

---

37 Friedrich Hayek, *Law, Legislation and Liberty, vol. 2: The Mirage of Social Justice* (London: Routledge, 1998), p. 67.

38 Friedrich Hayek et al., *Nobel Prize-Winning Economist Oral History Transcript*, (Los Angeles: Oral History Program, University of California, Los Angeles, 1983), p. 282, at archive.org

39 Hayek, *Law, Legislation and Liberty, vol. 2*, p. 27.

40 Ibid., p. 144.

required a moral framework that sanctioned wealth accumulation and inequality, promoted individual and familial responsibility, and fostered submission to the impersonal results of the market process at the expense of the deliberate pursuit of collectively formulated ends. It also required that moral obligations are limited to the requirement that we refrain from harming others, and do not require positive obligations to others.

This account of morals was deeply functionalist; the morals of the market, Hayek contended, function to sustain the only order that embraced 'nearly all mankind': the competitive market order.[41] Given that moral rules exist to support the market order, Hayek urged that 'conduciveness to that order be accepted as a standard by which all particular institutions are judged'.[42] This was Hayek's own version of the German ordoliberal conviction that economic policies must be *systemgerech*, or compatible with the whole economic system.[43] This market-conduciveness, or compatibility, gave the neoliberals a criterion for assessing claims to human rights that was more precise than a simple distinction between civil and political rights and social and economic rights: to the extent rights supported market relations, the neoliberals actively promoted them; when claims for rights interfered with the competitive market, by requiring state intervention and non-market forms of obligation and redistribution, they opposed them as though the fate of civilisation depended on it.

Today, much critical work on human rights is devoted to deflating the notion that human rights are the codification of a moral sense originating in human nature. Such a claim has little critical purchase on neoliberal accounts of human rights. Hayek, for instance, explicitly rejected the view that morals and rules are 'permanently implanted in an unalterable nature of man'.[44] His mentor Mises had put it in these blunt terms decades earlier: 'The fact is that Nature grants no rights at all'.[45] Rejecting the dichotomy between natural law and rationally constructed rules, Hayek argued that culture, institutions and morals are 'neither natural nor artificial, neither

---

41   Ibid., p. 113.
42   Ibid.
43   Ibid., n. 21, p. 188.
44   Ibid., p. 60.
45   Ludwig von Mises, *Socialism: An Economic and Sociological Analysis*, transl. J. Kahane (New Haven: Yale University Press, 1962), p. 62.

genetically transmitted nor rationally designed'.[46] Morals develop, he argued, through the unconscious selection of the values and institutions that provide those who submit to them with the greatest benefits. The morals of the market initially emerged in urban, commercial centres, Hayek argued, where substantive bonds were weaker and individuals more accustomed to cooler, more distant market relations with others.[47]

Hayek drew on the social theory of the Scottish Enlightenment to develop an evolutionary account of morality. Appropriating the work of Adam Smith and Adam Ferguson – for whom human history supposedly passed through a sequence of stages, from the hunter to the herdsman to the farmer to the trader – Hayek argued that the evolution from the 'small band' to the 'Great Society' required the abandonment of feelings of personal loyalty and egalitarian commitments more suitable to tribal existence. It required that the purpose-driven rules of small societies, in which individuals worked together towards shared ends, were replaced by abstract rules applicable to large numbers of strangers – and ultimately to all of humanity.[48] From this perspective, the transition to the market economy was achieved through (deeply resented) breaches of the solidarity that governed earlier social relations. 'Man', Hayek contended, 'has been civilized very much against his wishes.'[49]

---

46 Friedrich Hayek, 'Epilogue: The Three Sources of Human Values', in Friedrich Hayek, *Law, Legislation and Liberty: A New Statement of the Liberal Principles of Justice and Political Economy, vol. 3: The Political Order of a Free People* (London: Routledge, 1998), p. 155.

47 Hayek, *Law, Legislation and Liberty, vol. 2*, p. 146. Hayek drew partly on the philosopher H. B. Acton's defence of 'the morals of markets', in his 1971 book commissioned for the Institute for Economic Affairs by the Mont Pèlerin Society member Arthur Seldon. H. B. Acton, *The Morals of Markets: An Ethical Exploration* (London: Longman/IEA, 1971). He also relied on the work of the economic historian H.M. Robertson, whose 1933 study of the rise of economic individualism challenged Max Weber's account of the Calvinist influence on the 'spirit of capitalism' and argued that it was the development of industry and commerce that had brought about a shift in morals, not vice versa. H.M. Robertson, *Aspects of the Rise of Economic Individualism: A Criticism of Max Weber and his School* (New York: Kelly and Milliman, 1959).

48 Although Hayek hoped humanity would continue 'gradually to approach' a scenario in which the same rules applied to all humans, he warned that the attempt to realise this by allowing the free movement of people would re-awaken nationalist sentiments and set back the cause of freedom. While trade should be free to cross borders, the free movement of people remained an 'ultimate ideal' which should not be pursued impatiently. Hayek, *Law, Legislation and Liberty, vol. 2*, p. 57–8.

49 Hayek, 'Epilogue', p. 168.

In attributing the development of morality to the 'survival of the successful', Hayek presented a racialised narrative that took for granted that those Europeans who had developed commercial relations were more successful than others.[50] He saw their success as a result of their adoption of 'moral conceptions which do not prescribe particular aims but rather general rules limiting the range of permitted actions'.[51] In his contemporaries' demands for social justice and social and economic rights Hayek saw atavistic attempts on the part of 'the non-domesticated or un-civilized' members of society to resurrect the morals of a 'tribal society'.[52] From such a perspective, socialism and social democracy were not merely economic threats to the productivity and efficiency of economic relations; they were civilisational regressions, the return of 'suppressed primordial instincts' that threatened the moral foundations of the competitive market.[53]

One of my key arguments here is that the neoliberal argument for the competitive market was itself moral and political, rather than strictly economic. Early neoliberals attributed to the market a series of anti-political virtues: checking and dispersing power, facilitating social cooperation, pacifying conflict, and securing individual liberty and rights. They presented commercial or 'civil society' as a space of mutually beneficial, voluntary relations that contrasted with the violence, coercion and conflict of the political realm. Market coordination was less a means to enhance productivity and efficiency than a substitute for the violence, coercion and despotism that they argued were endemic to politics – and especially to mass politics. Only the widespread adoption of the morals of the market, Hayek argued, offered 'the distant hope of a universal order of peace'.

The Sweetness of Commerce

In extolling the pacifying virtues of the market, I argue that the neoliberals revived an older political argument for capitalism first identified by Albert Hirschman in his classic 1977 book *The Passions and the Interests*. There, Hirschman uncovered what he called the

---

50   Friedrich Hayek, *The Constitution of Liberty: The Definitive Edition*, ed. Ronald Hamowy (Chicago: University of Chicago Press, 2011), p. 112.
51   Hayek, *Law, Legislation and Liberty, vol. 2*, p. 144.
52   Ibid., p. 147.
53   Hayek, 'Epilogue', p. 165.

'*doux*-commerce' ('sweetness of commerce') thesis, which, he argued, was conventional wisdom in the mid eighteenth century. Hirschman's account of the moral virtues of the market began with a sentence in Baron de Montesquieu's *The Spirit of the Laws*, which he ultimately chose for his own book's epigraph: 'It is fortunate for men to be in a situation where, though their *passions* may prompt them to be wicked [*méchants*], they have nevertheless an interest in not being so.'[54] The view that the interests could check the passions, Hirschman argued, was a message of salvation for a world trapped between the violence of the passions and the seeming ineffectiveness of reason.[55] Far from viewing commerce as corrupting, as republican thinkers tended to do, Montesquieu praised it for its 'spirit of frugality, economy, moderation, work, wisdom, tranquility, order and rule'.[56] Commerce, he contended, is a source of gentleness, softness and polish, which 'cures destructive prejudices' and leads to more gentle mores.[57] For Montesquieu, those who pursued their interests through the market stood in a relation of mutual need, and thus the 'natural effect of commerce is to lead to peace'.[58]

Montesquieu wrote at a time when world trade was violent and dangerous, inseparable from colonial conquest and the slave trade. Marx mocked such accounts of the pacifying role of commerce in his writings on the 'primitive accumulation' of capital. After describing in garish detail the history of Dutch colonialism, with its secret prisons, assassinations, bribery and enslavement, he remarked sarcastically, 'That is peaceful [*doux*] commerce!' Yet, according to Hirschman, it was only when this violence 'came home' – with the French Revolution, the Napoleonic Wars and the social dislocation of the industrial revolution – that belief in the sweetness of commerce lost its grip on the European imagination. By the twentieth century, Hirschman concluded, no observer could still subscribe to this hopeful vision of the pacifying market. Its subsequent defenders therefore focused on its economic benefits, borrowing from Adam Smith to valorise the increased

---

54   Albert O. Hirschman, *The Passions and the Interests: Political Arguments for Capitalism before Its Triumph* (Princeton: Princeton University Press, 2013), p. xxii.

55   Ibid., p. 52.

56   Baron de Montesquieu, Baron, *The Spirit of the Laws* (Cambridge: Cambridge University Press, 1989), p. 48.

57   Ibid., p. 338.

58   Ibid.

productivity and efficiency made possible by the division of labour. For most critics, the neoliberal thinkers exemplified this shift from a political to an economic justification for capitalism.

Unlike Hirschman, I argue that a version of this justification of capitalism was central to neoliberal thought in the inauspicious circumstances of the twentieth century. For Hayek, who described his own project as doing 'for the twentieth century what Montesquieu had done for the eighteenth', and for his neoliberal colleagues, the challenge was to revive the argument that a society coordinated through the competitive market would replace the coercion, conquest and conflict endemic to politics with voluntary, mutually beneficial, harmonious social relations. The tendency to view neoliberalism as the dominance of the economy over all other spheres of life has obscured its distinctive *political* argument for the competitive market. Throughout the twentieth century, neoliberals argued that the demise of market competition was a threat to individual freedom that augured the rule of a coercive, bureaucratic power. They faulted socialism and social democracy for politicising distribution and replacing consensual market relations between individuals with violent sectional conflicts over ends. In the wars of the twentieth century, they saw the inevitable result of a turn away from the market economy.

Variants of Hirschman's thesis run through Mises's argument that, if not for the greater productivity of the division of labour, there would be *no* sentiments of sympathy or good will, but only 'endless bloody fighting'.[59] It is central to Hayek's description of the market as a 'catallaxy' – a term derived from the Greek verb *katallatein*, which meant both to exchange and 'to turn from an enemy into a friend'.[60] It informs Röpke's argument that allowing individuals to pursue their interests through the market leads to harmonious social coordination, while the pursuit of interests through the political process brings 'millions of conflicting interests' into play.[61] And it appears even in the positivist Friedman's argument that the use of 'political channels' strains the 'social cohesion essential for a stable society', while the use of the market

---

59 Ludwig von Mises, *Human Action: A Treatise on Economics* (San Francisco: Fox & Wilkes, 1996), p. 152.

60 Friedrich Hayek, 'The Confusion of Language in Political Thought', Institute of Economic Affairs Occasional Papers no. 20 (1968), p. 29.

61 Wilhelm Röpke, *The Moral Foundations of Civil Society* (New Brunswick: Transaction, 2002), p. 21.

reduces tensions by making it unnecessary for individuals to agree on ultimate ends.[62]

For the neoliberals, the competitive market was not simply a more efficient technology for the distribution of goods and services; it was the guarantor of individual freedom and rights, and the necessary condition of social peace. If neoliberal thinkers and human rights activists could find common cause, as I suggest they could, this is largely because the concerns of twentieth-century neoliberals were far less narrowly economic than existing accounts tend to allow.

What Do Neoliberal Human Rights Do?

The Chicago School economist Deirdre McCloskey holds up the drafting of the UDHR as evidence that market capitalism promotes the 'temperance to educate oneself in business and in life, to listen to the customer humbly, to resist the temptations to cheat, to ask quietly whether there might be a compromise here – Eleanor Roosevelt negotiating the United Nations Declaration of Human Rights in 1948'.[63] A recent defender of human rights similarly argues that the drafting of human rights standards provides a model for 'deliberative, nonviolent, and noncoercive processes of global governance and change' that could be extended to other areas.[64] No doubt the drafting of the UDHR required compromise between defenders of rival political, economic and religious systems. But one thing the drafters largely agreed on – and Roosevelt was no exception – was that the unrestrained market produced not sweetness and civility but conflict and disorder. Looking back in 1966, Hayek was far less complimentary than McCloskey about the compromises that produced the UDHR: the document, he argued, was an incoherent attempt to merge the liberal rights tradition with a starkly different one derived from 'the Marxist Russian Revolution'.[65]

---

62 Milton Friedman, *Capitalism and Freedom* (Chicago: University of Chicago Press, 2002), p. 23.

63 Deirdre McCloskey, *The Bourgeois Virtues: Ethics for an Age of Commerce* (Chicago: University of Chicago Press, 2006), p. 507. I take the question heading this subsection from the title of Talal Asad's excellent essay: Talal Asad, 'What Do Human Rights Do? An Anthropological Enquiry', *Theory and Event* 4: 4 (2000).

64 Kathryn Sikkink, *Evidence for Hope: Making Human Rights Work in the 21st Century* (Princeton, NJ: Princeton University Press, 2017), p. 16.

65 Hayek, *Law, Legislation and Liberty, vol. 2*, p. 103.

Throughout the book, I examine the neoliberal understanding of human rights alongside the diverse conceptions of rights and obligations that motivated the drafters of the UDHR and the two legally binding human rights covenants. Along with classical civil and political rights, these documents enshrined extensive lists of social and economic rights, and, in the case of the covenants, gave pride of place to the right of nations to self-determination. For the neoliberals of the time, the UN human rights process looked less like a model of peaceful market cooperation and more like the globalisation of the 'collectivism' that threatened at home. They believed the attempt to secure rights to social welfare and national self-determination would threaten the market order and 'Western civilisation'. However, I show that, despite their horror at the 'collectivism' and 'politicisation' that characterised the human rights process in the United Nations, the neoliberals did not simply turn away from human rights; rather, they developed their own account of human rights as moral and legal supports for a liberal market order.

In 1992 Friedman was asked about the original purpose of the Mont Pèlerin Society. There was 'no doubt', he replied, that its original purpose was 'to promote a classical, liberal philosophy, that is, a free economy, a free society, socially, civilly and in human rights'.[66] Coming from a thinker who described the authoritarian regime of Chile's General Pinochet as an economic and political 'miracle', this invocation of human rights appears out of place.[67] After all, human rights NGOs came to prominence in the 1970s precisely for contesting the torture and disappearances that accompanied neoliberal shock treatment in the Southern Cone. According to a prominent critical view, neoliberal emphases on competitive markets and austerity were 'inherently inimical to the protection of human rights', resting on completely different normative foundations.[68] As a recent primer on human rights puts it, 'neoliberalism is one logic in the world today; human rights is the other'.[69] From this perspective, the universalisation of human rights and the extension

---

66   David Levy, 'Interview with Milton Friedman', 1 June 1992, at minneapolisfed. org.

67   Milton Friedman, 'Passing Down the Chilean Recipe', *Foreign Affairs* 73: 1 (1994), p. 177.

68   Paul O'Connell, 'On Reconciling Irreconcilables: Neo-Liberal Globalisation and Human Rights', *Human Rights Law Review* 7: 3 (1 January 2007), p. 484.

69   Judith Blaue and Alberto Moncado, *Human Rights: A Primer* (Paradigm, 2009), p. 15.

of global capitalism and the world market are 'the two major, and often competing, globalising forces that strut the world stage'.[70]

But Friedman's account deserves to be taken seriously, even if it illuminates the time in which he was speaking more than it does the mid twentieth century. While one scholar has noted that human and political rights were 'notably absent' from the 1947 MPS statement of aims, at that time human rights were not yet an obvious aspect of a liberal tradition.[71] The phrase 'human rights' is similarly absent from the Oxford Manifesto, issued that same year by representatives from nineteen liberal parties as a statement of principles of the 'Liberal International'.[72] The discourse of human rights was still under construction, and there was no consensus even among liberals on the relationship between the newer language of human rights and earlier affirmations of the 'rights of man', 'fundamental rights', humanitarianism, or individual freedom under the rule of law. The neoliberals were active participants in that process of construction. Human rights played a significant and overlooked role in neoliberals' mid-century efforts to challenge socialism, social democracy and state planning, and neoliberal thinkers contributed more than has been acknowledged to the version of human rights that came to prominence decades later. By 1992, when Friedman spoke, the neoliberal argument that only a liberal market economy could foster human rights was taken as self-evident by many major international human rights NGOs.

The neoliberals saw human rights and competitive markets as mutually constitutive. In his bestselling polemic *The Road to Serfdom*, Hayek argued that all claims made on behalf of individuals could be attributed to the rise of the 'commercial spirit'. ' "The ideas of 1789" – liberty, equality, fraternity – are characteristically commercial ideals which have no other purpose but to secure certain advantages to individuals', he wrote.[73] For the author of *The Road to Serfdom* and his fellow neoliberals, the competitive market made individual rights possible, but the market's

---

70   David Kinley, *Civilising Globalisation: Human Rights and the Global Economy* (Cambridge/New York: Cambridge University Press, 2009), p. xii. Kinley argues that human rights and economic globalisation are in fact indispensable to each other and to a project that he calls 'civilising globalisation'. As I show, this 'civilising' mission is less innocent than it may appear.

71   Plehwe, 'Introduction', p. 25.

72   Liberal International, 'Oxford Manifesto – 1947', at liberal-international.org.

73   Hayek, *Road to Serfdom*, p. 183.

functioning also depended on the rule of law and the 'recognition of the inalienable rights of the individual, inviolable rights of man.'[74] Hayek's account of the rights of man owed much to his more utilitarian mentor Mises, whose 1922 study of socialism argued that individual rights had emerged 'hand in hand with the development of capitalism'. Once 'men' gained economic freedom, Mises argued, they soon desired it elsewhere, and sought 'legal recognition of the subjective rights of citizens.'[75] Rights, according to this perspective, do not inhere naturally in the human person; rather, they arise only when the capitalist division of labour allows individuals to pursue their own interests and values, freeing them from the arbitrary power of others. It was only capitalism, Mises argues, that made human relationships material and calculable, and brought freedom from the heavens down to earth: 'Such freedom is no natural right.'[76]

If the market order is the real basis of all the declarations of rights and charters of liberties, as Mises contended, then 'as soon as the economic freedom which the market economy grants to its members is removed, all political liberties and bills of rights become humbug.'[77] Like their Marxist critics, the neoliberals saw human rights as intimately bound up with the rise of capitalism. Indeed, it is Marx who Hayek credits as the first to recognise that 'the evolution of private capitalism with its free market had been a precondition for the evolution of all our democratic freedoms.'[78] For Marx, the freedom and equality enshrined in declarations of rights expressed the formal equality of market relations, while also sanctioning the egoism and inequality of civil society. Noting this parallel, Fredric Jameson suggests that Marx, in his account of freedom and democracy, argues, 'just like Milton Friedman, that these concepts and values are real and objective and are organically generated by the market system itself, and dialectically, indissolubly linked to it.'[79] The central difference is that while, for the neoliberals, there is 'no kind of freedom and liberty other than the kind which the market economy

74   Ibid., p. 120.
75   Mises, *Socialism*, p. 193.
76   Ibid., p. 194.
77   Mises, *Human Action*, p. 287.
78   Hayek, *Road to Serfdom*, p. 136.
79   Fredric Jameson, 'Postmodernism and the Market', in Ralph Miliband and Leo Panitch, *Socialist Register 1990: The Retreat of the Intellectuals* (Brecon: Merlin, 1990), p. 96.

brings about', for Marx, capitalist equality and freedom turn out to be inequality and un-freedom.[80]

In his early text, 'On the Jewish Question', Marx argued that the rights to equality, liberty, security and property enshrined in the eighteenth-century declarations amount to protections for the egoistic individual of civil society. In an article that challenges recent Marxist critiques of the complicity between human rights and neoliberalism, Samuel Moyn notes that the target of the young Marx's criticisms was the abstraction of political emancipation within the nation-state, not the transnational, NGO-driven, legalistic human rights dominant today. When human rights came to prominence in the 1970s, Moyn argues, they broke fundamentally with the statist paradigm of the revolutionary rights of man that Marx criticised. This transnational politics of human rights may have come to prominence at the same time as neoliberalism, he argues, but human rights NGOs were merely 'powerless companions' of neoliberalism.[81] Elsewhere, Moyn suggests that, while 'the notion that individuals have basic rights was shaped by the political economy that always affects so much else in moral ideals and social relations', this shaping was never complete, as human rights never reverted to their nineteenth-century role as protections of private property and freedom of contract.[82]

I argue that human rights were not simply shaped by an underlying economic reality; they were a central component of the neoliberal attempt to inculcate the morals of the market. This does not mean that contemporary human rights are reducible to protections of private property and contract. Clearly, they are not. But, just as human rights are distinct from the rights of man, neoliberalism is not the classical liberalism of the nineteenth century, and it is not reducible to a defence of property and contract either. One of the clearest and most succinct descriptions of the distinctiveness of neoliberalism comes from a 1951 paper by Friedman entitled 'Neo-Liberalism and its Prospects'. The 'basic error' of nineteenth-century liberalism, the young Chicago School economist argued, was to confine the role of the state to the mainte-nance of order and enforcement of contracts. Friedman framed

---

80 Mises, *Human Action*, p. 283.

81 Moyn, 'Powerless Companion', p. 153.

82 Samuel Moyn, *Not Enough: Human Rights in an Unequal World* (Harvard, MA: Harvard University Press, 2018), p. 175.

neoliberalism as a reaction to this basic error: 'Neoliberalism would accept the nineteenth-century liberal emphasis on the fundamental importance of the individual', he wrote, 'but it would substitute for the nineteenth-century goal of *laissez-faire* as a means to this end, the goal of the competitive order'.[83] This entailed much more scope for state intervention to create the conditions for competition than nineteenth-century *laissez-faire* had countenanced.

For all their undoubted diversity, the neoliberals of the early Mont Pèlerin Society were largely united around the programme outlined in Friedman's short paper. At the inaugural MPS meeting, Hayek argued that, while it is known that a functioning market relies on the 'protection of certain rights, such as property and the enforcement of contracts', it was only once this was accepted that 'the real problem begins'.[84] In *The Road to Serfdom*, he faulted previous liberals for neglecting the fact that a competitive market requires an 'appropriate legal system', and stressed that it was 'by no means sufficient that the law should recognise the principle of private property and freedom of contract'.[85] Human rights played an important role in the neoliberal attempt to develop an appropriate legal system and moral framework for a global capitalist market. The rights they formulated were not the rights of man that Marx had criticised. The correlate of seeing the competitive market as the sine qua non of peace, freedom and rights is that that neoliberal human rights exist not so much to protect the individual – even the egoistic individual – as to preserve the market order. To demonstrate this shift, let us look at how the neoliberals understood the four central rights that Marx criticised in 'On the Jewish Question'.

Liberty, Equality, Property and Security

In 'On the Jewish Question', Marx characterised the right to *liberty* as the right to do anything that does not harm others, and therefore as 'the right of separation' of a restricted individual. Liberty, or freedom, is the one value that neoliberal human rights would be expected to

---

83   Milton Friedman, 'Neo-Liberalism and Its Prospects', *Farmand*, 17 February 1951, p. 3.

84   João Rodrigues, 'The Political and Moral Economies of Neoliberalism: Mises and Hayek', *Cambridge Journal of Economics* 37: 5 (1 September 2013), p. 1002.

85   Hayek, *Road to Serfdom*, p. 87.

serve; but, examined closely, neoliberal freedom is largely indistinguishable from submission to what Mises called 'the sovereignty of the market'.[86] Unlike political sovereignty, the neoliberals saw market sovereignty as compatible with individual freedom. But they also maintained that the sovereign market requires individuals to adjust themselves to its imperatives, which means sacrificing egalitarianism and eschewing the project of collective freedom.[87] They believed that adjustment to the demands of the market was primarily secured by price fluctuations – that is, by what Marx called the 'silent compulsion of economic relations'.[88]

Writing about wages in an unregulated market, Mises contended that such fluctuations 'penalize disobedience' and 'recompense obedience' to the demands of the labour market. As this penal language makes clear enough, the market subject is not free in any expansive sense. The demands of the sovereign market, Mises states explicitly, 'submit the individual to a harsh social pressure' and 'indirectly limit the individual's freedom to choose his occupation'.[89] But he suggests that this pressure leaves the individual 'a margin in the limits of which he can choose between what suits him better and what less'.[90] It is only within this predetermined margin that the neoliberal individual is 'free to choose'. She may leave her home to pursue work in another city or stay at home and drive for Uber. She may not join a trade union, let alone struggle against the capitalist exploitation of waged labour. For Mises, 'this amount of freedom is the maximum of freedom that an individual can enjoy in the framework of the social division of labor'.[91] By pathologising mass politics as a threat to individual freedom, neoliberal liberty rights seek to confine human action within what I call the 'margin of freedom' offered by a liberal capitalist order. The

---

86   Mises, *Human Action*, p. 258.

87   In this sense, Brown is right that the contemporary liberal subject is so integrated into the goal of economic growth that she can easily be sacrificed to that end. And yet, rather than recent austerity politics ushering in a shift in neoliberal rationality 'from limitless to constrained, from freedom to sacrifice', as she puts it, the willingness to sacrifice individuals to the market was foundational to neoliberal thought. Brown, *Undoing the Demos*, p. 71.

88   Karl Marx, *Capital: A Critique of Political Economy, vol. 1*, transl. Ben Fowkes (London/New York: Penguin/New Left Review, 1981), p. 899.

89   Mises, *Human Action*, p. 599.

90   Ibid., p. 600.

91   Ibid.

neoliberal right to liberty is the right to do anything that does not harm the market.

The right to *equality*, Marx argued, was the equal right to be a self-sufficient, egoistic monad. The neoliberals broke decisively with the conception of equality enshrined in the declarations of the rights of man. 'Nowhere is the difference between the reasoning of the older liberalism and that of neoliberalism clearer and easier to demonstrate than in their treatment of the problem of equality', Mises wrote in 1927.[92] While eighteenth-century liberals' proclamations of universal human equality were often undercut by their support for economic inequalities and colonial rule, the neoliberals dispensed entirely with the belief in human equality. Nothing is as 'ill-founded as the assertion of the alleged equality of all members of the human race', in Mises's blunt formulation. 'Men are altogether unequal.'[93] Yet formal equality still played a central role in the neoliberal pantheon of rights. Equality before the law was central to their argument against state intervention; and the right to trade on equal terms played a key role in their argument against trade barriers and subsidies. As socialists demanded redistribution to secure greater economic equality, and anticolonialists invoked a new international law that would redistribute the fruits of colonial exploitation through 'corrective or compensatory inequality', the neoliberals argued that equality before the law made all redistribution impossible.[94] A neoliberal right to equality is a right of everyone to preserve their unequal wealth and power in the face of political demands for redistribution.

The right to *security*, according to Marx, was manifested in the police, who secured the universal egoism of civil society. With the global extension of capitalist social relations, neoliberal thinkers were met with the challenge of globalising this policing function. They believed that promoting a regime of rights would support the extension of the world market. 'People without rights', Mises warned, 'are always a menace to

---

92   Later, in the late 1940s, Mises rejected the label 'neoliberal' as implying a compromise with 'interventionism'. Here, he clearly placed himself in the camp of the 'neoliberals' who rejected the classical liberal natural-law presuppositions. This is the direct translation of the *neuen Liberalismus* of the original German, published in 1927.

93   Ludwig von Mises, *Liberalism: The Classical Tradition*, ed. Bettina Bien Greaves, transl. Ralph Raico (Indianapolis: Liberty Fund, 2005), p. 9.

94   Mohammed Bedjaoui, *Towards a New International Economic Order* (New York: Holmes & Meier, 1979), p. 249.

social order'.[95] They gave the state the role of protecting the competitive market from those who are unable to adjust themselves to its demands.[96] Mises was typically clear about the role of the state in a 'peaceful' liberal market order: noting that the market itself is free of coercion and the state must not interfere with it, he wrote that, in a liberal order, the state 'employs its power to beat people into submission solely for the prevention of actions destructive to the preservation and the smooth operation of the market economy'.[97] A central function of neoliberal human rights has been to globalise this function, legitimising state violence aimed at the global dissemination of capitalist social relations. The neoliberal right to security is a right for states to beat into submission those who threaten the market order.

The right to *property*, which Marx described as the foundation of the whole system, was, in his view, a right to self-interest. For earlier liberals, such as John Locke, property was justified as a means to 'improvement'. God meant the earth to be cultivated, and so gave it to the 'industrious and rational'.[98] Consistent with this justification, Mises bemoaned that much of the world's mineral wealth was located in areas 'whose inhabitants are too ignorant, too inert, or too dull to take advantage of the riches nature has bestowed upon them'.[99] As in the vision of earlier neoliberals, the right to private property ensured wealth was put in the hands of those most capable of utilising it. But they went further than this, stressing the institutional conditions in which such rights would be secure. If the governments of areas rich in resources prevented 'aliens' from exploiting this wealth, or their arbitrary conduct of public affairs threatened foreign investments, serious harm would result to all as a consequence. Preventing such harm required the 'right to keep foreign investments safe and to move capital freely across borders'.[100] A neoliberal right to property is the right to impose 'good governance' and the institutional structures that private investment requires across the globe.

---

95 Mises, *Socialism*, p. 77.
96 Mises, *Human Action*, p. 149.
97 Ibid., p. 257.
98 John Locke, *Two Treatises of Government and a Letter Concerning Toleration*, ed. Ian Shapiro (New Haven: Yale University Press, 2003), p. 114.
99 Mises, *Human Action*, p. 686.
100 Quinn Slobodian, *Globalists: The End of Empire and the Birth of Neoliberalism* (Cambridge: Harvard University Press, 2018), p. 123.

Humanity and Dignity: Neoliberalism and the Human Rights Revolution of the 1970s

Along with the rights to liberty, equality, property and security that contemporary human rights campaigns share with the older rights-of-man tradition, today's human rights are often justified as necessary to protect two key principles: 'humanity' and 'dignity'. For the young Marx, the split between the man and the citizen in the eighteenth-century declarations reflected the fact that the individual in bourgeois society leads a double life – a celestial life in the state (as an equal citizen) and a terrestrial life in civil society (as an unequal, egoistic individual).[101] The problem of the relation between man and citizen has similarly preoccupied much twentieth-century criticism of human rights. Faced with mass population expulsions in the wake of World War I, Hannah Arendt argued that those who lacked citizenship and had no other status than mere humanity were deprived even of the rights of man.[102] Many subsequent human rights defenders sought to overcome this gap between universal, humanist pronouncements and the territorial jurisdiction of independent sovereign states. Their efforts were central to the rise of a new, transnational human rights movement, which focused on securing the rights of those whose governments were 'unwilling or unable' to protect them.[103] The recognition that those who lacked the protection of a nation-state were also deprived of human rights ultimately licensed new forms of 'humanitarian' intervention that rationalized the projection of military might beyond the borders of sovereign territories as a means to secure humanity.

Humanity played a central role in the neoliberal challenge to political sovereignty and collectivism. The 'very concepts of humanity and therefore any form of internationalism are entirely products of the individualist view of man', Hayek wrote in *The Road to Serfdom*, 'and there can be no place for them in a collectivist system of thought'.[104] The neoliberals

101   Karl Marx, 'On the Jewish Question', in *Early Writings* (London: Penguin, 2000).

102   See in particular the collection Stephanie DeGooyer, Alastair Hunt, Lida Maxwell, Samuel Moyn and Astra Taylor, *The Right to Have Rights* (London: Verso, 2018).

103   International Commission on Intervention and State Sovereignty, 'The Responsibility to Protect: Research, Bibliography, Background. Supplementary Volume to the Report of the International Commission on Intervention and State Sovereignty' (Ottawa: International Development Research Centre, 2001).

104   Hayek, *Road to Serfdom*, p. 163.

mobilised this account of humanity against their own welfare states and postcolonial affirmations of sovereignty. In a world in which governments increasingly interfered with business, they argued, 'the principle of each nation's unrestricted sovereignty' is a challenge to all other nations.[105] When, later in life, Hayek formalised his account of the morals of the market, he argued that a 'universal humanism' required that we limit our moral obligations to others to the avoidance of harm.[106] Hayek believed that thinking in terms of humanity precluded domestic redistribution, which he framed as a throwback to tribal loyalties. The market order was the only one that potentially embraced all of humanity, the neoliberals believed, so defending humanity required preventing harm to the international market.

The term 'dignity' did not appear in those eighteenth-century rights declarations Marx examined, yet today it has become synonymous with human rights. The preamble of the UDHR begins by recognising the 'inherent dignity' of 'all members of the human family', and major human rights NGOs describe their *raison d'être* as upholding human dignity.[107] The founding statement of the Mont Pèlerin Society also begins with the warning that 'over large stretches of the Earth's surface the essential conditions of human dignity and freedom have already disappeared'.[108] For the Lebanese delegate Charles Malik, who drafted the UDHR's preamble, this reference to dignity reflected a Christian understanding of the human as a person, created in the image of God and requiring protection from the predations of mass politics and the state. Many early neoliberals had considerable sympathy with this Christian conception, and, for them too, upholding dignity meant restraining politics. Yet it meant more than this; for them, dignity retained some of the original sense of its Latin root *dignus*, which signified worth or desert. Just as dignity was originally a term of moral standing, the neoliberals believed that only the self-reliant and responsible could lead dignified lives. Seeking welfare from the state, from this perspective, was inherently undignified. For the neoliberals, dignity required a competitive order in which individuals were responsible for their own fates.

---

105   Mises, *Human Action*, p. 685.
106   Hayek, *Law, Legislation and Liberty, vol 2*, p. 149.
107   Human Rights Watch, 'About Us', 21 April 2015, at hrw.org.
108   'Statement of Aims', Mont Pèlerin Society Records, Stanford: Hoover Institution Archives, 4 April 1947, Box 5, Folder 16.

Throughout this book, I argue that the neoliberals of Mont Pèlerin reinvented human rights as the moral language of the competitive market. I show that they developed their own account of human rights as protections for the market order. This neoliberal vision of human rights was at its purest in the period of neoliberal ascendancy. It is clear in Margaret Thatcher's simultaneous denial that 'state services are an absolute right' and championing of a 'right to be unequal', and in Ronald Reagan's boastful statement, towards the end of his presidency, that 'from Central America to East Asia, ideas like free markets and democratic reforms and human rights are taking hold'.[109] It was taken up by the director of the World Trade Organisation (WTO), Pascal Lamy, who declared exuberantly in 2010: 'One could almost claim that trade is human rights in practice!' Lamy argued that 'human rights and trade rules, including WTO rules, are based on the same values: individual freedom and responsibility, non-discrimination, rule of law, and welfare through peaceful cooperation among individuals'.[110]

The liberal political theorist Michael Ignatieff expressed this vision clearly in 2001 when he argued that the civil and political rights of a 'capitalist rights tradition' are 'the most we can hope for'.[111] And Hayek's student, the international trade lawyer Ernst-Ulrich Petersmann, defended it most emphatically when he argued for the interdependence of human rights and international trade law. Eight years before the WTO embraced the idea of a mutual relation between human rights and competitive markets, Petersmann argued that the globalisation of human rights relies on the open markets, prohibition of economic discrimination and 'welfare-enhancing division of labour' enforced by the WTO, while human rights promote economic integration by 'protecting personal autonomy, legal and social security, peaceful change, individual savings, investments, production and mutually beneficial transactions across frontiers'.[112]

---

109   Ronald Reagan, 'President Reagan's 1986 State of the Union Address' (US House of Representatives, 4 February 1986), at reaganlibrary.gov/february-1986.

110   Pascal Lamy, 'Lamy Calls for Mindset Change to Align Trade and Human Rights', WTO, 13 January 2010, at wto.org.

111   Michael Ignatieff, *Human Rights as Politics and Idolatry* (Princeton, NJ: Princeton University Press, 2001).

112   E.-U. Petersmann, 'Time for a United Nations "Global Compact" for Integrating Human Rights into the Law of Worldwide Organizations: Lessons from European Integration', *European Journal of International Law* 13: 3 (1 April 2002), p. 621.

But the neoliberal human rights heritage was not only embraced by figures on the right. This neoliberal background can shed light on the apparent puzzle that the human rights politics of the late twentieth century, with its distinctive use of international advocacy to limit the power of the state, emerged, in Moyn's words, 'seemingly from nowhere'.[113] I show that organisations like Amnesty International, Human Rights Watch and Médecins sans Frontières drew (explicitly in some cases, implicitly in others) on an account of rights developed by the neoliberals since the 1940s. For them, too, decolonisation had generated a desperate need for new standards to constrain postcolonial states. They focused their attention on what Hayek argued was the complement of the 'taming of the savage': the 'taming of the state'.[114] The attempt to discipline postcolonial states held a much larger place in the new politics of human rights than did the concerns with economic welfare and self-determination of previous decades.

Neoliberalism and the 'Human Rights Revolution' of the 1970s

Although human rights NGOs came to prominence in the context of the evisceration of social welfare protections and public services, these concerns rarely entered the frame of their early advocacy. In his major biography of the 'International Human Rights Movement', Aryeh Neier, the former head of Human Rights Watch, suggests that the rise of human rights coincided with a shift of Cold War rhetoric, from a focus on economic competition between communism and capitalism to one on the political conflict of 'repression, or totalitarianism, versus liberty, or human rights'.[115] I argue that major international human rights and humanitarian NGOs embraced the central neoliberal dichotomy between commercial or 'civil society' – understood as a realm of freedom, voluntary interaction and distributed, private power that checked the centralised power of the state – on the one hand, and politics, understood as violent, coercive and conflictual on the other. They defended

---

113   Samuel Moyn, *The Last Utopia: Human Rights in History* (Cambridge: Belknap, 2010), p. 3.

114   Hayek in Alan Ebenstein, *Hayek's Journey: The Mind of Friedrich Hayek* (New York: Palgrave Macmillan, 2003), p. 218.

115   Aryeh Neier, *The International Human Rights Movement: A History* (Princeton, NJ: Princeton University Press, 2012), p. 13.

the same (anti-)political virtues the neoliberals attributed to the market: restraining political power, taming violence and facilitating a margin of individual freedom.

Like the neoliberals, major international human rights NGOs initially embraced law to restrain politics, while avoiding engagement with those social and economic rights that could only be achieved through political action, not judicial sanction. The methodology of many human rights NGOs, as Kenneth Roth, the director of the US-based Human Rights Watch notes, consists in the ability 'to investigate, expose, and shame', which involves identifying a particular violation, a specific violator, and a clear remedy.[116] This has made these NGOs both reluctant and unsuited to challenge the structural and impersonal effects of market processes. Nevertheless, while supposedly eschewing coercion, major human rights NGOs, including Roth's, have been quite prepared to call on the military might of the most powerful states to intervene in the name of securing human rights and universalising a distinctive moral order. In the process, they often aligned with the neoliberal embrace of a 'strong security state, stripped of its social capacity' so as to protect the market and enforce the morals of the market across the globe.[117]

Then, as today, the content of human rights was a product of political struggle. Human rights are not given by nature, and there has never been a single human rights movement capable of securing general agreement about a list of rights and their order of priority, let alone realising these rights for all. But to stop at pointing out that 'human rights' lacks a unitary meaning, as Susan Marks notes in a related context, is 'silently to signal that these phenomena are isolated problems, unrelated to wider processes, tendencies and dynamics at work in the world'. By leaving unexamined the tendencies and dynamics that bring such transformations about, as Marks notes, we occlude an understanding of what would be necessary to achieve genuine change.[118] Such 'false contingency' neglects the ways in which political possibilities are framed by systemic constraints. Specifically, the belief that

---

116   Kenneth Roth, 'Defending Social and Economic Rights', in *International Human Rights* (Oxford: Oxford University Press, 2013), 295.

117   Jeanne Morefield, *Empires Without Imperialism: Anglo-American Decline and the Politics of Deflection* (Oxford: Oxford University Press, 2014), p. 139.

118   Susan Marks, 'False Contingency', *Current Legal Problems* 62: 1 (1 January 2009), p. 17.

human rights are endlessly polyvalent treats them as free-floating, disconnected form the structures of contemporary capitalism, unmoored from the historical conditions and defeats that brought them into being. It obscures the fact that not all figures of the human and of community are equally capable of 'signifying within the text of human rights'.[119]

This book begins in the late 1940s, with the drafting of the Universal Declaration of Human Rights and the founding of the Mont Pèlerin Society. The early parts of the book explore those strands of neoliberal thought that were particularly focused on the requirements of a 'civilisation' that early neoliberals depicted as indistinguishably moral, racial and economic. In the first three chapters, I focus predominantly on early neoliberalism, and on the leading figures associated with the Austrian School of economics and the ordoliberalism of the German Freiburg School. The central characters of these first chapters are Austrian School figures Mises and Hayek, British economist Lionel Robbins, German ordoliberals Wilhelm Röpke and Alexander Rüstow, Swiss diplomat and economist William Rappard, and French philosopher Bertrand de Jouvenel – though many others make cameo appearances. While not without their significant disagreements with one another, these figures were united by a concern with world order (as Quinn Slobodian has highlighted), and by the conviction that international economic integration presupposed what Röpke called 'extra-economic integration (social-political-moral-institutional-legal integration)'.[120]

In Chapter 1, I read debates about civilisational hierarchies during the drafting of the UDHR against neoliberal attempts to defend what they portrayed as a threatened Western civilisation. I show that, while anticolonialists succeeded in ridding the UDHR of the language of 'civilisation', the neoliberals constructed a new standard of civilisation that would secure submission to the international market. Chapter 2 turns to social and economic rights. I show that the neoliberals rejected

---

119   Golder, *Foucault and the Politics of Rights*, p. 88.
120   Wilhelm Röpke, 'Economic Order and International Law', *Recueil des Cours* 86 (1954), p. 211. Slobodian uses the term 'Geneva School', to refer to a similar group of thinkers, drawing attention to the formal and informal relations that bound these thinkers to the Graduate Institute of International Studies, headed by Rappard, and to their shared 'globalist' focus on developing a new liberal order for the world. Slobodian, *Globalists*.

mid-century welfarism, which they argued confused society with a household and was therefore 'totalitarian'. Nonetheless, I also argue that, in defining social and economic rights as flexible standards that did not imply binding obligations on states, the drafters of the UDHR developed an account of social and economic rights that was ultimately compatible with a privatised, neoliberal approach to the management of poverty. Chapter 3 turns to the question of colonialism. It shows that, as the anticolonial struggle for a right to self-determination focused increasingly on economic self-determination, the neoliberals challenged Marxist theories of imperialism by defining imperialism as a problem of politics, not capitalism. I argue that, in promoting a dichotomy between the market as a realm of mutually beneficial, free, peaceful exchange, and politics as violent, coercive and militaristic, the neoliberals sought to inculcate the morals of the market and pathologise those political struggles which threatened the assigned places of postcolonial societies in the international division of labour.

In the second half of the book, I turn to the 1970s and 1980s, as the neoliberals embraced the language of human rights promoted by a new generation of human rights NGOs, and these NGOs in turn adopted the neoliberal dichotomy between violent politics and peaceful civil society. I show that the earlier neoliberal critiques of the UN human rights process were now replaced by far more ambivalent attitudes, as the neoliberals recognised that this new interventionist human rights language might assist them in their own goals of enshrining a moral order for global capital. These chapters show that earlier European neoliberals' concerns with the moral, legal and subjective conditions for competitive markets were far more central to the Chicago School and to later neoliberal development theory than is often understood. Chapter 4 examines the role of neoliberal thinkers in General Augusto Pinochet's violent imposition of a new economic and institutional order in Chile. I argue that the central neoliberal concern was to depoliticise Chilean society and secure submissive subjects. It was in this context that human rights NGOs came to prominence, for contesting the junta's violence. The problem, I argue, was not that the human rights NGOs allowed the neoliberals to obscure the relation between their economic shock and the political violence necessary to impose it, as is often suggested. Rather, in conceptualising the *problem* as politics and the *solution* as law, the human rights NGOs bolstered the neoliberal dichotomy between violent politics and peaceful markets, secured by constitutional restrictions. Chapter 5 examines the foundation Liberté sans Frontières (LSF), established by the French leadership of the respected humanitarian organisation Médecins sans Frontières in the mid 1980s. It shows that, in this period, the language of human rights was directly aligned with neoliberal challenges to the postcolonial attempt to formulate a New International Economic Order. Far from being powerless companions, the figures of LSF worked alongside neoliberal development economists such as Peter Bauer to combat demands for postcolonial economic justice.

What I call neoliberal human rights are not the only form of human rights that have existed historically. As many scholars have pointed out, and as I show in detail throughout this book, social democrats, socialists and anticolonialists used the language of human rights throughout the twentieth century for ends that were at odds with neoliberal perspectives of the period, including to demand social welfare, national self-determination and racial equality.[121] Nor do I claim that today's human rights campaigns necessarily further neoliberal ends. My focus is on hegemonic conceptions of human rights, rather than uses of human rights by marginalised and subaltern groups. It is no doubt true, as theorists of rights have argued, that the claiming of rights can generate a site of 'creativity and agency', and that a politics of rights can open up a democratic space for 'perspectival claims' that seek to persuade rather than to shut down political contestation.[122] But I do contend that the neoliberal contribution to human rights has been far more widely influential than most contemporary human rights defenders would like to admit – and not only on the political right or in the halls of power.

---

121   Joseph R. Slaughter, 'Hijacking Human Rights: Neoliberalism, the New Historiography, and the End of the Third World', *Human Rights Quarterly* 40: 4 (2018); Paul O'Connell, 'On the Human Rights Question', *Human Rights Quarterly* 40: 4 (2018); Steven L. B. Jensen, *The Making of International Human Rights: The 1960s, Decolonization, and the Reconstruction of Global Values* (Cambridge: Cambridge University Press, 2016); Baxi, *Future of Human Rights*; Carol Anderson, *Eyes Off the Prize: The United Nations and the African American Struggle for Human Rights, 1944–1955* (Cambridge: Cambridge University Press, 2003); Michael E. Goodhart, ed., *Human Rights: Politics and Practice*, 3rd edn (Oxford/New York: Oxford University Press, 2016).

122   Kiran Kaur Grewal, *The Socio-Political Practice of Human Rights: Between the Universal and the Particular* (London: Routledge, 2016), p. 4; Karen Zivi, *Making Rights Claims: A Practice of Democratic Citizenship* (Oxford: Oxford University Press, 2012), p. 42.

Without coming to terms with that influence, social movements and struggles that wield the language of human rights to contest neoliberalism may instead find that they strengthen its hold.[123] The story I tell here is the story of how neoliberal thinkers made human rights the morals of the market.

123   Radha D'Souza, *What's Wrong with Rights? Social Movements, Law and Liberal Imaginations* (London: Pluto, 2018).

1

'The Central Values of Civilization Are in Danger'

The spirit of the barbarians, which the Western peoples thought they had tamed by centuries of struggle, is abroad again and threatens to destroy the civilizing work of all these centuries.

Wilhelm Röpke

The civilized world can only seek and find a universal philosophy that, by its total humanity, will be able to maintain the tradition of civilization in spite of a totally inhuman enemy.

Walter Lippmann

The statement of aims of the neoliberal Mont Pèlerin Society (MPS) begins with a warning: the 'central values of civilization are in danger'.[1] In language that echoes that of the Universal Declaration of Human Rights (UDHR), which was being drafted across the Atlantic at the same time, the 1947 statement signalling the consolidation of neoliberalism declared that the essential conditions of 'human dignity and freedom' had largely disappeared.[2] In his opening address at the society's inaugural meeting, Friedrich Hayek said that the experience of the 'actual decay of civilization' had taught European thinkers lessons not yet learnt in the

---

1 'Statement of Aims', Mont Pèlerin Society Records, Stanford: Hoover Institution Archives, 4 April 1947, Box 5, Folder 16.
2 Ibid.

UK and the United States.[3] In a foreword to the 1956 American edition of *The Road to Serfdom* the Austrian economist explained that the book aimed to show that state economic controls and public monopolies could destroy the market economy and 'gradually smother the creative powers of a free civilization.'[4] This threat, Hayek believed, long preceded the outbreak of World War II; everywhere, liberal ideals and free markets were threatened by the rise of collectivist mass politics, and only those who could remember the period before World War I knew what a liberal world was like.

The early neoliberals saw themselves as fighting for more than an economic programme; at stake, they believed, was the survival of 'Western civilization'. Faced with widespread demands for socialism, state welfare provision and economic planning, they turned their attention to the moral values and subjective qualities underpinning a competitive market order. 'Self-discipline, a sense of justice, honesty, fairness, chivalry, moderation, public spirit, respect for human dignity, firm ethical norms – all of these are things which people must possess before they go to market and compete with each other', wrote the German ordoliberal, Wilhelm Röpke.[5] The neoliberals portrayed these moral and subjective qualities as the products of a civilisation whose foundations were in Greece, Rome and Christianity, and whose 'basic individualism' was the inheritance of Erasmus, Montaigne, Cicero, Tacitus, Pericles and Thucydides.[6] This construction of Western civilisation was deeply anachronistic. Neither the ancient Greeks nor the Romans understood themselves as part of 'the West', and nor were their various conceptions of the self and the subject compatible with neoliberal individualism.[7] Yet the claim to speak on behalf of Western civilisation allowed the neoliberals to recast their adversaries not merely as representative of rival political and economic movements but as threats to civilisation and the freedoms and rights it provides.

3   Friedrich Hayek, *Studies in Philosophy, Politics and Economics* (Chicago: University of Chicago Press, 1967), p. 150.

4   Friedrich Hayek, *The Road to Serfdom: Texts and Documents*, ed. Bruce Caldwell (Chicago: University of Chicago Press, 2007), p. 44.

5   Wilhelm Röpke, *A Humane Economy: The Social Framework of the Free Market*, transl. Elizabeth Henderson (Chicago: Institute for Philosophical and Historical Studies, 1961), p. 125.

6   Hayek, *Road to Serfdom*, p. 68.

7   Georgios Varouxakis, 'The Godfather of "Occidentality": Auguste Comte and the Idea of "The West"', *Modern Intellectual History*, October 2017.

All this was laid out clearly in the MPS's original statement of aims, which condemned central economic direction because it conflicts with the 'right of each individual to plan his own life'. Like the preamble of the UDHR, the neoliberal statement stressed freedom of speech, thought and expression, and restraint of arbitrary power. Rejecting now-outdated nineteenth-century *laissez-faire*, it framed the competitive market as the product of an appropriate institutional framework and a rule of law. It also noted that the trends leading towards 'totalitarianism' were not confined to the economic realm but had also emerged in morality, philosophy and the interpretation of history. Conflating communism, fascism and social democracy, the neoliberals argued that all systems that organise social efforts towards a single goal 'are totalitarian in the true sense of this new word which we have adopted to describe the unexpected but nevertheless inseparable manifestations of what in theory we call collectivism'.[8] A free society, in contrast, required a competitive market economy, and what the MPS statement called a 'widely accepted moral code' governing collective as well as individual action.[9]

The attempt to produce such a shared moral code as a response to a civilisational crisis was also central to the drafting of the Universal Declaration of Human Rights. 'Disregard and contempt for human rights', its preamble notes, 'have resulted in barbarous acts which have outraged the conscience of mankind'. In contrast to its pride of place in the Mont Pèlerin statement, however, the word 'civilisation' does not appear in the UDHR, and nor do its cognates 'civilised' and 'uncivilised'. While all the attendees at the initial meeting of the MPS came from Europe, the United Kingdom or the United States, the drafting of the UDHR involved delegates from the East and West, from colonial powers and recently independent nations, from Christian and Muslim societies, and from trade unions and religious organisations. The inclusiveness of its drafting should not be overstated; more than half of the world's people still lived under colonial rule and were therefore unable to influence its account of 'universal' humanity.[10] Nonetheless, unlike the

---

8 Hayek, *Road to Serfdom*, p. 100.

9 MPS 'Draft Statement of Aims' in Philip Mirowski and Dieter Plehwe, eds, *The Road from Mont Pèlerin: The Making of the Neoliberal Thought Collective* (Cambridge: Harvard University Press, 2009), p. 23.

10 Johannes Morsink, *The Universal Declaration of Human Rights: Origins, Drafting, and Intent* (Philadelphia: University of Pennsylvania Press, 1999), p. 96.

neoliberals, who believed firmly in the superiority of 'Western civilisation', delegates at the UDHR were soon embroiled in conflicts about the perpetuation of civilisational hierarchies in a document supposed to specify the rights of all human beings.

The contested category of 'civilisation' provides a unique lens through which to view the evolution of both human rights and neoliberalism, both of which have been criticised as new iterations of a colonial civilising mission. Critics of neoliberalism have noted that structural adjustment programmes implemented by the international financial institutions – the International Monetary Fund (IMF), the World Bank, and the World Trade Organization (WTO) – have had dramatic effects on societies of the Global South, remaking both economies and subjectivities along Western capitalist lines. Critics of human rights have also pointed to the parallels between contemporary human rights universalism and the mixture of humanitarian moralism, economic interest and brute violence of colonial rule. Such criticisms extend to human rights organisations based in the Global North, which have been charged with revitalising the 'international hierarchy of race and color' that privileges white people as models and saviours, and portrays racialised subjects as either victims or 'savages'.[11]

Such claims for continuity with older civilising projects are not made only by critics. The political theorist Jack Donnelly argues that human rights provides a new iteration of the so-called classical 'standard of civilisation', according to which membership in the 'family of nations' was reserved for those who fulfilled certain moral, legal and economic criteria, and restrained 'shockingly uncivilized practices' such as slavery, piracy and polygamy, while protecting individual rights and freedom of commerce.[12] The International Commission on Intervention and State Sovereignty (ICISS), which reframed humanitarian intervention as the 'Responsibility to Protect' notes that human rights are often seen as 'the contemporary Western values being imposed in place of Christianity and the "standard of civilisation" in the 19th and early 20th century'.[13]

---

11   Makau Mutua, *Human Rights: A Political and Cultural Critique* (Philadelphia: University of Pennsylvania Press, 2002), p. 155.

12   Jack Donnelly, 'Human Rights: A New Standard of Civilization?', *International Affairs* 74: 1 (January 1998), p. 5.

13   International Commission on Intervention and State Sovereignty, 'The Responsibility to Protect: Research, Bibliography, Background. Supplementary Volume to the Report of the International Commission on Intervention and State Sovereignty' (Ottawa: International Development Research Centre, 2001), p. 11.

The Chicago School economist and virtue ethicist Deirdre McCloskey is one of the most explicit contemporary defenders of the thesis that commerce is sweet and civilising; she argues that, in making it necessary to negotiate mutually beneficial market exchanges, 'as a civilized people must', capitalism instils a series of 'bourgeois virtues': prudence, temperance, justice, courage, love, faith and hope.[14] For many contemporary advocates of neoliberalism and human rights, the racism that animated the older standard of civilisation may be distasteful, but the need for international moral and legal standards that facilitate and 'civilise' the economy, and establish criteria for membership in the 'international community' has not gone away.[15]

Following the fall of the Berlin Wall, human rights organisations largely dispensed with the language of 'backward races' and 'civilised nations' that was still central to liberalism in the early twentieth century, while advocates of neoliberalism replaced explicit racial hierarchies with a seemingly objective discourse of economic development, economic growth, good governance and economic freedom. Today, the rise of what Daniel Pipes of the Middle East Forum refers to as 'Pro-Christendom, Pro-European and Pro-Western' 'civilisationist' parties is often understood as a populist reaction against both human rights and neoliberalism, which are associated with universalism, non-discrimination and equality before the law.[16] Such a characterisation stumbles upon the fact that many of these same parties and leaders, notably US President Donald Trump, combine explicit appeals to Western civilisation and anti-immigrant, anti-Muslim racism with fiscal discipline, corporate tax cuts and further retrenchment of the remnants of the welfare state. This chapter demonstrates that this combination is not new; it had an important place among the preoccupations of the early neoliberals, for whom defending 'the West' meant developing a moral framework to protect the competitive market.

Faced with the rise of collectivist mass politics, mid-twentieth-century neoliberalism was a defensive liberalism. Breaking with the optimism of the eighteenth and nineteenth centuries, the early neoliberals believed the survival of the competitive market required the

---

14   Dierdre McCloskey, *The Bourgeois Virtues: Ethics for an Age of Commerce* (Chicago: University of Chicago Press), pp. 26, 31.

15   David Kinley, *Civilising Globalisation: Human Rights and the Global Economy* (Cambridge/New York: Cambridge University Press, 2009), p. 3.

16   Daniel Pipes, 'The Rise of Western Civilisationism', *Australian*, 14 April 2018.

re-establishment of its moral foundations. It was through this lens that they viewed human rights. Redefined to exclude social protections, human rights, they believed, could protect the market order by securing property and private investment and fostering the morals of the market. From the neoliberal perspective, the UN human rights process, with its expansion of membership beyond the bounds of the 'civilised' family of nations, and its challenges to racial hierarchies, threatened the continuity of civilisation. But the neoliberals saw the potential for the language of human rights to provide that 'generally observed and undisputed code of moral norms and principles of behavior' which, the German ordoliberal Wilhelm Röpke argued, was the precondition of economic integration.[17] Human rights, from this perspective, were not a product of international consensus. They were a product of 'Western civilisation', and their role was to support the extension of capitalist social relations by fostering the legal security, morals and forms of subjectivity conducive to an international market order.

The Standard of Civilisation

During the early drafting of the UDHR, the Soviet delegate, Vladimir Koretsky, rebuked the great French jurist René Cassin for his use of the phrase 'civilised nations'. Framing civilisational hierarchies as an anachronism from the age of the tsars, Koretksy argued the phrase had 'no meaning at the present time'.[18] Noting that the UK's draft declaration also referred to 'civilised nations', the future judge at the International Court of Justice (ICJ) asked that the committee 'not follow old documents too blindly but find a new track for itself'.[19] The Soviet bloc delegates framed the drafting of an international bill of rights as an opportunity to move beyond the civilisational hierarchies of pre-war international relations. At a time of deep international conflict between defenders of starkly different political and economic systems, the campaign against

---

17   Wilhelm Röpke, *International Economic Disintegration* (London: William Hodge, 1942), p. 72.

18   Vladimir Koretsky (USSR), 'Summary Record of the Third Meeting of the Drafting Committee of the Commission on Human Rights', 11 June 1947, in William A. Schabas, ed., *The Universal Declaration of Human Rights: The Travaux Préparatoires*, Vol. 1 (Cambridge: Cambridge University Press, 2013), p. 728.

19   Ibid., p. 732.

civilisational hierarchies was one aspect of a broader effort to prevent the universalisation of one rival system under the name of human rights.

In defence of his country's draft, the UK delegate noted that the phrase 'civilized nations' was used in the statute of the ICJ, attached to the UN Charter, which the Soviet Union had also signed.[20] Indeed, the statute of the World Court listed the 'principles of law accepted by civilized nations' among the sources of international law. Evoking the continuity and authority of a long tradition, the UK submission grounded human rights in these general principles, which it claimed also found expression in phrases like the 'law of nature' or *jus gentium* ('law of nations') that informed the 'fundamental rights of man'.[21] That the language of civilisation had a long history was not in question, however questionable may have been the UK delegate's conflation of it with the history of the law of nations.[22] Throughout the nineteenth century, claims about civilisation served to demarcate sovereign states from societies deemed incapable of self-government, and so lacking in legal personality.[23] The classical 'standard of civilisation' made a state's recognition under international law contingent on its transformation of its internal and external relations, including by guaranteeing the basic rights of foreign traders. It carried a vision of civilisation defined by the superiority of European law over indigenous legal orders, and of capitalist industry, private property and labour discipline over cooperative forms of social life. It required that 'inalienable rights were associated with the freedoms of trade, travel and proselytizing'.[24] It was therefore a key technology for the inculcation of the morals of the market.

According to the typical story, recounted by the nineteenth-century legal scholar John Westlake, a civilised state was one in which 'people of

---

20 Geoffrey Wilson (UK), in Ibid., p. 732.

21 Division of Human Rights, 'Textual Comparison of the Draft International Bill of Human Rights submitted by the Delegation of the United Kingdom to the Drafting Committee of the Commission on Human Rights, and the Draft Outline of an International Bill of Rights' in Schabas, *The Universal Declaration of Human Rights*, vol. 1, p. 327.

22 Ian Hunter, 'Spatialisations of Justice in the Law of Nature and Nations: Pufendorf, Vattel and Kant', unpublished draft paper, n.d. – available at researchgate.net.

23 Martti Koskenniemi, *The Gentle Civilizer of Nations: The Rise and Fall of International Law 1870–1960* (Cambridge: Cambridge University Press, 2004), p. 138.

24 Gerrit W. Gong, *The Standard of 'Civilization' in International Society* (Oxford: Clarendon, 1984), p. 36.

a European race' could live as they were accustomed to living at home.[25] Westlake's story made purported European standards the embodiments of civilisation, and European powers the ultimate judges of whether a state had reformed sufficiently to warrant recognition. A central test of whether a non-European state was 'civilised' was whether it had the capacity, and the inclination, to protect European commerce, to enter into binding contracts, and to secure the basic rights to 'life, dignity and property' of European traders.[26] The protection of rights, the rule of law, and a centralised state with a monopoly on the use of violence and a capacity to enter into contracts were all preconditions for 'the incorporation of the periphery into an uneven yet fundamentally global system of exploitation and commodity circulation'.[27] The Berlin Conference of 1884–85 – which carved up the African continent between European states (the 'Scramble for Africa') while claiming to break with the rapacious imperialism of the past – framed commerce as a civilising force that would enable 'backward' peoples to enter the world market. As the British statesman Joseph Chamberlain put it, 'We develop new territory as Trustees of Civilization for the Commerce of the World.'[28] The benevolence of European rule, the civilising role of commerce, and the attempt to extend a list of basic rights were deeply intertwined.

This language of civilisation legitimised 'hierarchies of wealth, power and privilege' by taxonomising and ranking peoples.[29] Its racial hierarchies were typically understood in evolutionary terms, as stages of a single process. The nineteenth-century Scottish international lawyer James Lorimer gave the clearest account of the rights adequate to such a hierarchical ordering of humanity. Lorimer was a vituperative critic of equality, both of nations and classes, and his hierarchical vision was predicated on a distinction between civilised, barbarian and savage states. In opposition to the anthropology of his time, he contended that 'primitive man' threw little light on the characteristics of humanity. 'For

---

25   See Antony Anghie, *Imperialism, Sovereignty and the Making of International Law* (Cambridge: Cambridge University Press, 2004), p. 85.

26   Gong, *The Standard of 'Civilization'*, p. 27.

27   Ntina Tzouvala, 'Civilisation', in Jean d'Aspremont and Sahib Singh, eds, *Concepts for International Law: Contributions to Disciplinary Thought* (Cheltenham: Edward Elgar, 2018).

28   Antony Anghie, 'Civilization and Commerce: The Concept of Governance in Historical Perspective', *Villanova Law Review* 45: 5 (2000), p. 904.

29   Adolph Reed Jr, 'Marx, Race, and Neoliberalism', *New Labor Forum* 22: 1 (2013), p. 49.

our purposes', he wrote, in a typically racist passage, 'the single life of Socrates is of greater value than the whole existence of the negro race.'[30] According to Lorimer's natural law theory, human capacities (or 'gifts of Providence') were unequally distributed, and the role of law, in declaring rights, was to recognise and vindicate this underlying factual inequality; 'to create rights', he wrote, 'is as impossible as to create the individual in whom they inhere, to add a cubit to his stature, or to raise him from the dead; and to declare rights in excess of his faculties is simply to declare what is not'.[31] The consequence of this position was that 'higher' races had more rights, while, within a state, the most 'gifted' and educated individuals had more rights than the poor.

Although he wrote in the late nineteenth century, when the 'Scottish Enlightenment had certainly run out of steam', Lorimer's approach to international law echoes that of his Scottish forebears more than has often been noticed.[32] Although Lorimer drew on pseudo-biological theories to advance arguments that were more explicitly racist than those of Adam Smith, Adam Ferguson or their contemporaries, he nonetheless adopted their basic evolutionary assumption that civil society gradually developed from the 'savage' condition of tribal existence to the 'polished' life of a commercial society. Like Hayek, who drew on such stadial histories to develop his account of the morals of the market, Lorimer saw the extension of the division of labour as integral to the process of civilisation.

A conservative critic of the French Revolution, Lorimer considered free trade to be the 'only novel and fruitful application of the principle of fraternity', and he saw the division of society into classes as central to material progress.[33] Economic and racial categorisations blurred in this presentation; Lorimer argued that a state's wealth might furnish the 'only means available for international purposes of estimating the moral and intellectual qualities of citizens', and he regularly compared the domestic poor to 'barbarians'.[34] Sanctifying wealth by treating it as

---

30   James Lorimer, *The Institutes of Law: A Treatise of the Principles of Jurisprudence as Determined by Nature* (Edinburgh: T. & T. Law, 1872), p. 53.

31   Ibid., p. 204.

32   Gerry Simpson, 'James Lorimer and the Character of Sovereigns: The Institutes as 21st Century Treatise', *European Journal of International Law* 27: 2 (2016), p. 434.

33   Lorimer, *Institutes of Law*, pp. 395–6.

34   Cited in Martti Koskenniemi, 'Race, Hierarchy and International Law: Lorimer's Legal Science', *European Journal of International Law* 27: 2 (2016).

evidence of superiority, Lorimer argued that, even if the same means of culture could be placed within the reach of all, 'men's powers of availing themselves of it differ so widely, that, relatively at least, the barbarian, like "the poor", we shall "have with us always".[35]

This slippage between race and economics persisted even as the standard of civilisation appeared to establish neutral and universal criteria for membership in the 'family of nations'. On the surface, the standard held out the possibility that independent, non-colonised states like Japan and Siam (now Thailand) could be admitted to this 'family' if they transformed their international and external relations.[36] In reality, ascriptive racial hierarchies remained central, even if they were no longer framed as static biological accounts of racial difference. The British imperialist Cecil Rhodes exemplified this shift. A firm believer in white supremacy, Rhodes appealed to Dutch Afrikaners in 1897 by promising 'equal rights for every white man south of the Zambesi'. Two years later, he instead promised 'equal rights for every civilized man'.[37] In 1900, he told the South African League that he had 'used the word civilised to cover the coloured people' (a category that did not include the black majority) and others worthy of the rights of voters.[38] In a short period of time, the white race became the civilised – a category ultimately extended to certain (wealthy and literate) people of colour. What remained consistent was the hierarchical ordering of humanity, and the belief that this hierarchy was indissolubly racial and economic.

The drafting of the UDHR saw a similarly significant shift in the language of classification and ranking, even as it purported to codify the rights of a universal humanity. The United States, which was both less invested than the UK and France in the old order of European colonialism and more anxious about allowing the Soviets to monopolise the language of progress, worked to construct a civilisational discourse adequate to a new era of universal rights. Eleanor Roosevelt told the delegates that while there were 'peoples of different levels of development in various parts of the world', this did not mean they were naturally inferior, but that they had not had the same opportunities for

---

35   The internal citation is to the biblical passage Mathew 26.
36   Anghie, *Imperialism, Sovereignty and the Making of International Law*, p. 67.
37   Gong, *Standard of 'Civilization'*, p. 52.
38   'Cecil Rhodes's Great Speech', *Examiner*, 13 November 1900.

development.[39] Such arguments would become central to the neoliberal civilising missions of the later twentieth century.

William Rappard and the Sacred Trust of Civilisation

In his opening address at the inaugural MPS Conference, the Swiss economist and diplomat William Rappard depicted his colleagues as the inheritors of both Adam Smith's economic science and his liberal politics. What Smith did not realise, this well-travelled diplomat argued, was that the 'economic man' underpinning his science was 'like Smith himself, a Scotchman who preferred to work and to save rather than idly to enjoy idleness'. Rappard contrasted this 'Scotch brand of *homo economicus*', for whom work was a virtue and saving a characteristic trait, with the Algerian Arabs he had witnessed in Algiers five years earlier, shunning work and enjoying themselves by sitting idly on the pavements. Had Smith been 'reared among the sun-baked race of Arabs who prefer leisure to work' and equality to liberty, he speculated, 'would his semi-tropical economic man not have led him quite consistently to preach a very different doctrine?'[40] Smith's liberal economics, Rappard believed, could only thrive in conditions inhabited by a very distinctive subject. It was not only his international experience that had taught Rappard that Smith's particular brand of *homo economicus* was not a 'natural man'. Even the 'European economic man' was today clamouring for 'social security and equality much more than for economic progress and freedom', he noted.[41] Reviving international liberalism, he believed, would require an institutional and moral order to cultivate that Scottish *homo economicus* that a liberal market presupposed.

Few people were as familiar with the relations between commerce, civilisation and human rights as Rappard. In 1920, the Swiss economist was appointed director of the Mandates Section of the League of Nations, and so tasked with overseeing the territories confiscated from Germany

---

39 Eleanor Roosevelt (Chair), 'Summary Record of the Third Meeting of the Drafting Committee of the Commission on Human Rights', 11 June 1947, in Schabas, *The Universal Declaration of Human Rights*, vol. 1, p. 732.

40 William Rappard, 'Opening Address to the Mont Pèlerin Society', Mont Pèlerin Founding Meeting, Mont Pèlerin: Hoover Institution Archives, 1947, Box 5, Folder 12.

41 Ibid.

and the Ottoman Empire in the wake of World War I.[42] These areas, according to the League of Nations Covenant, were 'inhabited by peoples not yet able to stand by themselves under the strenuous conditions of the modern world', whose development formed 'a sacred trust of civilisation'.[43] Reflecting the belief in a hierarchical ordering of peoples, the mandated territories were ranged on a scale from A to C. A mandates (Iraq, Syria, Palestine and Lebanon) were classed as sufficiently 'advanced' to expect independence in the near future, while C mandates (Namibia and Germany's former Pacific territories) were considered so undeveloped that they should be governed as integral parts of the territories of their administering powers. Rappard presented the interests of the 'native inhabitants' of the mandates as his paramount concern.[44] Yet, as a founding member of the MPS, he had no doubt that these interests would be best served by private capital investment and integration into the world market.

Rappard was deeply involved in both the practical administration of mandate territories and the development of neoliberalism. He was a close friend of Hayek, who wrote to him in the wake of the success of *The Road to Serfdom* that 'there are still many more people who feel on the whole as we do than I had ever dared hope'.[45] As the co-founder of the Graduate Institute of International Studies in Geneva, Rappard provided a wartime institutional home to a group of neoliberal thinkers that included Ludwig von Mises, Wilhelm Röpke and Luigi Einaudi.[46] The long-time MPS executive-secretary, Albert Hunold, wrote that, 'stone by stone', Rappard's institute was building 'a solid foundation of our western way of life, the very essence of which is freedom and the

---

42   For an excellent historical account of the mandates, see Susan Pedersen, *The Guardians: The League of Nations and the Crisis of Empire* (Oxford: Oxford University Press, 2015).

43   League of Nations, 'The Covenant of the League of Nations (Including Amendments Adopted to December, 1924)' (The Avalon Project, Yale Law School, 1924), at avalon.law.yale.edu.

44   William Rappard, 'The Practical Working of the Mandates System', *Journal of the British Institute of International Affairs* 4: 5 (1925), p. 211.

45   Cited in Angus Burgin, *The Great Persuasion: Reinventing Free Markets since the Depression* (Cambridge: Harvard University Press, 2012), p. 93.

46   Plehwe, 'Introduction', in Mirowski and Plehwe, Road from Mont Pèlerin, p. 13. Quinn Slobodian refers to the branch of neoliberalism that emerged around Rappard as the 'Geneva School' neoliberals, and notes their shared preoccupation with world order. Quinn Slobodian, *Globalists: The End of Empire and the Birth of Neoliberalism* (Cambridge: Harvard University Press, 2018).

dignity of man'.[47] Rappard provided a bridge between the 'civilising' work of the mandate system and the neoliberal attempt to save civilisation from the threat of collectivism. He brought an internationalist perspective to neoliberal thinking, and a belief that the international extension of the competitive market required the cultural and subjective transformation of non-capitalist societies.

The mandates have been described as experimental laboratories for techniques of governance and rule.[48] These experiments, I suggest, deeply influenced the neoliberal attempt to submit sovereignty to rules that support a flourishing market and to inculcate the morals of the market. While the locus of sovereignty in the mandates was a topic of great controversy, mandatory powers were generally not considered to be sovereign.[49] Rather, the mandates were held in trust, and the presupposition of a trust, as the conservative thinker Edmund Burke outlined in his famous indictment of the British East India Company, is that any power set over people must be exercised for their benefit.[50] On this basis, Burke told the House of Commons in 1783 that, if England were to be driven out of India on this day, 'nothing would remain, to tell that it had been possessed, during the inglorious period of our domination, by anything better than the ourang-outang or the tiger'.[51] The mandate system represented the face of an 'enlightened imperialism', which sought to distance itself from what was portrayed as the rapacious colonial exploitation of the past.

In contrast to the monopolist practices of the old trading companies, the mandate system guaranteed 'equal economic opportunity' in the mandates for all League members. Rappard framed this 'Open Door' policy as a recognition that international commerce led to peace. We have seen that this sweetness-of-commerce thesis can be traced back to the eighteenth century, but Rappard credited it to the 'great trade emancipator and peacemaker' Richard Cobden. In 1842 (at the height of his

---

47   Albert Hunold, 'Preface', in Albert Hunold, ed., *Freedom and Serfdom: An Anthology of Western Thought* (Dordrecht: D. Reidel, 1961), p. 7.

48   Anghie, *Imperialism, Sovereignty and the Making of International Law*, p. 136.

49   Sir Arnold McNair's advisory opinion to the ICJ (1950) in Carsten Stahn, *The Law and Practice of International Territorial Administration: Versailles to Iraq and Beyond* (Cambridge: Cambridge University Press, 2008), p. 88.

50   Edmund Burke, *The Writings and Speeches of Edmund Burke, Vol. 5: India: Madras and Bengal: 1774–1785*, ed. P.J. Marshall and William B Todd (Oxford University Press, 1981).

51   Ibid.

campaign against the Corn Laws), Cobden argued that the 'colonial system, with all its dazzling appeals to the passions of the people, can never be got rid of except by the indirect processes of Free Trade.'[52] In contrast, as a typical *neoliberal*, Rappard was not prepared to leave the fortunes of commerce to *laissez-faire*. In his search for a body of international norms to secure a competitive market order, the peculiar juridical status of the mandates proved to be both a blessing and a curse.

The curse was starkly outlined by Rappard's colleague on the Permanent Mandates Commission (PMC), Lord Lugard: without a sovereign state to guarantee investments and secure contracts in the mandates, this former East Africa Company employee and then British colonial official argued, private investors lacked confidence to invest. From this perspective, the mandates lacked key determinants of 'civilisation': the capacity to enter into binding contracts, and to protect property rights and investments. Rappard took the problem very seriously, arguing that it was no good to respond that, in deterring capitalists, the mandate system had protected its beneficiaries from exploitation. Although coming from 'the home of Rousseau', the Swiss diplomat added, 'I shall refrain from denouncing the evils of civilisation and singing the praises of the state of nature!'[53] Civilisation, Rappard made clear, was synonymous with economic development, and required an attractive climate for private capital investment.

Rappard's solution would have significant consequences for the development of the mandates and for later neoliberal responses to decolonisation. He successfully proposed that the League make clear it would not approve any cessation or transfer of the mandate (including in the event of eventual independence) without advance assurance that the new government would 'accept responsibility for the fulfilment of the financial obligations regularly assumed by the former Mandatory Power', and respect 'all rights regularly acquired' under its administration.[54] The people of the mandates would not be considered ready to

---

52   William Rappard, 'Foreword', in Benjamin Gerig, ed., *The Open Door and the Mandates System: A Study of Economic Equality before and since the Establishment of the Mandates System* (London: George Allen & Unwin, 1930), p. 11.

53   Rappard, 'Practical Working of the Mandates System', p. 211.

54   Benjamin Gerig, *The Open Door and the Mandates System: A Study of Economic Equality before and since the Establishment of the Mandates System* (London: George Allen & Unwin, 1930), p. 169.

'stand by themselves' until they guaranteed the rights of private capital and respected contracts made without their consent.

The PMC, which Rappard headed, broke with a naturalistic faith in markets in order to develop a body of rules to foster investment and capital accumulation. Its experiment in the use of transnational bodies to bind states in the interests of capital influenced neoliberal techniques of government. It inspired not only the Bretton-Woods institutions and the WTO, but also the European Union (EU), which much later used similar techniques – and similar racialised accusations of laziness and absent entrepreneurialism – to impose austerity on 'backward' southern European nations. In Rappard's description, the PMC was an 'umpire' ensuring that the game was played fairly, which must be clearly independent of governments. Otherwise 'the game would be up, because no one could be expected to play the game if the umpire was suspected of having been unduly influenced'.[55] A central lesson of the mandate system, and one that the neoliberals would often insist on, was that the needs of capital would be best served by a transnational body of rules overseen by 'impartial' umpires imposing rules on all players. It is fitting, then, that the Centre William Rappard in Geneva is now home to the WTO.[56]

Perhaps more surprisingly, the mandates were also a laboratory for the transnational monitoring of human rights. In a 1946 article, 'Human Rights in Mandated Territories', Rappard noted the strangeness of the UN Charter's claim to protect human rights.[57] Refusing the 'deplorable cynicism' of dismissing this new language as pious wishes, he sought to distil a conception of human rights from the work of the PMC. Human rights were best understood as the individual's 'general freedom from oppression', he argued, which meant that, in protecting freedom of conscience and religion and suppressing the slave trade, the mandate system had always been serving human rights.[58] Rappard's key lesson, however, concerned the *means* of promoting human rights. The PMC comprised diplomats and former colonial officials with no coercive powers, he wrote; its only resource was its 'moral authority', which

---

55 Rappard, 'Practical Working of the Mandates System', p. 222.

56 Slobodian provides a rich account of the role of neoliberals in the founding of the WTO in, *Globalists*.

57 William Rappard, 'Human Rights in Mandated Territories', *Annals of the American Academy of Political and Social Science* 243: 1 (1946), p. 118.

58 Ibid., p. 119.

enabled it to shame governments in front of their own citizens. Such impartiality and independence, he wrote in another essay of the same year, allowed the PMC to function as 'an international or rather a super-national moral authority'.[59]

Rappard argued that a body of independent experts who wielded moral authority and the threat of publicity offered the best means of 'enlightening and influencing public opinion within and beyond national boundaries'. It was because he believed that the mandate system had at least partially succeeded in this task that Rappard saw it as a model for the UN's new human rights project.[60] In the subsequent years, as the drafting of the UDHR commenced, Rappard's lessons seemed to have been ignored by delegates who clashed over political and economic questions and challenged the civilisational hierarchies that motivated the mandate system. His model of the transnational moral authority of impartial experts from the Global North would have to wait several decades to be revived as the dominant model of international human rights activism. When a new generation of human rights NGOs emerged that wielded moral authority and expertise in the public sphere, they flourished alongside concerted attempts to bind postcolonial states to the interests of private capital.

Universal Human Rights and the Fading of the Standard of Civilisation

The UN human rights process of the 1940s, which gave each sovereign state an equal vote, broke starkly with the elite moral authority Rappard distilled from the mandate system. The involvement of non-European states and representatives of the Soviet bloc in the drafting process seemed to the neoliberals to be a reflection of the crisis of civilisation, not a solution to it. During the drafting of the UDHR, delegates from China and Saudi Arabia, among others, sought to relativise 'Western civilisation' and remind the European powers that a declaration of *human* rights could not be based on a single cultural tradition. The

---

59   William Rappard, 'The Mandates and the International Trusteeship Systems', *Political Science Quarterly* 61: 3 (1946), p. 412. As Susan Pedersen notes, most of these 'independent experts' had close ties to their own governments, or were under instruction from them. Pedersen, *The Guardians*, p. 2.

60   Rappard, 'Human Rights in Mandated Territories', p. 122.

presence of delegates who had once been excluded from 'civilised' law-making bodies changed the terms of the debate. China had long been forced to accept humiliating concessions in the form of incursions by European traders and missionaries.[61] Muslim societies existed outside that group of states that, before they became 'civilised nations', had been known simply as 'Christendom'.[62] Delegates from these societies, and from recently independent countries – notably India – were unwilling to allow the attempt to formulate a list of human rights to enshrine the superiority of Western civilisation.

Early in the drafting process, Eleanor Roosevelt reflected on an early meeting over tea between herself, the Chinese delegate Peng Chun Chang, the Lebanese delegate Charles Malik and the Canadian Director of the UN Secretariat's Division on Human Rights John Humphrey:

> Dr Chang was a pluralist and held forth in charming fashion on the proposition that there is more than one kind of ultimate reality. The Declaration, he said, should reflect more than simply Western ideas and Dr Humphrey would have to be eclectic in his approach. His remark, though addressed to Dr Humphrey, was really directed at Dr Malik, from whom it drew a prompt retort as he expounded at some length the philosophy of Thomas Aquinas. Dr Humphrey joined enthusiastically in the discussion, and I remember that at one point Dr Chang suggested that the Secretariat might well spend a few months studying the fundamentals of Confucianism![63]

At this point, Roosevelt reflects, the conversation became 'so lofty' that she was unable to follow', and so she refilled the tea cups and 'sat back to be entertained by the talk of these learned gentlemen'.[64]

Chang, who earned a PhD in the United States studying with the American pragmatist philosopher John Dewey, was committed to ensuring the declaration avoided metaphysical presuppositions and reflected both the diversity and the interpenetration of cultures and

---

61   Teemu Ruskola, *Legal Orientalism: China, the United States, and Modern Law* (Cambridge: Harvard University Press, 2013), p. 125.
62   Henry Wheaton, *Elements of International Law: With a Sketch of the History of the Science* (Philadelphia: Carey, Lea & Blanchard, 1836).
63   Eleanor Roosevelt, *On My Own* (New York: Harper, 1958), p. 77.
64   Ibid.

traditions.[65] In a drafting meeting in June 1948, he drew attention to the influence of Chinese thought on Enlightenment thinkers such as Voltaire, Quesnay and Diderot, who had embraced China as a model of a moral order without superstition. Resisting the idea that 'European civilisation' was hermetically sealed, he told the drafters that 'Chinese ideas had been intermingled with European thought and sentiment on human rights at the time when that subject had first been speculated upon in modern Europe.'[66] In articulating a vision of human rights that drew on diverse cultural traditions, Chang resisted civilisational hierarchies, pre-empting subsequent theorists who have depicted the universalism of human rights as a product of an 'overlapping consensus' between diverse political, religious and economic systems.[67]

The Saudi Arabian delegate, Jamil Baroody, criticised Chang's ecumenical position, arguing that the UDHR was 'based largely on Western patterns of culture, which were frequently at variance with the patterns of culture of Eastern states.'[68] Today, the argument that human rights are a 'Western construct with limited applicability' to the non-Western world (as a highly influential article put it), is often depicted as a product of the turn towards autocracy in postcolonial states.[69] In the 1940s, however, Baroody and others already suspected that the new human rights language could become a means for coercive interventions into non-Western societies. With far less faith than Chang that human rights could be detached from ethnocentrism and civilisational hierarchies, Baroody anticipated more recent criticisms of the 'dominant influence of Western liberal thought and philosophies' on the key human rights texts.[70]

It was challenges from outside Europe, more than the often-cited post-war loss of faith among Europeans in their own civilisation, that

---

65   Jun Zhao, 'China and the Uneasy Case for Universal Human Rights', *Human Rights Quarterly* 37: 1 (2015), pp. 32–3.

66   Morsink, *Universal Declaration of Human Rights*.

67   The idea of an 'overlapping consensus' comes from John Rawls, and has been applied to human rights by scholars including Martha Nussbaum and Charles Taylor. See Charles R. Beitz, *The Idea of Human Rights* (Oxford: Oxford University Press Oxford, 2011), p. 76.

68   Jamil Baroody (Saudi Arabia), 'Summary Record of the Ninety-First Meeting of the Third Committee', 2 October 1948, in Schabas, *The Universal Declaration of Human Rights*, vol. 3, p. 2057.

69   Adamantia Pollis and Peter Schwab, 'Chapter 1: Human Rights: A Western Construct with Limited Applicability', in Adamantia Pollis and Peter Schwab, eds, *Human Rights: Cultural and Ideological Perspectives* (New York/London: Praeger, 1980).

70   Mutua, *Human Rights*, p. 154.

helped rid the UDHR of the language of civilisation. It is commonly argued that wartime atrocities made legal distinctions between civilised and uncivilised societies anachronistic.[71] From this perspective, the UDHR's affirmations of human equality indicated that chastened European powers had renounced racial and civilisational hierarchies in favour of universal humanism. But the view that the horrors of the war destabilised the distinction between the civilised and the uncivilised tacitly accepts that only atrocities committed against Europeans, and not colonial genocide, massacre and slavery, were sufficient to render European claims to civilisational superiority suspect. Two years after the adoption of the UDHR, the Martiniquian poet and politician Aimé Césaire argued that 'the very distinguished, very humanistic, very Christian bourgeois' is unable to forgive the Nazis not for the '*crime against man*' as such, but rather for 'the crime against the white man . . . and the fact that he applied to Europe colonialist procedures which until then had been reserved exclusively for the Arabs of Algeria, the coolies of India, and the blacks of Africa'.[72] Césaire charged what he termed 'pseudo-humanism' with promoting a conception of the rights of man that was fragmented, limited, narrow and 'sordidly racist'.[73] This conception of rights still maintained its hold during the drafting of the UDHR, as delegates from colonial powers sought to preserve civilisational hierarchies and colonial rule in the face of a variety of challenges.

For the neoliberals, the very attempt to find an international, cross-cultural consensus on a list of human rights was a profound mistake. In contrast to the model of elite moral authority mobilised by the League of Nations' mandate process, they viewed the UN as a false bureaucratic unity at odds with the spiritual unity of Europe.[74] Europe, Röpke argued, is 'more than catch-words, rhetoric and an empty excuse for conferences'; its 'spiritual heritage' of Greek culture, Christianity, individual freedom and economic freedom made it 'the home of humanity, tolerance, reason and

---

71   Brett Bowden and Leonard Seabrooke, *Global Standards of Market Civilization* (London: Routledge, 2006), p. 6.

72   Aimé Césaire, *Discourse on Colonialism*, transl. Joan Pinkham (New York: Monthly Review, 1972), p. 3.

73   Ibid., p. 3.

74   In contrast, Marco Duranti has decisively demonstrated the influence of this latter conception on the drafting of the European Convention of Human Rights. Marco Duranti, *The Conservative Human Rights Revolution: European Identity, Transnational Politics, and the Origins of the European Convention* (Oxford: Oxford University Press, 2017).

religion veneration.[75] For the neoliberals, the horrors of World War II were not a product of Western civilisation, but the results of the collectivist challenge to the liberalism that had previously defined it. They depicted civilisation as the product of the spread of commerce and the division of labour and a moral order that facilitated the pursuit of individual interest and trade. This meant that any restriction of trade was a civilisational regression – a return from the morals of the market to the egalitarianism and shared purposes of what Hayek described as a tribal morality.

Ludwig von Mises's Market Civilisation

In March 1938, the Gestapo ransacked the apartment of the leading Austrian School economist Ludwig von Mises, confiscating twenty-one boxes of papers and sealing the apartment behind them. Two years later, Mises, who had initially left Vienna for Rappard's Institute for International Affairs, fled Europe altogether for the United States.[76] He wrote to Hayek that he was reluctantly saying 'adieu to a Europe about to disappear forever'.[77] A decade earlier, Mises had been cautiously optimistic that fascist movements had saved Europe from the crisis of Bolshevism. 'It cannot be denied that Fascism and similar movements aiming at the establishment of dictatorships are full of the best intentions and that their intervention has, for the moment, saved European civilization', he wrote – adding that the 'merit that Fascism has thereby won for itself will live on eternally in history'.[78] Although he warned that fascism was no more than an 'emergency makeshift', he stressed that it emerged not among 'barbarians', as had Bolshevism, but in Europe, where 'the intellectual and moral heritage of some thousands of years of civilization cannot be destroyed at one blow'.[79] Fascist movements would therefore always remain under the influence of liberalism, he predicted and, once the indignation at Bolshevik 'murders and atrocities' had passed, fascism would become more 'moderate'.[80]

---

75   Wilhelm Röpke, *International Order and Economic Integration* (Dordrecht: D. Reidel, 1959), pp. 48–50.

76   Jörg Guido Hülsmann, *Mises: The Last Knight of Liberalism* (Auburn: Ludwig von Mises Institute, 2007), p. 685.

77   In Richard M. Ebeling, *Monetary and Economic Policy Problems Before, During, and After the Great War* (Indianapolis: Liberty Fund, 2012), p. lvi.

78   Ludwig von Mises, *Liberalism: The Classical Tradition*, ed. Bettina Bien Greaves, transl. Ralph Raico (Indianapolis: Liberty Fund, 2005), p. 30.

79   Ibid.

80   Ibid.

When this Jewish liberal intellectual ultimately abandoned Europe to the Nazis, this did not dent his faith in the inextricable relation between the competitive market and civilisation, but it did signal the end of an era in the development of neoliberalism. Mises's private seminar, held between 1920 and 1934 in his office in the Vienna Chamber of Commerce, was formative for a generation of neoliberal thinkers, among them Hayek, the philosopher Alfred Schütz, and the prominent economists Gottfried Haberler and Fritz Machlup.[81] One day, as Mises looked out of the window of his chamber offices onto Vienna's opulent grand boulevard (Ringstrasse), he told Machlup, 'Maybe grass will grow there, because our civilization will end.'[82] Mises was first among the MPS members to devote sustained attention to the problem of civilisation. By 1946, when Hayek proposed the formation of a new liberal institute, Mises could argue that 'eminent citizens' had been attempting to prevent civilisation's demise and stem the tide of totalitarianism for more than sixty years.[83]

For the Austrian milieu that nourished Mises and Hayek, the entire twentieth century was marked by decline. Mises came of age in Vienna under the multi-ethnic and supranational Austro-Hungarian Empire. In 1871, when the economist Carl Menger wrote what became the founding text of the Austrian School of economics, *Principles of Economics*, only 4 per cent of the population of Vienna were eligible to vote. They used their voting power to support liberal reforms, including freedoms of speech, assembly, religion and faith, as well as academic freedom.[84] Mises acknowledged later that the Liberal Party's position in the House of Deputies was not due to popular support; rather, the liberals benefited from an electoral system that privileged the upper middle class and the intelligentsia, and 'withheld the right to vote from the masses'.[85] The fatal contradiction of the Liberal Party, he suggested, was that it was a supposedly democratic party with a pronounced 'aversion to

81   Hülsmann, *Mises*, p. 465.

82   Richard M. Ebeling, 'Mises the Man and His Monetary Policy Ideas Based on His "Lost Papers"', *Mises Wire*, 7 April 2018, at mises.org.

83   Ludwig von Mises, 'Observations on Professor Hayek's Plan', *Libertarian Papers* 1: 2 (2009), p. 1.

84   Eugen Maria Schulak and Herbert Unterköfler, *The Austrian School of Economics: A History of Its Ideas, Ambassadors, and Institutions*, transl. Arlene Oost-Zinner (Auburn: Ludwig von Mises Institute, 2011), p. 4.

85   Ludwig von Mises, 'On the History of German Democracy', Bettina Bien Greaves, ed., in *Nation, State, and Economy*, transl. Leland B. Yeager (Indianapolis: Liberty Fund, 2006), p. 102.

democracy'.[86] Writing in the immediate aftermath of World War I, he attributed that party's ruin to the specific circumstances of the Austro-Hungarian Empire. But the fatal contradiction he identified was not confined to central Europe nor to the nineteenth century. Neoliberalism too combined a defence of liberal democracy with anxiety that unrestrained democracy threatened the liberal economic order.

Like his contemporaries Raphael Lemkin (1900–59), who initiated the Genocide Convention, and Hersch Lauterpacht (1897–1960), who pioneered the legal concepts of the 'crime against humanity' and transnational human rights, Mises grew up in Lemberg (today the major Ukrainian city of Lviv/Lwów), on the border of the Russian Empire. Mises came from a modernising assimilated Jewish family, and strongly identified with what he saw as the civilising influence of the Habsburg Empire's German elite, whose culture was often depicted as 'fertilizer for an otherwise barren east'.[87]

Writing in the immediate wake of World War I, he noted that, until the mid nineteenth century, Germans in the Habsburg Empire had taken their cultural superiority and dominance for granted; 'Whoever rose became German', he wrote.[88] When the Empire's other nationalities rejected this civilising path and demanded national independence, it was a painful realisation for the liberal German milieu. From this point on, they threw their support behind the monarchy, Mises recounted, and rejected demands for national autonomy and democratisation, which would have subjected Germans to the rule of Slavic majorities.[89]

Faced with the breakup of the Austro-Hungarian Empire in the wake of World War I, and the rise of social democracy and then fascism, the Austrian School neoliberals were preoccupied with what another resident of Vienna, the psychoanalyst Sigmund Freud, identified in the title of his *Civilization and Its Discontents* (1930). Freud saw his contemporaries' hostility to civilisation as originating in the revolt of 'the primitive roots of the personality still unfettered by civilizing influences' against the discipline and constraint of civilisation.[90] For Mises and his

86   Ibid., p. 102.

87   Pieter M. Judson, *The Habsburg Empire* (Harvard: Harvard University Press, 2016), 73.

88   Mises, 'On the History of German Democracy', p. 94.

89   Ibid., p. 95.

90   Sigmund Freud, *Civilization and Its Discontents* (New York: W. W. Norton, 2017), p. 70.

fellow Austrian School members, the restraint most essential to civilisation was submission to the demands of the market. They believed that, in creating a web of mutually beneficial relations, commerce was civilising, and that the most civilised peoples were therefore those with the most extensive division of labour. For Mises, the 'destiny of modern civilization as developed by the white peoples in the last two hundred years is inseparably linked with the fate of economic science'.[91] Although Mises criticised the metaphysical ideas of constant progress, he identified a form of compulsion at work in the division of labour. It was always in the interests of the most 'advanced' societies to draw others into the web of social cooperation, both in the interests of greater productivity and because such cooperation fostered peace, he argued. The outbreak of World War I brutally shattered 'the dream of an ecumenical society' that Mises had believed was heralded by the 'opening up of the backward regions of the Near and Far East, of Africa and America' and the extension of the world market.[92]

In conceptualising a civilised society as a market society with a highly developed division of labour, Mises drew on the thought of Adam Smith, whom he credited with the discovery of the eternal law of social evolution that every civilisation must follow if it is not to fall back into barbarism.[93] Mises placed himself within in a tradition that stretched back to the Baron de Montesquieu's belief that commerce 'polishes and softens [adoucit] barbarian ways', which informed Scottish Enlightenment thinkers, including Smith and Adam Ferguson, for whom the history of civil society was one of slow and gradual progression from the 'rude and infant state' of unsettled tribes, to the industry, arts, sciences and class divisions of 'polished' commercial nations.[94] This reference to the polishing function of commerce is likely to be the root of the term 'polished nations', which the Scots used to refer to civilised, commercial nations, in contrast to 'rude' ones.[95] In Ferguson's great *Essay on the History of*

91 Ludwig von Mises, *Human Action: A Treatise on Economics* (San Francisco: Fox & Wilkes, 1996), p. 10.

92 Ludwig von Mises, *Socialism: An Economic and Sociological Analysis*, transl. J. Kahane (New Haven, CT: Yale University Press, 1962), p. 308.

93 Ludwig von Mises, *Theory and History: An Interpretation of Social and Economic Evolution* (Auburn: Ludwig von Mises Institute, 2007), p. 167.

94 Adam Ferguson, *An Essay on the History of Civil Society*, ed. Fania Oz-Salzberger (Cambridge: Cambridge University Press, 2001), p. 74.

95 Albert O. Hirschman, *The Passions and the Interests: Political Arguments for Capitalism before Its Triumph* (Princeton: Princeton University Press, 2013), p. 60.

Civil Society, a polished nation is defined by its refinement and sensibility as well as its commerce, division of labour and wealth. The idea that commerce was civilising gave impetus to the dichotomy later expressed under the oppositions 'civilised–uncivilised', 'advanced–backward', and 'developed–undeveloped'.[96]

In appropriating this tradition, Mises portrayed civilisation as inextricably economic and racial. While he rejected the biological racism of the French eugenicist Arthur de Gobineau, Mises sought to rescue its 'germ' for a 'modern' race theory that ascribed racial hierarchies to an evolutionary process that gave certain races 'so long a lead that members of other races could not overtake them within a limited time'.[97] The North American poltical scientist Adolph Reed Jr and others have emphasised the historical variance of racial classifications and the narratives that elaborate them.[98] For Mises, what distinguished races was not only an inequality of intelligence and willpower, but also an unequal ability to form societies based on an extensive division of labour. The 'better races', he argued, have a special aptitude for social cooperation through the market. Consequently, the 'peoples who have developed the system of the market economy and cling to it are in every respect superior to all other peoples'.[99] While he sought to show that all races derive advantages from cooperation, he also contended that so-called inferior races could only progress by protecting private property and individual rights, adopting an extensive division of labour, and adapting themselves to the margin of freedom enabled by a market society.[100]

While he rejected the natural-law belief in human equality, Mises embraced individual rights as key components of the liberal heritage. Mises contrasted 'Western man' – 'entirely a being adjusted to life in freedom and formed in freedom' – with the 'Asiatics', who he depicted as the apathetic inhabitants of stagnant societies.[101] While Adam Smith had based a similar judgment of China on its refusal of foreign trade, Mises attributed the disintegration of the once-powerful

---

96   Ibid.
97   Mises, *Socialism*, p. 325.
98   Reed, 'Marx, Race, and Neoliberalism'.
99   Mises, *Human Action*.
100   Mises, *Socialism*, p. 326.
101   Ludwig von Mises, *The Anti-Capitalistic Mentality* (Auburn: Ludwig von Mises Institute, 2008), p. 102.

empires of Japan, India and China to their absence of individual rights. 'The East', he claimed, 'never tried to stress the rights of the individual, against the power of rulers.'[102] Deprived of rights, the wealthy were exposed to the resentment of the masses and the permanent threat of expropriation. Mises also believed that the absence of individual rights had made barbaric abuses a matter of course in 'the East': 'slavery, serfdom, untouchability, customs like sutteeism or the crippling of the feet of girls, barbaric punishments, mass misery, ignorance, superstition, and disregard of hygiene'.[103] It was the absence of a culture of individual rights, he argued, that attracted the people of the East to socialism.[104] In such a picture, the absence of the competitive market economy was inseparable from violations of freedom and bodily integrity, while socialism was aligned with foot-binding and slavery. 'Freedom is indivisible', Mises remarked, and so preventing such practices required a competitive market underpinned by a system of individual rights.[105]

In the course of the twentieth century, Mises and his neoliberal colleagues cast state planning, medical and employment insurance, protective tariffs and welfare states not simply as economic threats, but as threats to individual rights – and ultimately to civilisation itself. Like his Scottish predecessor Adam Ferguson, Mises believed that while the 'most remarkable races of men ... have been rude before they were polished', the 'polished' nations might nonetheless slide back along the evolutionary scale.[106] While Ferguson warned that a people might be corrupted by its commercial success, Mises believed it was socialism that was hastening the decline of civilisation. In Asia, he warned, antagonists of European civilisation were gathered under the banner of socialism. And if they were allowed to destroy the division of labour, 'nomad tribes from the Eastern steppes would again raid and pillage Europe, sweeping across it with swift cavalry'.[107]

The key distinction between East and West, according to Mises, is that the East was 'foreign to the Western spirit that has created capitalism'. As a result, he contended that, 'if the Asiatics and Africans really

---

102   Ibid., p. 103.
103   Mises, *Theory and History*, p. 376.
104   Ibid.
105   Ibid.
106   Ferguson, *Essay on the History of Civil Society*, p. 107.
107   Mises, *Socialism*, p. 511.

enter into the orbit of Western civilisation, they will have to adopt the market economy without reservation'.[108] Adopting the market did not merely mean adopting a technical means of allocating goods; it required a profound cultural, moral and subjective transformation. Market peoples are peace loving, Mises warned, but would fight to the death against anyone who interfered with this division of labour, and 'repel the barbarian aggressors whatever their numbers may be'.[109] Earlier, he had suggested that, if only some nations became socialist, the cause would not be lost. The remaining capitalist ones – driven by the 'fundamental social law' to extend the global division of labour – would 'impose culture upon the backward nations or destroy them if they resisted'.[110] Conversion or destruction were the only options available to those who sought to exist outside the world market.

Moral Integration: The Neoliberals Against *Laissez-Faire*

Freiburg economist and early MPS member Walter Eucken was typical of early neoliberalism in his belief that nineteenth-century liberalism had failed. This failure, Eucken wrote to his fellow German neoliberal Alexandre Rüstow, was not due to its religious and metaphysical foundations. Rather, when liberalism 'lost its religious and metaphysical content, it decayed'.[111] Eucken, one of the founders of Germany's postwar social-market economy, shared the dominant MPS view that securing a competitive market order could not be left to the invisible hand. The experience of the political polarisation and crisis of Weimar Germany had alerted the German liberals to the moral, institutional and legal conditions for a competitive market order. Whatever their differences, the early neoliberals largely accepted that the survival of civilisation required state action to produce the conditions for a competitive market, including by promoting a conducive moral climate. Even the Chicago School's Milton Friedman – who would later describe the invisible hand as Smith's 'great achievement' – argued in 1951 that the collectivist faith in the state was 'an understandable reaction to a basic error of

---

108   Mises, *Human Action*, p. 671.
109   Ibid.
110   Mises, *Socialism*, p. 512.
111   Eucken, cited in Nils Goldschmidt, 'Walter Eucken's Place in the History of Ideas', *Review of Austrian Economics* 26: 2 (2013), p. 143.

nineteenth-century individualist philosophy' and its embrace of *laissez-faire*.[112]

Few were as vocal in their rejection of *laissez-faire* as the German ordoliberals Röpke and Rüstow. During the war, both men lived in Istanbul, where President Kemal Atatürk's attempt to secularise and modernise Turkey prompted them to focus on the moral and religious foundations of a competitive market economy.[113] Rüstow criticised the call to *laissez-faire* as both a 'summons to honour God and an adjuration not to allow short-sighted human anxieties to interfere in the eternal wisdom of the natural law'.[114] He believed it had led previous liberals into an overly 'care-free' faith that, left alone, the market would improve 'moral standards'.[115] The ordoliberals accepted that, by promoting mutual dependence, 'the division of labour can be conceived as one of the most potent civilizing factors'.[116] But theirs was not a straightforward 'sweetness of commerce' thesis; they regarded competition as morally dangerous and believed that, left alone, the market would not produce the necessary 'lubricant of morals, sentiments and institutions'.[117] Röpke derided the invisible hand as a ' "philosopher's stone" that turned the base metal of callous business sentiments into the pure gold of common welfare and solidarity'.[118] A competitive market order, the ordoliberals argued, required an institutional framework and 'a generally observed and undisputed code of moral norms and principles of behavior'.[119]

If moral integration was crucial within the borders of a single state, they argued that it was even more so in the international sphere, where the greater precariousness of order and the absence of a central state with a single authoritative body of laws placed a premium on shared legal and moral standards. It was only by finding a workable international substitute for the sovereign state, they believed, that the eighteenth and nineteenth centuries had achieved that 'socio-political

---

112   Milton Friedman, 'Neo-Liberalism and Its Prospects', *Farmand*, 17 February 1951.

113   Antonio Masala, 'Wilhelm Röpke and Alexander Rüstow in Turkey: A Missed Legacy?' (Istanbul: Yıldız Technical University, 2016).

114   Alexander Rüstow, 'Appendix', in Röpke *International Economic Disintegration*, p. 270.

115   Ibid.

116   Röpke, *International Economic Disintegration*, p. 70.

117   Ibid., p. 70.

118   Ibid., p. 67.

119   Ibid., p. 72.

integration of the civilized world' without which no world economy would have been possible.[120] By this stage, the neoliberals had already lived through the shock of Britain's 1931 withdrawal from the gold standard, which they regarded as a central plank of an 'international legal and moral system' whose violation represented 'the act of men without honour, honesty or scruples'.[121] The international economic integration of the past two hundred years, Röpke argued, had required an 'undisputed moral code'.[122] For Mises, too, the gold standard had been about much more than commodity prices and foreign exchange: it had 'born Western civilization into the remotest parts of the earth's surface, everywhere destroying the fetters of age-old prejudices and superstitions, sowing the seeds of new life and well-being, freeing minds and souls to create riches unheard of before'.[123]

If economic disintegration was a product of moral disintegration, then a revival of dreams of perpetual peace required the development of moral and legal standards to support the global spread of the competitive market by protecting private property and human dignity. The market economy, Röpke argued, 'belongs essentially to a liberal social structure and one which respects individual rights', while non-market, collectivist coordination is coercive, ignoring such rights.[124] The attempt to draft a universal human rights declaration might have made a contribution to the revival of such shared moral standards. But, of course, everything depended on how those rights were understood. For the neoliberals, human rights could only play this role if they broke with the rationalism of the French Revolution and fostered submission to the market order. While Christianity could not provide history or the market with a providential guarantee, they believed it could secure the moral foundations of a competitive market order 'truly compatible with human dignity'.[125]

120   Ibid., p. 74.
121   Wilhelm Röpke, *Economics of the Free Society*, transl. Patrick M. Boarman (Chicago: Henry Regnery Company, 1963), p. 49.
122   Röpke, *International Economic Disintegration*, p. 72.
123   Mises, *Human Action*, p. 173.
124   Wilhelm Röpke, *The Moral Foundations of Civil Society* (New Brunswick: Transaction, 2002), p. 5.
125   Rüstow, 'Appendix', p. 280.

Commerce and Christianity

In his masterful account of the Christian embrace of human rights in the twentieth century, the historian of human rights Samuel Moyn stresses how radically the version of human rights promoted by Catholics in the mid twentieth century differed from the revolutionary rights-of-man tradition, which the Church bitterly opposed throughout the eighteenth and nineteenth centuries. To a 'rather disturbing extent', he writes, 'human rights and especially human dignity had no necessary correlation with liberal democracy'.[126] Moyn doubts that the embrace of liberal principles by conservative Christians was a victory for liberalism. Could it be, he asks, that Christianity and conservatism changed liberalism more than vice versa, as the language of rights was 'extricated from the legacy of the French Revolution' and tethered to a religious, conservative agenda?[127] This transformation, I suggest, did not simply come from outside. In attempting to free human rights from the French Revolution, conservative Christians tapped into an internal transformation of liberalism pioneered by the figures associated with the MPS, who sought to re-establish liberalism on secure moral foundations.

This was clear in Hayek's opening address to the Society's inaugural conference, which deplored the rationalistic liberalism of the French Revolution. Unless the 'breach between true liberalism and religious convictions can be healed', he argued, 'there is no hope for a revival of liberal forces'.[128] The importance of Christianity to the new liberal project was reflected in a session at that conference on 'Liberalism and Christianity', which included twelve speakers drawn from across Europe, the UK and the United States. Although none of the Society's founders were active representatives of the Catholic faith, Röpke noted in 1957, this 'circle of technicians' soon turned its attention to the relation between Christianity and freedom. They became conscious, he suggests, that liberals and Christians, 'concerned for freedom and human dignity', shared common ground they did not share with their collectivist enemy.[129]

---

126   Samuel Moyn, *Christian Human Rights* (Philadelphia: University of Pennsylvania Press, 2015), p. 8.

127   Ibid., p. 9.

128   Friedrich Hayek, *Studies in Philosophy, Politics and Economics* (Chicago: University of Chicago Press, 1967), p. 155.

129   Wilhelm Röpke, 'Liberalism and Christianity', *Modern Age* 1: 2 (1957), p. 128.

The neoliberal embrace of Christianity was not necessarily a product of faith. Hayek was himself agnostic, but he believed that Christianity was essential for cultivating the morals of the market and the willingness to submit to the market order.[130] A 'refusal to submit to anything we cannot understand', he warned in *The Road to Serfdom*, 'must lead to the destruction of our civilization'.[131] Hayek believed that the rise of rationalism made people unwilling to submit to anything they did not understand. Through this refusal, he argued, the rationalist may become the 'destroyer of civilization', and we will be 'thrown back into barbarism'.[132] The Austrian economist acknowledged that this submission has historically been achieved by religions, traditions and superstitions 'which made men submit to those forces by an appeal to his emotions rather than to his reason'.[133] But he made clear this was preferable to the preoccupation with reason he saw in his own time.

The Chicago School's Frank Knight was relatively isolated in his belief that communism and the Catholic Church shared the same principles and were similarly undemocratic. The year after the UDHR was adopted, Knight suggested that the Church at least deserved credit for 'not pretending to believe in democracy or individual liberty'.[134] As Moyn notes, however, the position of the Church was also changing in the face of the threat that socialism and fascism represented to its autonomy and to the freedoms of conscience and worship. The drafting of the UDHR therefore attracted the attention of conservative Christians, who were similarly concerned with the re-establishment of moral standards and saw in human rights a means to protect the dignity and conscience of the human person and preserve intermediate institutions (like the Church and the family) in the face of the rise of 'totalitarianism'.

For the neoliberals, communism was not simply a competing European political movement; communism was 'a pseudo-religion within the shell of the Russian state, a sort of secularized Islam', in

---

130   Jessica Whyte, 'The Invisible Hand of Friedrich Hayek: Submission and Spontaneous Order', *Political Theory*, 7 November 2017.

131   Hayek, *Road to Serfdom*, p. 211.

132   Friedrich Hayek, '"Conscious" Direction and the Growth of Reason', in *The Collected Works of F. A. Hayek: Studies on the Abuse and Decline of Reason*, vol. 13 (Chicago: University of Chicago Press, 2010), p. 154.

133   Ibid.

134   Frank H. Knight, 'World Justice, Socialism and the Intellectuals', *University of Chicago Law Review* 16: 3 (1949), p. 440.

Roepke's words, communists were emissaries of an empire bent on world domination.[135] With this 'Communist Pseudo-Islam' there could not be 'one world', but only a mobilisation of Europe against the threat of fanatical hordes from the East.[136] This assimilation of communism, totalitarianism and Islam recurred frequently in the writings of the neoliberals, who drew on orientalist tropes of inassimilable otherness to discredit their adversaries. Mises, whose beloved Habsburg Empire had long been viewed as the bulwark against the Ottoman Empire, argued that, while socialism's rapid expansion had been compared to that of Christianity, it would be more appropriate to compare it to Islam, 'which inspired the sons of the desert to lay waste ancient civilizations, cloaked their destructive fury with an ethical ideology and stiffened their courage with rigid fatalism'.[137] In 1961, MPS vice-president, Albert Hunold, criticised those intellectual leaders he deemed ignorant of 'the real nature of totalitarianism' and 'incapable of pointing out the ways and means by which a check can be imposed upon this "new Islam" and a policy initiated that is worthy of the dignity and strength of our western civilisation and culture'.[138]

Here, too, the neoliberals were close to conservative Christians. Such views were echoed by the Lebanese UN delegate Charles Malik, who drafted the Universal Declaration's preamble with its ringing assertion that the 'inherent dignity of the equal and inalienable rights of all members of the human family is the foundation of freedom, justice and peace in the world'. For Malik, who insisted on the inclusion in the UDHR of 'religious ciphers' such as 'inherent', 'inalienable', 'endowed', it was 'Western civilization' that contained at its core 'the truest reality of human dignity'.[139] In contrast, he argued that 'certain elements in Islam admit of an interpretation that accords with Communism'.[140] Malik singled out the 'blind fatalism of Marx', and called on the West to take action to ensure that the 'alliance between Communism, radical nationalism, anti-Westernism, xenophobia and religious reaction and

---

135 Röpke, *International Order and Economic Integration*, p. 60.
136 Ibid., pp. 60, 74.
137 Mises, *Socialism*, p. 461.
138 Hunold, 'Preface', p. 7.
139 On ciphers, see Alexandre Lefebvre, *Human Rights and the Care of the Self* (London: Duke University Press, 2018), p. 161; Charles Malik, 'Human Rights and Religious Liberty', *Ecumenical Review* 1: 4 (1949), p. 408.
140 Charles Malik, 'Call to Action in the Near East', *Foreign Affairs*, 34:4 (1956), p. 640.

fanaticism need not be the last word'.[141] Several years earlier, in the course of posing the question 'Whither Islam?', Malik had depicted Arab history as dominated by the 'overwhelming numbers of lower classes and the absence of the middle class', which had had led to the domination of 'the masses and of the mob'.[142] All these considerations came to the fore as UN delegates debated the right to change one's religion. Christian advocacy on behalf of missionaries would ultimately bolster the neoliberal attempt to enshrine new standards to protect the rights of traders across the globe.

The Right to Change One's Religion and the Mission of Human Rights

One of the most intractable debates about human rights concerns the legitimacy of intervention across borders to prevent their violation. Whether or not such legitimacy is legitimate is often thought to hinge on the answer to another question: How universal is the provenance of human rights? While some attempt to construct a multicultural Whig history by identifying the origins of human rights in ancient Hindu texts or the writings of Confucius, it is more common to point to the participation of delegates from Lebanon, China, Saudi Arabia or India in the drafting of the UDHR as evidence that human rights have a cross-cultural legitimacy capable of grounding human rights interventions.[143] For critics, on the other hand, human rights universalism is marked by a history of European colonialism, and serves both to facilitate and to obscure the coercive reconstruction of societies on capitalist lines. The anthropologist Talal Asad, for instance, situates human rights in a lineage stretching back to the Spanish colonisation of the Americas, for which the extension of European law was explicitly viewed as a project of cultural and religious transformation; most human rights theorists, Asad argues, 'don't address

---

141   Ibid.

142   Charles Malik, 'The Near East: The Search for Truth', *Foreign Affairs* 30: 2 (1952), p. 256.

143   For the former, see Paul Gordon Lauren, *The Evolution of International Human Rights: Visions Seen* (Philadelphia: University of Pennsylvania Press, 2011). For the latter, see Kathryn Sikkink, *Evidence for Hope: Making Human Rights Work in the 21st Century* (Princeton, NJ: Princeton University Press, 2017).

seriously enough the thought that human rights is part of a great work of conversion'.[144]

These debates were prefigured during the drafting process of the UDHR. It was in the course of the drafting debates about freedom of conscience and conversion that the relation of human rights to earlier patterns of coercive intervention became a topic of fierce dispute. Charles Malik, who championed the right to freedom of conscience, has been portrayed as a figure at the 'crossroads of many cultures, and personally and professionally shaped by both Christianity and Islam'.[145] But the Lebanese diplomat was hardly an ideal mediator between religious traditions. An Orthodox Christian by birth, though with a strong predilection for Roman Catholicism, Malik would later align – during his active participation in Lebanon's civil war – with the Christian Maronite sect. Malik's role as an active participant in his own country's sectarian conflicts has not dented his image in human rights scholarship as a figure who embraced tolerance and mutual understanding. The Palestinian intellectual Edward Said, whose mother's cousin was married to Malik, gives a very different account, describing Malik as 'the symbol and the outspoken intellectual figurehead of everything most prejudicial, conflicted, and incompatible with the Arab and largely Islamic Middle East'.[146] Malik was not the 'surrogate for the absent Muslim voice' on the commission on human rights that he has often been portrayed as.[147]

Malik's Christianity deeply informed his stress on a spiritually unified 'West'. In a 1952 essay, he wrote that 'the West is unthinkable apart from Christianity and the East apart from Islam'.[148] Malik was more committed than many of the European delegates to constructing an idea of 'the West' characterised by 'Greece, Rome, Christianity', the democracy of the 'Anglo-Saxon experience' and the French Revolution.[149] The argument that this Christian influence was inclusive, with 'broad appeal

144   Talal Asad, 'What Do Human Rights Do? An Anthropological Enquiry', *Theory and Event* 4: 4 (2000).

145   Lauren, *Evolution of International Human Rights*, p. 207.

146   Edward W. Said, *Out of Place: A Memoir* (New York: Alfred A. Knopf, 1999), p. 263.

147   Ali A. Allawi, *The Crisis of Islamic Civilization* (New Haven, CT: Yale University Press, 2009), p. 189.

148   Malik, 'Near East', *Foreign Affairs* 30: 2 (1952), p. 239.

149   Charles Malik, 'The Relations of East and West', *Proceedings of the American Philosophical Society* 97: 1 (1953), p. 1.

across many cultures', obscures the extent of Malik's universalist Christian commitment to the transformation of non-Western socie-ties.[150] Like Rüstow and Röpke, with whom he shared a conservative Christian fear of the intrusions of politics, Malik took the view that global economic integration required moral transformation; if the 'undeveloped countries' wished to develop their economies, he argued in 1953, they would need to absorb not only Western techniques but also three thousand years of Western scientific tradition and a commit-ment to 'the inherent dignity of the human person'.[151]

Malik portrayed freedom of conscience as the central value of this Western heritage. This provenance meant that 'not all claims of conscience are therefore seen as being equal in the UDHR.'[152] Not only did Malik assume the religious and Christian contours of conscience; he also argued, more controversially, that the right to change one's religion was a necessary aspect of this 'Platonic–Christian tradition'.[153] Malik saw such a right as central to upholding freedom of conscience in the face of two key adversaries: a 'mass' (working-class and communist) politics whose focus on economic welfare threatened to reduce the human to a material, rather than a spiritual, being; and Islam, which, according to Malik's Orientalist depiction, lacked reason and distinction, and fused different orders (God and the universe, man and God, man and animal, and past and future) so that, in Islam, 'man – as to his origin, his powers, his state, and his destiny – is exceedingly ambiguous'.[154]

The final text of Article 18, which Malik promoted, reads as follows: 'Everyone has the right to freedom of thought, conscience and religion; this right includes freedom to change his religion or belief, and freedom, either alone or in community with others and in public or private, to manifest his religion or belief in teaching, practice, worship and obser-vance.' While freedom of conscience had a long history, there was no consensus that it required a right to change religion. Kathryn Sikkink argues that Malik based his support for such a right 'not on a Western

150   Mary Ann Glendon, 'The Influence of Catholic Social Doctrine on Human Rights', in *15th Plenary Session* (Catholic Social Doctrine and Human Rights, Vatican City: Pontifical Academy of Social Sciences, 2010), p. 70.

151   Charles Malik, 'Some Reflections on Technical and Economic Assistance', *Bulletin of the Atomic Scientists* X: 3 (1954), p. 96.

152   Tobias Kelly, 'A Divided Conscience', *Public Culture* 30: 3 (1 September 2018), p. 375.

153   Malik, 'Human Rights and Religious Liberty', p. 404.

154   Malik, 'Relations of East and West', p. 2.

precedent, but on his country's experience accepting religious refugees, some of whom fled persecution resulting from religious conversions'.[155] But the very idea of Lebanon as a 'Christian refuge', as Lebanese historian Fayyaz Traboulsi notes, was bound to an idea of its distinctiveness with respect to 'Arab identity and Islam, both part of "barbaric Asia"'.[156]

The strongest opposition to the right to change one's religion came from Baroody, the delegate from Saudi Arabia. Baroody was representing a repressive, theocratic state, and scholars have been quick to identify his challenge to this right, and Saudi Arabia's abstention from the final UDHR, as a product of the prohibition on apostasy in conservative Wahhabi interpretations of Islam.[157] But the picture is more complicated than that. Baroody, like Malik, was a Lebanese Christian. In opposing the right to change one's religion, he never referred to Islamic law, but instead framed this new right as a right for missionaries. Proselytising Christians had historically become the vanguards of political interventions, he argued, and 'peoples had been drawn into murderous conflict by the missionaries' efforts to convert them'.[158] Baroody depicted Article 18 as a right to open up non-Western societies for trade and exploitation. Such concerns resonated with Chang, who responded: 'For the countries of the Far East, the nineteenth century, with its expansion of Western industrialism, had not always been very kind', and missionaries had not always limited themselves to their religious missions.[159]

Chang would have known well that, when the First Opium War ended in 1842 with the Treaty of Nanking, which forced China to open to Western commerce, this led to great evangelical and commercial excitement back in Britain. Trade, even when forced upon a country by gunboats, was a vehicle for spreading the word of the gospels and promoting universal brotherhood. 'Those who denied their people access to truth, and to the manufactures of the West', in contrast, 'were

---

155 Sikkink, *Evidence for Hope*, p. 86.

156 Fawwaz Traboulsi, *A History of Modern Lebanon* (London: Pluto, 2007), p. 83.

157 Glenn Mitoma, 'Charles H. Malik and Human Rights: Notes on a Biography', *Biography* 33: 1 (12 June 2010), p. 227; Abdulaziz M. Alwasil, 'Saudi Arabia's Engagement in, and Interaction with, the UN Human Rights System: An Analytical Review', *International Journal of Human Rights* 14: 7 (27 May 2010).

158 Baroody, 'Summary Record of the Hundred and Twenty-Seventh Meeting of the Third Committee', 9 November 1948, in Schabas, *The Universal Declaration of Human Rights*, vol. 3, p. 2489.

159 Peng Chun Chang (China), in ibid., p. 2496.

infringing on an inherent human right'.[160] When the Second Opium War ended with the 1858 Treaties of Tianjin, traders were granted almost unlimited access to China's territory, and missionaries were guaranteed the freedom to evangelise their faith.[161] The status of missionaries had long played an important role in European attempts to determine which states were sufficiently 'civilised' to enter the family of nations, and the forcible imposition of unequal treaties was a consequence of falling short of this standard in European eyes. The imposition of this standard meant the coercive transformation of China's legal, political and economic systems to make its territory safe for commerce, conversion and capital accumulation. Despite this history of proselytising as precursor to commercial and military interventions, Chang spoke in favour of the right to change one's religion, leaving Baroody to declare him 'over-optimistic' in allowing missionaries to repeat their past mistakes.[162]

Both Baroody and Malik had significant personal experience with missionaries. Both men were graduates of the American University of Beirut (AUB), established by Protestant missionaries (originally as the Syrian Protestant College) in 1866. That formative experience shaped Malik's emphasis on freedom of conscience; in 1923, when he arrived at the AUB, its new president, Baynard Dodge, used his inaugural address to assure his students that the university did not intend to proselytise: 'To us, Protestantism means religious freedom.'[163] Yet the AUB was not just an island of religious tolerance; it was also evidence of the tight bond between commerce and Christianity. The university was established using the fortunes of the Dodge family, whose mining interests in the United States had given them a particular interest in the 'civilising' of indigenous peoples, upon whose un-ceded land they built mines. Those who built the Dodge fortune also committed themselves to the 'assimilation and uplift' of African-Americans in the South during Reconstruction – but only after the failure of their preferred option of resettlement in Liberia.[164] Both Baroody and Malik were products of the

---

160   Lydia He Liu, *The Clash of Empires* (Cambridge, MA: Harvard University Press, 2004), p. 134.

161   Brian Stanley, ' "Commerce and Christianity": Providence Theory, the Missionary Movement, and the Imperialism of Free Trade, 1842–1860', *Historical Journal* 26: 1 (1983), p. 90.

162   Baroody, in ibid., p. 2502.

163   Mitoma, 'Charles H. Malik and Human Rights', p. 229.

164   Robert Vitalis, *America's Kingdom: Mythmaking on the Saudi Oil Frontier* (Redwood City, CA: Stanford University Press, 2007), p. 39.

Dodges' civilising mission in the Middle East – but with very different outcomes.

Baroody's interpretation of the UDHR's right to change religion as a right for missionaries was largely accurate. The freedom of missionary activities was a key concern of those Protestant and Catholic non-governmental organisations Malik credited for their important role in the formulation of the draft article on religious freedom.[165] The codification of the right to change one's religion had been a particular concern for the Commission of the Churches on International Affairs, and was grounded in concerns about barriers to missionary work, particularly in the Middle East. For the churches, the right to religious freedom necessarily included the right to hear the gospel, and thus required freedom of proselytism, especially in the face of the strictures of Islamic law.[166]

It would nonetheless be mistaken to portray the debates over this right as a 'clash of civilisations' between Christianity and Islam. Such a position not only ignores a history of mutual borrowing and interactions among Christians, Jews and Muslims, but, as Asad writes, it attributes to a people an identity (European, Islamic) that 'depends on the definition of a selective civilizational heritage of which most of the people to whom it is attributed are in fact almost completely ignorant'.[167] Moreover, delegates from countries with Muslim majorities were split on the right to change religion. Pakistan's representative and foreign minister, Sir Mohammed Zafrullah Khan, actively embraced the missionary implications Baroody saw in Article 18, arguing that, as Islam was also a proselytising religion, Muslims must insist that conscience is free and able to change its judgment. In support of this position, he cited the Koran: 'Let he who chooses to believe, believe, and he who chooses to disbelieve, disbelieve.'[168]

While Baroody framed his opposition to Article 18 as a rejection of what Makau Mutua calls 'proselytism, coupled with force and power',

---

165   Malik, 'Human Rights and Religious Liberty', p. 406.

166   Linde Lindkvist, *Religious Freedom and the Universal Declaration of Human Rights* (Cambridge: Cambridge University Press, 2017), p. 80.

167   Talal Asad, *On Suicide Bombing* (New York: Columbia University Press, 2007), p. 10.

168   Mohammed Zafrullah Khan (Pakistan), 'Verbatim Record of the Hundred and Eighty-Second Plenary Meeting of the United Nations General Assembly', 10 December 1948, in Schabas, *Universal Declaration of Human Rights*, vol. 3, 3054. Lindkvist, *Religious Freedom*, p. 64.

there was nonetheless an irony to his advocacy of non-intervention.[169] Whatever his own personal commitments, which were largely Arabist in tenor, Baroody represented a kingdom whose participation in the inaugural UN conference was funded by the US Oil Company Aramco, and which owed its existence as an independent state largely to these same US oil interests. 'The transformation of the landscape that became Saudi Arabia', as the political scientist Robert Vitalis writes, 'was wrought in great part by foreigners, arriving in increasing numbers in the 1940s and 1950s, financed by foreign investment, foreign private and public aid, and large loans secured by future oil royalties.'[170] By the time Baroody was representing Saudi Arabia, David Dodge, the son of his old AUB president, was himself working for Aramco as a senior figure in its government relations department – a position in which he would have exerted significant influence over the Saudi state.

Baroody may have represented a US client state, but the arguments he made during the drafting of the UDHR would become increasingly worrying for the neoliberals. In rejecting the missionary implications of the new human rights discourse, he challenged the legitimacy of the attempt to establish global standards to secure the integration of the world market. As the UDHR was being drafted, Baroody gave a paper in New York, where he warned that, in the event of another global conflict, the 'Arab East . . . may become one of the major battlegrounds and graveyards of the clashing modern civilizations'.[171] It was essential, he warned perceptively, that this region's resources, especially its oil, not become 'war fuel'. The biggest danger, he argued, was that 'the old blind belligerent forces may plunge the world into a ghastly global conflict'.[172] By drawing attention to the violence of previous attempts at conversion, Baroody worked to challenge the legitimacy of European civilizing missions. In this sense, it is accurate to depict his argument as a 'relatively mild' foretaste of the anti-imperialism that later became prominent in UN forums.[173] In response, the neoliberals would draw the missionary and interventionist implications of the new human rights language, which framed

---

169   Mutua, *Human Rights*, p. 100.
170   Vitalis, *America's Kingdom*, p. 6.
171   Jamil M. Baroody, 'Economic Problems of the Arab East', *Problems of the Middle East* (New York, 1947), p. 2.
172   Ibid., p. 3.
173   Cited in Lindkvist, *Religious Freedom*, p. 99.

human rights as a means to enforce global standards to support the old rights of private capital.

For the neoliberals, the Christian emphasis on freedom of conscience provided a foundation for the freedom of individual choice that a market order required. They nonetheless gave their own twist to this freedom. In 1945, Hayek wrote:

> To the accepted Christian tradition that man must be free to follow *his* conscience in moral matters if his actions are to be of any merit, the economists added the further argument that he should be free to make full use of *his* knowledge and skill, that he must be allowed to be guided by his concern for the particular things of which *he* knows and for which *he* cares, if he is to make as great a contribution to the common purposes of society as he is capable of making.[174]

In post-war Europe and the United States, the neoliberals watched with horror as faith in the market was increasingly displaced by concerns with the welfare and economic security of the working classes. Malik likewise criticised the West for its wrong turn, and demanded its repentance for having offered the East only the 'false Gods of modern Western civilization: nationalism, materialism, Communism.'[175] To Malik's despair, these 'false Gods' were embraced by many of his fellow diplomats during the drafting of the Declaration.

In the wake of the war, 'civilisation' was retooled in a social-democratic direction, and even liberals increasingly recognised that competing with the temptations on the left and the right required them to recognise the social and economic needs of the working classes. 'To be civilized, in the old liberal sense', the historian Mark Mazower notes, 'was not necessarily to be modern.'[176] On the contrary, it was to prioritise a set of civil liberties and property rights that increasingly appeared

---

174   Friedrich Hayek, 'Individualism: True and False', in *Individualism and Economic Order* (Chicago: University of Chicago Press, 1958), p. 14 (emphases in original).

175   Malik, 'Near East', p. 256.

176   Mark Mazower, 'The End of Civilization and the Rise of Human Rights', in Stefan-Ludwig Hoffman, ed., *Human Rights in the Twentieth Century* (Cambridge: Cambridge University Press, 2010), p. 37.

antiquated.[177] The promise of social welfare gave a new impetus to the language of civilisation by associating it with rising living standards and material welfare. Within less than three years of the adoption of the UDHR, Malik warned that human rights were under threat from the ultimate danger of materialism, which he argued inverted the hierarchy that should place civil and political rights above social and economic ones. 'Certain rights', he complained, 'are assuming exaggerated importance; it is hard to keep them in their place. Who is not clamouring today for his economic rights, for what is called a decent standard of living?'[178] For the neoliberals, too, these developments threatened to subject the whole world to totalitarianism. The threat to the central values of civilisation, identified in the MPS statement of aims, was, first of all, a threat to market competition in the face of the 'revolt of the masses'.

---

177   Ibid.
178   Charles Malik, 'Human Rights in the United Nations', *International Journal* 6: 4 (1951), p. 278. This text is based on a lecture that Malik gave in 1945.

2

There Is No Such Thing as 'the Economy': On Social and Economic Rights

The masses demand, unabated, a minimum of vital security.

Louis Rougier

In a searing 1966 critique, Friedrich Hayek described the Universal Declaration of Human Rights as an incoherent attempt 'to fuse the rights of the Western liberal tradition with an altogether different conception derived from the Marxist Russian Revolution'.[1] Hayek praised the document's first twenty-one articles for following the eighteenth century precedent and enshrining the 'classical civil rights'.[2] But he heavily criticised the remaining articles, which laid out a long list of social and economic rights, including rights to social security, work, rest and leisure, food, clothing, housing, medical care, social security and education, and to form and join trade unions.[3] Hayek believed such guarantees fundamentally misunderstood the nature of rights. Not only were they too vague for a court to enforce, he argued; they were ultimately meaningless, as no declaration of rights could actually guarantee anyone

---

1   Friedrich Hayek, 'Justice and Individual Rights: Appendix to Chapter Nine', in Friedrich Hayek, *Law, Legislation and Liberty: A New Statement of the Liberal Principles of Justice and Political Economy, 2: The Mirage of Social Justice* (London: Routledge, 1998), p. 103. This essay was first published in 1966 in the seventy-fifth anniversary issue of the Norwegian journal *Farmand* (Oslo, 1966) with the title 'Misconception of Human Rights as Positive Claims'.

2   Ibid.

3   Neier, *The International Human Rights Movement: A History* (Princeton: Princeton University Press, 2012), p. 59.

a certain standard of material welfare. In scathing terms, he wrote that the 'conception of a "universal right" which assures to the peasant, to the Eskimo, and presumably to the Abominable Snowman, "periodic holidays with pay" shows the absurdity of the whole thing.'[4]

Addressing young people born into welfare states, Hayek challenged the social philosophy underpinning social and economic rights. There is no such thing as a 'society' with a duty to care for its members, he argued, anticipating Margaret Thatcher. Hayek contended that 'society' is simply a 'spontaneous order' that emerges as individuals and families pursue their welfare on the market. In social and economic rights, he saw the influence of a conflicting social philosophy, which viewed 'society' as a 'deliberately made organization'. Hayek gave law and rights a central role in his own account of a free society predicated on the division of labour. Far from dismissing human rights, he criticised the drafters for weakening the concept of 'right' and destroying all respect for it. A declaration of rights should do no more than the 'time-honoured political and civil rights' have always done, he argued: 'delimit individual domains' in which private initiative, entrepreneurialism, and personal responsibility can flourish.[5]

By the time Hayek made these remarks, such views were gaining ground. That year, two legally binding human rights covenants were adopted by the United Nations. Unable to replicate the compromises that had led to the Universal Declaration of Human Rights (UDHR) in a document destined to become binding international law, the drafters produced both an International Covenant on Civil and Political Rights, and an International Covenant on Economic, Social and Cultural Rights. Among those that refused to sign on to the latter was the United States, where it was often viewed with suspicion as a 'Covenant on Uneconomic, Socialist and Collective Rights'.[6] Nor did its social and economic rights attract any significant domestic support in the United States, 'even from within the human rights community, which has . . . always been assumed to be its natural constituency'.[7]

When a new generation of international human rights NGOs came to prominence in the late 1970s, they largely pursued a narrow agenda of

---

4   Hayek, 'Justice and Individual Rights', p. 105.
5   Ibid., pp. 101–2.
6   Philip Alston, 'US Ratification of the Covenant on Economic, Social and Cultural Rights: The Need for an Entirely New Strategy', *American Journal of International Law* 84: 2 (April 1990), p. 366.
7   Ibid.

protecting what Hayek termed 'classical civil rights', rather than promoting social and economic rights. Aryeh Neier, the former head of the US-based Human Rights Watch (HRW), noted with displeasure that, in enshrining a list of social and economic rights, the UDHR marked a 'radical break with its predecessors'.[8] 'Not everybody can have everything', Neier contended in 2006, and the role of human rights should be to specify those few things to which *everyone* is entitled.[9] Even as major human rights NGOs, including HRW, have gradually shifted their attention to social and economic rights, they have largely restricted their focus to discrimination in the provision of welfare, where it is possible, as HRW's current director Kenneth Roth explained, to identify specific violators and perpetrators. Human rights NGOs flourished in a period of neoliberal ascendancy, in which Hayek's contention that it was meaningless to declare that 'everyone' was entitled to food, housing, clothing and medical care had begun to seem self-evident.

In stark contrast, in the late 1940s, delegates charged with drafting an international bill of rights depicted social and economic rights as evidence of the social progress won by workers' movements. Rights to work, leisure, social security and a 'decent standard of living', as the Ecuadorian delegate put it, were the 'real triumph of the twentieth century'.[10] China's P. C. Chang warned that neglecting 'freedom from want' would produce a document that would 'ill accord with the times'.[11] Chile's Hernán Santa Cruz, a tireless advocate of social and economic rights, argued for adjusting production and distribution to secure general welfare, in order to transform 'the political democracy of the nineteenth century into an economic democracy'.[12] Defenders of social and economic rights stressed the need to go beyond the 1789 Declaration

---

8 Neier, *International Human Rights Movement*, p. 59.

9 Aryeh Neier, 'Social and Economic Rights: A Critique', *Human Rights Brief* 13: 2 (2006), p. 2.

10 Carrera Andrade (Ecuador), 'Verbatim Record of the Hundred and Eighty-Second Plenary Meeting of the United Nations General Assembly', 10 December 1948, in William A. Schabas, ed., *The Universal Declaration of Human Rights: The Travaux Préparatoires*, vol. 3, (Cambridge: Cambridge University Press, 2013), p. 246.

11 Peng Chun Chang (China), 'Summary Record of the Fourteenth Meeting of the Commission on Human Rights', 4 February 1947, in Schabas, *Universal Declaration of Human Rights*, vol. 1, p. 201.

12 Hernando Santa Cruz (Chile), 'Summary Record of the Sixty-Ninth Meeting of the Economic and Social Council', 14 March 1947, in Schabas, *Universal Declaration of Human Rights*, vol. 1, p. 246.

of the Rights of Man and Citizen, which Hayek's mentor Ludwig von Mises termed 'the programme of the liberal philosophy of the State'.[13] Following Marx's notorious critique of the egoism of the rights of man, the Yugoslav delegate argued that the 1789 Declaration treated 'man' as an isolated individual independent of his social conditions.[14]

Few delegates outside the Soviet bloc endorsed this same delegate Ljubomir Radovanovic's argument that the French Revolution had abolished feudal slavery only to 'reintroduce slavery within the framework of a new social capitalistic order'.[15] But the majority agreed that a twentieth-century rights declaration must offer protection from the 'dependence and economic subjugation' of a capitalist market.[16] Meeting in the wake of the Great Depression, they were deeply aware of what the republican political theorist Hannah Arendt termed 'the terrifying predicament of mass poverty'.[17] The previous decades had made clear that individual effort and personal responsibility were painfully inadequate in the face of mass unemployment and social dislocation – and that state inaction risked fostering rebellion. The rise of socialism and communism had placed 'the social question' on the international political agenda – including at the United Nations.

Nonetheless, there was less 'unanimity as to the inclusion of economic and social rights in the Universal Declaration' than the welfarist, postwar climate would suggest.[18] Early in the drafting, the UK delegate defended his own country's draft declaration, which contained no social and economic rights, by telling the assembled delegates that the 'world needed freedom and not well-fed slaves'.[19] In liberal societies, the delegate of the Ukrainian Soviet Socialist Republic, Michael Klekovkin, shot back: 'Men are free but are dying of hunger'.[20] In a critique that resonated

---

13   Ludwig von Mises, *Socialism: An Economic and Sociological Analysis*, transl. J. Kahane (New Haven, CT: Yale University Press, 1962), p. 58.

14   Ljubomir Radovanovic (Yugoslavia), 'Verbatim Record of the Hundred and Eighty-Third Plenary Meeting of the United Nations General Assembly', 10 December 1948, in Schabas, *Universal Declaration of Human Rights*, vol. 3, p. 3074.

15   Ibid.

16   Ibid.

17   Hannah Arendt, *On Revolution* (London: Penguin, 1990), p. 24.

18   Samuel Moyn, *Not Enough: Human Rights in an Unequal World* (Cambridge: Harvard University Press, 2018), p. 58.

19   Charles Dukeston (UK), cited in Johannes Morsink, *The Universal Declaration of Human Rights: Origins, Drafting, and Intent* (Philadelphia: University of Pennsylvania Press, 1999), p. 223.

20   Michael Klekovin (USSR), cited in Morsink, *Universal Declaration*, p. 224.

with that of the neoliberals, Charles Malik opposed social and economic rights because 'the government controls that would be needed to realize these rights would mean the destruction of free institutions in a free world'.[21]

Like the welfare states that preceded them, the social and economic rights in the UDHR were products of compromise, and many delegates sought to ensure that these rights implied no obligations on states. The United States delegation led the attempt to detach these rights from more radical political challenges to an economic order based on private appropriation and labour exploitation. Drawing on the experience of the New Deal, the US delegation sought a compromise that would transform political demands for redistribution into flexible standards, adjustable in line with policy considerations, and thus never on the same level as civil and political rights. While T. H. Marshall, who pioneered the idea of a progressive movement from civil to political to economic rights, sought to extend the 'status of freedom' to combat a 'hierarchical caste-like system of class', the drafters of the UDHR were more concerned to ensure that social and economic rights did not unduly disrupt the status inequalities of civil society.[22] They reasserted a gendered division of labour, in which secure male employment and female domestic labour would be bolstered by the state provision of a social safety net. The colonial powers (notably France and the United Kingdom), along with the United States, also sought to preserve racial segregation and colonial exploitation by bolstering the legitimacy of racial discrimination as a mechanism for determining entitlement.[23]

This did not prevent the neoliberals of the 1940s from treating social and economic rights as a threat to freedom, individual rights and personal morality. Any attempt to organise society to provide for economic wellbeing, Hayek suggested, would destroy the spontaneous market order. Reorganising society on the model of the household was 'totalitarian', he argued. Today the word 'totalitarianism' evokes images of gulags and death camps. For the neoliberals who helped to pioneer the concept, its semantic sphere was much broader, encompassing all

---

21 Cited in Morsink, *Universal Declaration*, p. 224.

22 For a powerful account of Marshall on the status of freedom, see Anna Yeatman, 'Gender, Social Policy and the Idea of the Welfare State', in Sheila Shaver, ed., *Gender and Social Policy* (Cheltenham: Edward Elgar, 2018).

23 The following chapter is devoted to the conflicts over colonialism during the human rights drafting process.

'collectivist' interventions into the market order. 'The common features of all collectivist systems', Hayek wrote, 'may be described, in a phrase ever-dear to socialists of all schools, as the deliberate organization of the labors of society for a definite social goal.'[24] The various collectivisms differed in the goals towards which they wished to direct society, he acknowledged; but they all differed from liberalism in refusing the supremacy of individual ends, and were therefore 'totalitarian in the true sense of this new word which we have adopted to describe the unexpected but nevertheless inseparable manifestations of what in theory we call collectivism'.[25] In demands for 'freedom from want', the neoliberals of the 1930s and 1940s saw a threat to freedom, to morality, and to 'Western civilisation' itself.

Neoliberalism and the State as Household

In 1968, soon after his critique of the UDHR, Hayek published a brief essay on the term 'economy'. Much confusion had been caused by the use of the same word to refer to two distinct phenomena, he argued: on the one hand, 'economy' referred to the deliberate arrangement of resources in the pursuit of a unitary hierarchy of ends, as in a household, an organisation or an enterprise; on the other, it referred to the overall structure produced by the interrelation of these households, organisa-tions and enterprises, which we often call 'a social, or national, or world "economy" and often also simply an "economy"'.[26] According to Hayek, the use of the term 'economy' to refer to the overall market order smug-gled in the idea that society as a whole should be organised on the model of the household in order to provide for people's needs. This confusion, he argued, had brought about a profound transformation in both law and morals; while a spontaneous order requires abstract, universal rules that enable each individual to preserve 'his' own 'protected domain', the rules of an organisation are directed to the achievement of specific ends.[27] Hayek believed that his contemporaries' preference for the

---

24   Friedrich Hayek, *The Road to Serfdom: Texts and Documents*, ed. Bruce Caldwell (Chicago: University of Chicago Press, 2007), p. 100.

25   Ibid.

26   Friedrich Hayek, 'The Confusion of Language in Political Thought', Institute of Economic Affairs Occasional Papers No. 20 (1968), p. 28.

27   Ibid., p. 16.

pursuit of such deliberate ends reflected a decline of the morals of the market and the revival of a 'tribal' morality suited to the small group.

In seeking to confine the term 'economy' to organisations such as the family and the enterprise, Hayek drew on its ancient Greek origins in the word *oikonomia*, which signified the management of a household – an *oikos*. The multiple economic relations that defined the ancient *oikos* – those between masters and slaves, fathers and children, husbands and wives – were governed to ensure the household's well-ordered functioning. The freedom that characterised Greek political life, for that minority of the population who could participate in it, relied on the labour of slaves and women, who were confined to the *oikos*. The household was devoted not to freedom but to the necessities of biological life, and was ruled by a household head with 'uncontested, despotic powers'.[28] Against this household model, Hayek borrowed the term 'catallaxy' to refer to the extended market order.[29] Derived from the Greek verb *katallatein*, which meant both to exchange and 'to turn from an enemy into a friend', *catallaxy* embodied the neoliberal belief that the market was a peaceful realm of voluntary relations grounded in mutual interest. It served to distinguish a market society from the coercion and despotism the neoliberals took to be intrinsic to the political pursuit of shared ends.

Hayek's critique of the household model of the economy was not original. The nineteenth-century political philosopher John Stuart Mill was the first to criticise the belief that political economy 'is to the state, what domestic economy is to the family'.[30] The management of a household is not a science but an art, Mill contended in 1844; it is, in Aristotle's terms, a form of *phronesis* or practical wisdom, governed by maxims of prudence, and aimed at securing the greatest physical comfort or enjoyment with a given means. Political economy, in contrast, was not a

---

28   Hannah Arendt, *The Human Condition* (Chicago: University of Chicago Press, 1998), p. 27.

29   The term was initially used by the nineteenth-century political economist Richard Whately in an attempt to free the new science of political economy from its association with the less than elevated concerns of the household. Richard Whately, 'Introductory Lectures on Political Economy', Online Library of Liberty, 1831, at oll. libertyfund.org.

30   John Stuart Mill, 'On the Definition of Political Economy; and on the Method of Investigation Proper to It', *Essays on Some Unsettled Questions of Political Economy* (London: Batoche Books, 2010); Gunnar Myrdal, *The Political Element in the Development of Economic Theory*, transl. Paul Streeten (London: Routledge, 2002), p. 16.

governmental paradigm, but a scientific one; not the art of household management writ large, but a science with its own laws and truths. In 1930, the Swedish economist Gunnar Myrdal, with whom Hayek would share the 1974 Nobel Prize in Economics, had referred to Mill to criticise economists for depicting society on the model of a household, with a single common purpose, and treating economics as 'social housekeeping'.[31]

A decade before Hayek, in 1958, Hannah Arendt had drawn on Myrdal to criticise the modern tendency to model 'the people' on the family and entrust their care to 'a gigantic nation-wide administration of housekeeping'.[32] For both Myrdal and Arendt, the collective establishment of ends was necessarily political, and could not be determined on the despotic model of the household head. For Hayek and the neoliberals, in contrast, the critique of the household model served to discredit all politics and to privilege the market as resource-allocator. For them, there were only two options: the simple conditions in which 'the father can supervise the entire economic management', as Mises put it, or a system of monetary calculation and market prices in which decisions on the allocation of resources are removed entirely from political oversight.[33]

The neoliberals attributed the breakdown of the 'open' market society and the rise of the household model to what the conservative Spanish philosopher José Ortega y Gasset called the 'revolt of the masses'. Writing in 1930, Ortega y Gasset argued that standards built up over centuries of European dominance were being torn down by 'persons not specially qualified', who no longer knew their place. He traced this levelling to the French Revolution's rights of man and citizen, which he argued had given the 'average man' a new sense of mastery and dignity.[34] The neoliberal thinkers were deeply ambivalent about what Röpke called the 'Janus-faced revolution'. While the 'ideas of 1789' had created the air which all now breathed, Röpke wrote in 1942, nonetheless 'the revolution was a catastrophe'.[35] The neoliberals claimed the 1789 Declaration of the Rights

---

31   Ibid., p. 146.

32   Arendt, *Human Condition*, p. 28.

33   Ludwig von Mises, *Economic Calculation in the Socialist Commonwealth*, transl. S. Adler (Auburn: Ludwig von Mises Institute, 2012), p. 15.

34   Ortega y Gasset was invited to the Walter Lippmann Colloquium, but was unable to attend. Jurgen Reinhoudt and Serge Audier, eds, *The Walter Lippmann Colloquium: The Birth of Neo-Liberalism* (London: Palgrave Macmillan, 2018); José Ortega y Gasset, *The Revolt of the Masses* (London: Unwin Books, 1969), p. 11.

35   Wilhelm Röpke, *The Social Crisis of Our Time*, transl. Annette Schiffer Jacobsohn and Peter Schiffer Jacobsohn (Chicago: University of Chicago Press, 1950 [1942]), p. 41.

of Man and of the Citizen as part of the liberal heritage – the ideas of 1789, liberty, equality, and fraternity, as Hayek put it, were 'characteristically commercial ideas'.[36] But in the (Jacobin) Declaration of 1793, which granted sovereignty to the people and stressed the 'common welfare', they saw the beginning of the transformation of society into a single organisation. The years 1789 to 1792 'were those of the liberal revolution for freedom', the German ordoliberal Alexander Rüstow argued. 'In 1792, the totalitarian revolution for domination was begun'.[37]

The neoliberals attributed the French revolution's 'totalitarian' turn to the demands of the masses for economic welfare, and to the introduction of 'state control of prices, commandeering of supplies, [and] compulsory rationing'.[38] Here, their analysis was close to that of Arendt, who depicted the French Revolution's turn towards economic equality as the eruption of the concerns of the household into the political sphere. Arendt argued that, just as for pre-moderns, the distinction between rich and poor was natural and unavoidable; the French revolutionaries asserted the rights of the people against 'tyranny and oppression, not against exploitation and poverty'.[39] In the transformation of the rights of man into the 'rights of the Sans-Culottes' (rights to 'dress, food and the reproduction of the species'), Arendt saw the turning point of all subsequent revolutions.[40] For the neoliberals, too, the attempt to deal with poverty by political means marked the ruin of freedom. The 'finest opportunity ever given to the world was thrown away', Hayek wrote, citing the Catholic liberal Lord Acton, 'because the passion for equality made vain the hope for freedom'.[41]

The French philosopher and early member of the Mont Pèlerin Society (MPS), Bertrand de Jouvenel, paid particular attention to the role of the French Revolution in the decline of liberty. Jouvenel, who was born into an aristocratic family and inherited the title of 'Baron', upheld

---

36   Hayek, *Road to Serfdom*, p. 183.

37   Alexander Rüstow, *Freedom and Domination: A Historical Critique of Civilization*, ed. Dankwart A. Rüstow, transl. Salvador Attanasio (Princeton, NJ: Princeton University Press, 1978), p. 341.

38   Walter Eucken, *The Foundations of Economics: History and Theory in the Analysis of Economic Reality*, transl. T. W. Hutchison (Berlin: Springer-Verlag, 1992), p. 92.

39   Arendt, *On Revolution*, p. 74.

40   Ibid., p. 60.

41   Friedrich Hayek, 'Individualism: True and False', in Friedrich Hayek, *Individualism and Economic Order* (Chicago: University of Chicago Press, 1958), p. 31.

the fate of individual rights during the revolution as proof that all revolutions augment power, rather than restricting it. In *On Power*, first published in 1945, he argued that, despite its striking proclamation that 'man, as man, had certain sacred rights', the French Revolution had annihilated the rights it claimed to protect.[42] Identifying a fundamental conflict between democratic sovereignty and the rule of law, Jouvenel contended that the Revolution had ultimately placed a new, unified national subject on the throne, and elevated the rights of the whole over those of the individual.

In returning to the French Revolution in the immediate wake of World War II, Jouvenel sought a 'usable history' with which to challenge his contemporaries' 'attacks on those same individual rights which in 1789 had had their sacredness proclaimed'.[43] For this man of the right, whose sympathies lay with the Vichy regime, the primary threat to individual rights was not fascism, but the promise of a 'larger social welfare'.[44] It was US President Franklin D. Roosevelt, he believed, who embodied the sacrifice of individual rights for social rights.[45] Jouvenel criticised those narratives that were so common during the drafting of the UDHR, for which social and economic rights were a progressive extension of the older civil and political rights. 'The new rights of man are given out as coming to complete those already proclaimed in the eighteenth-century', he wrote. But instead, 'they contradict and abrogate them'.[46] While the old rights decreed liberty and made individuals responsible, he argued, the new social rights replaced this adult responsibility with tutelage. The old liberty was thereby sacrificed for a new security, he argued; the new promises 'close the cycle which was opened by the declarations of earlier days'.[47]

Neoliberalism was never a narrowly economic doctrine. The early neoliberals were wary of the very idea of the economy, and horrified by what Hayek described as the reinterpretation in economic terms of the old political ideals of liberty, equality and security.[48] Repeatedly, they

---

42 Bertrand de Jouvenel, *On Power: Its Nature and the History of Its Growth* (Boston: Beacon, 1962), p. 229.

43 Ibid., p. 309.

44 Ibid.

45 Ibid., p. 330.

46 Ibid., p. 350.

47 Ibid.

48 Hayek, *Road to Serfdom*, p. 210.

singled out President Roosevelt's 1941 'Four Freedoms' speech – which added 'freedom from want', and 'freedom from fear' to the more traditional freedoms of speech and worship – as evidence of the contemporary confusion of the market and household. Roosevelt ended his speech by declaring that freedom 'means the supremacy of human rights everywhere'. For the neoliberals, in contrast, Roosevelt's speech marked the demise of all human rights. Hayek argued that Roosevelt had transformed an 'older liberal tradition of human rights', entailing limits to the power wielded over individuals, into positive claims for benefits.[49] These new rights, Hayek argued, could not be legally enforced without destroying the liberal order that the old civil rights aimed to secure. Social and economic rights would only be possible, he argued – speaking specifically of the UDHR – if 'the whole of society were converted into a single organization, that is, made totalitarian in the fullest sense of the word'.[50]

A New Deal

In a 1932 speech in Detroit, where 223,000 people were then unemployed, Franklin Delano Roosevelt announced a new vision of economic life.[51] From 'the days of the cave man to the days of the automobile, the philosophy of "letting things alone" has resulted in the jungle law of the survival of the so-called fittest', the man who would soon be president told the assembled crowd.[52] Far from being a peaceful realm of mutually beneficial, voluntary relations, the market, Roosevelt said, was governed by the 'jungle law' of free competition and individual responsibility. The stock market crash of 1929 had discredited *laissez-faire* liberalism, which had launched its fight against the feudal order partly as a critique of state paternalism in the name of individual freedom and rights.[53] Against the 'jungle law' of the free market, Roosevelt outlined

---

49   Hayek, 'Justice and Individual Rights', pp. 103–4; Friedrich Hayek, 'Epilogue: The Three Sources of Human Values', in *Law, Legislation and Liberty*, p. 203.

50   Hayek, 'Justice and Individual Rights', p. 104.

51   Tompkins Bates, *The Making of Black Detroit in the Age of Henry Ford* (Chapel Hill: University of North Carolina Press, 2013), p. 156.

52   Franklin D. Roosevelt, 'Campaign Address at Detroit, Michigan', ed. Gerhard Peters and John T. Woolley, American Presidency Project, 1932, at presidency.ucsb.edu.

53   Norberto Bobbio, *Liberalism and Democracy* (London: Verso, 2005), p. 17.

a corporatist vision of a reconciled human family, in which government would provide worker's compensation, child support, old-age pensions, unemployment insurance and public health programmes. Roosevelt drew on the 1931 papal encyclical *Quadragesimo anno*, which declared it an 'intolerable abuse' for mothers to be forced to work outside the home 'to the neglect of their proper cares and duties'. Noting that the followers of *laissez-faire* had decried state welfare measures as 'paternalistic', he responded: 'All right, if they are paternalistic, I am a father.'[54]

In declaring himself the father of Detroit's working class, Roosevelt placed himself in a position long occupied by the industrial magnate Henry Ford, who had pioneered a paternalist mode of government predicated on high wages, working-class consumption, women's unpaid labour in the home, intense disciplinary surveillance of working-class households, and brutal suppression of industrial action. As president, Roosevelt's New Deal took over central planks of Henry Ford's model by combining welfare provision with racial segmentation and discrimination, a gendered division of labour, state paternalism and social pacification. He established a racialised compact that mediated the struggle between state, labour and business, and positioned a 'white working class' in jobs that were more secure and better paid than those of non-white workers.[55]

The same year he made his Detroit speech, local police and security personnel from the Ford Motor Company opened fire with machine-guns on a 'hunger march' of unemployed workers. The workers were bound for Ford's River Rouge Plant to present a list of demands, which included not only the rehiring of the unemployed and fuel to tide them over through winter, but also an end to racial discrimination and the right to unionise.[56] In this climate of radical political agitation and violence (the attack on the march had killed five and injured more than twenty others), Roosevelt sought to depoliticise economic welfare. 'I am afraid that some of you people today in Detroit have been talking politics', he told his audience. 'Well, I am not going to. I want to talk to you about Government. That is a very different thing.'[57]

54   Roosevelt, 'Campaign Address at Detroit, Michigan'.

55   Lisa Tilley and Robbie Shilliam, 'Raced Markets: An Introduction', *New Political Economy* 23: 5 (2017), p. 535.

56   Beth Tompkins Bates, *The Making of Black Detroit in the Age of Henry Ford* (Chapel Hill, NC: University of North Carolina Press), p. 159.

57   Roosevelt, 'Campaign Address at Detroit, Michigan'.

Roosevelt may have sought to distinguish government from politics, but, for the neoliberals, any challenge to the role of the market in distributing resources was a political threat to an open society. If the neoliberals were vehement opponents of the New Deal (and of the post-war welfare state), this was certainly not because they wanted to 'talk politics', or because they objected to the perpetuation of a sexual division of labour and racial segmentation. Rather, they believed that state-welfarism cushioned people from the consequences of their actions, and thereby undermined 'the moral and social health of the nations'.[58] Wilhelm Röpke provided a succinct description of the difference in social philosophies that divided liberals from defenders of the welfare state. Those, like himself, who were concerned with the foundations of liberal civilisation, he argued, held up 'the ideal of the well-ordered house – security through individual effort supplemented by mutual aid'.[59] On the other side was a philosophy of collectivism, massification and family breakdown, which was embraced by demagogues and used to manipulate the masses. Holding up Roosevelt as the paradigmatic figure of such demagoguery, Röpke put the point in blunt terms: all talk of 'freedom from want' kills genuine freedom.[60]

Wilhelm Röpke and the Revolt of the Masses: Conservative Neoliberalism

To date, the bulk of scholarship on the intersection between neoliberalism and socially conservative family-values politics has focused on the United States, in an attempt to understand how seemingly amoral neoliberal economists made common cause with the moralism of the neoconservative right. In her brilliant account of the place of the family in neoliberalism, Melinda Cooper argues that, although they eschewed the 'overt moralism of social conservatives', Chicago and Virginia School neoliberals rejected the sexual liberation movements of the 1960s and 1970s because they worried about the economic costs of family breakdown and the weakening of the family's privatised social-welfare

---

58   Cited in Wilhelm Röpke, *A Humane Economy: The Social Framework of the Free Market*, transl. Elizabeth Henderson (Chicago: Institute for Philosophical and Historical Studies, 1961), p. 163.

59   Cited in ibid., p. 177.

60   Röpke, *Social Crisis of Our Time*, p. 165.

function.[61] Cooper follows the pioneering approach of Wendy Brown, whose 'American Nightmare' explains the compatibility of the 'fierce moral-political rationality' of neoconservatism with 'market-political rationality' as a product of the neoliberal weakening of democratic values, which enables the 'moralism, statism, and authoritarianism' of neoconservatism – even as the latter aims to compensate for some of the former's effects.[62] Such accounts undoubtedly illuminate our understanding of the United States, where Chicago economists such as Gary Becker mused about replacing marriage entirely with voluntary, short-term contractual relations between individuals of any gender, while social conservatives promoted 'traditional marriage' and railed against the breakdown of the nuclear family.

But neoliberalism, as scholars like Philip Mirowski and Dieter Plewhe remind us, is not simply a North American phenomenon. Rather, it was a transnational movement from the beginning.[63] Social conservatism was not an external supplement to the development of neoliberalism. Conservative moralism, including an explicit defence of religion and family values, was foundational to the neoliberal attempt to reinvent the liberal project beyond *laissez-faire*. It was the German ordoliberals who paid the most attention to the moral breakdown they saw as endemic to the revolt of the masses. Röpke, in particular, formulated a distinctive account of the rise of the masses and its implications for freedom, morality and family life. His argument that the competitive market required a moral foundation and the re-establishment of strong families to promote self-reliance and 'dignity' would go on to exert a significant influence on the neoliberal critique of the welfare state – including in the United States.[64]

---

61   Melinda Cooper, *Family Values: Between Neoliberalism and the New Social Conservatism* (New York: Zone, 2017), p. 8.

62   Wendy Brown, 'American Nightmare: Neoliberalism, Neoconservatism, and De-Democratization', *Political Theory* 34: 6 (2006), pp. 691, 703.

63   Philip Mirowski and Dieter Plehwe, eds, *The Road from Mont Pèlerin: The Making of the Neoliberal Thought Collective* (Cambridge: Harvard University Press, 2009).

64   Quinn Slobodian provides an excellent account of the embrace of Röpke by the US New Right in the 1960s. Quinn Slobodian, *Globalists: The End of Empire and the Birth of Neoliberalism* (Cambridge: Harvard University Press, 2018), pp. 146–81. And Miriam Bankovsky's groundbreaking work on the household economics of Alfred Marshall shows that early neoclassical welfare economics in the United States also had its own ethical account of the family as central to the training of 'moral sensibility' and the cultivation of an understanding of the social value of work. Miriam Bankovsky, 'Alfred Marshall's Household Economics: The Role of the Family in Cultivating an Ethical Capitalism', *Cambridge Journal of Economics* 43: 1 (17 January 2019).

In July 1936, Röpke participated in a conference organised by the Rockefeller Foundation to consider the problem of economic stabilisation, alongside future members of the MPS, including Ludwig von Mises, William Rappard, Lionel Robbins and Gottfried Haberler. Wary that the Rockefeller Foundation's proposal to establish a central observatory to gather and coordinate economic data would result in an unnecessary bureaucracy and economic interventionism, the participants decided instead to fund several research projects, including one by Röpke on protectionism. Eschewing a narrow economic analysis, Röpke argued that the rise of the masses threatened the economic integration enabled by nineteenth-century liberalism and its standards of civilisation. Drawing on Ortega y Gasset's work, he coined the term *Vermassung* ('enmassment') to define the levelling process he believed threatened the survival of the world economy and Western civilisation.[65] 'Capitalism, liberalism, individual initiative and responsibility, competition and adaptability are to-day at a heavy discount', he wrote; 'they are old-established rulers against whom a mass rebellion has broken out'.[66]

Röpke's was a deeply conservative critique aimed at the uprooting effects of capitalism, the loss of hierarchal order, the 'diminished differentiation in the social status' and the 'emancipation from natural bonds and communities'.[67] He depicted the rise of the masses as a phenomenon of proletarianisation, which deprives large sections of the population of property and the liberty it provides, rendering them dependent. For Röpke, factory life was at the root of mass demands for the reorganisation of society. The revolt of the masses led to the 'progressive displacement of spontaneous order and coherence by organization and regimentation'.[68] This critique of massification drew on a Roman model of independence, associated with property ownership (including ownership of slaves) and the possession of legal personality. Independence was a status constituted in opposition to the dependence of those who worked for someone else for a living, and therefore lacked legal personality. With the rise of industrial capitalism, this model of independence was increasingly claimed by white working men, whose new-found

---

65 Wilhelm Röpke, *International Economic Disintegration* (London: William Hodge, 1942), p. 239.
66 Ibid., p. 238.
67 Ibid., p. 240.
68 Ibid.

freedom and juridical status contrasted with the subordination and lack of personality of a new series of 'dependents': women, paupers, colonial subjects and slaves.[69]

Röpke regularly used racial tropes and metaphors of primitivism and barbarism to characterise these dependent proletarian masses. He shared this with Hayek, who found evidence in Ortega y Gasset's work that 'the first attempt to emerge from the tribal into an open society' failed because individuals were employed in regimented organisations before they 'had time to learn the morals of the market'.[70] For Hayek, the revolt of the masses represented the failure of the 'taming of the savage'.[71] For Röpke, newly proletarianised peasants from the country-side were a culturally alien force and a threat to a civilised society. In language that has since become all too familiar on today's anti-immigrant right, he complained that 'the country of Goethe, the Humboldts and even of Nietzsche' had been 'swamped by countless millions which came too quickly and in too great numbers to be absorbed culturally'; a 'nation', Röpke warned, 'may beget its own barbarian invaders'.[72]

This racialisation of independence was particularly intense in a slave society like the United States, where 'liberty, property, and whiteness were inextricably enmeshed'.[73] Faced with the gap between republican ideals of freedom and independence and the realities of wage labour, white workers, 'disciplined and made anxious by fear of dependency', struggled to distinguish themselves from dependent and right-less slaves by configuring independence as a property of whiteness.[74] The racial refiguring of the masculine ideal of independence in a

---

69   Nancy Fraser and Linda Gordon, ' "Dependency" Demystified: Inscriptions of Power in a Keyword of the Welfare State', *Social Politics* 1: 1 (1994).

70   Friedrich Hayek, 'The Discipline of Abstract Rules and the Emotions of the Tribal Society', in *Law, Legislation and Liberty: A New Statement of the Liberal Principles of Justice and Political Economy* (London: Routledge, 1998), p. 146.

71   'The Taming of the Savage' was Hayek's plan for the title of his final book, which was ultimately published as 'The Fatal Conceit'. See Alan Ebenstein, *Hayek's Journey: The Mind of Friedrich Hayek* (New York: Palgrave Macmillan, 2003), p. 225.

72   Röpke, *International Economic Disintegration*, p. 241, n. 2. Röpke was referring here to the work of Marcel Dutheil in his book *La population allemande; les variations du phénomène démographique, leur influence sur la civilisation occidentale* (Paris: Payot, 1937).

73   Saidiya V. Hartman, *Scenes of Subjection: Terror, Slavery, and Self-Making in Nineteenth-Century America* (Oxford: Oxford University Press, 1997), p. 119.

74   David R. Roediger, *The Wages of Whiteness: Race and the Making of the American Working Class* (London: Verso, 2007), p. 14.

white-supremacist key obscured the wage-dependence and labour discipline of industrial capitalism. It also rendered invisible the dependence of white male workers on white women's domestic labour, and the dependence of the capitalist social order on slave labour and colonial exploitation.[75] Independence formed a powerful myth that bolstered the political standing of white working men, fused property ownership and legal personality, and relegated those construed as 'dependent' to a sphere of diminished rights.

It was this myth that Ronald Reagan would draw on decades later when he used the term 'emancipation' to refer to 'freeing' poor families from welfare dependence.[76] At stake in this emancipatory language was an attempt to mobilise the republican valorisation of freedom and independence against a welfare system that was implicitly racialised and aligned with slavery, blackness and dependence. But the centrality of this myth of independence to neoliberal attacks on welfare goes back much further than Reagan, as does the association of state welfare provision with moral hazard and family breakdown. For Röpke, the most serious symptom of the revolt of the masses was the decline of the family. As the family is 'the natural sphere of the woman, the proper environment for raising children and indeed the parent cell of the community', the German neoliberal argued that women were the real victims of a welfare state that prevented them fulfilling their 'vital functions'.[77]

Women may have been the primary victims of the welfare state, from this conservative perspective, but this did not mean that men benefited from it. Röpke regularly cited the remark of the nineteenth-century French political theorist Alexis de Tocqueville, whose 1835 text *Democracy in America* warned that, in a democracy, individuals would entrust their private needs to an 'immense tutelary power' that would reduce them to 'a flock of timid and industrious animals, of which the government is the shepherd'.[78] Writing a decade after World War I, Röpke argued this threat had been realised by the welfare state, which 'takes care of the sort of comfortable stall-feeding of the domesticated

---

75   On the genealogy of dependence as a keyword in welfare politics in the United States, see Fraser and Gordon, ' "Dependency" Demystified'.

76   Ronald Reagan, 'Address Before a Joint Session of Congress on the State of the Union,' The American Presidency Project, 4 February 1986, https://www.presidency.ucsb.edu/documents/address-before-joint-session-congress-the-state-the-union.

77   Röpke, *Social Crisis of Our Time*, p. 16.

78   Cited in Röpke, *Humane Economy*, p. 159.

masses'.[79] Röpke sought the measure of 'respect for human personality' in the masses' responsibility for their own welfare, remarking that it is hardly progress to treat increasing numbers of people as 'economic minors' under the 'tutelage of the state'.[80]

Such views were already common among neoliberals by the 1938 Walter Lippmann Colloquium, where the French philosopher Louis Rougier used his opening address to warn: 'The masses are willing to abandon their freedom in the hands of the one, chief or messiah, who promises them security'.[81] A year earlier, Rappard had given his own twist to the idea of the welfare state as a strictly gendered household. In the midst of the mass unemployment and desperate poverty of the Great Depression, he argued, quite extraordinarily, that the individual in all the countries that experienced modern revolutions now resembled a 'pampered old bachelor who has a very faithful cook' and has come to depend on her. Singling out the United States of the New Deal, Rappard argued that the individual had 'jeopardised his possession of that freedom for which his ancestors fought and bled'.[82] By the time Hayek wrote *The Road to Serfdom*, he complained that it was 'no longer independence but security which [gave] rank and status', and that a man was now considered eligible for marriage not because he had the capacity to provide for a family, but because he has 'the certain right to a pension'.[83]

It was Röpke who distilled the tone of the neoliberal discussions of the mid twentieth century: while the desire for security is natural, he argued, it can become an obsession 'which is ultimately paid for by the loss of freedom and human dignity'.[84] The human dignity that the MPS statement of aims warned was disappearing was threatened, first of all, by the welfare state. This neoliberal critique of welfare would continue to resonate for decades, before ultimately being adopted by governments in the 1970s and 1980s. The neoliberal argument against state welfare was not confined to the economic threat it posed to a free-enterprise system. Rather, neoliberals like Röpke positioned the welfare

---

79   Ibid., p. 170.
80   Ibid., p. 155.
81   Louis Rougier, 'Address by Professor Louis Rougier', in Reinhoudt and Audier, *Walter Lippmann Colloquium*, p. 101.
82   William Rappard, 'The Relation of the Individual to the State', *Annals of the American Academy of Political and Social Science* 189: 1 (1937), p. 216.
83   Hayek, *Road to Serfdom*, p. 154.
84   Cited in Röpke, *Humane Economy*, p. 163.

state as a political threat to a social order founded on the nuclear family and racial hierarchy, and as a moral threat to the values of self-reliance, independence, responsibility and human dignity. From this perspective, while the drafters of the UDHR also dedicated themselves to human dignity, their commitment to social and economic rights would ultimately be its ruin.

'Himself and His Family': The Subject of Social and Economic Rights

From a neoliberal perspective, the UDHR's adoption of social and economic rights seemed evidence of a desire for security, which would enable the state to usurp the traditional role of the family. But many of the UDHR's drafters were concerned to uphold the family as what its Article 16 (initiated by Charles Malik) calls 'the natural and fundamental group and unit of society'. The pacifying, governmental approach of Roosevelt's New Deal deeply informed the social and economic rights in the declaration. Just as Roosevelt sought to avoid 'talking politics', the drafters sought to detach social and economic rights from political challenges to the exploitation of labour, the existing division of labour and the reproductive role of the nuclear family, and transform them into minimalist guarantees for the most needy.

The struggle over social and economic rights came to a head during the drafting of what is now Article 25 of the UDHR. In its final form, Article 25 reads as follows:

(1) Everyone has the right to a standard of living adequate for the health and well-being of himself and of his family, including food, clothing, housing and medical care and necessary social services, and the right to security in the event of unemployment, sickness, disability, widowhood, old age or other lack of livelihood in circumstances beyond his control.

(2) Motherhood and childhood are entitled to special care and assistance. All children, whether born in or out of wedlock, shall enjoy the same social protection.

Article 25 reveals the gendered social vision underpinning the declaration's social and economic rights. This social vision resists easy dichotomies between questions of wealth redistribution, on the one hand, and juridical status and subordination on the basis of gender, race and sexuality, on the other. The 'economy' was not an autonomous realm divorced from the gendered and racial regimes in which labour is ordered, and in which wealth (and increasingly debt) are accumulated and handed down from one generation to the next.[85] And the subject of social and economic rights was emphatically not an abstract, universal subject. Rather, race and gender marked the borders of entitlement, and designated this subject as a white, male, heterosexual, 'breadwinner' or head of a family.

The explicitly masculine subject 'himself' appears twice in the declaration, as the subject of social welfare (Article 25) and as the subject of the right to work (Article 23). Previous scholarship has tended to explain away what one historian calls this 'oversight involving a worker and "his family"' as an aberration from the universalist thrust of the declaration, whose social and economic rights could just as easily have been expressed in 'neutral, nonsexist terminology'.[86] Such explanations obscure the delegates' shared commitment to the family as the primary site of welfare and social reproduction. The centrality of unwaged women's labour to the Fordist settlement in the United States was matched by the Soviet Union's dramatic reversal of post-revolutionary policies such as easier divorce, equal rights for women in marriage, and collective cafeterias and childcare centres designed to free women from housework.[87] In stark contrast to the Russian revolutionary Alexandra Kollontai's argument that 'communism liberates woman from her domestic slavery and makes her life richer and happier', the Soviet delegates at Lake Success emphasised the 'protection which the State must give the home'.[88]

The Latin American delegates, who did most to advance the declaration's social and economic rights, were also fierce defenders of the family. Challenging the neoliberal dichotomy between state and family

---

85   See Cooper, *Family Values*.

86   In the major history of the drafting of the UDHR, Johannes Morsink argues that the 'women's lobby' largely expunged sexist language from the declaration, and that this 'oversight' does not detract from the commitment of the drafters to equality between the sexes. Morsink, *Universal Declaration*, p. 120.

87   Valerie Bryson, 'Feminism Between the Wars', in Roger Eatwell and Anthony Wright, eds, *Contemporary Political Ideologies* (London: Continuum, 1999), p. 211.

88   Alexandra Kollontai, 'Communism and the Family', *Worker*, 1920. Alexandre Bogomolov cited in Morsink, *Universal Declaration*, p. 254.

responsibility, they nonetheless argued, as the Chilean delegate Hernán Santa Cruz's draft article suggested, that the state had a duty 'to assist parents in the maintenance of adequate standards of child welfare within the family circle'.[89] Santa Cruz was perhaps an unlikely defender of familial responsibility: 'on one occasion while his family was out of town', the US State Department noted, he 'sold the entire household effects, including his wife's clothing, and gave the proceeds to his mistress'.[90] Nonetheless, the familial model of welfare was widely shared. Even the Commission on the Status of Women, which fought bitterly to remove all references to 'man' and 'men', did not challenge the 'historically specific gender norms' reflected in the male-breadwinner model.[91] In inscribing this social model in a declaration of the rights of 'all members of the human family', the drafters presented the nuclear family as the civilised endpoint of social evolution, and as a model for the world.

'Organization Thinking': The International Labour Organization and the Right to a Standard of Living

The initial draft of the Universal Declaration's Article 25, with its reference to 'himself and his family' was prepared by the International Labour Organization (ILO), which drew on its own long history of promoting a family-based welfare system. When Hayek later criticised the UDHR, he argued it was 'couched in that jargon of organization thinking which one has learnt to expect in the pronouncement of trade union officials or the International Labour Organization'.[92] The pacifying vision of social order expressed in the UDHR did owe much to the ILO's founding premise that labour conditions involving 'injustice, hardship and privation to large numbers of people' would lead to 'unrest'

89   Inter-American Juridical Committee, 'Draft Declaration of the International Rights and Duties of Man' (Rio de Janeiro: United Nations Economic and Social Council, 8 January 1947), at un.org.

90   Cited in Brian A. W. Simpson, *Human Rights and the End of Empire: Britain and the Genesis of the European Convention* (Oxford: Oxford University Press, 2004), p. 364.

91   Glenda Sluga, 'René Cassin: Les Droits de l'homme and the Universality of Human Rights, 1945–1966', in Stefan-Ludwig Hoffman, ed., *Human Rights in the Twentieth Century* (Cambridge: Cambridge University Press, 2011), p. 116.

92   Hayek, 'Justice and Individual Rights', p. 105.

and imperil the 'peace and harmony of the world'.[93] The foundation of the ILO, and its commitment to social justice, were a recognition of the threat that demands for equality and economic rights posed to social peace and to the 'political integrity of existing empires and states'.[94] Comprising representatives of governments, employers and workers, the ILO was formed to set standards, with the assistance of labour statisticians, and secure social progress and class compromise, rather than conflict.

In the early 1920s, soon after its establishment in 1919 under the Treaty of Versailles, the ILO prepared a major report on 'Family Allowances' that laid out arguments for ensuring men could support their families; family allowances, the report suggested, would secure a better distribution of the nation's wage bill by directing more to men with dependent families.[95] The social benefits would include reduced infant mortality, improved child health, and the development of the physical and intellectual capacities of a future generation of workers. Family allowances would ensure there was 'less need for the mother to go out to work, and thus she has more time to give proper care to her children'; recognition of the value of mothers would lead in turn to the 'raised status of women'.[96] The ILO stressed the benefits of this social model for both state and capital: family allowances would promote the health of the population and ensure social stability, the report argued, as men who supported families at home would be more reliable workers (and presumably less likely to go on strike.)

Decades later, this vision still informed the drafting of the UDHR. Much of the early drafting debate concerned whether the language of a right to 'a standard of living' provided by the ILO draft was sufficient, or whether it was necessary to specifically mention rights to medical care, housing, food and clothing. The language of the standard of living was a key aspect of what Hayek correctly identified as ILO 'jargon'; and as he recognised, there was more at stake in this language than a question of semantics. The real conflict was over whether social and economic

---

93   International Labour Organization, 'Constitution of the International Labour Organization (ILO)' (1919), at ilo.org.

94   Glenda Sluga, *Internationalism in the Age of Nationalism* (Pennsylvania: University of Pennsylvania Press, 2013), p. 124.

95   International Labour Organization, 'Family Allowances: The Remuneration of Labour According to Need', Series D (Wages and Hours) (Geneva, 1924).

96   Ibid., p. 14.

rights entailed corresponding state duties or could be secured through private consumption. Speaking as the representative of the United States, Eleanor Roosevelt stated that the ILO text was 'both complete and adequate'.[97] Despite her own personal commitment to social welfare, Roosevelt represented a country in which the consensus that underpinned the New Deal was giving way in the face of the anti-communism of the nascent Cold War. She was receiving instructions from US Undersecretary of State Robert A. Lovett, who was reportedly 'confused' by the UN's work on human rights, and particularly concerned by social and economic rights.[98] In a memo of March 1948, Roosevelt was informed that Lovett 'felt that if these were expressed they could far better be expressed in terms of 'better standards' rather than a right to a "decent living"'.[99]

In contrast to rights, which are (at least in theory) absolute, standards are relative and variable, and so enable flexibility and compromise. To speak of 'better standards' is to eschew absolutes. Like the term 'standard' – which can refer both to the ordinary ('bog standard') and to a standard of measurement ('the gold standard') – definitions of the standard of living oscillated between bare subsistence and aspirational opulence. Accounts of social and economic rights similarly moved between these two poles: for some, they ensured the bare minimum necessary for survival; for others, in a more republican key, social and economic rights freed people from the demands of necessity and enabled collective freedom. This gap was reflected in the distance between the original draft of the UDHR, penned by the Canadian socialist who headed the UN Secretariat's human rights division, John Humphrey, and the original US submission. Humphrey's draft went far beyond securing the conditions of mere survival to articulate rights to 'good food and housing and to live in surroundings that are pleasant and healthy'. The US submission, in contrast, outlined a 'right to enjoy *minimum* standards of economic, social and cultural well-being'.[100] The

---

97 Roosevelt ultimately accepted the inclusion of rights to 'food, clothing, housing and medical care'. 'Summary Record of the Seventy-First Meeting of the Commission on Human Rights', 14 June 1948, in Schabas, *Universal Declaration of Human Rights*, vol. 2, p. 1872.

98 Allida Black, ed., *The Eleanor Roosevelt Papers, vol. I: The Human Rights Years, 1945–1948* (Charlottesville: University of Virginia Press, 2010), p. 754.

99 Ibid.

100 'United States Proposals Regarding an International Bill of Rights', 28 January 1947, in Schabas, *Universal Declaration of Human Rights*, vol. 1, p. 103 (my emphasis).

language of the standard of living served to temper the utopian aspiration to a good life expressed in the rights Humphrey borrowed from various Latin American constitutions. In emphasising *minimum* standards, the US delegation sought to detach social and economic rights from egalitarianism, reconciling them with a privatised and consumerist conception of welfare.[101]

Prior to the drafting of the UDHR, the ILO and the League of Nations had been sites for conflicts between the standard of living, which was viewed as an 'American obsession' with materialism and individual consumption, and a European focus on a 'manner of life', characterised by non-market concerns with taste, quality and preference.[102] Between 1929 and 1931, the ILO had done extensive work on determining an adequate standard of living, sponsored by the department store magnate Edward Filene and the Ford Corporation, which wanted to pay workers in its European plants wages equivalent to those paid in Detroit to secure what one Ford manager called 'the maximum efficiency of the worker'.[103] The ILO subsequently developed nutrition standards and calorie guidelines, and correlated wages with the cost of an average food basket. While Latin American members were strong advocates for this work on nutrition, the ILO resisted Peruvian and Chilean policies of price controls, which aimed to keep the price of food staples low, and state-run *restaurantes populares* to feed the poor.[104]

The language of the standard of living expressed the rising prestige of consumption as the path to working-class welfare and political inclusion. Embracing a position central to neoliberal understandings of the social, one Australian ILO delegate argued that consumption would 'revitalize international democracy', as the 'consumer could articulate

---

101   In contrast, Moyn sees the minimalist focus on basic needs that became prominent later as a break with the prevalent welfarism and egalitarianism that informed the drafting of the UDHR, Moyn, *Not Enough*.

102   Patricia Clavin, 'What's in a Living Standard? Bringing Society and Economy Together in the ILO and the League of Nations Depression Delegation, 1938–1945', in Sandrine Kott and Joëlle Droux, eds, *Globalizing Social Rights: The International Labour Organization and Beyond* (New York: Palgrave Macmillan, 2013), p. 243.

103   Victoria De Grazia, *Irresistible Empire: America's Advance through Twentieth-Century Europe* (Cambridge, MA: Belknap, 2005), p. 79.

104   Corinne A. Pernet, 'Developing Nutritional Standards and Food Policy: Latin American Reformers between the ILO, the League of Nations Health Organization, and the Pan-American Sanitary Bureau', in Sandrine Kott and Joëlle Droux, eds, *Globalizing Social Rights: The International Labour Organization and Beyond* (New York: Palgrave Macmillan, 2013), p. 257.

his or her preferences to the market, to governments and to international organizations.'[105] This model of individual consumption and liberal improvement was the key US contribution to the UDHR's social and economic rights. When questioned by her government's committee on social policy about whether Article 25's proposed rights to health, food, clothing and medical care implied 'socialization', Eleanor Roosevelt replied: 'No, it merely sets standards, a flexible one'.[106] The language of the living standard lodged the consumer at the heart of the UDHR's economic and social rights, ultimately making them compatible with neoliberal welfarism. It was the seed of that minimalist focus on basic needs that would come to typify human rights in a later period of neoliberal ascendancy.[107]

It Is Not Enough to Talk About Standards of Living

During the drafting of the UDHR, both opponents and supporters of social and economic rights argued that they required more resources than civil and political rights. 'Economic and social rights, in order to be fully realised, require material assistance to be furnished by the state', France's René Cassin argued.[108] This assumption has since been challenged, both on the practical grounds that an effective justice system and political enfranchisement require material resources and state action, and on conceptual grounds, by those – notably Étienne Balibar – who have contested the very split between liberty and equality that underpinned the discourse of 'old' and 'new' rights.[109] In the immediate wake of World War II, the difference struck most delegates as obvious. The Czech delegate echoed Cassin's point: while a 'purely legal and formal instrument' would be sufficient for the implementation of civil

105   Frank McDougall cited in Patricia Clavin, *Securing the World Economy: The Reinvention of the League of Nations, 1920–1946* (Oxford: Oxford University Press, 2013).

106   Allida Black, ed., *Eleanor Roosevelt Papers*, vol. I, p. 709.

107   Moyn, *Not Enough.*

108   Cited in Morsink, *Universal Declaration*, p. 227.

109   Office of the High Commissioner for Human Rights, 'Statement on Visit to the USA, by Professor Philip Alston, United Nations Special Rapporteur on Extreme Poverty and Human Rights*', 15 December 2017, at ohchr.org; Étienne Balibar, ' "Rights of Man" and "Rights of the Citizen" ', in Étienne Balibar, *Masses, Classes, Ideas: Studies on Philosophy and Politics Before and After Marx* (London: Routledge, 1994).

and political rights, he argued, 'to render the right to social security effective it had to have a proper basis – an economic basis without which there could be no social security properly so-called'.[110]

The strongest supporters of social and economic rights contested the flexibility of the 'standard of living', arguing that the state should take responsibility for welfare functions that had previously been relegated to the home. The Chinese delegate P. C. Chang and the Soviet delegate Alexei Pavlov fought hardest to ensure that rights to food, clothing, housing and medical care in Article 25 were not subsumed under a right to a standard of living, but were turned into obligations on the state. When the UK delegate objected to these rights, Chang responded that he 'did not see what possible objection there could be to that phrase when millions of people throughout the world were deprived of food and clothing'.[111] While Chang often evoked the long lineage of a concern for welfare in the Confucian tradition, as the drafting took place he anxiously watched the advance of a Communist revolution that would ultimately overthrow the Nationalist government he represented. The promotion of labour welfare was seen as an important means 'to legitimize the moderate, reformist policy of the Nationalist Government' and compete with the growing influence of the Chinese Communist Party (CCP).[112] With a revolution in train in his own country, Chang's vision of social welfare ultimately went further than the pacifying vision of the ILO's 'standard of living'.

Rejecting the language of the standard of living in total, the Soviet bloc delegates sought to amend the ILO text to read that the state and community 'should take all necessary measures, including legislative ones, to insure for every person *real* possibilities of enjoying all these rights'.[113] The USSR's position went beyond merely admitting a principle to stipulate that the rights in question would be guaranteed by legal

110   Jiri Nosek (Czechoslovakia) 'Summary Record of the Hundred and Thirty-Eighth Meeting of the Third Committee', 15 November 1948, in Schabas, *Universal Declaration of Human Rights*, vol. 3, p. 2588.

111   Jun Zhao, 'China and the Uneasy Case for Universal Human Rights', *Human Rights Quarterly* 37: 1 (2015), p. 37.

112   Yifeng Chen, 'The International Labour Organisation and Labour Governance in China 1919–1949', in Roger Blanpain, ed., *China and ILO Fundamental Principles and Rights at Work* (Alphen aan den Rijn: Kluwer Law International, 2014), p. 21.

113   Alexei Pavlov (USSR), 'Summary Record of the Seventy-First Meeting of the Commission on Human Rights', 14 June 1948, in Schabas, *Universal Declaration of Human Rights*, vol. 2, p. 1874.

measures. 'It was not enough', Pavlov argued, 'to talk about standards of living and well-being.'[114] Instead, they pointed to the model of the 1936 Soviet Constitution (the Stalin Constitution), which combined an enumeration of rights with discussions of their implementation. These constitutional protections have been described as 'an analogue of socialist realism', which presented an accessible representation of an idealised reality that did not exist in the present.[115] The majority of drafters reacted strongly to the idea of a legal requirement of states to provide their citizens with food, clothing, housing and medical care. In conceptualising social and economic rights as flexible standards that would mitigate extreme poverty without challenging economic or status inequalities, they developed a model of social and economic rights compatible with a neoliberal approach to poverty management.

'By Means Not Inimical to the Market': Neoliberal Poverty-Management

In the wake of the Great Depression, the *laissez-faire* tenets of an earlier liberalism no longer seemed tenable to any but the most intransigent opponents of state intervention. Ludwig von Mises found himself largely isolated at the inaugural meeting of the MPS when he argued that all public relief should be abolished, as private charity was sufficient to 'prevent the absolute destitution of the very restricted hard core of unemployables'.[116] The majority of the neoliberals, in contrast, sought to avoid what Röpke called the false choice between the 'social Darwinism' of *laissez-faire* and a 'cradle to the grave' welfare system.[117] The former, they believed, had neglected the conditions necessary to sustain a labour force and created a backlash against the competitive market. Against the latter, they revived a series of objections the ILO had canvassed back in the 1920s: the welfare state was a 'foretaste of communism' that would undermine the responsibility of workers to provide for their families,

---

114   Ibid., p. 1875.

115   Mark B. Smith, 'Social Rights in the Soviet Dictatorship: The Constitutional Right to Welfare from Stalin to Brezhnev', *Humanity* 3: 3 (2012), p. 388.

116   William Rappard, 'On Reading von Mises', in Mary Sennholz, ed., *On Freedom and Free Enterprise: Essays in Honor of Ludwig von Mises* (Auburn: Ludwig von Mises Institute, 2008), p. 19.

117   Röpke, *Social Crisis of Our Time*, p. 164.

remove the incentive for wage labour, increase bureaucracy, and (in a Malthusian vein) increase the profligacy of the poor and the growth of the population.[118] Rather than rejecting all state assistance, however, the neoliberals focused on the forms of welfare that would be compatible with a market economy. Among the areas for further study outlined in the inaugural MPS statement of aims was the 'possibility of establishing minimum standards by means not inimical to initiative and the functioning of the market'.[119]

The form that a distinctly liberal approach to poverty should take had preoccupied neoliberal circles since the 1938 Walter Lippmann Colloquium. There, Rougier had posed the opening question: 'can economic liberalism meet the social demands of the masses?' The neoliberals worried that it was the planned economy's promise to guarantee a 'vital minimum' that 'attracts the masses to the totalitarian states'.[120] In *The Good Society*, Lippmann himself had argued that what the classical economists dismissed as 'frictions and disturbances' in the market order were, in the eyes of their victims, 'cruel injustices, misery, defeat and frustration'.[121] The success of the competitive market, he argued, required a social policy that would assist people to adapt themselves to the market's demands. There could be no question of 'taking from the rich and giving doles to the poor'; rather, social insurance should help people make choices within the margin of freedom the market allowed, by tiding them over while they learnt the skills for new occupations or moved elsewhere in search of work.[122] The question for the neoliberals was whether providing a vital minimum could be compatible with a functioning competitive market.

They determined that any state welfare provision must be what Walter Eucken called *systemgerecht* – that is, 'in conformity with the whole system'.[123] Eucken moved neoliberalism beyond earlier debates about intervention versus non-intervention by focusing on the *style* of

118   International Labour Organization, 'Family Allowances', p. 21.

119   Statement of Aims of the MPS, cited in Dieter Plehwe, 'Introduction', in Philip Mirowski and Dieter Plehwe, eds, *The Road from Mont Pèlerin: The Making of the Neoliberal Thought Collective* (Cambridge: Harvard University Press, 2009), p. 25.

120   Rougier, 'Address by Professor Louis Rougier', p. 101.

121   Walter Lippmann, *The Good Society* (London: Billing & Sons, 1943), p. 208.

122   Ibid., p. 228.

123   Eucken cited in Slobodian, *Globalists*, p. 205.

intervention. Under his influence, Röpke and the other German ordo-liberals drew a line between compatible and incompatible interventions – that is, between 'those that are in harmony with an economic structure based on the market, and those which are not'.[124] Compatible interventions secured the regulating function of the price mechanism; incompatible interventions paralysed it, and therefore required a cascade of further interventions. The paradigmatic incompatible intervention was rent control, which neoliberals argued prevented supply and demand from governing the distribution of housing, granted privileges to those with rent-controlled apartments, prevented property-owners from profiting from their own property, reduced investment in new housing, and led to housing shortages and unemployment in the building sector, necessitating further intervention. A state that intervenes in incompatible ways, Röpke argued, had 'joined the battle with all the forces of the market which must be fought to the finish'.[125]

This theme was central to Röpke's presentation at the 1958 MPS meeting at Princeton. Röpke spoke on a panel on the welfare state, which also included contributions from Jouvenel and from the US industrialist William J. Grede, the Cambridge economist Walter Hagenbuch, and the Finnish economist Bruno Suviranta.[126] By that time, faced with weakening of the egalitarianism that had sustained the welfare state, the neoliberals had hardened their position. Allowing himself a hint of triumphalism, Hagenbuch noted that, while ten years ago people in Britain had believed everyone should receive a basic income from the state as 'his social birthright', this view had largely been abandoned.[127] The turning point was the 1951 election, which saw the Conservative Party return to power, partly by mobilising middle-class women in 'Housewives' Committees' that protested 'the hardships that are being imposed on them' – notably shortages of luxury goods, high taxes, and what one middle-class housewife called the gradual disappearance of 'the things that made life gracious in the past'.[128] In this climate, the neoliberals were in no mood for compromise.

---

124 Röpke, *Social Crisis of Our Time*, p. 160.
125 Ibid., p. 161.
126 The latter circulated a long paper for the panel but did not present it.
127 Walter Hagenbuch, 'The Welfare State and Social Policy', 9th Mont Pèlerin Society Meeting, Princeton: Hoover Institution Archives, 1958, Box 12, Folder 5, p. 8.
128 Ina Zweiniger-Bargielowska, 'Rationing, Austerity and the Conservative Party Recovery after 1945', *Historical Journal* 37: 1 (1994), p. 180.

That same year, Röpke published his major work, *The Humane Economy*, which included a blistering attack on the welfare state and proclaimed the need for 'resistance to the destruction of dignity' that it brought about.[129] Röpke's book also directly confronted the question of the ethical foundations of a market economy. Is a competitive market society amoral, 'drowning all values in the icy water of egotistical calculation?' he asked, citing Marx and Engels. Or, he asked, referring directly to the origins of the sweetness-of-commerce thesis: 'can we still subscribe to that astonishing eighteenth-century optimism which made Samuel Johnson say: "There are few ways in which man can be more innocently employed than in getting money"?'[130] Röpke's own answer was that the morals of the market were neither those of saints nor those of the battlefield; echoing the sweetness-of-commerce thesis, according to which the cooler interests act to check the violent passions, he described market morality as 'lukewarm, without passions' and characterised by the following features:

> Reliance on one's own efforts, initiative under the impulse of the profit motive, the best possible satisfaction of consumer demand in order to avoid losses, safeguarding one's own interests in constant balance with the interests of others, collaboration in the guise of rivalry, solidarity, constant assessment of the weight of one's own performance on the incorruptible scales of the market, constant struggle to improve one's own real performance in order to win the prize of a better position in society.

Referring back to the 'distinguished ancestors' of this market morality, including Montesquieu, Röpke argued that the central contribution of 'bourgeois' liberal philosophy was to teach that 'there is nothing shameful in the self-reliance and self-assertion of the individual taking care of himself and his family' without which our civilisation is unthinkable.[131]

When it came to welfare, system conformity was not simply a technical matter. What really mattered was ensuring that the provision of a vital minimum did not interfere with the moral and subjective qualities

---

129   Röpke, *Humane Economy*, p. 58.
130   Ibid., p. 113.
131   Ibid., p. 119.

underpinning a competitive market order. In his contribution to the Princeton MPS panel, Röpke told his colleagues that, if they did not want to leave the individual entirely alone to face the 'vicissitudes of life', they must develop rules, principles and distinctions to ensure that concessions to state provision did not legitimise the welfare state, which 'we are all convinced, is the ruin of a free and prosperous society and of the dignity of the self-respecting individual'.[132] A compatible policy had to avoid the weakening of the family, individual responsibility and the will to work for a living.[133]

This theme was taken up in even stronger terms by Grede, a rabidly anti-union representative of the US Chamber of Commerce and a founder of the far-right anti-immigration and anti-civil rights John Birch Society. Grede, who was invited to the Princeton MPS meeting in an attempt to build stronger links between its members and US business, was representative of a broader convergence between free enterprise and right-wing religious conservatism. Grede argued that the superior economic development of the United States was due to its moral and religious foundations and its Bill of Rights, which protected individual freedom from government and, more importantly, from the masses. In contrast, he argued that cradle-to-grave welfare usurped individual responsibility and weakened the 'moral fibre' of a free society. By freedom, he clarified, he did not mean licence; on the contrary, a free society relied on the 'moral pressures of people with deep religious convictions'. Grede charged the welfare state with weakening such pressure; 'with loose morality comes loose law enforcement', he argued, and consequently the breakdown of freedom.[134]

The neoliberals believed that a market-conforming social policy must not stifle the system of risks and incentives that produced familial responsibility and submission to the market. Concretely, this meant that any government payments must be *minimalist* (sufficient to prevent destitution, but no more) and *targeted* at the poorest citizens through strict means-testing. There could be no universal provision, no expectation of social insurance 'as of right', and certainly no use of welfare to redistribute wealth in the interest of greater equality.

132 Wilhelm Röpke, 'Discussion on the Welfare State', 9th Mont Pèlerin Society Meeting, Princeton: Hoover Institution Archives, 1958, Box 12, Folder 6, p. 2.

133 Röpke, *Humane Economy*, p. 166.

134 Grede, 'Moral Effects of the Welfare State', 9th Mont Pèlerin Society meeting, Princeton: Hoover Institution Archives, 1958, Box 12, Folder 6, pp. 2–3.

As his more libertarian critics like to point out today, Hayek had already proposed such a minimalist, market-conforming welfare policy in *The Road to Serfdom*.[135] In a relatively wealthy society, Hayek acknowledged, 'some minimum of food, shelter, and clothing, sufficient to preserve health and capacity to work, can be assured to everybody'; but security against 'undeserved loss' can never be. Although we may sympathise with someone who finds all his hopes disappointed through no fault of his own, he argued, we cannot remedy his situation without destroying the competitive market order.[136] The risk of such loss was necessary to discipline individuals to submit to the market order and adapt themselves to its imperatives. To compensate those whose risks do not pay off would interfere with the feedback mechanism through which the market directs our activities where they are most needed.[137] Hayek contended that the discipline of the market could only be escaped by a retreat to the security of the barracks. If we wished to maintain our (margin of) freedom, he averred, we must ask the state for nothing more than a minimum of subsistence. Anything more would be to set off along the road to serfdom.

Despite general agreement about minimalist welfare, Hayek noted that there remained difficult questions about the 'precise standard'.[138] Early neoliberalism was deeply sceptical about the statistical and standardising practices embraced by the ILO. They saw the attempt to 'tame chance' by using statistics and social surveys to calculate and insure against risks at the level of the population as hubristic.[139] Hayek developed his critique of pretensions to knowledge in the course of the socialist calculation debate of the 1920s and 1930s.[140] In the course of that debate, socialists, notably the Austrian economist and philosopher Otto Neurath, had proposed that detailed inventories of the standard of living (*Lebenslage*) would make it possible to assess social institutions and economic organisation according to the criteria of how well they

---

135   For a typical example, see Hans-Hermann Hoppe, 'Why Mises (and Not Hayek)?', *Mises Daily*, 4 October 2011, at mises.org.

136   Hayek, *Road to Serfdom*, p. 150.

137   Ibid., p. 150.

138   Ibid., p. 148.

139   Ian Hacking, *The Taming of Chance* (Cambridge: Cambridge University Press, 2010).

140   Hayek joined the fray alongside Mises, who argued that rational planning was impossible in the absence of private ownership of capital goods and a system of market prices. See Mises, *Economic Calculation*.

improved people's lives by increasing the availability of everything from food and clothing, to entertainment, leisure time and health.[141]

Against such projects, Hayek's central contribution was to stress the superiority of the market in distributing dispersed knowledge. In so doing, he challenged not only socialist planning but also the positivism of neoclassical economics, telling both, in Michel Foucault's words, 'you cannot [act] because you do not know'.[142] In his most influential article, *The Role of Knowledge in Society* (1945), Hayek distinguished between scientific knowledge of general laws and contextual knowledge of time and place, arguing that the specific knowledge possessed by individuals cannot be adequately aggregated or expressed in statistical form.[143]

Any attempt to achieve sufficient knowledge of individual needs to produce a uniform standard of living would override the diversity of individual preferences and prevent individuals from using their own knowledge to further their own best interests. Mises took this line of thought further in his major work *Human Action*, where he claimed that the very idea of a 'physiological minimum of subsistence' was an invention of 'demagogues'. The claim that 'a definite quantity of calories is needed to keep a man healthy and progenitive, and a further definite quantity to replace the energy expended in working', was untenable, he argued. In the attempt to determine human needs, Mises saw an attempt to make humans the material of a despotic system of 'breeding and feeding' that deprived them of their margin of freedom.[144] Not only did he conceive the attempt to develop nutritional standards as a politically motivated attempt to justify interference with the market; as Mike Hill and Warren Montag note, Mises also believed it would also 'rob human beings, or at least those who labor, of their dignity and reduce them to the status of domestic animals'.[145]

---

141   Otto Neurath, 'Inventory of the Standard of Living' [1937] Thomas E. Uebel and Robert S. Cohen eds, *Economic Writings: Selections 1904–1945*, (Dordrecht: Springer Science and Business Media, 2006).

142   Michel Foucault, *The Birth of Biopolitics: Lectures at the Collège de France 1978–1979*, ed. Michel Senellart, transl. Graham Burchell (New York: Palgrave Macmillan, 2008), p. 283.

143   Friedrich Hayek, 'The Use of Knowledge in Society', *American Economic Review* 35: 4 (1945), p. 520.

144   Ludwig von Mises, *Human Action: A Treatise on Economics* (San Francisco: Fox & Wilkes, 1996), p. 604.

145   Mike Hill and Warren Montag, *The Other Adam Smith* (Redwood City, CA: Stanford University Press, 2014), p. 327.

The German ordoliberals similarly criticised what Rüstow called the 'idolisation of the standard of living'.[146] They rejected the materialism of what Röpke dismissively dubbed 'standard-of-life-ism', and the attempt to fight the Cold War on the terrain of economic productivity.[147] Both men saw consumerism as a key marker of a materialistic mass society, and they bemoaned the fact that, in West Germany, social status was increasingly measured in 'radiograms, television sets, refrigerators'.[148] Drawing on the Catholic principle of subsidiarity, which devolves responsibility to the individual, the family and the local community, the ordoliberals articulated what Rüstow called a *Vitalpolitik*, which aimed to overcome massification and secure the dignity and contentment of the individual.[149] While Mises even disputed that there is a natural need for a fixed number of daily calories, the ordoliberals sought to re-naturalise the family within the social order. *Vitalpolitik* aimed to reinforce what Rüstow called the 'eternal family' – that is, the natural, anthropological unit, rooted in human nature, with responsibility for the welfare of its members.[150]

If these different neoliberal positions could unite, it was because their rejection of the standard of living was primarily a response to the threat that standardising would lead to *equalising*. Hayek's colleagues largely shared his endorsement of *minimal* state provision for the truly impoverished. In *The Humane Economy*, Röpke contrasted 'a state which occasionally rescues some unfortunate individual from destitution' with another, where, in the name of equality, private income is diverted through the welfare state.[151] With typical nostalgia, he argued that, in 'the old days', public assistance was intended as a temporary substitute for self-provision, and was therefore 'meant to safeguard only a certain minimum'. Now, in contrast, public services were becoming the rule, 'often with the hardly veiled intention of meeting maximal, or indeed,

146   Alexander Rüstow, 'Organic Policy (Vitalpolitik) versus Mass Regimentation', in Albert Hunold, ed., *Freedom and Serfdom: An Anthology of Western Thought* (Dordrecht: D. Reidel, 1961), p. 186.

147   Wilhelm Röpke, 'Economic Order and International Law', *Recueil des Cours* 86 (1954), p. 209.

148   Rüstow, 'Organic Policy', p. 186.

149   Mitchell Dean, 'Rethinking Neoliberalism', *Journal of Sociology* 50: 2 (2012), pp. 150–63.

150   Rüstow, 'Organic Policy', p. 177.

151   Röpke, *Humane Economy*, p. 157.

luxury standards'.[152] Posing what was then a 'heretical question', Röpke wondered if it would be better if the welfare state were abolished, 'except for an indispensable minimum', and the money saved directed to non-governmental social services.[153] Responding to the Labour Party's demand that the poverty line and welfare payments should rise to give welfare recipients a share in rising prosperity, Hagenbuch similarly retorted: 'In a society of millionaires, the purpose of the Welfare State would be to ensure that the sick, the unemployed and the aged were millionaires also.'[154]

As well as being minimal, a compatible social policy would be *targeted*, employing 'much more discrimination in the payment of benefits'.[155] The neoliberals sought to return to the time prior to the British economist William Beveridge's proposal, which influenced the introduction of the welfare state, to provide social insurance 'as of right and without means test'.[156] The neoliberals harked back to the household means-test, which was one of the most hated aspects of the poverty-relief of the 1930s. Like the Ford Company's intrusive paternalism, the family means-test had subjected relief recipients to invasive and humiliating investigations of their finances and savings. Continuing a history of deterrence that had characterised poor relief since the Poor Law of 1834, the means-test treated accepting relief as a matter of social disgrace.[157] Like the earlier Poor Laws, it was an object of 'passionate resentment and embittered feeling' among working people, as the General Council of the Trade Union Council put it, adding: 'We hate it with the same intensity that we hate the thought of the workhouse.'[158] By treating the family as an economic unit for the purposes of determining eligibility, the means-test undermined unemployed men's status in the

---

152   Ibid., p. 159.
153   Ibid., p. 167.
154   Hagenbuch, 'Welfare State and Social Policy', p. 5.
155   Ibid., p. 5.
156   William Beveridge, 'Social Insurance and Allied Services', Inter-departmental Committee on Social Insurance and Allied Services, 1942, p. 7.
157   Noel Whiteside, 'The Beveridge Report and Its Implementation: A Revolutionary Project?', *Histoire@Politique* 3: 24 (2014). For a penetrating account of the attempt by the Chicago School neoliberals to resurrect this poor law tradition in the United States, see Cooper, *Family Values*.
158   Cited in Susan Pedersen, *Family, Dependence, and the Origins of the Welfare State: Britain and France, 1914–1945* (New York: Cambridge University Press, 1993), p. 313.

family, forcing them to depend on the wages of their wives or, more commonly, their children. By putting white working-class men in a position of dependence long reserved for women and children, the family means-test was widely interpreted as a crisis of both masculinity and the working-class family.

Neoliberal Paternalism

It has often been noted that a liberal revival that came to prominence as a critique of the paternalism of the welfare state ended up expanding state involvement in the welfare system. Neoliberal welfarism, critics note, enlists the state to coerce welfare recipients into the worst, lowest-paid jobs and subjects them to invasive supervision and income-management. Such 'neoliberal paternalism' is often understood as the product of a tactical alliance between free-market neoliberals and family-values social conservatives who found common cause in opposition to the 'ungovernability' of the social movements of the 1960s.[159] But the social conservatism of a figure like Lawrence Mead, whose 'new paternalism' inspired US workfare policies, was prefigured decades earlier by European neoliberals. Mead's 1986 exhortation that the state must demand 'acceptance of the verdict of the market place' was central to neoliberal discussions of welfare from the 1930s.[160]

In a paper prepared for the 1958 MPS meeting, Jouvenel described the 'violent reluctance' to target assistance to 'the needy', as the result of a modern 'gain in personal dignity'.[161] It was no longer acceptable to ask whether someone who falls sick had personal means, he complained; 'the same help is to be afforded to the wealthy and to the poor', to the mother of three children married to a labourer and the mother married to the chairman of the corporation that employs him.[162] This gain in 'dignity' is reflected in Article 23 of the UDHR, which declares that

---

159   See, for example, Cooper, *Family Values*; and Joe Soss, Richard C. Fording and Sanford F. Schram, *Disciplining the Poor: Neoliberal Paternalism and the Persistent Power of Race* (Chicago: University of Chicago Press, 2011).

160   Mead, cited in Soss, Fording, and Schram, *Disciplining the Poor*, p. 28.

161   Bertrand de Jouvenel, 'Broodings on the Welfare State', in *Mont Pèlerin Society*, 9th Mont Pèlerin Society Meeting, Princeton: Hoover Institution Archives, 1958, Box 12, Folder 5, p. 6. Jouvenel's paper was circulated but not presented.

162   Ibid., p. 6.

'everyone who works has the right to a just and favourable remuneration ensuring for himself and his family an existence worthy of human dignity and supported, if necessary, by other means of social protection'. While they rejected both the idea of a just wage and the idea that social protection was a right, the neoliberals upheld both this gendered vision of family welfare and the association of dignity with work. They sought to turn back the clock to when there was nothing dignified about seeking state assistance. Dignity, for them, was a status that applied only to responsible and self-reliant adults, capable of supporting themselves and their families.

At the Walter Lippmann Colloquium, Hayek had laid out two models of relief: one gives the unemployed worker a dole at the level of his former wage; 'the other is designed on the model of the poor law in England'.[163] The former threatened to trespass on the margins of neoliberal freedom, making workers unwilling to submit to the market and move for work. Only the deterrence of the latter could reconcile relief with a market-pricing mechanism. For all their criticisms of the paternalism of the welfare state, the neoliberals believed that those destitute few who were eligible for state relief had forfeited their independence, their personal responsibility – and possibly their freedom too.

In *The Road to Serfdom*, Hayek suggested that government relief posed difficult questions about whether those who received it were entitled to the freedom enjoyed by others.[164] The neoliberals were not so far from earlier punitive and privatised conceptions of poverty-management, which made the individual and the family fully responsible for social welfare. John Locke, who is today considered among the great liberals, saw no contradiction between advocating freedom and rights and arguing that children older than three whose families were unable to feed them should be sent to work.[165] The paternalism of contemporary neoliberal welfare systems is rooted in the same contention that those who draw on state assistance forfeit their independence and renounce a freedom that is inseparable from submission to the verdict of the market, and from personal responsibility for risk. The Chicago School's Milton Friedman inherited aspects of this earlier

---

163   Cited in Reinhoudt and Audier, *Walter Lippmann Colloquium*, p. 155.
164   Hayek, *Road to Serfdom*.
165   Cited in Domenico Losurdo, *Liberalism: A Counter-History* (London: Verso, 2011), p. 70.

neoliberal tradition. 'Freedom is a tenable objective only for responsible individuals', he contended. 'Paternalism is inescapable for those whom we designate as not responsible.'[166]

As the paternalism of neoliberal welfarism suggests, the neoliberals' real problem with the welfare state was never really its paternalism. 'The language of the old paternal government is still current and so are its categories', Röpke noted in 1958, 'but all this is becoming a screen that hides the new crusade against anything which dares exceed the average, be it in income, wealth, or performance.'[167] Although they criticised the welfare state for depriving individuals of their freedom and independence, what really horrified the neoliberals was this crusading pursuit of equality. If the problem of relief to the 'weak and helpless' were taken as a pretext for 'levelling out all differences in income and wealth', Röpke argued, that was the path of 'social revolution.'[168] Decades earlier, Hayek had identified this same spectre lurking behind the paternalist arguments sustaining the New Deal. The demand for freedom from want, he argued, was 'only another name for the old demand for an equal distribution of wealth.'[169] Much later he bemoaned the 'unfortunate' fact that 'the endeavour to secure a uniform minimum for all who cannot provide for themselves has become connected with the wholly different aims of securing a "just" distribution of incomes.'[170] Poverty relief, the neoliberals believed, must never interfere with the inequalities of civil society.

In the summer of 1940, Hayek was pondering the fate of his own family. Then living in London, the Austrian economist believed it likely that he might soon be killed by enemy bombing. Fearing the worst, he considered a number of offers to place his small children with 'some unknown family', who would presumably continue to raise them if he did not survive the war. In the most concrete terms, he considered the relative merits of sending his children to the United States, Argentina or Sweden, on the assumption that their social position in the country would be determined largely by chance. From behind this veil of ignorance, Hayek decided that 'the very absence in the US of the sharp social distinctions

---

166   Milton Friedman, *Capitalism and Freedom* (Chicago: University of Chicago Press, 2002), p. 33.
167   Röpke, *Humane Economy*, p. 156.
168   Cited in ibid., p. 176.
169   Hayek, *Road to Serfdom*, p. 78.
170   Hayek, 'Epilogue', p. 55.

which would favour me in the Old World should make me decide for them in favour of the former'. The absence of aristocratic hierarchies and the relative social equality produced by the New Deal, he recognised, would give his children the best possible chance in life. As if as an after-thought, Hayek then added a bracketed qualifying sentence: '(I should perhaps add that this was based on the tacit assumption that my children would there be placed with a white and not with a coloured family.)'[171] In the midst of an anecdote that Hayek introduced in order to justify the impersonal allocation of social positions through the market, white supremacy appeared between two brackets, as a 'tacit assumption' underpinning a narrative of success through hard work and chance. Hayek's Rawlsian thought experiment thus exemplified Saidiya Hartman's claim that 'abstract equality produces white entitlement and black subjection'.[172] The ignorance that Hayek often argued prevents us from altering the distributional outcomes of the market was, patently, what Charles Mills calls 'white ignorance', which makes the liberal social contract a 'racial contract'.[173]

Even in cases in which the unequal starting positions of individuals are 'determined by earlier unjust acts or institutions' – as the racial inequality that he tacitly acknowledged in the United States surely was – Hayek argued that it would generally be 'impracticable' to correct it. It would be preferable, he suggested, to 'accept the given position as due to accident and simply from the present onwards to refrain from any measures aiming at benefiting particular individuals or groups'.[174] Hayek acknowledged that, given the centrality of the family in a child's initial social position, inequalities between families would be perpetuated over time. In fact, he endorsed inherited wealth precisely because such a perpetuation of inequality supposedly created a better elite.[175] Yet he took for granted that, wherever his children were placed, their welfare would be the sole responsibility of their new family. However much his children's hopes were frustrated by 'unmerited disappointment', there was no justification for state action to equalise their chances. In

171   Friedrich Hayek, 'Notes: Chapter Ten: The Market Order or Catallaxy', in Hayek, *Law, Legislation and Liberty, vol. 2*, p. 189.

172   Hartman, *Scenes of Subjection*, p. 116.

173   Charles W. Mills, *White Ignorance* (Oxford: Oxford University Press, 2017), p. 49.

174   Hayek, *Law, Legislation and Liberty, vol. 2*, p. 131.

175   Ibid.

privatising welfare and foreclosing redistribution, the neoliberals entrenched economic inequalities while naturalising gender subordination within the family and sanctioning race as the 'natural ordering principle of the social'.[176]

Any intrusion into the private sphere of the family, even for the purpose of rectifying historical injustices or providing children with more equal starting positions, would be totalitarian, the neoliberals contended. In their more melodramatic moments, they depicted any form of state-licensed redistribution as leading directly to the policies of Nazi Germany or Soviet Russia. This path might begin with a government that 'wants to make it possible for poor parents to give more milk to their children', Mises warned, in an almost caricatured version of the 'road to serfdom thesis', but in 'proceeding step by step on this way it finally reaches a point in which all economic freedom of individuals has disappeared. Then socialism on the German pattern . . . of the Nazis emerges'.[177] Hayek struck a similar tone decades later when he criticised the drafters of the UDHR for imagining themselves as 'Platonic philosopher-kings' and seeking a 're-organization of society on totalitarian lines'.[178]

In reality, the social and economic rights in the UDHR were hardly as threatening to the market order as Hayek and his comrades seemed to believe. Framed in minimalist terms, and orientated towards securing the racial and gender order of mid-twentieth-century capitalism, these social and economic rights were ultimately far more compatible with a liberal market than the neoliberals initially feared. Far from ushering in a 'social revolution' that overturned hierarchies of status and inequalities of wealth, social and economic rights increasingly came to signify merely the aspiration to realise over time a basic minimum for the most impoverished.[179] As Hayek correctly noted in 1976, proclaiming rights to food, education, health, housing and clothing was a very different matter from actually securing food, education, health, housing or clothing for all.

While Hayek attributed the UDHR's social and economic rights to the Marxism of the Russian Revolution, the Soviet delegates shared much of his cynicism about the practical effects of declaring such rights.

---

176   Hartman, *Scenes of Subjection*, p. 121.

177   Mises, *Socialism*, p. 595.

178   Hayek, 'Justice and Individual Rights', 105.

179   For an important account of the subsequent transformation of human rights into aspirations to secure minimalist standards of 'sufficiency', see Moyn, *Not Enough*.

In a capitalist country, the Soviet bloc delegates argued, there would always be a 'flagrant contradiction' between what was said in the declaration and the reality. The declaration of a right to rest, for instance, 'had a hollow ring in a society in which a small group always rested, while the overwhelming majority worked all the time'.[180] The fundamental transformation necessary to secure such a right was far from the minds of the majority of diplomats who drafted the UDHR. Nonetheless, as they met at Lake Success and at the Palais De Chaillot in Paris, another dramatic transformation was underway as the great age of decolonisation gained momentum. Those colonial subjects whose subjugation, labour and resources underpinned the welfare and freedom of the people of the metropolis were demanding freedom for themselves. Even more significantly, they were refusing Hayek's claim that it was 'impractical' to correct the inequalities deriving from unjust acts or institutions, and were demanding economic transformations to secure real control over their lands and resources.

---

180   Dimitry Manuilsky (Ukrainian Soviet Socialist Republic), 'Verbatim Record of the Hundred and Eightieth Plenary Meeting of the General Assembly', 9 December 1948, in Schabas, *Universal Declaration of Human Rights*, vol. 3, p. 3036.

3

Neoliberalism, Human Rights and the 'Shabby Remnants of Colonial Imperialism'

Let us assume that the United Nations had been established in the year 1600 and that the Indian tribes of North America had been admitted as members of this organization. Then the sovereignty of these Indians would have been recognized as inviolable. They would have been given the right to exclude all aliens from entering their territory and from exploiting its rich natural resources which they themselves did not know how to utilize. Does anybody really believe that any international covenant or charter could have prevented these Europeans from invading these countries?

Ludwig von Mises

In 1966, almost twenty years after the United Nations' human rights process began, the UN General Assembly adopted two legally binding human rights covenants – the International Covenant on Civil and Political Rights (ICCPR) and the International Covenant on Economic, Social and Cultural Rights (ICESCR). By then, successful anticolonial struggles had almost doubled the UN's membership. As the covenants were adopted, the Nigerian delegate expressed pride that his country, though unable to participate in the drafting of the Universal Declaration of Human Rights (UDHR), had achieved independence in time to make a 'meager contribution' to the drafting of the covenants.[1] The

---

1   A. A. Mohammed (Nigeria) 'Official Record of the 1496th Plenary Meeting of the United Nations General Assembly', 16 December 1966, p. 11, at undocs.org.

enthusiastic presence of representatives of newly independent states seemed to show that the universal aspirations embodied in the UDHR had triumphed over those civilisational hierarchies the colonial powers had sought to consolidate back in 1948. In a particularly exuberant speech, the Mexican delegate announced: 'Like a chrysalis, long enveloped in its cocoon, the Covenants now, spreading their glorious wings, are ready to improve the lot of mankind.'[2] For anticolonialists, the cause for celebration was twofold: not only had former colonies participated in the drafting of the covenants as independent sovereign states; they had also succeeded in adopting the right of peoples to self-determination as the first human right.

The Mexican delegate's optimism seems to challenge the oft-heard critique of the abstraction of human rights discourse, its indifference to the particularity that it is the stuff of lived experience. On the contrary, it seemed to be precisely *because* the universal human inscribed in the texts of human rights is abstract that it has proved so capable of expanding to include those who were once excluded. From this perspective, both the subjects and borders of rights are structurally in flux, and so the language of human rights can always be taken up by new excluded subjects to affirm their inclusion in the category of humanity. Such a strategy – what the French philosopher Jacques Rancière calls 'verifying equality' – entails seizing and taking seriously what is often dismissed as a groundless claim (that all human beings are born free and equal in rights, for instance) and using it to stage a dispute.[3] In the historiography of human rights, this approach is most forcefully articulated by the historian Lynn Hunt, who argues that declarations of rights have a tendency to cascade, including ever more people as subjects of rights.[4]

The period that separated the adoption of the UDHR in 1948 from the adoption of the human rights covenants in 1966 seems at first to have been a period of just such cascading rights claims. Victorious anticolonial movements drastically changed both the composition of the UN and the terms of human rights debates. In 1955, delegates from twenty-nine African and Asian countries gathered at Bandung in Indonesia, and declared that the right of peoples and nations to

---

2   Cuevas Cancino (Mexico) Ibid., p. 3.
3   Jacques Rancière, *On the Shores of Politics* (London: Verso, 2006), p. 47.
4   Lynn Hunt, *Inventing Human Rights: A History* (New York: W. W. Norton, 2007).

self-determination is 'a pre-requisite for the full enjoyment of all funda-mental Human Rights'.[5] Two years later, in 1957, Ghana became the first sub-Saharan African nation to win its independence; in 1960, dubbed the 'Year of Africa', it was followed by seventeen more African nations, including Nigeria, whose delegate was so proud to participate in the drafting of the human rights covenants. Much had changed since the early days of the drafting of the UDHR, when delegates from colonial powers had sought to defend civilisational hierarchies and exclude their colonial subjects from human rights.

Yet, even as what Hunt terms the 'bulldozer force of the revolutionary logic of rights' was in full gear, anticolonialists were recognising that their new-found freedom and sovereign equality did not grant them the inde-pendence for which they had fought.[6] Just prior to the adoption of the human rights covenants, Kwame Nkrumah, the first president of inde-pendent Ghana, coined the termed 'neo-colonialism' to refer to the subtle mechanisms that perpetuated colonial patterns of exploitation in the wake of formal independence. Nkrumah argued that the achievement of formal sovereignty had neither freed former colonies from the unequal economic relations of the colonial period nor given them political control over their territories. A 'state in the grip of neo-colonialism,' he wrote, 'is not master of its own destiny'.[7] Among the mechanisms of neocolonialism, Nkrumah singled out international capital's control of the world market, exploitative uses of international aid and aid conditionality, and the moral pressure exerted by US labour organisations, missionaries and NGOs.[8] Neocolonialism emerged, as Upendra Baxi has noted, just as struggles for independence appeared to succeed.[9] The struggle against neocolonialism took the form of new demands for economic rights, including rights to development and to 'Permanent Sovereignty Over Natural Resources'.[10]

5   Asian-African Conference, 'Final Communiqué of the Asian-African Conference of Bandung' (Djakarta: Centre Virtuel de la Connaissance sur l'Europe, 24 April 1955), p. 6.

6   Hunt, *Inventing Human Rights*, p. 168.

7   Kwame Nkrumah, *Neo-Colonialism: The Last Stage of Imperialism* (New York: International, 1966), p. x.

8   Ibid., p. 243.

9   Upendra Baxi, *The Future of Human Rights* (Oxford: Oxford University Press, 2008), p. 51.

10   Resolution 1803 on Permanent Sovereignty Over Natural Resources was adopted by the UN General Assembly in December 1962, 'Permanent Sovereignty over Natural Resources, General Assembly Resolution 1803 (XVII) ', at legal.un.org.

For the neoliberals, this attempt to politicise the postcolonial economic order was a threat to the world market and international peace. They argued that this postcolonial economic project was the inheritance of mid-century colonialism, which had abandoned the free-trade policies of the earlier British Empire in favour of economic planning. Faced with rising anticolonialism, the neoliberals sought to change the terms of the debate over imperialism and colonialism. They argued that imperialism was not the 'highest stage of capitalism', as Vladimir Lenin had argued, but the result of the *politicisation* of the economy. Summing up the shared neoliberal perspective, Wilhelm Röpke complained that imperialism was one of the 'sad results of the politicization of the economy into which we lapse the more we increasingly abandon the principles of the market economy'.[11] Against postcolonial demands for economic self-determination, the neoliberals mobilised their dichotomy between the market as a realm of mutually beneficial, free, peaceful exchange, and politics as violent, coercive and militaristic. Separating political sovereignty from economic ownership, they argued, would enable all parties to purchase the raw materials of former colonies on the open market, rendering colonisation and conquest unnecessary.

At the 1957 meeting of the Mont Pèlerin Society, the Stanford agricultural economist Karl Brandt drew on the myth of the market as a *catallaxy* that transforms enemies into friends to lay out a neoliberal approach to decolonisation. The problem for an 'enlightened liberalism', he argued, was not 'how to rid the colonial areas of the white people'; rather, it was 'how to create, as soon as possible, conditions in the colonial areas under which the white people not only can stay but where more of them can enter the areas as welcome partners and friends'.[12] Creating the conditions in which 'the white people' could stay meant ensuring that their rights were protected. Breaking with the optimism of nineteenth-century *laissez-faire*, the neoliberals argued that the future

---

This was one of a suite of resolutions that attempted, as Sundhya Pahuja puts it paraphrasing Nkrumah, 'to re-assert the "political kingdom" over the economic". Sundhya Pahuja, *Decolonising International Law: Development, Economic Growth, and the Politics of Universality* (Cambridge: Cambridge University Press, 2011), p. 86.

11   Wilhelm Röpke, *The Social Crisis of Our Time*, transl. Annette Schiffer Jacobsohn and Peter Schiffer Jacobsohn (Chicago: University of Chicago Press, 1950), p. 107.

12   Brandt, cited in Angus Burgin, *The Great Persuasion: Reinventing Free Markets since the Depression* (Cambridge: Harvard University Press, 2012), p. 120.

of the world market depended on the creation of a legal and moral framework to restrain postcolonial sovereignty, protect property and investments, and secure the existing international division of labour. Against the postcolonial human rights project, the neoliberals developed a competing human rights project – 'market-friendly' human rights, which aimed to protect the right to trade, and to license transformative interventions to uphold this right.[13] More importantly, neoliberal human rights were designed to inculcate the morals of the market and shape liberal subjects. What Nkrumah called neocolonialism was, for the neoliberals, a project.

Social Democratic Colonialism and the Problem of Human Rights

In 1947, the Labour government that built the UK's welfare state sent its delegate to Lake Success with instructions to ensure the new human rights declaration contained no social and economic rights.[14] Charles Dukes, the retired trade unionist representing the UK, presented his country as a bastion of freedom, social justice and equality. At the same time, he was tasked with deflecting challenges to Britain's colonial empire, which then comprised thirty-eight territories with a combined population of 60 million people.[15] The Colonial Office viewed the drafting of an international human rights document as a serious threat. Wary of the Foreign Office's enthusiasm for the Cold War potential of human rights, a 1947 Colonial Office memo warned that the UK should not commit to a conception of human rights based too closely on the political and social conditions of 'advanced Europeanized countries'; if such a conception were accepted, the memo warned, '(attractive as this might be for "having a go at the totalitarians") we shall expose our colonial flank'.[16]

---

13   Baxi, *Future of Human Rights*.

14   Lord Dukeston, 'Text of the Letter from Lord Dukeston, the United Kingdom Representative on the Human Rights Commission, to the Secretary-General of the United Nations', 5 June 1947), in William A. Schabas, ed., *The Universal Declaration of Human Rights: The Travaux Préparatoires*, Vol. 1, (Cambridge: Cambridge University Press, 2013), p. 288–99.

15   In the course of the drafting, Dukes was honoured with the title Lord Dukeston. Brian A. W. Simpson, *Human Rights and the End of Empire: Britain and the Genesis of the European Convention* (Oxford: Oxford University Press, 2004), p. 341.

16   Simpson, *Human Rights and the End of Empire*, p. 341.

The fear of exposing its 'colonial flank' shaped the approach to the drafting of the UDHR taken by the UK and by the other major colonial power, France. Dukes was instructed in the Colonial Office position: 'colonial status is not a cause of backwardness; it is a remedy'.[17] The Colonial Office stipulated five prerequisites for self-government: a healthy and vigorous people; adequate technical skill and knowledge; adequate production; a commodity for export; and, finally, honest and efficient administration and governance.[18] This represented a turn away from the free trade of the nineteenth-century British Empire, as the state took on direct responsibility for economic development. From the neoliberals, there was little to defend in this social democratic colonialism. They watched with horror as the 'totalitarian' social democracy they had condemned at home was exported to the former colonies. Before turning to their response, it is worth considering in more detail the contours of the social democratic colonialism against which they developed their own understanding of the world market and the rights it entailed.

Less than a decade after the UDHR's adoption, the Swedish social democrat Gunnar Myrdal proclaimed that the welfare state, which was becoming a reality in all 'advanced nations', should be transformed into a 'welfare world'.[19] This dream was undercut by the reality of colonial exploitation. The same year that the UDHR was adopted, the UK's minister of economic affairs, Sir Stafford Cripps, contended that Britain's very survival depended on 'a quick and extensive development of our African resources'.[20] The demand to increase production in the colonies made the UK very wary of extending economic rights. For anticolonialists, who were accustomed to the gap between universal pronouncements and colonial realities, the seeming contradiction between welfarism at home and the denial of economic rights at an international level provided a lens through which to illuminate the post-war economic order.

It was Nkrumah who grasped most clearly that the colonies were not simply an exception to the extension of social welfare and rights.

---

17   Ibid., p. 375.
18   Ibid., p. 298.
19   Gunnar Myrdal, *An International Economy: Problems and Prospects* (New York: Harper & Brothers, 1956), p. 321.
20   Frederick Cooper, *Decolonization and African Society: The Labor Question in French and British Africa* (Cambridge: Cambridge University Press, 2010), p. 204.

Colonial exploitation, he argued, constituted the condition of possibility for economic rights in the metropolis. Faced with popular expectations that the end of the war would be marked by welfare and higher living standards, he argued that 'no post-war capitalist country could survive unless it became a "welfare state".[21] As a greater share of the proceeds of colonial exploitation were redirected to the working classes in the interests of social pacification, the Ghanaian President noted, two principles central to early capitalism were sacrificed: the subjugation of the working classes within each country, and the exclusion of state control of capitalist enterprise. Nkrumah argued that substituting free trade with welfare states exported class struggle to the international stage and made colonial exploitation newly central to the stability of capitalism.[22] The colonies were not simply latecomers to the welfare world. If there was no 'rights cascade' when it came to social and economic rights, this was, not least, because the exploitation of the colonies made these rights possible in the metropolis.

In the decades leading up to the drafting of the UDHR, strikes and labour disputes across the Caribbean and the African continent forced colonial officials to deal with questions of labour and living standards. Despite the arguments of the UK Treasury, which warned against creating a colonial 'dole', the Colonial Office successfully won passage of the Colonial Development and Welfare Act (1940), which enabled metropolitan spending on water, health, housing and education in the colonies.[23] The act was predicated on a social theory that assumed improved standards of living and social services would succeed in 'cooling colonial anger and restoring imperial honour'.[24] This gave a progressive gloss to colonial rule, as state supervision and planning were portrayed as necessary to protect the people of the colonies from market fluctuations. The reality, in the context of the war, was starkly different: real wages in African cities were plummeting, and colonial governments were more focused on lifting productivity than on

---

21 Nkrumah, *Neo-Colonialism*, p. xii.
22 Ibid., p. 255.
23 Frederick Cooper, 'Modernizing Bureaucrats, Backward Africans, and the Development Concept', in Randall M. Packard, ed., *International Development and the Social Sciences: Essays on the History and Politics of Knowledge* (Berkeley: University of California Press, 1997), p. 67.
24 Cooper, *Decolonization and African Society*, p. 114.

raising the living standards of the people they governed.[25] In such a context, colonial powers were particularly wary about international declarations of human rights.

Fabianising the Empire

By 1947, when the drafting of the UDHR began, the UK Labour government had begun what the Labour Party's *Tribune* newspaper called 'Fabianising the Empire'. Established in 1884 with the goal of reconstructing British society to secure 'the general welfare and happiness', by the twentieth century the Fabians had turned their attention from 'civilising' the British working class to developing the Empire. In 1926, the Russian revolutionary Leon Trotsky had described the Fabian Society as an anachronism of the Victorian era, when the 'benevolent bourgeoisie' did cultural and educational work among the poor.[26] The neoliberals were no more complimentary. Hayek, who taught at the Fabian-founded London School of Economics, reflected that his Fabian colleague Harold Laski was 'frightfully offended' by *The Road to Serfdom*, which he believed was written specifically against him.[27] Laski was not entirely mistaken. Hayek wrote the book with one clear purpose, he recalled later: to persuade his 'Fabian colleagues that they were wrong'.[28] In the book itself, he criticised the imperialism of the Fabians, arguing that their enthusiasm for planning went along with a veneration of large states and a 'glorification of power' that was akin to that of the Nazis.[29]

As the UDHR was drafted, the Fabian Colonial Bureau was the main vehicle for the UK's 'progressive' colonial policy, and it was against this Fabian imperialism that the neoliberals would develop their own response to the question of the colonies. For the Fabians, colonial development was too important to be left to the market; the benevolent hand of the state was necessary to secure order and prepare colonial subjects

25   Ibid., p. 115.

26   Leon Trotsky, 'The Fabian "Theory" of Socialism', in *Chapter IV: Trotsky's Writings on Britain* (London: New Park, 1974).

27   Friedrich Hayek et al., *Nobel Prize-Winning Economist Oral History Transcript* (Los Angeles: Oral History Program, University of California, Los Angeles, 1983), p. 113, at archive.org.

28   Ibid., p. 423.

29   Friedrich Hayek, *The Road to Serfdom: Text and Documents*, ed. Bruce Caldwell (Chicago: University of Chicago Press, 2007), pp. 163–4.

for the demands of an efficient modern economy. For the neoliberals, in contrast, mid-twentieth-century colonial policy represented a dangerous step away from the liberalism and free trade of the earlier British Empire. In the Fabian commitment to economic planning, they saw the politicisation of the economy and a cause of international friction and imperialist conflict. Much later, neoliberal development economists would look back on this period and argue that, at independence, postcolonial leaders were 'handed a system of close economic controls which placed the bulk of the population at their mercy'.[30] In the British government's embrace of economic planning, the neoliberals discerned the origins of postcolonial 'totalitarianism'.

The social democratic imperialism of the late 1940s sought legitimacy in the claim that it was lifting living standards in the colonies. Once again, the ILO played an important role in what Frederick Cooper calls 'imperialism internationalized'.[31] A founding premise of the ILO was that the failure of any one country to adopt 'accepted international minimum standards' was an obstacle to the promotion of such standards in all other countries.[32] As an 'avant-garde of global governance', the ILO helped to shape a moral discourse and a vision of global order to be administered from Europe.[33] It aimed to stabilise the colonies and normalise wage labour through the extension of minimum standards of welfare and labour regulation. This also entailed globalising a normative vision of the family. As ILO officials believed 'the disruption of family life' threatened stability, they promoted the phasing out of children's employment and the regulation of the employment of women, and advised that employers of migratory workers take account of 'their normal family needs'.[34]

At the ILO's 1947 Convention, the Indian workers' delegate, Shanta Mukherjee, noted the almost total absence of workers from the colonies. 'Can any policy which has not freedom as its declared objective secure the well-being and happiness of dependent peoples?', she asked.[35] By

---

30   Peter Bauer and Basil Yamey, 'Black Africa: The Living Legacy of Dying Colonialism', *Encounter*, February 1984, p. 56.

31   Cooper, *Decolonization and African Society*, p. 217.

32   Ibid., p. 217.

33   Yifeng Chen, 'The International Labour Organisation and Labour Governance in China 1919–1949', in Roger Blanpain, ed., *China and ILO Fundamental Principles and Rights at Work* (Alphen aan den Rijn: Kluwer Law International, 2014), p. 28.

34   Cooper, *Decolonization and African Society*, p. 219.

35   Ibid., 219.

updating older civilisational and racial hierarchies for new welfarist times, the 'progressive' colonial policy of the period sought to forestall such questions. In 1946, Rita Hinden of the Fabian Colonial Bureau clashed with Nkrumah at a conference on the 'Relation between Britain and the Colonial Peoples'. 'When Mr Nkrumah said "we want absolute independence", it left me absolutely cool', she reflected. 'British socialists are not so concerned with ideals like independence and self-government, but with the idea of social justice.'[36] By taking the emphasis off the political question of independence, the Fabians portrayed colonial rule as necessary to protect colonial subjects from market fluctuations. The year the UDHR was adopted, the Fabian and colonial secretary, Arthur Creech Jones, proclaimed that, with British help, he could see 'Africans shaking off the shackles of ignorance, superstition and cramping custom, becoming aware and self-reliant and marching with other free people down the great highways of the world to keep their rendezvous with destiny.'[37] In drawing on the metaphorics of slavery, Creech Jones portrayed Africans as shackled by their own customs and ignorance, and colonial rule as a force of emancipation.

It was in the context of the Boer War, which pitted the British Empire against the Boer states, the South African Republic (Transvaal) and the Orange Free State, in an attempt to maintain its position in southern Africa, that the Fabians committed themselves to an imperialism stripped of 'old-fashioned Free Trade talk'.[38] The 1900 pamphlet, 'Fabianism and the Empire', edited by George Bernard Shaw, embraced this imperialist role, arguing that a 'Great Power' like the United Kingdom, must 'govern in the interests of civilization as a whole'.[39] Shaw's widely discussed pamphlet argued for rescuing the Empire from the 'strife of classes and private interests' through effective social organisation. Everywhere the Empire's ships sailed, it argued, they should bring factory codes and minimum-wage legislation; 'civilization must follow the flag'.[40] In contrast to the neoliberals, the Fabians measured civilisation not by the extent of the division of labour, but by labour

---

36   Rita Hinden, quoted in Partha Sarathi Gupta, *Imperialism and the British Labour Movement 1914–1964* (London: Macmillan, 1975), p. 326.

37   Cooper, *Decolonization and African Society*, p. 208.

38   Bernard Shaw, ed., *Fabianism and the Empire: A Manifesto by the Fabian Society* (London: Grant Richards, 1900), p. 12.

39   Ibid., p. 12.

40   Ibid., p. 7.

regulations and living standards; 'no flag that does not carry a reasonable standard of life with it shall be the flag of a Great Power', Shaw
wrote.[41] This civilising mission aimed to prevent political conflict and
class struggle, eradicate disease and crime, and increase the efficiency of
colonial production. For the neoliberals, the support of the Fabians for
the Boer War was evidence that socialism and imperialism shared what
Röpke called a 'common ideological breeding ground'.[42]

The Fabians in the Labour government were the inheritors of the
utilitarianism and paternalism of the nineteenth-century liberal J. S.
Mill, who famously declared that despotism was legitimate in governing
those he termed 'barbarians' – 'provided the end be their improvement'.[43]
Mill's account of improvement was framed as a critique of a rapacious
colonialism of conquest and exploitation practised by 'selfish usurp-
ers'.[44] Equally, the Fabians portrayed themselves as opponents of an
older colonialism of exploitation and conquest. But for them, as for Mill,
the claim to be preparing the colonised for eventual self-government
provided a moral justification for continuing subjugation. Comparing
the colonised to children, Mill had argued that different civilisations
required different institutions, just as children of different ages required
different lessons.[45] This pedagogical conception continued to inform
British colonial policy into the 1940s. 'The colonial system', a UK
Colonial Office official told a UN committee in 1947, 'was a practical
illustration of democracy under tuition.'[46]

The Fabians also inherited Mill's scepticism about the universalist
belief that political institutions suitable for England or France are 'the
only fit form of government for Bedouins and Malays'.[47] In 1901, Shaw

41   Ibid., p. 55.
42   Röpke, *Social Crisis of Our Time*, pp. 60, 75.
43   John Stuart Mill, *On Liberty* (Indianapolis: Hackett, 1978), p. 504. In 1936, the
British Fabian political theorist and economist Harold Laski noted that the 'typical
English socialism was Fabian, a body of doctrine upon which the emphasis of John
Stuart Mill's ideas was far more profound than that of Marx'. Harold J. Laski, *The Rise of
European Liberalism (Works of Harold J. Laski): An Essay in Interpretation* (Abingdon:
Routledge, 2015), 241.
44   Mill, cited in Karuna Mantena, *Alibis of Empire: Henry Maine and the Ends of
Liberal Imperialism* (Princeton, NJ: Princeton University Press, 2010), p. 31.
45   Ibid., p. 31.
46   In Simpson, *Human Rights and the End of Empire*, p. 294.
47   John Stuart Mill, 'Considerations on Representative Government', in J. M.
Robson, ed., *Essays on Politics and Society* (Toronto: University of Toronto Press, 1977),
p. 394.

noted that the British Empire was no longer 'a Commonwealth of white men and baptised Christians', and argued against extending democratic institutions to subjects who were 'black, brown, or yellow', and whose creed was 'Mahometan, Buddhist or Hindu'.[48] The belief in collective, cultural requirements for civilisation shaped Mill's account of rights, and went on to influence the Fabians in the Labour government. Following in the utilitarian tradition of Jeremy Bentham, for whom natural rights were 'nonsense upon stilts', Mill argued that rights are simply claims that a society should protect in the interests of general utility. In the colonies, there was little utility in granting rights to those who lacked the pre-requisite for liberty: the capacity to improve themselves through reasoned discussion. Rather, he believed it was in the interest of all humanity that the Empire guide the colonised to civilisation, just as a parent guides a child into adulthood. He therefore demarcated those who were ready for rights from those who required a 'vigorous despotism' to lead them to a higher level of civilisation.[49]

During the drafting of the UDHR, the UK was still concerned to ensure that no proclamation of rights interfered with its capacity to wield such despotism throughout its Empire. Hayek, in contrast, set himself against Mill's belief that, until people were capable of being guided by conviction or persuasion, 'there is nothing for them but implicit obedience to an Akbar or Charlemagne, if they are so fortunate to find one'.[50] In Hayek's view, the assumption that people must be morally autonomous before they can be free reversed the order of priority between morality and freedom; only in a free society could people act on their own moral convictions, he argued.[51] But it was not the civilising mission of Mill, or of the Fabians, per se that offended Hayek and his fellow neoliberals. As we have seen, they had their own project of spreading civilisation across the globe. What they objected to most in social democratic colonialism was not the colonialism but the social democracy. Mill was responsible for the idea of social justice, Hayek argued, and and his influence had consequently 'done a great deal of

48 Shaw, *Fabianism and the Empire*, p. 16.

49 Mill, 'Considerations on Representative Government', p. 567.

50 Friedrich Hayek, 'The Moral Element in Free Enterprise', *The Freeman*, July 1962, p. 46.

51 Friedrich Hayek et al., *Nobel Prize-Winning Economist Oral History Transcript*, (Los Angeles: Oral History Program, University of California, Los Angeles, 1983), p. 282, at archive.org.

harm'.[52] In Mises's estimation, Mill was 'the great advocate of socialism' in comparison with whom 'all other socialist writers – even Marx, Engels, and Lassalle – are scarcely of any importance'.[53] The interventionism and socialism of Mill's disciples on the British left was evidence of the perniciousness of these developments. 'Fabian and Keynesian "unorthodoxy"', Mises warned hyperbolically, 'resulted in a confused acceptance of the tenets of Nazism'.[54] Against this Fabian colonial vision, the neoliberals developed their own critique of colonialism. At mid-century, they still hoped that independence from colonial rule could mark the return to a liberal world order.

Imperialism and the Sweetness of Commerce

In 1927 Ludwig von Mises published a scathing attack on European colonialism, which he described as antithetical to all the principles of liberalism. Mises traced modern imperialism to the 1870s, when the industrial countries had abandoned free trade in order to compete for colonial markets in Africa and Asia. More than twenty years later, the Belgian delegate to the United Nations was still defending his country's record in this period by arguing that Belgium had not forcibly conquered the Congo, but freed it from the 'scourge of the slave trade . . . at very considerable sacrifice to itself'.[55] Mises flatly rejected such arguments. The basic idea of colonial policy in this period, he argued, was to take advantage of the superior weaponry of the 'white race' to subjugate, rob and enslave weaker peoples. But, even as he criticised colonial imperialism, Mises argued that the British Empire was different; she pursued 'grand commercial objectives', he argued, and her free-trade policies benefited her colonial subjects and the whole world.[56]

---

52   Friedrich Hayek et al., *Nobel Prize-Winning Economist Oral History Transcript*, p. 201.

53   Mises, 'Appendix', *Liberalism*, p. 154.

54   Ludwig von Mises, *Omnipotent Government: The Rise of the Total State and Total War* (Auburn: Ludwig von Mises Institute, 2010), p. 228.

55   Commission on Human Rights, 'Summary Record of the 295th Meeting of the Third Committee of the United Nations General Assembly', 27 October 1950), p. 161 at hr-travaux.law.virginia.edu/document/iccpr/ac3sr295/nid-1845.

56   Ludwig von Mises, *Liberalism: The Classical Tradition*, ed. Bettina Bien Greaves, transl. Ralph Raico (Indianapolis: Liberty Fund, 2005), pp. 92–3.

Writing with a nervous eye on rising anticolonial movements from India to the Philippines, Mises warned that, if independence damaged the integration of the colonies in global circuits of trade, it would be 'an economic catastrophe of hitherto unprecedented proportion'.[57] Despite his liberal scruples about coercive rule, he believed that political independence was of minor significance compared to the future of an international market civilisation. 'European officials, troops, and police must remain in these areas', he wrote,

> as far as their presence is necessary in order to maintain the legal and political conditions required to insure the participation of the colonial territories in international trade. It must be possible to carry on commercial, industrial, and agricultural operations in the colonies, to exploit mines, and to bring the products of the country, by rail and river, to the coast and thence to Europe and America. That all this should continue to be possible is in the interest of everyone, not only of the inhabitants of Europe, America, and Australia, but also of the natives of Asia and Africa themselves.[58]

Writing during World War II, Mises predicted that the establishment of a United Nations would lead to autonomy for the people of Africa and Asia, but insisted that 'there are today no such things as internal affairs of a country which do not concern the rest of mankind'.[59] If anti-imperialism in the colonies developed into anti-capitalism, Mises and his fellow neoliberals believed, it would be a catastrophe for all of humanity.

To forestall this possibility, the neoliberals sought to transform popular understandings of imperialism. Their aim was to refute the contention, made popular by J. A. Hobson's influential 1902 text *Imperialism: A Study*, that imperialism was a product of market capitalism. Hobson had attributed imperialism, which he distinguished from the establishment of settler-colonies, to manufacturers, investors and financiers engaged in a 'cut-throat struggle' for new markets and investments.[60] Rejecting the idea that nations exist in a Hobbesian state of nature marked by a

---

57 Ibid., p. 96.
58 Ibid.
59 Mises, *Omnipotent Government*, p. 279.
60 J. A. Hobson, 'Imperialism, A Study – Introductory: Nationalism and Imperialism', at marxists.org.

war of all against all, Hobson argued elsewhere that it was only because 'the power of the people is usurped by bosses' that international relations were marked by conflict and strife.[61] Hobson attributed the imbalance between production and consumption that drove the imperialist competition for new markets to the weak consuming power of the working classes of the imperialist countries. Imperialism, in this picture, was the fruit of unequal economic distribution at home, and would only be overcome by domestic social reform to lift the living standards of the poor.

Hobson's study raised a question that continued to be posed by critics of imperialism across the next century: If imperialism was the result of the 'selfish interests of certain industrial, financial and professional classes', he asked, then why did it garner such broad support?[62] His answer was that imperialists attached themselves to those movements that portrayed themselves as doing good in the world, and represented their own motives in humanitarian terms. In Britain, he noted, there existed a substantial minority with 'a genuine desire to spread Christianity among the heathens, to diminish the cruelty and other sufferings which they believe exist in countries less fortunate than their own, and to do good work about the world in the cause of humanity'.[63] Hobson did not question the sincerity of what he framed as these 'disinterested' aims, but did argue that imperialists latch onto these elevated sentiments in order to create a 'moral justification' for their actions.[64] The combination of strong interested forces with weak disinterested ones, he wrote, 'is the homage which imperialism pays to humanity'.[65]

It was Hobson's association of imperialism with commercial interests that the neoliberals set out to displace. This became more urgent when Vladimir Lenin went beyond Hobson's 'bourgeois social reformism' to define imperialism as the 'highest stage of capitalism'.[66] Writing in 1916, Lenin described imperialism as a phenomenon of monopoly capitalism, with its territorial division of the world between financial and industrial

---

61   J. A. Hobson, 'The Ethics of Internationalism (1906–7)', in Peter Cain, ed., *Writings on Imperialism and Internationalism* (Abingdon: Routledge, 2013), p. 28.
62   Hobson, 'Imperialism, A Study', p. 196.
63   Ibid., p. 197.
64   Ibid., p. 199.
65   Ibid., p. 200.
66   V. I. Lenin, 'Imperialism: The Highest Stage of Capitalism', in Paul Le Blanc, ed., *Revolution, Democracy, Socialism: Selected Writings* (Pluto, 2008), p. 236.

cartels and competing imperial blocs. Lenin indicted monopoly and violence as the reality lurking behind the myth of peaceful, mutually beneficial exchange. As capitalism developed, he argued, the concentration of production and capital led to the transformation of free competition into monopoly. Far from creating peaceful international relations of mutual understanding and benefit, the Bolshevik theoretician contended, war and Great Power rivalry were endemic to capitalism. Lenin reserved his greatest scorn for those who predicted a further stage of 'ultra-imperialism' in which a union of imperialist powers would come together in a single political entity, whereby 'wars shall cease under capitalism'.[67] For Lenin, the dream of perpetual peace, which continued to animate mid-century neoliberalism, would remain a dream for as long as capitalism persisted.

The neoliberals sought to rescue capitalism from the charge that it led to war and violence. Imperialism, they argued, was a product of *politics* and the pursuit of national glory, not of capitalism. As early as 1919, the Austrian School economist Joseph Schumpeter (a participant in Mises's private seminar) rejected Marxist arguments, defining imperialism as an atavistic remnant of absolutist autocracy. Inverting the sweetness-of-commerce thesis, Schumpeter argued that the beneficial effects of capitalism had been inhibited by the persistence of pre-capitalist institutions and attitudes.[68] Capitalism, Schumpeter argued, directs the productive energies once spent on wars of conquest into productive labour, and a 'purely capitalist world therefore can offer no fertile soil to imperialist impulses'.[69] The more capitalist social relations penetrated the economy and the mind, he argued, the more anti-imperialism and pacifism would thrive. The problem was not capitalism itself, but the fact that it had not been strong enough to alter decisively the social structure or mentality of the pre-capitalist age, with its 'disaster-bound addiction to heroic antics'.[70]

Just as figures like the Baron de Montesquieu and James Steuart had argued that commerce was sweet and pacifying – in an age when the slave trade was at its peak, and when 'trade in general was still a

---

67   Ibid., p. 240.

68   Albert O. Hirschman, *The Essential Hirschman*, ed. Jeremy Adelman (Princeton: Princeton University Press, 2013), p. 231.

69   Joseph Schumpeter, *Imperialism and Social Classes*, transl. Heinz Norden (New York: Meridian, 1966), p. 22.

70   Hirschman, *Essential Hirschman*, p. 233.

hazardous, adventurous and often violent business' – the neoliberals of the twentieth century sought to sanitise the capitalism of their time.[71] An unrestricted competitive market, they argued, would replace violent conflicts over territory and resources with peaceful and mutually beneficial commerce. The cause of conflict, they argued, lay elsewhere – in the politicisation of the economy and the confusion between political sovereignty and the ownership of a territory's natural resources.

This argument was made with the greatest force by the British economist Lionel Robbins, in a series of lectures at William Rappard's Geneva Institute of Graduate Studies. In 1939, as another war broke out in Europe, Robbins challenged Lenin's argument that the previous Great War was an imperialist war – 'an annexationist, predatory, war of plunder' for the division of the world and 'the partition and repartition of colonies'.[72] Robbins depicted war as inimical to a 'Great Society' based on private property and the division of labour, and finance capital as a pawn of government, not a prime mover.[73] In geopolitical matters, he argued, bankers are a 'pacific influence'.[74] If war was contrary to the interests of capital, Robbins argued its cause lay elsewhere – in politics, and especially in the existence of independent sovereign states. 'Not capitalism', Robbins argued, 'but the anarchic political organization of the world is the root disease of our civilization.' Imperialism, from this perspective, was a result of the abandonment of free trade, and of liberalism's 'strict distinctions between territory and property'.[75]

Röpke, who was in the audience during Robbin's lecture and enjoyed it 'tremendously', borrowed terms from Roman law to define this vision of liberal peace.[76] A liberal economy, he argued, separates *imperium* from *dominium*, ownership from sovereignty, and therefore prevents conflicts over resources. Referring back to the liberalism of David Hume and Adam Smith, he described the (old) liberal principle as that of the 'thorough separation between the spheres of the government and of

71 Albert O. Hirschman, *The Passions and the Interests: Political Arguments for Capitalism before Its Triumph* (Princeton, NJ: Princeton University Press, 2013), p. 63.

72 V. I. Lenin, 'Preface to the French and German Editions', in *Imperialism, the Highest Stage of Capitalism* (Seaside, OR: Rough Draft Printing, 2014), p. 8.

73 Lionel Robbins, *The Economic Causes of War* (New York: Howard Fertig, 1968), p. 15.

74 Ibid., p. 56.

75 Ibid., p. 74.

76 Susan Howson, *Lionel Robbins* (Cambridge: Cambridge University Press, 2011), p. 328.

economy, between sovereignty and the apparatus which provides material goods, between the Imperium and the Dominium, between the political power and the economic power'.[77] It was a central article of faith for the neoliberal thinkers that a state that rules an area rich in natural resources does not *own* those materials, which are owned by private individuals who may enter into mutually beneficial relations for their sale. Multilateral relations of trade allow industrial nations to obtain raw materials by running their export chains through several countries, neutralising state borders and making the political rule of regions rich in resources unnecessary, Röpke argued.[78] The goal, as Quinn Slobodian puts it in his striking account of neoliberal 'globalism', was a liberal world in which 'nobody would mistake the lines on the map for meaningful marks in the world of dominium'.[79]

For the neoliberals, it was the confusion of sovereignty with ownership that made territorial control the precondition of economic exploitation and led to international conflict. Once states take over the ownership of the materials within their border, Robbins argued, 'the distinction between territorial jurisdiction and property disappears and, *for that very reason*, the fact of geographical inequality becomes a permanent cause of disharmony'.[80] He once again contrasted this situation with the free trade of the old British Empire, in which, for 'cultivated Britons', the 'dominions of the empire' were a 'ceremonial fiction', not a concrete reality; in a free-trade economy based on the principle of the open door, any private investor can buy a country's raw materials on the market on equal terms, he argued, and so has no need to resort to conquest.[81] Mises put the same point more concretely: 'It is of no advantage for an English buyer of Australian wool that Australia is part of the British Empire; he must pay the same price that his Italian or German competitor pays.'[82]

In depicting the British Empire as peaceful, Robbins obscured not only the great naval force that ensured its supremacy over its rivals, but

77 Wilhelm Röpke, *International Order and Economic Integration* (Dordrecht: D. Reidel, 1959).

78 Wilhelm Röpke, *Economics of the Free Society*, transl. Patrick M. Boarman (Chicago: Henry Regnery, 1963), p. 75.

79 Quinn Slobodian, *Globalists: The End of Empire and the Birth of Neoliberalism* (Cambridge, MA: Harvard University Press, 2018), p. 117.

80 Robbins, *Economic Causes of War*, p. 97 (emphasis in original).

81 Ibid., p. 74.

82 Mises, *Omnipotent Government*, p. 100.

also the genocidal violence wielded against indigenous and First Nations peoples in the process of establishing its distinctive white-settler colonies. Also absent from his narrative was what Mike Davis refers to as the 'late Victorian holocausts' by which British exploitation and commitment to Malthusian doctrines and free trade dramatically exacerbated the effects of climate to produce extraordinary famines, notably in India.[83] In praising the peaceful trade of the British Empire, he engaged in an imperial politics of 'deflection' that turned attention away from empire's violence by insisting on its fundamental liberality.[84]

Mises was more explicit about the brutal state violence necessary to uphold 'peaceful' commerce. He justified the wars waged by England to expand her empire by arguing that, had India and China not been forcefully opened to trade, not only 'each Chinese and each Hindu, but also each European and each American would be considerably worse off'.[85] Depicting the extension of the international division of labour as being in the interests of all of humanity, he argued that developed nations could not remain indifferent to those who wished to maintain their independence at a lower level of civilisation. Mises developed a 'just war' argument for postcolonial times: any country that deprived others of access to its natural resources did an injury to all of humanity, he argued, and could legitimately be compelled to trade.[86]

On these grounds, he praised the Opium Wars that had 'opened' China to British trade; 'no barriers ought to be put in the way even of the trade in poisons', he argued, it being up to each individual to restrain himself.[87] The unequal and extraterritorial treaties imposed on China established a precursor for neoliberal forms of empire 'predicated on legally protected freedom of trade without formal territorial control'.[88] In a different context, the challenge for the neoliberals was to conceptualise the institutional and legal conditions that would compel postcolonial states to offer their resources on the market's terms.

---

83   Mike Davis, *Late Victorian Holocausts: El Niño Famines and the Making of the Third World* (London: Verso, 2001).

84   Jeanne Morefield, *Empires Without Imperialism: Anglo-American Decline and the Politics of Deflection* (Oxford: Oxford University Press, 2014).

85   Ludwig von Mises, *Socialism: An Economic and Sociological Analysis*, transl. J. Kahane (New Haven, CT: Yale University Press, 1962), p. 235.

86   Ibid., p. 233.

87   Ibid., p. 234.

88   Teemu Ruskola, *Legal Orientalism: China, the United States, and Modern Law* (Cambridge: Harvard University Press, 2013), p. 204.

Neoliberalism and the 'Taming of the State'

Although the neoliberals harked back to an earlier era of free trade, they also broke with the *laissez-faire* anti-imperialism of nineteenth-century liberalism and its assumption that free trade would naturally lead to harmony. Writing during World War II, Mises argued that, while earlier liberals had correctly recognised that there could be no conflicts between correctly understood interests, they had drastically overestimated the ability of the masses to understand their own interests. In typically aristocratic mode, he argued that liberalism had failed because 'most men are too dull to follow complex chains of reasoning'. If even the Germans had proved incapable of recognising that their interests lay in market competition, not conquest, he despaired, 'how can we expect that the Hindus, the worshippers of the cow, should grasp the theories of Ricardo and of Bentham?'[89] Just as Rappard had pointed out that Smith's economic argument for free trade presupposed a distinctly Scottish *homo economicus*, Mises contended that the success of a liberal market relied on an institutional and legal order that would shape liberal subjects. 'The essential feature of the advanced West was not its technique', he wrote (in terms that resonated with Charles Malik's arguments at Lake Success), 'but its moral atmosphere'; a competitive market would thrive only in a society that encouraged saving, entrepreneurship, and peaceful competition.[90]

The question for the neoliberals was how to secure a legal and institutional structure that would foster the moral environment on which an international division of labour depended. In seeking to answer this, they drew on the experiments in international governance and supervision pursued by Rappard and the Permanent Mandates Commission, and by the earlier British Empire, which Mises depicted as a 'mandatory of European Civilization'.[91] In the wake of World War II, the challenge for the neoliberals was how to provide new standards of civilisation for a world of independent states. They believed that world commerce required binding legal standards to protect traders, and prevent confiscations and discriminatory treatment of non-nationals. Judged by 'Western standards', Robbins wrote, 'the appeals of traders and investors

---

89 Mises, *Omnipotent Government*, p. 283.
90 Ibid., p. 102.
91 Ibid., pp. 97–8.

for protection against arbitrary confiscation, discriminating justice and administrative corruption, have often had much justification.[92] Faced with growing anticolonial movements, the neoliberals sought to ensure that political self-determination did not enable the people of the former colonies to claim their natural resources as their own property or subject them to political control.

While states were necessary to enforce labour discipline and security, and create the conditions for market competition, they had to be shielded from the demands of their own people and prevented from interfering with the market. As Hayek put it, the 'taming of the savage' must be followed by the 'taming of the state'.[93] What was necessary was 'a set of rules which define what a state may do, and an authority capable of enforcing these rules'.[94] It was essential that the post-war period avoid a return to 'unfettered sovereignty' – especially in former colonies.[95] Here, the neoliberals were broadly in agreement, but they were still grappling with the question of what those rules would look like, and how they would be enforced. They were nonetheless clear that the problem of securing a liberal economy was not a technical one, and that the new order would need to amount to more than economic rules. Mises contended that the preconditions of an international economy were 'social, legal, constitutional and political'.[96] Röpke stipulated that a truly international economic order must be based on 'fundamental liberty and equality of rights'.[97] Against economic autarky, the neoliberals sought to develop a moral order for all humanity. 'No human cooperation and no lasting peace are conceivable', Mises concluded, 'if men put loyalty to any particular group above loyalty to humanity, moral law, and the principle of every individual's moral responsibility and autonomy.'[98]

---

92   Robbins, *Economic Causes of War*, p. 87.
93   Hayek in Alan Ebenstein, *Hayek's Journey: The Mind of Friedrich Hayek* (New York: Palgrave Macmillan, 2003), p. 218.
94   Hayek, *Road to Serfdom*, p. 231.
95   Ibid.
96   Mises, *Omnipotent Government*, p. 101.
97   Wilhelm Röpke, *The Moral Foundations of Civil Society* (New Brunswick: Transaction, 2002), p. 229.
98   Mises, *Omnipotent Government*, p. 239.

Making Haste Slowly: The Human Rights Covenants and the Problem of Universalism

As the drafting of the human rights covenants began, less than a year after the adoption of the UDHR, neoliberal fears that postcolonial states would withdraw from the international division of labour seemed exaggerated. The first preoccupation of diplomats from newly independent countries was far more modest: ensuring that the covenants were as universal as the UDHR, which included the unprecedented guarantee that its rights would apply to 'everyone', including inhabitants of territories under 'trust, non-self-governing or under any other limitation of sovereignty'. During the drafting of the UDHR, representatives of the colonial powers had fought hard against the inclusion of this guarantee, even arguing that it was *discriminatory* to mention colonial subjects specifically as subjects of human rights. Back then, delegates representing colonial powers had spoken forcefully against what the UK delegate called the 'apparent discrimination' of 'especially mentioning the trust and non-self-governing territories'.[99] To specify that colonial subjects were subjects of human rights, they argued then, would be to call into question the universality of the category 'everyone'. Now, faced with drafting a legally binding covenant, delegates of these same states proposed colonial exclusion clauses to prevent the automatic application of the covenants in the territories they controlled. Despite having succeeded in removing references to 'civilised nations' from the UDHR, anticolonialists were again forced to challenge metropolitan arguments that colonial subjects lacked the civilisational requirements to be bearers of human rights. Rejoining this challenge, the Soviet delegate Alexei Pavlov argued that his own delegation's draft covenant, which contained no colonial exclusion clauses, 'avoided any suspicion of discrimination' and made it difficult for colonial powers to 'dodge their obligations'.[100]

The French delegate René Cassin led the campaign for the colonial clause, arguing that it might not be the most progressive clause that

---

99 Geoffrey Wilson (United Kingdom), 'Summary Record of the Seventy-Seventh Meeting of the Commission on Human Rights' in Schabas, *Universal Declaration of Human Rights*, vol. 2, p. 1931.

100 Alexei Pavlov (USSR), 'Summary Record of the 129th Meeting of the Commission on Human Rights' (Lake Success: United Nations Economic and Social Council, 27 June 1949), p. 14, at uvallsc.s3.amazonaws.com.

would lead most surely to progress.[101] Cassin, a key drafter of the UDHR, is regularly celebrated as a great universalist, but his universalism coexisted with a deep belief in the civilising role of colonial rule, and the legitimacy of violence in sustaining it.[102] As the French state jailed nationalist electoral candidates in Algeria and Britain waged violent counterinsurgencies in Palestine and Malaya, both delegations argued for colonial clauses to take account for the fact that the territories under their administration were 'constantly progressing along the road to self-government and independence', as the UK delegate put it.[103] Cassin too relied on an idea of measured progress to argue that applying covenants automatically to non-self-governing territories would 'result in a general alignment at the level of the most backward people', as France could not impose progressive measures that her subjects were unable to understand 'on account of their attachment to their own traditions'.[104]

Prefiguring more contemporary arguments, Cassin singled out France's North African territories, arguing that Muslim families could not be held to the same standards as families in metropolitan France. Cassin was committed to the view that the rights of man were a Judeo-Christian inheritance, and he saw the status of women as both 'a marker of a society's capacity to value and enact human rights and, concurrently, a basis for

101   René Cassin (France) in ibid., p. 15.

102   In December 1941, as permanent secretary to the Council of Defense of the Empire, he had travelled from Palestine, Lebanon and Egypt to Indochina and the Cameroons to collect information on support for the French Republic in these territories. In the late 1950s, Cassin, now vice-president of France's Conseil d'État, authorised emergency powers to combat anticolonial resistance in Algeria. Glenda Sluga, 'René Cassin: Les Droits de l'homme and the Universality of Human Rights, 1945–1966', in Stefan-Ludwig Hoffman, ed., *Human Rights in the Twentieth Century* (Cambridge: Cambridge University Press, 2011).

103   Lord MacDonald, Commission on Human Rights, 'Summary Record of the 294th meeting of the Third Committee', 26 October 1950, p. 150, at hr-travaux.law. virginia.edu. On Algeria see Alistair Horne, *A Savage War of Peace: Algeria 1954–1962* (New York Review of Books, 2011). In Malaya, British colonial authorities responded to workers' revolts in the rubber plantations with emergency legislation, detaining more than 30,000 people without trial, destroying the property of communist sympathisers, using chemical defoliants to destroy crops, and rationing food to starve out guerrillas. By then, rubber exports from Malaya provided Britain with its largest income from the Empire, which was used partly to fund the welfare state. Patricia Owens, *Economy of Force: Counterinsurgency and the Historical Rise of the Social* (Cambridge: Cambridge University Press, 2015), p. 182.

104   René Cassin (France), 'Summary Record of the 129th Meeting of the Commission on Human Rights', pp. 14, 16.

denying the universal application of human rights in culturally differenti-
ated communities.[105] Transforming the rights of the family, which might
take several months in metropolitan France, he argued, would take a long
time in the overseas territories, and might 'endanger public order, since
the peoples would not be ready for such changes'.[106] Cassin's argument for
slow and steady progress drew a sarcastic response from the
Czechoslovakian delegate; the 'advice to make haste slowly seemed rather
reactionary in an era of jet-propelled planes', he remarked.[107]

At this point, the anticolonialists were the universalists, and they too
spoke in the name of humanity. Rejecting the relevance of cultural difference, they argued that, while colonial clauses may be acceptable in agree-
ments on 'road traffic, customs duties or narcotic drugs', they were out of
place in a covenant devoted to human rights.[108] Women, including
women representing countries with Muslim majorities, played a particularly significant role in undercutting Cassin's paternalistic arguments.
Iraq's delegate, Bedia Afnan, wondered how 'the degree of evolution of a
people could prevent it from enjoying rights' that Cassin himself had
acknowledged were 'inherent in human nature'. Women had been
granted equal rights in Syria, Iraq and Egypt, where 'the tradition of
Islam was allied with political freedom', she argued, but not in the dependent territories, Algeria, Morocco, Tunisia and Libya.[109] For opponents of
the colonial clause, it was colonialism, not cultural or religious difference, that was the barrier to the universal extension of human rights.

Although opponents of the colonial clause rejected Cassin's advocacy
of 'the instrument of progress, the colonial clause', they too relied on
narratives of progress to depict human rights as civilising technologies.[110] Reversing colonial arguments that civilisation was the

105 Sluga, 'René Cassin', p. 118.
106 René Cassin (France) 'Summary Record of the 294th Meeting of the Third
Committee of the United Nations General Assembly', 26 October 1950, p. 152, at
hr-travaux.law.virginia.edu.
107 Adolf Hoffmeister (Czechoslovakia), 'Summary Record of the 295th Meeting
of the Third Committee of the United Nations General Assembly', 27 October 1950, p.
157, at hr-travaux.law.virginia.edu.
108 Peng Chun Chang (China), ibid., p. 159.
109 Bedia Afnan (Iraq), 'Summary Record of the 296th Meeting of the Third
Committee of the United Nations General Assembly,' (27 October 1950), p. 163, at
hr-travaux.law.virginia.edu.
110 Cassin (France) 'Summary Record of the 294th Meeting of the Third
Committee', p. 152.

prerequisite for human rights, they argued that dependent peoples needed human rights in order to progress from what the Belorussian delegate called their 'backward condition'.[111] The 'fact that certain countries were backward in comparison with others', the Ethiopian delegate agreed, was not grounds for denying their human rights. Rather, 'the reason for their backward condition was that their population had for so long been denied the opportunity to enjoy fundamental freedoms'.[112] The delegate of the Philippines contested Cassin's arguments, contending that the 'right to progress could not be withheld from such peoples just because of their primitive evolution'.[113] The Chilean delegate also argued that the 'low level of civilization' of a people did not justify the denial of human rights; 'civilization was not learnt from books' he stressed. Rather, 'it could only be learnt by personal experience and . . . the enjoyment of human rights was the best teacher of the subject'.[114]

As implied by the Czech delegate's jest about jet-propelled planes, opponents of the colonial clause sought to accelerate the process of modernisation. In arguing that human rights were prerequisites for civilisation, they accepted the directional account of progress that underpinned colonial civilising claims. On the one hand, they challenged metropolitan arguments that the culture of the colonised constituted an insuperable barrier to the exercise of human rights, and contested the metropolitan prerogative to determine when 'native' culture had been sufficiently reformed. On the other hand, they largely accepted the necessity of such reform, and depicted the exercise of human rights as a civilising practice that would promote the modernisation of 'backward' or 'primitive' peoples.[115] Faced with the cultural-relativist arguments of the colonial powers, most opponents of the colonial clause now distanced themselves from the Saudi delegate Jamil Baroody's earlier warnings that the UDHR was based primarily on Western philosophies and cultural patterns. They

---

111   Mr. Koussoff (Byelorussian Soviet Socialist Republic), 'Summary Record of the 296th Meeting of the Third Committee', p. 165.

112   Imru Zelleke, 'Summary Record of the 294th Meeting of the Third Committee', p. 155.

113   Benigno Aquino (Philippines) 'Summary Record of the 129th Meeting of the Commission on Human Rights', p. 16–17.

114   Carlos Valenzuela (Chile) "Summary Record of the 296th Meeting of the Third Committee', p. 168.

115   This was a critique of colonialism that, as Sundhya Pahuja writes in a related context, 'fails to question the ostensibly axiomatic need for the transformation of colonised societies'. Pahuja, *Decolonising International Law*, p. 84.

accepted, at least rhetorically, the superiority of the self-possessed, modern individual of human rights over the 'primitive' native condition. In doing so, they unwittingly prefigured the later repurposing of human rights; in a changed geopolitical context, the civilising mission of human rights would license coercive interventions to remake societies, subjectivities and economies in the interests of global capitalism.

Alexander Rüstow and the 'Shabby Remnants of Colonial Imperialism'

At the 1956 meeting of the Mont Pèlerin Society, devoted to 'The Challenge of Communism and the Response of Liberty', the German ordoliberal Alexander Rüstow praised the 'tremendous, epoch-making importance' of the previous year's Bandung conference.[116] Held in the mountainous West Javan capital, Bandung, in Indonesia, the Asian-African conference was sponsored by the prime ministers of Burma, Ceylon (Sri Lanka), India, Indonesia and Pakistan, all of which had gained their independence during the previous decade. Representatives of twenty-nine countries, representing half the world's population, travelled to Bandung to build political and economic cooperation. The conference's final communiqué condemned the racial discrimination and 'denial of the fundamental rights of man' in the existing colonies, and declared colonialism in all its manifestations 'an evil which should speedily be brought to an end'.[117] At the same time, it stressed the urgency of economic development, including through foreign capital investment. Even more significantly for those committed to the cause of freedom, Rüstow told his neoliberal colleagues, was that 'Western colonial imperialism was lined up for comparison with Soviet imperialism'. To draw the advantages of this, he argued, Europe must liquidate its 'shabby remnants of colonial imperialism'.[118]

The Bandung conference, as Rüstow was quick to note, was marked by conflicts about the nature of imperialism and the significance of human rights. Despite the prevalence of the language of anticolonial

---

116   Alexander Rüstow, 'Crossword Puzzle Moscow', 7th MPS Meeting, Berlin: Hoover Institution Archives, 1956, Box 7, Folder 12. p. 11.
117   Asian-African Conference, 'Final Communiqué', p. 6.
118   Rüstow, 'Crossword Puzzle Moscow', p. 11.

solidarity, Cold War splits were already evident, and delegates from South Vietnam, Pakistan and Ceylon argued that Soviet colonialism was a greater threat than the European variant. The Iraqi delegate also warned of the danger of jumping 'from the pan into the fire', declaring the new imperialism of the Soviet Union to be 'much deadlier than the old one'. The Pakistani delegate argued against being 'misled into opening our doors to a new and more insidious form of imperialism that masquerades in the guise of liberation'.[119] This Cold War framing also played out in debates about human rights. When Charles Malik proposed that the final communiqué endorse the UDHR, he was supported by many of these same anti-communist states and opposed by China, India, Indonesia and North Vietnam.

The debate at Bandung largely played out within the terms of universalism. Obiora Chinedu Okafor has suggested that 'the tension between the universality and relativity of human rights (in almost all its shades) was present at Bandung, however subtly'.[120] It is nonetheless important to note that, while delegates argued over the legitimacy of the UDHR's claim to be a 'common standard of achievement for all peoples and all nations', those who resisted endorsing it largely avoided the language of cultural relativism later made prominent in the so-called 'Asian-Values Debate'. Instead, they followed the Chinese premier, Zhou Enlai, who pointed out that his country (like many others) had been excluded from the drafting of this 'universal' declaration and from the UN (China's UN seat having been given to Taiwan in the wake of China's 1949 Communist Revolution).[121] Ultimately, this argument was resolved through what Malik considered a 'very satisfactory' compromise: the final communiqué 'took note' of the UDHR, while condemning colonialism 'in all its forms', leaving delegates to interpret this as they wished.[122]

---

119   Roland Burke, *Decolonization and the Evolution of International Human Rights* (Philadelphia: University of Pennsylvania Press, 2010), p. 28.

120   Okafor writes 'it is clear that [then] Communist China could hardly have subscribed fully to this very strong universalist approach, at least not at the relevant time, and many other Afro-Asian states (such as Singapore and Malaysia) would later reject this strong universalism, albeit to varying extents'. Obiora Chinedu Okafor, 'The Bandung Ethic and International Human Rights Praxis: Yesterday, Today, and Tomorrow', in *Bandung, Global History, and International Law: Critical Pasts and Pending Futures*, ed. Michael Fakhri, Vasuki Nesiah, and Luis Eslava (New York: Cambridge University Press, 2017), 518–19.

121   Burke, *Decolonization and the Evolution of International Human Rights*, p. 28.

122   Ibid., p. 24.

For Rüstow, all this provided fertile ground for severing anticolonialism from anti-capitalism. Rüstow was distinctive among neoliberal thinkers in the period of decolonisation in his conviction that colonialism was 'a bloody stain on the historic record of humanity, an endless chain of gravest crime against humanitarianism'. Along with his pragmatic concerns about the propaganda value the Soviets were drawing from European colonialism, he grounded his critique in natural law, which he depicted as 'the legal armory of the struggle for freedom and human rights'. Singling out the cruelty of the Spanish *conquistadores*, he denounced the sharp contrast between their 'unrestrained bestiality' and their 'professions of Christianity and the values of their Western civilization'.[123] Challenging the rhetoric of the civilising mission, he denounced the colonial powers for trampling on the 'human dignity of the colonial peoples', and labelled their claims to be carrying out the 'white man's burden' pure hypocrisy.[124]

Rüstow's indictment of colonialism seemed little different to Mises's 1927 criticisms of the hypocrisy, robbery and enslavement perpetuated by colonial powers. But the embrace of sovereignty by postcolonial states had changed the terms of the neoliberal debate. In the great period of decolonisation, the neoliberal majority was preoccupied with the danger that independent postcolonial states would refuse to submit to their existing positions in the international division of labour. They had become increasingly anxious that a 'dangerous liaison' between supporters of planning in developed and developing countries threatened the market system.[125] Emerging agendas of industrialisation, import substitution and economic planning threatened to recapitulate the 'totalitarian' Fabian model, while demands for economic self-determination politicised the economy and eroded the separation of *dominium* and *imperium*.

Rüstow has been depicted as the figure *against* whom the neoliberal perspective on colonialism was developed.[126] It is true that, in a context

---

123 Alexander Rüstow, *Freedom and Domination: A Historical Critique of Civilization*, ed. Dankwart A. Rüstow, transl. Salvador Attanasio (Princeton, NJ: Princeton University Press, 1978), p. 663.

124 Ibid., p. 662.

125 Dieter Plehwe, 'The Origins of the Neoliberal Economic Development Discourse', in Philip Mirowski and Dieter Plehwe, eds, *The Road from Mont Pèlerin: The Making of the Neoliberal Thought Collective* (Cambridge: Harvard University Press, 2009), p. 240.

126 Ibid.

of armed anticolonial struggles and Soviet anti-imperialism, his fellow MPS members reacted angrily to his criticisms of European colonial powers. But Rüstow also contributed more positively to the neoliberal discourse on colonialism. Like Schumpeter, Robbins and Mises before him, he defined colonial imperialism as a phenomenon of politics, not capitalism. Challenging Rosa Luxemburg's argument that imperialism was driven by a capitalist search for new markets, he replied that, for the economist, every market is simply an exchange. Monopoly capitalism, which Rudolf Hilferding and later Lenin had seen as the source of imperialism, was a degeneration of the market economy, he argued, produced by a political motive ('feudal atavism'), not by economic imperatives. Like Schumpeter, Rüstow believed that, within the capitalist economy, 'war and imperialism are nothing but bad business and undesired economic disturbances: they are not the logic but the illogic of capitalism'.[127] For Rüstow, market relations were peaceful and consensual; freed of political distortions, capitalism would be a force of peace.

Although Rüstow, and his closest neoliberal colleague Röpke, are generally – and rightly – understood to have been more concerned than many of their fellow MPS members with the negative impacts of competitive markets on social integration, when it came to imperialism these 'sociological liberals' were great exponents of the 'sweetness of commerce'. Echoing earlier arguments that the virtue of commerce lay in checking the violent passions, Röpke portrayed war as a matter of 'instincts, feelings and passions', while the 'atmosphere created by free market economics, i.e. the principle of economic organisation inherent in "capitalism", serve[d] rather to curb and suppress atavistic, bellicose emotions than to stir them up'.[128] Röpke depicted imperialism and the rule of the passions as the results of 'an age dominated by mass movements and mass instincts'.[129] On this account, the 'optimistic rationalism of earlier days' had underestimated the continuing hold of instincts, passions and feelings, and the obstacles these posed to a liberal market.[130]

While Rüstow attributed colonial imperialism to the 'warlike spirit' of states, his real concern was not with the state per se, which he believed needed to be strong in order to depoliticise civil society.[131]

---

127 Rüstow, *Freedom and Domination*, p. 94.
128 Röpke, *International Order and Economic Integration*, pp. 84–5.
129 Ibid., p. 85.
130 Ibid., pp. 84–5.
131 Rüstow, *Freedom and Domination*, p. 95.

Rather, he traced the 'cult of the great Leviathan' not to Thomas Hobbes, but to Jean-Jacques Rousseau and the tradition of revolutionary popular sovereignty.[132] As anticolonialists struggling for self-determination were drawn to Rousseau's theorisation of the 'will of the people', Rüstow, in common with much neoliberal opposition to popular sovereignty, positioned the Swiss philosopher at the origin of modern totalitarianism.[133] 'Rousseau', he wrote, 'explicitly and emphatically rejects any constitutional limitation on the totalitarian omnipotence of the state, any reservation of human rights of the individual'.[134] Rüstow's attribution of colonialism to a tradition of popular sovereignty was central to the development of the great neoliberal dichotomy between the pacifying market and violent politics, and would later inform attempts to contest 'totalitarian' postcolonial sovereignty in the name of human rights.

Rüstow prefigured this later anti-totalitarian politics of human rights in another way also – by articulating a human rights discourse that broke decisively with the defences of self-determination as a human right that echoed in the speeches at Bandung. In his paper 'Human Rights or Human Duties?', presented at the 1960 MPS meeting, Rüstow laid out a human rights–based duty to bring freedom to the world. In contrast to the common assumption that neoliberal human rights are individualistic, he argued that freedom is *social*, and that human rights therefore presuppose social relations mediated by the competitive market.[135] What Rüstow elsewhere described as the 'manly fight for human rights' generated a robust duty to defend capitalism.[136] Rüstow's position was universalist, and, by extension, interventionist: we live in 'one world', he argued, and therefore have a duty to realise a vision of freedom for all humanity. The endpoint of this vision was a radically federalist global arrangement in which political options were limited by human rights, 'ethics and legal standards'.[137] In Rüstow's neoliberal 'anti-colonialism', we see the emerging outlines of a world whose dominant

---

132   Ibid., p. 523.

133   Peter Hallward, 'Fanon and Political Will', *Cosmos and History: The Journal of Natural and Social Philosophy* 7: 1 (2011), pp. 104–27.

134   Rüstow, *Freedom and Domination*, p. 519.

135   Alexander Rüstow, 'Human Rights or Human Duties?', 11th MPS Meeting, Kassel: Hoover Institution Archives, 1960, 6, Box 15, Folder 6-8.

136   Rüstow, *Freedom and Domination*, 504.

137   Rüstow, 'Human Rights or Human Duties?', p. 10.

human rights ideology entails a duty to enmesh all of humanity in the capitalist division of labour.

Self-Determination and the Sad History of Private Investment

In a 1952 lecture at the San Francisco Public Library, Mises singled out the promise of the first prime minister of independent India, Jawaharlal Nehru, that private businesses would not be expropriated in the ten years following independence. 'You can't expect people to invest if you tell them you will expropriate them at some time in the future', Mises retorted.[138] Describing Nehru's Fabian-inspired socialism as a step backwards even from late British rule, Mises broke starkly with what Gunnar Myrdal was then praising as India's 'heroic attempt' at grand-scale planning. For Myrdal, this attempt was the only alternative to 'continued acquiescence in economic and cultural stagnation or regression'.[139] For Mises, in contrast, the refusal of peaceful commerce brought back the threat of war. If resource-rich 'backward countries' refuse access to foreign corporations on the market's terms, he asked rhetorically, 'can anyone expect that the people of the civilized countries will forever tolerate this state of affairs?'[140] Mises warned ominously that the world was returning to a state in which it was not possible to access raw materials without conquest. World peace depends on unrestricted foreign investment, he argued, 'not on the boy scouts of the United Nations'.[141]

In the UN, things were looking increasingly gloomy from a neoliberal perspective. As more states gained their independence, the campaign against the colonial exclusion clause soon morphed into a struggle for a right to self-determination, including economic self-determination. With decision-making power in the Bretton-Woods international financial institutions weighted towards wealthy states, the UN became the site of what one historian has called 'a strangely secluded and artificial

---

138   Ludwig von Mises, *Marxism Unmasked: From Delusion to Destruction* (Irvington, NY: Foundation for Economic Education, 2006).
139   Cited in Peter Bauer, *From Subsistence to Exchange and Other Essays* (Princeton: Princeton University Press, 2000), pp. 119–20. The description of Myrdal is also Bauer's.
140   Mises, *Marxism Unmasked*.
141   Ibid.

version of the broader struggle for independence.'[142] This created a new relationship between the human rights project and broader debates about development and the rights of people to sovereignty over their natural resources. In its final form, the Covenant on Economic, Social and Cultural Rights embodies this new focus. According to its Article 1.2, 'All peoples may, for their own ends, freely dispose of their natural wealth and resources.'[143] Realising the neoliberals' worst fears, delegates from recently independent states increasingly pursued an agenda of permanent sovereignty over natural resources, which sought to secure the 'inalienable right' of sovereign states to dispose of the resources located in their territories, including by nationalising the foreign companies that had hitherto exploited them. 'Today's "human rights" as formulated by the UN', Röpke wrote in a 1965 letter, 'include the sacred right of a state to expropriate a power plant.'[144]

The shift towards economic self-determination has often been viewed as displacing the individual as the subject of human rights in favour of proclaiming what one historian calls 'state rights' against private capital.[145] But the shift from a focus on civil and political rights to an emphasis on economic self-determination cannot easily be mapped onto a shift from protecting the individual to empowering the state. The liberal approach to human rights, which sequestered the world economy from political challenge, was supported by many of the world's most powerful states, and licensed their interventions on behalf of their corporations. The capacity of human rights to protect individuals across borders was always one-sided: 'No major Euro-American nation would subject itself to Third World institutional scrutiny and critique of its human rights performance.'[146] In a period of US-sponsored military coups and continuing exploitation by former colonial power, postcolonial attempts to secure the societies of newly independent nations from outside intervention were not merely rationales for authoritarianism.

142   Vanessa Ogle, 'State Rights against Private Capital: The "New International Economic Order" and the Struggle over Aid, Trade, and Foreign Investment, 1962–1981', *Humanity: An International Journal of Human Rights, Humanitarianism, and Development* 5: 2 (2014), p. 213.

143   United Nations General Assembly, 'International Covenant on Economic, Social and Cultural Rights' (United Nations Human Rights Office of the High Commissioner, 16 December 1966), at ohchr.org.

144   Cited in Slobodian, *Globalists*, p. 124.

145   Ogle, 'State Rights against Private Capital'.

146   Baxi, *Future of Human Rights*, p. 170.

For more radical anticolonialists of the period, individualistic languages of dignity and liberty were the means by which neocolonialists distracted the people of the colonies from what the Martiniquan psychiatrist and anticolonialist Frantz Fanon called their basic requirements: 'bread, clothing, shelter'.[147] Fanon's 'stretched Marxism' foregrounded race as the basis for settlers' entitlement to 'the material benefits of colonial capitalism'.[148] In proposing to do justice to 'human dignity', Fanon argued that neocolonialism addressed itself to the middle classes of the colonial country, who had internalised its civilisational hierarchies and sought to constitute themselves in the place of the colonial elites. While the West held up both its economic system and its 'humanist superiority' for emulation, Fanon urged the people of the colonies to find their own distinctive paths. Upholding a 'new humanism', he argued that, if the people of former colonies were to create new political and human possibilities for themselves, they had to stop honouring the 'notorious "rights" of the occupant' whose guarantee had been presented as the price for independence.[149]

Nkrumah similarly argued that, although the African continent harboured extraordinary untapped wealth, this was being used to enrich Europe, not the continent's people. Embracing the economic policies, if not the racist paternalism, of the Fabians, Nkrumah argued that, in attempting to 'raise the living standards of its people', Africa could not industrialise in 'the haphazard *laissez-faire* manner of Europe', but must pursue 'comprehensive socialist planning'.[150] Going beyond the Fabians, he also argued for political unity to challenge the liberal myth of the market as a free space of mutually beneficial exchange, and alter terms of sale of raw materials. Noting that 'decolonisation' was a word much used by imperialist spokesmen to describe the transfer of *political* sovereignty, he argued that colonialism still controlled that sovereignty, and former colonies still provided the raw materials for their former rulers' manufactures. 'The change in the economic relationship between the new sovereign states and the erstwhile masters is only one of form', Nkrumah manitained. 'Colonialism has achieved a new guise.'[151]

---

147   Frantz Fanon, *Toward the African Revolution*, transl. Haakon Chevalier (New York: Grove Press, 1967), p. 122.

148   Robert Knox, 'Valuing Race? Stretched Marxism and the Logic of Imperialism', *London Review of International Law* 4: 1 (2016), pp. 81–126.

149   Frantz, *Toward the African Revolution*, pp. 122–6.

150   Nkrumah, *Neo-Colonialism*, p. 11.

151   Ibid., p. 31.

By 1958, when the MPS gathered in Princeton a year after the independence of Ghana, Mises despaired that the recent history of *laissez-faire* capitalism had been 'very sad'.[152] Disparaging governments and the UN for their negative view of private investment, he complained that, while such investment had succeeded economically everywhere, politically it had succeeded 'only in a few civilized countries of Europe and America', while elsewhere it ended in expropriation, confiscation and 'anti-capitalistic' policies that amounted to simple sabotage.[153] Although less than 5 per cent of foreign-owned firms were nationalised at the high-point of decolonisation, some high-profile cases sent shock-waves through business circles, especially in the mineral and petroleum industries, and galvanised opposition to self-determination.[154] Mises singled out the Egyptian nationalisation of the Suez Canal two years earlier, in 1956, as the turning point. The Canal held a symbolic place in the neoliberal imagination; its opening in 1869 had fostered the expansion of international trade by allowing ships to pass between Europe and Asia without circumnavigating Africa. At the Walter Lippmann Colloquium, Mises had cited the Canal as an example of those 'works of vital importance' that could only have been achieved by the largest of corporations.[155]

Mises did not mention the strict police control exercised by the British over the migrant workers who built the canal, but they played a starring role in Egyptian President Gamal Abdel Nasser's speech announcing the nationalisation.[156] 'Egypt undertook to supply labour to dig the Canal by *corvée* of which 120,000 died without getting paid', he told his audience, as Egyptian troops reclaimed the canal.[157] The Canal Company, the Arab nationalist leader argued, had been restored to its

---

152 Ludwig von Mises '"Undeveloped Countries": Discussion on Two Papers Submitted by Peter Bauer to the 9th Meeting of the Mont Pèlerin Society, Princeton, September 1958', in Albert Hunold ed. Mont Pèlerin Quarterly, 1:1 (April 1959), p. 20.

153 Ibid.

154 This figure applies to the period from 1960 to 1976. Stephen J. Kobrin, 'Expropriation as an Attempt to Control Foreign Firms in LDCs: Trends from 1960 to 1979', *International Studies Quarterly* 28: 3 (1984), p. 329. The most high-profile case was Mohammed Mossadegh's 1951 nationalisation of the Anglo-Iranian Oil Company, which prompted a US-backed coup.

155 Jurgen Reinhoudt and Serge Audier, eds, *The Walter Lippmann Colloquium: The Birth of Neo-Liberalism* (London: Palgrave Macmillan, 2018), p. 125.

156 Timothy Mitchell, *Colonising Egypt* (Berkeley: University of California Press, 1991), p. 96.

157 Gamal Abdel Nasser, 'Speech Announcing the Nationalization of the Suez Canal Company', 26 July 1956 at cvce.eu.

rightful owners, the Egyptian people, who were fighting for 'political and economic independence' against the domination of 'imperialists and exploiters'.[158] To Mises, this blurring between sovereignty and ownership, as much as the leverage that control of the Suez Canal gave to those who wished to disrupt world trade, was a threat to the international division of labour, and therefore to civilisation. Decolonisation was undermining the human right to trade. It was on the terrain of human rights that the neoliberals would launch their counter-attack.[159]

'There is Nothing as Timid as a Million Dollars': Securing the Rights of Capital

In 1957 the Mont Pèlerin Society returned to the Swiss Alps to convene in the mountain village of Saint Moritz. Looking out from his window, one participant from the United States was struck by the green trees trimmed in white after a night of heavy snow. Even more pleasing to Leonard E. Read of the Foundation of Economic Education was the presence of the man who had presided over the first meeting in Mont Pèlerin, 'the patriarch of our Society, the eighty-some-year-old and internationally famous William Rappard'.[160] The 1957 meeting was the occasion of the first MPS discussion of a topic dear to the heart of the Swiss diplomat, who had devoted so much of his life to the liberal civilising mission: 'Liberalism and Colonialism'. While Rappard was appointed to chair the session, his active life was nearing its end, and he would not participate in the development of the neoliberal response to anticolonialism. When Read greeted him effusively, Rappard told him, 'this will be the last time you will see me. I am old.'[161] That night, he had a stroke. He would die the following April. At the same time, his neoliberal colleagues would increasingly despair at the failure of the liberal teleology underpinning Rappard's life's work. As newly independent nations demanded

---

158   Ibid.

159   For an excellent account of the Suez Crisis as the birthplace of an 'Americanised global economy, premised upon an openness to investment, free trade, non-discrimination and the international management of resources in the decolonised world', see Anne Orford, *International Authority and the Responsibility to Protect* (Cambridge: Cambridge University Press, 2011).

160   Leonard E. Read, 'Leonard E. Read Journal – August 1957' (Foundation for Economic Education, 1957), at history.fee.org.

161   Ibid.

sovereignty over their natural resources, the neoliberals meeting in the mountains turned their minds to saving the international division of labour from a resurgence of 'tribal' morals.

The rise of anticolonialism made neoliberals increasingly defensive of European colonialism and its supposed civilising role. Their problem, as the Dutch philosopher-economist Justus Meyer put it, reprising late colonial stereotypes, was that the colonised 'wards' had proved far less rational and amenable to civilisation than the liberal colonialists assumed; they clung to their own customs, they lacked the IQs to embrace education, and (like those Algerians who William Rappard had viewed as a challenge to Adam Smith's economics), they were generally 'not inclined to work more than necessary' to provide their accustomed standard of living. Faced with such intransigence, Meyer claimed that 'liberalistic colonialism is at its wits' ends'.[162] In an unintegrated world, it would be all very well to leave those who refused Western pedagogy alone. But, given the commercial relations developed over centuries, granting self-determination to colonial subjects 'would dry up the sources of tropical raw materials, oil and many things the rapidly progressing western world cannot do without'.[163] Against the normative principles of liberal humanitarianism, which he believed had failed in practice, Meyer held up as an 'elementary law' of self-preservation' that the 'historically grown relations between colonial powers and their colonies not be broken off abruptly without something sensible to take the place of historical patterns interwoven with the economic system of the Western world'.[164] The question for the neoliberals was what 'sensible' arrangement would confine former colonies to their allotted roles in the global division of labour as providers of raw materials and cheap labour, while shaping market subjects.

Rüstow's fellow panellists at the 1957 'Liberalism and Colonialism' session reacted violently to his critique of European colonialism. Yet they too sought to develop a language to pathologise postcolonial sovereignty and transform the postcolonial state into a barrier against the

---

162   Justus Meyer, 'The Concept of Colonialism', Stanford: Hoover Institution Archives, 1957, 15, Box 11, Folder 2. The neoliberal response to anticolonialism followed the pattern that Karuna Mantena has identified in the later period of the British Empire, when liberal imperialist disillusionment in the face of resistance to the 'civilising' mission was followed by recourse to culturalist rationalisations for failure which served as 'alibis of empire'. Mantena, *Alibis of Empire*.

163   Ibid.

164   Ibid.

popular aspirations of its people – not a vehicle for their realisation. For the neoliberals, sovereignty had never been the *telos* of the civilising mission. Quite the opposite, their challenge was always to restrain popular sovereignty, to prevent 'the masses' from capturing the state and refusing the discipline imposed by the competitive market order. Freed from its relation to popular sovereignty and economic self-determination, the language of human rights offered them a means to legitimise transformative interventions and subject postcolonial states to universal standards aimed at protecting the international market.

In an extraordinary reversal, neoliberals in the period of decolonisation portrayed colonialism as a means of pluralistic international cooperation, humanity and inclusion, and anticolonialism as xenophobic, exclusionary, discriminatory and racist. Karl Brandt, the Stanford economist who had posed the problem of how to ensure that 'the white people' could return as friends, told the conference that, if independence led to 'rule by narrow-minded racial nationalism and hostility towards international economic cooperation', this would lower 'levels of living'.[165] The core problem, he argued, was to ensure that economic and social progress were not brought at the expense of 'loss of individual liberty, society's respect for human dignity, government by law, and due process and justice'. His fellow panellist Edmond Giscard d'Estaing – the father of France's President Valéry Giscard d'Estaing and head of a company that oversaw economic transactions with the French colonies – argued that the slogan of 'liberation from colonialism' was licensing an 'explosion of xenophobia' and 'primitive hatred' and disrupting the work of global integration.[166] If independence meant that the world would fall apart into 'sealed off compartments', Brandt argued, this would be a profound blow to freedom.[167]

The freedom that mattered most to the neoliberals was the freedom to trade across borders on non-discriminatory terms, which they represented as the necessary foundation of all freedoms and rights. 'The institution of a free market, of competition among enterprises, freedom of

---

165 Karl Brandt, 'Liberal Alternatives in Western Policies Toward Colonial Areas', 8th MPS Meeting, St Moritz: Hoover Institution Archives, 1957, Box 11, Folder 3, pp. 1–13.

166 Edmond Giscard d'Estaing, 'Libéralisme et Colonialisme', 8th MPS Meeting, St Moritz: Hoover Institution Archives, 1957, Box 12, Folder 18, p. 1. D'Estaing was President of the Société Financière Française et Coloniale.

167 Brandt, 'Liberal Alternatives', pp. 2, 9.

entry and freedom of exit to professions and any sort of business are the safeguards and anchors of freedom and justice for the people in under-developed areas', Brandt made clear.[168] While he looked forward to the 'gradual abolition of the privileged status of the white people', this move towards equality was predicated on newly independent states accepting market discipline. Self-government was conditional on newly inde-pendent countries submitting to the demands of the market and respect-ing the rights of foreign traders. The neoliberals envisioned what B. S. Chimni calls a 'borderless global space' in which the role of Third World nation-states is to 'facilitate the expansion of global capitalism through promoting free trade, lifting constraints on movements of capital, and ensuring infrastructure development'.[169] Creating such a space could not be left to *laissez-faire*; it required enforceable international standards – and the right to intervene when they were flouted.

This project inspired the neoliberals in their contributions to the founding of the World Trade Organization, with its binding rules and enforcement of non-discriminatory trade.[170] Yet binding trade rules were not sufficient for supporting a competitive world market. In a book on the philosophy of history published in 1957 – the year of the MPS discussion of colonialism – Mises attributed mass penury in Asia to the absence of 'a legal and constitutional system which would have provided the opportu-nity for large-scale capital accumulation'.[171] Mises identified the funda-mental problem as that of an egalitarian moral economy, which had licensed the confiscation of private property. China lacked the morals of the market he suggested, and without a transformation of mentality and morality, aid and industrialisation would be followed only by expropria-tion and the consolidation of centralised state structures. Here, he and his frequent antagonist Rüstow agreed: while Rüstow worried that the social dislocation that would follow the imposition of Western civilisation on 'natives' who were still living in the 'Stone Age' would provide an opening for communism, he nonetheless argued that as 'long as the present structure of these countries continues, we might as well convert any

---

168   Ibid., p. 12.

169   B. S. Chimni, 'Anti-Imperialism', in Eslava, Fakhri and Nesiah, eds, *Bandung, Global History, and International Law*, p. 35.

170   On the role of neoliberals, notably Gottfried Haberler in that process see Slobodian, *Globalists*.

171   Ludwig von Mises, *Theory and History: An Interpretation of Social and Economic Evolution* (Auburn: Ludwig von Mises Institute, 2007), p. 216.

investment of ours into roubles'.[172] For the neoliberals, a conducive climate for foreign investment required a profound social transformation, or conversion, and the adoption of the morals of the market. Exporting capital meant exporting capitalist social relations and a morality that fostered capital accumulation. Liberal philosophy 'could triumph', Mises argued, 'only within an environment in which the ideal of income equality was very weak'.[173] What was needed in the East was a cultural shift, and a set of institutions to foster wealth accumulation. 'What the East Indies, China, Japan, and the Mohammedan countries lacked', Mises wrote, 'were institutions for safeguarding the individual's rights'.[174]

This focus on the legal and institutional preconditions of development would become increasingly central to neoliberal development discourse in the subsequent decades. By 1990, the previously human rights–averse World Bank began to argue that, through its lending programme, it had always been promoting human rights. Its post-Washington-consensus focus consolidated this shift; as the bank moved from 'market fundamentalism to governance fundamentalism', it focused on public administration, the rule of law, accountability and transparency, and identified a lack of human rights as evidence of bad governance.[175] Rather than breaking with neoliberalism, the World Bank increasingly concentrated on legal and governance structures that 'put international property rights centrestage and included "human" rights as an integral component of [an] international risk-governance mechanism' that increasingly incorporated '"civil society" actors' into economic governance.[176] This shift coincided with the heyday of an interventionist politics of human rights that justified the use of massive military force as a means to prevent grave human rights violations. However 'disinterested' many supporters of such interventions may have been, their activism helped give a humanitarian stamp to what Hobson described as the 'strong interests' of imperialism.

Both trends were prefigured by the neoliberals of Mont Pèlerin in the period of decolonisation. Wary that demands for self-determination

172   Rüstow, 'Crossword Puzzle Moscow', p. 13.
173   Ludwig von Mises, *Human Action: A Treatise on Economics* (San Francisco: Fox & Wilkes, 1996), p. 842.
174   Ibid., p. 500.
175   Radha D'Souza, *What's Wrong with Rights? Social Movements, Law and Liberal Imaginations* (London: Pluto, 2018), pp. 160–9.
176   Ibid., p. 164.

would lead to the breakdown of the international division of labour, they focused their attention on producing a legal and institutional framework to constrain postcolonial states. They saw the potential that the language of human rights could be used to justify supervision of postcolonial states to ensure they protected the rights of traders. They upheld a universal humanity, with an interest in the greatest possible division of labour, and sang the praises of an open world economy (even as they were ambivalent about, and often downright antagonistic towards, mass migration). Depicting the market as a source of sweetness, gentleness and universal friendship, and politics as violent and conflictual, they sought to depoliticise social relations. Politicisation, they increasingly argued, was the key barrier to the subjective qualities – notably entrepreneurialism – that were necessary for economic advancement.

At the 1958 MPS meeting, the Mexican law professor Gustavo Velasco argued that such politicisation in his country was the consequence of underdevelopment. The harmful effects of inflation in Mexico had been primarily psychological, he argued. 'Mexico has had and still has inflation because it has lived beyond its means.'[177] Velasco attributed the underlying causes of inflation to three factors: the welfare state, the desire for economic betterment, and the desire for economic development. Inflation, he argued, resulted from access to subsidised goods and services (provided by a government that acted as a 'third-dimensional Santa Claus'), upward pressure on wages as a result of trade union action, and over-investment by the government.[178] Velasco was pessimistic about the possibility of reversing these trends. High popular expectations and the politicisation of economic life made it impossible to keep inflation under control. By 1958, Velasco had not countenanced what would be necessary to lower these expectations and depoliticise the economy. It would take another decade and a half before the neoliberals found their solution in Chile.

---

177   The Mont Pèlerin Society, 'The Mont Pèlerin Quarterly', *Journal of the Mont Pèlerin Society* I: 1 (April 1959), p. 12.

178   Ibid., p. 13.

4

Human Rights in Pinochet's Chile: The Dethronement of Politics

For you to be a Communist or a Socialist is to be totalitarian. For me, not so. I believe man is free when he has an economic position that guarantees him work, food, housing, health, rest and recreation. I am the founder of the Socialist Party and I must tell you that I am not totalitarian, and I think Socialism frees man.

Salvador Allende

Don't confuse totalitarianism with authoritarianism. I don't know of any totalitarian governments in Latin America. The only one was Chile under Allende. Chile is now a great success. The world shall come to regard the recovery of Chile as one of the great economic miracles of our time.

Friedrich Hayek

In late 1977 – as the Chilean military junta extended the state of siege in place since its 1973 coup and formally dissolved all political parties – Friedrich Hayek wrote a letter to a German newspaper, the *Frankfurter Allgemeine Zeitung*, to protest what he depicted as unfair international criticism of the regime of General Augusto Pinochet. When his article was rejected, he wrote to the editor expressing disappointment that the newspaper lacked the 'civil courage' to resist popular anti-Pinochet sentiment.[1] Hayek singled out the human rights organisation Amnesty

1 Hayek, cited in Andrew Farrant, Edward McPhail and Sebastian Berger, 'Preventing the "Abuses" of Democracy: Hayek, the "Military Usurper" and Transitional Dictatorship in Chile?', *American Journal of Economics and Sociology* 71: 3 (2012), p. 517.

International – which had been awarded the Nobel Peace Prize earlier that year – for turning 'slander [into] a weapon of international politics'.[2] After accepting an invitation to lecture in Chile, he complained, he was inundated with phone calls, letters and anti-Pinochet material by 'well-intentioned people I did not know but also from organizations like "Amnesty International"', who asked him to cancel his visit.[3] Amnesty's materials on Chile from this period detail the Junta's widespread use of arbitrary imprisonment, execution, systematic torture and the 'disappearance' of political detainees, 1,500 of whom then remained unaccounted for. In a style Amnesty helped pioneer, its 1977 report on Chilean political prisoners combined legal analysis with moving accounts of missing individuals. To take only one example, it recounted that José Baeza Cruces, a trader from Santiago, had been arrested in his shop in July 1974 by personnel of the Air Force Intelligence Service. Cruces was taken to a basement in the Ministry of Defence and later to the Air Force Academy of War, where, according to witnesses, he was tortured every day for at least six months. After that the witnesses were transferred and contact with Cruces was lost.[4]

This combination of vivid description of individual cases with legal analysis would ultimately become central to a new wave of international NGO-led human rights activism that looked dramatically different to postcolonial demands for self-determination and economic sovereignty. This new human rights activism had little impact on Hayek, who travelled to Chile and declared the dictatorial regime 'an example at the global level'.[5] Hayek's fellow Mont Pèlerin Society member, the Chicago School economist Milton Friedman, later echoed this assessment, describing Chile as an economic and political 'miracle'.[6] Neither Hayek nor Friedman were detached observers of this 'miracle'. Both men gave advice to Pinochet, and both had disciples in his authoritarian regime

---

2 Ibid.

3 Farrant, McPhail, and Berger, 'Preventing the "Abuses" of Democracy', pp. 517–18. Hayek's own doctoral student, Ralph Raico, was among those who sent him Amnesty reports and called on him to reconsider his visit. Bruce Caldwell and Leonidas Montes, 'Friedrich Hayek and His Visits to Chile', *Review of Austrian Economics* 28: 3 (2015).

4 Amnesty International, *Disappeared Prisoners in Chile* (London: Amnesty International Publications, 1977), pp. 1, 3, 22–3.

5 Farrant, McPhail, and Berger, 'Preventing the "Abuses" of Democracy', p. 520.

6 Milton Friedman, 'Passing down the Chilean Recipe', *Foreign Affairs* 73: 1 (1994), p. 177.

– Friedman among the Chicago-trained *técnicos* (or 'Chicago Boys'), who formulated the regime's economic 'shock' programme, and Hayek among the conservative Catholic *gremialistas*, who produced an institutional order to protect the economy from political challenge. These two civilian elite factions were to define the economic and political orientation of Pinochet's regime.

Given Hayek's support for Pinochet's regime and his criticisms of Amnesty International, it seems surprising that some have criticised the new politics of human rights for helping to sanitise neoliberalism. Focusing on the role of Friedman and the 'Chicago Boys' in guiding the junta's economic reforms, Naomi Klein, for instance, criticises Amnesty International for obscuring the relationship between neoliberal 'shock therapy' and political violence.[7] Noting that the Southern Cone was a 'laboratory' for both neoliberalism and grassroots human rights activism, she argues that, in its commitment to impartiality, Amnesty occluded the reasons for the torture and killing, and thereby 'helped the Chicago School ideology to escape from its first bloody laboratory virtually unscathed'.[8] Samuel Moyn, on the other hand, contests the claim that the human rights movement was complicit in the rise of neoliberalism, deeming Klein's account 'exaggerated and implausible'. The success of the human rights movement, he argues, is at least partly due to 'the left's own failure either to escape savage repression' or to bring about coalitions to denounce dictatorship with as much success.[9]

Viewed from another angle, Moyn's comment raises the question of why, in the period of neoliberal ascendancy, international human rights organisations flourished, largely escaping the repression that was pursued so furiously against leftists, trade unionists, rural organisers and indigenous people in countries such as Chile. As Pinochet's regime engaged in a systematic campaign to eradicate the Chilean left, it allowed overseas human rights organisations such as Amnesty International, the International Commission of Jurists, and Americas Watch (a precursor to Human Rights Watch) to enter the country, and gave them extensive

---

7   Naomi Klein, *The Shock Doctrine: The Rise of Disaster Capitalism* (New York: Picador, 2008), p. 118.

8   Ibid.

9   Samuel Moyn, 'A Powerless Companion: Human Rights in the Age of Neoliberalism', *Law and Contemporary Problems* 77 (2015), p. 158.

freedom of movement.[10] While the CIA-trained National Intelligence Directorate had instructions to carry out the 'total extermination of Marxism', the junta, anxious to present Chile as a modern, Western, Catholic and 'civilised' nation, did not disavow the language of human rights, even at the height of the repression.[11] Moreover, despite Hayek's displeasure at Amnesty's anti-Pinochet activism, the neoliberals did not eschew the language of human rights; on the contrary, they argued that their own proposals were necessary in order to secure freedom, human dignity and human rights.

As the regime unleashed a brutal programme of torture, assassination and extra-judicial killing aimed primarily at Hayek's own antagonists – leftists, social democrats and trade unionists – he remarked that he had 'not been able to find a single person even in much maligned Chile who did not agree that personal freedom was greater under Pinochet than it had been under Allende.'[12] Rather than simply dismissing this claim, we should look more closely at the neoliberal idea of freedom, and the place of rights and law within it. This means departing from the standard story, according to which the neoliberals in Chile focused on their area of technical economic expertise while turning a blind eye to the repression necessary to implement their economic agenda. On the contrary, not even the most technical of the Chicago economists justified their work in Chile simply on economic grounds. Rather, they argued that the junta had saved Chile from a totalitarian regime, reversing a history of planning and state intervention and making possible individual freedom and human rights. Despite the fact that neoliberals had devoted sustained attention to rights, law and human dignity since the 1940s, little attention has been paid to the distinctively political vision of neoliberalism in Chile – or the place within it of human rights.

The problem was not that the neoliberals obscured the connection between a competitive liberal economy and human rights, as critics

---

10   When he once barred a UN human rights committee from the country, Pinochet justified his stance based on supposed bias in human rights investigations, not by criticising human rights language, asking: 'How many commissions did they send to Cuba, the USSR, Vietnam?' Cited in Pamela Constable and Arturo Valenzuela, *A Nation of Enemies: Chile under Pinochet* (New York: W. W. Norton, 1993), p. 64.

11   Ibid., p. 91; Jan Eckel, 'Under a Magnifying Glass', in Stefan-Ludwig Hoffman, ed., *Human Rights in History* (Cambridge: Cambridge University Press, 2010), p. 331.

12   Farrant, McPhail, and Berger, 'Preventing the "Abuses" of Democracy', p. 513.

such as Klein contend. Rather, they were explicit that human rights and civil freedoms presupposed a functioning competitive market. If, as Mises had put it much earlier, 'as soon as the economic freedom which the market economy grants to its members is removed, all political liberties and bills of rights become humbug', then defending human rights meant defending economic freedom.[13] In line with the argument I have traced over the course of this book, the neoliberals in Chile mobilised a stark dichotomy between politics as violent, coercive and conflictual, and market relations as peaceful, voluntary and mutually beneficial. It was in Chile that a neoliberal human rights discourse was consolidated. This neoliberal version of human rights justified constitutional restraints and law as necessary to preserve the individual freedom that only a competitive market could secure. If human rights were a product of a functioning market, as the neoliberals consistently argued, they were also necessary to protect the market from egalitarian political movements. Rather than protecting individuals from state repression, neoliberal human rights operated primarily to preserve the market order by depoliticising society and framing the margin of freedom compatible with submission to the market as the only possible freedom.

In focusing their attention on state violence and unlawful political mobilisations while upholding civil (or market) society as a realm of freedom and voluntary cooperation, human rights NGOs lent credence to the great neoliberal dichotomy between coercive politics and free and peaceful markets. Allende's government had challenged the myth of the market as a realm of voluntary, non-coercive and mutually beneficial relations. The junta (with the aid of the Chicago Boys and the *gremialistas*) sought to undo this politicisation, decimate collective political identities, and inculcate norms of submission, personal responsibility and self-reliance. The human rights movement, with its politely worded reports about torture and disappearance, offered little threat to the junta's ideal of a liberalised market society free from class struggle and political conflict. In challenging the junta's torturous means, human rights NGOs arguably helped to restrain the worst of its violence, but they did so at the cost of abandoning both the political conflict over ends and the economy as a site of political struggle.

---

13   Ludwig von Mises, *Human Action: A Treatise on Economics* (San Francisco: Fox & Wilkes, 1996), p. 287.

In framing their human rights agenda as apolitical, and without implications for economic arrangements, NGOs such as Amnesty International sought to avoid the violent political conflicts between rival economic and political visions that marked Allende's rule. But, in accepting the dichotomy between violent politics and pacific civil society, they further discredited political challenges to the inequalities and impersonal domination of market society. The human rights politics consolidated in Chile followed only one of the paths laid down decades earlier by the drafters of the Universal Declaration of Human Rights (UDHR), who also sought to render visible the heavy costs of economic deprivation and the compulsion exerted by hunger and want. In abandoning the political conflict over ends, human rights NGOs could do little to contest the terms of a 'return to democracy' that combined neoliberal policies with the language of individual freedom, human dignity and the subjection of politics to law.

Allende's Regime, Dependency and the Market

In 1986, Friedman and his Chicago School colleague Arnold Harberger participated in a symposium on the relations between economic, political and civic freedom organised by the Fraser Institute, a pro-market Canadian think tank. The symposium's premise was that economic freedom and civil liberties could flourish in conditions in which political freedom was absent, as majority rule had 'no particular virtues, especially if the majority decides to abuse the rights of the minorities'.[14] For Harberger, who had spent decades overseeing the training of economics students from Latin America, this relationship between political and economic freedom was a 'dilemma'. Latin Americans, he told the symposium, were beset by a 'predilection to romanticism', a 'tremendous, incredible vulnerability to demagogy' and a collective tendency towards 'self-pity'. Military governments, he contended, were 'best at leading them to think their way out of that, but it is a terrible dilemma for us as freedom-loving individuals'.[15] If romanticism was a barrier to economic

---

14   Michael A. Walker, 'Preface', in Michael A. Walker, ed., *Freedom, Democracy and Economic Welfare: Proceedings of an International Symposium* (Vancouver: Fraser Institute, 1988), p. xi.

15   Arnold Harberger, 'Capitalism and Freedom in Latin America: Discussion', in Walker, *Freedom, Democracy and Economic Welfare*, p. 273.

freedom, Harberger wondered, was it legitimate to use political repression to shatter it?

Harberger's 'dilemma' highlights the concern with questions of culture, politics, morality and subjectivity lurking behind the value-free positivist veneer of Chicago economics. Although Chicago economists were less preoccupied than European neoliberals with these questions, they too intuited that their economic proposals presupposed what William Rappard had astutely called a 'Scottish *homo economicus*', who was often absent in other parts of the world. The primary barrier to 'good economics' in Latin America, Harberger believed, was therefore cultural and subjective. 'Asians think self-reliance in any situation in which you put them', he argued. 'Anything that happens to them was done by fate', and they take responsibility for changing their situations. Such a comportment was also central to Hayek's account of the morals of the market. While in the nineteenth century, people still believed that an 'economic crisis, a loss of a job, a loss of a person, was as much an act of God as a flood or something else', the Austrian economist contended, the loss of this fatalistic attitude had made people unwilling to 'accept certain moral traditions' and submit to their market-dispensed fates.[16] For Harberger, this problem was particularly pronounced in Latin America, where people 'are forever explaining that somebody else did it to them; they didn't do it to themselves'.[17]

Harberger was responding to a paper by the Uruguayan economist Ramón Díaz, who argued that 'Latin American democracy has sought its inspiration very much in Rousseau, and very little in Locke' – that is, it has prioritised popular sovereignty over property and individual rights.[18] It was this culture of romanticism and popular political mobilisation that Harberger saw as the source of Chilean socialism. On returning from his regular trips to Santiago, Harberger (the former Chicago student and development economist Andre Gunder Frank recalled) would describe Chile's health and education systems as 'absurd attempts to live beyond its underdeveloped means'.[19] Forcing Chileans

---

16   Friedrich Hayek et al., *Nobel Prize-Winning Economist Oral History Transcript*, (Los Angeles: Oral History Program, University of California, Los Angeles, 1983), p. 161, at archive.org.

17   Harberger, 'Capitalism and Freedom in Latin America', p. 273.

18   Ramón P. Díaz, 'Capitalism and Freedom in Latin America', in Walker, *Freedom, Democracy and Economic Welfare*, p. 253.

19   Gunder Frank, cited in Klein, *Shock Doctrine*, p. 61.

to live within their means and submit fatalistically to the judgment of the market would be the central task of Harberger's 'Chicago Boys'.

Harberger oversaw a US government–sponsored partnership between the Catholic University of Chile and the University of Chicago, which, he reflected, spawned more than a dozen key ministers, Central Bank presidents and budget directors.[20] The Chile Project stretched back to the era of import-substitution industrialization of the 1950s – a time, he reflected, when the watchwords across Latin America were 'interventionism, paternalism, nationalism, and socialism'.[21] The Chicago Boys' opposition to the politicisation of the economy preceded Allende's victory by decades; but his socialist government's economic planning, Keynesian demand-stimulation and wealth redistribution provided their ideal adversary, and brought them to the attention of Chile's business elites. From the Chicago-inspired perspective of these *técnicos*, Allende's proposals amounted to an ignorant violation of the laws of the economy and the destruction of a free society.

Allende's first speech as president, in November 1970, exemplified the 'romanticism' Harberger believed blighted Chile's economy. Allende urged his fellow Chileans to rebuild their country 'according to our dreams' – to rebuild a country in which 'all children begin life equally, with equal medical care, education and nutrition'.[22] His government sought to ameliorate existing inequalities in wealth and power by displacing the market as the key allocator of basic commodities. It significantly expanded spending on health, education and housing, distributed free powdered milk to young children, heavily subsidised public transport, mandated pay rises, introduced price controls, and established popular resorts (*balnearios populares*) devoted to socialised leisure.[23]

More disturbing to neoliberals was the government's move to nation-alise Chile's largest US-owned copper mines. US law required 'adequate, prompt and effective compensation' for expropriated US companies. As

---

20   Arnold Harberger, 'Good Economics Comes to Latin America, 1955–95', *History of Political Economy* 28: supplement (1996), p. 302.

21   Ibid., p. 303.

22   Salvador Allende, 'First Speech to the Chilean Parliament', Marxists Internet Archive, 1970, at marxists.org.

23   Social spending was 50 per cent higher under Allende than his predecessor Eduardo Frei. Marcus Taylor, *From Pinochet to the 'Third Way': Neoliberalism and Social Transformation in Chile* (London: Pluto, 2006), p. 26.

the campaign for Permanent Sovereignty over Natural Resources discussed in Chapter 3 intensified, Allende received a standing ovation in the United Nations General Assembly when he explained that his government would deduct 'excess profits' amounting to US$774 million from the compensation it paid the two biggest US mining companies, leaving them with a *debt* to the Chilean government.[24] What Allende termed Chile's 'reasoned rebellion' challenged the inequalities of the global economy, giving substance to the demand for economic self-determination.[25]

In an address to delegates of sixty-three nations at the United Nations Conference on Trade and Development (UNCTAD) in Santiago one year before the coup, Allende stressed the need to rectify an unfair international division of labour based on 'age-old exploitation' and a 'dehumanized concept of mankind'.[26] Chile's delegate to the UNCTAD conference was Hernán Santa Cruz, who had struggled decades earlier to secure the social and economic rights in the UDHR. At the UNCTAD conference, Santa Cruz stressed that the realisation of the UDHR's social, economic and cultural rights required a just international economic order. Only days after the *New York Times* had revealed plotting between the CIA and the ITT telecommunications company to prevent Allende becoming president, Santa Cruz told the plenary that any external attempt to deprive a country of its right to dispose freely of its natural resources was a 'flagrant violation of the principles of self-determination and non-interference', and a threat to international peace and security.[27]

To Harberger and the Chicago Boys, Santa Cruz's emphasis on social and economic rights reflected the influence of 'nationalist, protectionist, distributive mythologies', notably the dependency theory of the Argentinean economist Raúl Prebisch, executive secretary of the UN's

24   Excess profits were profits over 12 per cent of the book value of the company between 1955 and 1970. Tanya Harmer, *Allende's Chile and the Inter-American Cold War* (Chapel Hill, NC: University of North Carolina Press, 2011), p. 309.

25   Ibid., p. 62.

26   Salvador Allende, 'Address to the Third UN Conference on Trade and Development (UNCTAD)', in James D. Cockcroft, ed., *Salvador Allende Reader* (Brighton: Ocean Press, 2000).

27   Daniel J. Whelan, '"Under the Aegis of Man": The Right to Development and the Origins of the New International Economic Order', *Humanity: An International Journal of Human Rights, Humanitarianism, and Development* 6: 1 (2015), p. 103.

Economic Commission for Latin America (ECLA).[28] Prebisch's account of unequal trade between the centre and the periphery challenged the neoclassical assumption that market relations are free, voluntary and mutually beneficial. In opposition to the myth of the sweetness of commerce, Prebisch highlighted the centrality of domination to the operations of the world economy. To Harberger, this stress on the external determinants of economic development – the international economic system, commodity prices, multinational corporations, and what Allende termed 'neo-colonial exploitation' – elevated the Latin American tendency to assume that 'somebody else did it to them' to the level of theory.[29]

The US government, guided by the Monroe Doctrine, and alarmed both by Chile's domestic policies and by the threat they offered to US regional hegemony, devoted substantial funding and efforts to sabotaging Allende's progress in 'establishing a totalitarian Marxist state in Chile'.[30] The Unidad Popular (UP) government's expropriation policy led to increasingly strident demands for a harder US line, not only on Chile but on the entire postcolonial economic agenda. The US Treasury secretary, John Connally, argued that preventing a snowballing trend of expropriations across Latin America and the Caribbean required that Chile be made an example. (Even he could not have imagined that Chile would soon offer an example of radical market reform that, forty years later, would be hailed by the *Wall Street Journal* as a model for Egyptian generals who had just seized power from the elected government of the Muslim Brotherhood's Mohammed Morsi.)[31] As Harberger noted, it was ultimately a military government, and a particularly brutal one, that induced Chileans to 'think their way out' of the attempt to transform their collective situation, and instead submit to their (market-dispersed) fates.

---

28 Harberger, 'Capitalism and Freedom in Latin America: Discussion', p. 273.
29 Salvador Allende, 'Address to the Third UN Conference on Trade and Development'.
30 From a 1971 US memo, cited in Harmer, *Allende's Chile*, p. 62.
31 'After the Coup in Cairo', *Wall Street Journal*, Review & Outlook, 7 July 2013.

Capitalism and Freedom

Chile's transformation into an exemplary laboratory of neoliberalism owed much to Harberger's Chicago Boys. On 12 September 1973, the morning after the coup, their 189-page economic programme, *El Ladrillo* ('The Brick') was on the desk of every major figure in the new regime. It called for trade liberalisation and tariff reductions; widespread privatisation, including of social security; and a regressive value-added tax. In 1993, Harberger noted with satisfaction that this vision was now overwhelmingly accepted by all of Chile's major parties, while, at the time, the Chicago programme was 'too market-oriented, too open-economy, and too technocratic' even for the traditional Chilean right.[32] In 1975, Friedman met with Pinochet to convince him that Chile's economy required 'shock treatment', primarily in the form of a drastic reduction in public spending. The general, Friedman noted, 'was sympathetically attracted to the idea of a shock treatment but was clearly distressed at the possible temporary unemployment that might be caused'.[33] In the wake of his visit, Friedman wrote to Pinochet to stiffen his resolve: 'There is no way to end the inflation that will not involve a temporary transitional period of severe difficulties, including unemployment'.[34]

Following the argument of the Chilean diplomat Orlando Letelier, Naomi Klein has argued that this economic 'shock', which led to a massive transfer of wealth to the wealthiest individuals and monopolies, required the political shock of the junta's torture chambers. This relation was obscured, she contends, by the reports of human rights organisations, which treated the torture and disappearances in isolation from the economic agenda. Letelier had argued that the assumption that 'economic freedom' and political terror were independent of each other allowed the neoliberal economists to 'support their concept of "freedom" while exercising their verbal muscles in defence of human rights'.[35] According to the Chilean diplomat, the '*laissez-faire* dreams and

---

32   Arnold Harberger, 'Secrets of Success: A Handful of Heroes', *American Economic Review* 83: 2, 'Papers and Proceedings of the Hundred and Fifth Annual Meeting of the American Economic Association' (1993), p. 345.

33   Milton Friedman and Rose D. Friedman, *Two Lucky People: Memoirs* (Chicago: University of Chicago Press, 1998), p. 399.

34   Milton Friedman and Rose D. Friedman, 'Appendix A, Chapter 24 (Chile): Documents', in Friedman and Friedman, *Two Lucky People*, p. 592.

35   Letelier, cited in Klein, *Shock Doctrine*, p. 99.

political greed of the old landowning oligarchy and upper bourgeoisie' required both the technical respectability provided by the Chicago economists and the violence of the junta. There was an 'inner harmony' between the political and the economic, he argued, and those who advocated economic shock therefore shared responsibility for the brutal methods used to implement it.[36]

It is true that, faced with protests in the wake of his visit to Chile, Friedman presented his advice to the regime in apolitical, technical terms; despite his 'profound disagreement with the authoritarian political system of Chile', he wrote, he did not consider it 'as an evil for an economist to render technical economic advice to the Chilean Government, any more than I would regard it as evil for a physician to give technical medical advice to the Chilean Government to help end a medical plague'.[37] He depicted his own recommendations (the abolition of price controls and subsidies, and the loosening of employment regulations, to make it possible to 'eliminate waste') as aimed simply at removing obstacles to the efficient operation of the market.[38] It is also true that Friedman continued to profess his support for human rights. Two years later, he summarised his own political message as follows: 'Property rights are not in conflict with human rights. On the contrary, they are themselves the most basic of human rights and an essential foundation for other human rights.'[39] On closer examination, however, it is clear that Friedman's argument in Chile was not that political freedom and economic freedom were 'entirely unrelated', as Letelier and Klein both argue.[40] Rather, he argued that they were intimately related: property rights are the essential foundation of all other human rights, he contended, and a free market is necessary for realising the 'equal right to freedom'.[41]

Friedman never departed from his argument that economic freedom is both a central component of human freedom and the necessary

---

36   Orlando Letelier, 'Economic 'Freedom's' Awful Toll; The "Chicago Boys" in Chile', *Review of Radical Political Economics* 8: 3 (1976), p. 52.

37   Friedman, cited in Eric Schliesser, 'Friedman, Positive Economics, and the Chicago Boys', in Ross B. Emmett, ed., *The Elgar Companion to the Chicago School of Economics* (Cheltenham: Edward Elgar, 2010), p. 185.

38   Friedman and Friedman, *Two Lucky People*, 'Appendix A', p. 593.

39   Ibid., 'Appendix B', p. 605.

40   Klein, *Shock Doctrine*.

41   Milton Friedman, Milton Friedman, *Capitalism and Freedom* (Chicago: University of Chicago Press, 2002), p. 195.

condition for all other freedoms. He stressed the necessary relation between economics and politics even during his visit to Chile, and by his own account this was as big a shock to his audiences as his argument for dramatic austerity. In what he later called his 'anti-totalitarian talk' to students at the Catholic University of Chile in Santiago, his key theme was 'the fragility of freedom'.[42] He told his audience that Chile's present difficulties were almost entirely due to 'the forty-year trend towards collectivism, socialism and the welfare state', and depicted the welfare state as the key threat to free societies. Today, after decades of neoliberal hegemony, the characterisation of state intervention into the economy as a threat to freedom is ubiquitous. Friedman's students, in contrast, received his message with 'an attitude of shock'.[43] Such talk, however, was classic Friedman. His major work, *Capitalism and Freedom*, explicitly contested the 'delusion' that political freedom could be combined with a socialist economy.[44] Historically, political freedom came into being along with the free market and the emergence of capitalism, he argued, while social planning and welfarism had required 'trampling rough-shod on treasured private rights'.[45]

Although Letelier recognised this aspect of Friedman's argument, he argued that, in Chile, 'when the economic theories he advocates coincide with an absolute restriction of every type of democratic freedom', Friedman had instead disentangled economics and politics.[46] In rendering Friedman's argument, Letelier, perhaps unconsciously, distorted it. The central argument of *Capitalism and Freedom* is not that economic liberalism is necessary for political *democracy*, but that it is necessary for political *freedom* – defined as the absence of coercion by one's 'fellow men'.[47] Although it seems obvious that Pinochet's torturous regime fundamentally violated this condition, the coercion that most concerned Friedman took the form of political interference with the market. By 'removing the organization of economic activity from the control of political authority', he argued, 'the market eliminates the source of

---

42   Milton Friedman, 'Commanding Heights: Milton Friedman', Public Broadcasting Service, 1 October 2000, at pbs.org; Friedman and Friedman, *Two Lucky People*, p. 400.

43   Friedman and Friedman, *Two Lucky People*, p. 400.

44   Friedman, *Capitalism and Freedom*, p. 8.

45   Ibid., p. 11.

46   Letelier, cited in Schliesser, 'Friedman, Positive Economics, and the Chicago Boys', p. 185.

47   Friedman, *Capitalism and Freedom*, p. 15.

coercive power.'[48] Following Mises's account of market sovereignty, Friedman depicted the market as a superior *political* model, a 'system of proportional representation' in which (in his typically trivial example) 'each man can take a vote, as it were, for the color of tie he wants and get it' without having to submit to the preference of the majority.[49] It was an 'utter fallacy' to assume that the equal weight of each individual implies majority rule, he argued at the California symposium; 'All that each person has equal weight implies is that nobody has a right to violate anybody else's rights.'[50]

Despite their apolitical presentation, the Chicago Boys followed Friedman in attributing a series of what I have called '(anti)-political virtues' to a competitive market order, among them the absence of coercion, impersonal rule, non-discrimination, and, pre-eminently, individual freedom. Their advocacy of free-market reform was predicated on a stark dichotomy between politics (defined by coercion and conflict) and the market (which enabled non-coercive, mutually beneficial, voluntary social interchange). Pablo Baraona, a Chicago graduate who later became minister of the economy, outlined this dichotomy in the starkest terms. Chile's problems, he argued, were all attributable to politics – 'the quest for power for its own sake and increasing unrestrained demagoguery.'[51] In contrast, the market was 'the economic manifestation of freedom and the impersonality of authority.'[52] The leading 'Chicago Boy', Sergio de Castro, who served as both minister of economy and minister of finance under Pinochet, believed that (economic) freedom was best secured by 'authoritarian' government with its 'impersonal' mode of exercising power.[53] Just as Mises had argued that economic autarky was a just cause for war, the argument that a functioning market was the necessary condition for domestic peace licensed state violence 'to crush the onslaught of peace-breakers'.[54]

Long before Friedman, Mises described the market order as the real basis of all the declarations of rights and charters of liberties, which

48   Ibid., p. 15.
49   Ibid., p. 15.
50   Milton Friedman, 'A Statistical Note on the Gastil-Wright Survey of Freedom: Discussion', in Walker, *Freedom, Democracy and Economic Welfare*, p. 143.
51   Baraona, cited in Juan Gabriel Valdés, *Pinochet's Economists: The Chicago School in Chile* (Cambridge: Cambridge University Press, 1995), p. 29.
52   Baraona, cited in ibid., p. 31.
53   Constable and Valenzuela, *Nation of Enemies*, p. 186.
54   Mises, *Human Action*, p. 149.

remained a 'dead letter' without economic freedom.[55] The freedom of a market society, as we have seen, operated within strict margins; there is no freedom to challenge the market as the key allocator of goods and social positions, to ameliorate the inequalities it produces, or to establish ends collectively. Rather, individual freedom is subject to the 'harsh social pressure' of the sovereign market, and the pursuit of individual values through consumption is limited by personal finances.[56] Mises spelled out the necessary relation between market freedom and political repression most clearly: there is 'in the operation of the market no compulsion or coercion', he argued. Therefore, the state 'employs its power to beat people into submission solely for the prevention of actions destructive to the preservation and the smooth operation of the market economy'.[57] The neoliberals knew all too well that their vision of freedom was indistinguishable from the violence that secured submission to the market.

In the Chilean case, what is most striking about the relation between the economists and the junta's repression is not that they ignored it, but how willingly they embraced it. Friedman wrote to Pinochet to assure him that Allende's regime represented the 'terrible climax' of a trend towards socialism, and that the general had been 'extremely wise in adopting the many measures you have already taken to reverse this trend'.[58] In 1977, the Chicago human capital theorist, Gary Becker, wrote of his pride in his Chilean students, whose 'willingness to work for a cruel dictator and start a different economic approach was one of the best things that happened to Chile'.[59] Harberger later dismissed those who protested the junta's repression, saying: 'if you look at human rights violations or political violations, you will find them in any Asian country almost at that time, in multiples of whatever was happening in Chile'.[60] Hayek told the right-wing Chilean newspaper *El Mercurio* that, while he did not support permanent dictatorship, he saw Pinochet's 'transitional dictatorship' as a 'means of establishing a stable democracy

---

55   Ibid., p. 287.
56   Ibid., p. 599.
57   Ibid., p. 258.
58   Friedman and Friedman, 'Appendix A', p. 593.
59   Cited in Verónica Montecinos, 'Economics: The Chilean Story', in Verónica Montecinos and John Markoff, eds, *Economists in the Americas* (Cheltenham: Edward Elgar, 2009), p. 153.
60   Arnold Harberger, 'Commanding Heights: Arnold "Al" Harberger', Public Broadcasting Service, 3 October 2000, at pbs.org.

and liberty, clean of impurities'.[61] Within Chile, de Castro reflected that, as public opinion was very much against the Chicago Boys, it was 'our luck that President Pinochet understood and had the character to withstand criticism'.[62]

Contra Klein and Letelier, the neoliberals did not treat their technical economic agenda and the junta's political repression as 'entirely unrelated'.[63] On the contrary, neoliberalism in Chile, as elsewhere, was always a *political* (or anti-political) project that found its normative justification in its claim to enhance the form of freedom that only a competitive market could provide.[64] Faced with a brutal dictatorship prepared to implement his economic agenda, Friedman was not a technician focused on his area of expertise to the exclusion of the political fallout. Rather, Pinochet's dictatorship offered a solution to a seemingly intractable neoliberal problem: how to replace popular sovereignty with the sovereignty of the market. It demonstrated what was necessary, in a context defined by strong collective politics and norms of solidarity, to induce subjects to abandon romanticism and the political contestation of ends, and adopt the morals of the market.

Pinochet's Political Miracle

In 1982, Friedman claimed that Pinochet's Chile was a 'miracle'. The previous year, Hayek had called Chile's economic recovery 'one of the greatest miracles of our time'.[65] For Friedman, Chile was not simply an *economic* miracle – it was 'an even more amazing political miracle'. Despite having facilitated a massive transfer of wealth to the rich, Friedman contended that, by substituting market mechanisms for state control, the dictatorship had replaced 'control from the top with control from the bottom'.[66] There was, nonetheless, something surprising about

61   Farrant, McPhail, and Berger, 'Preventing the "Abuses" of Democracy', p. 522 (my emphasis).

62   Constable and Valenzuela, *Nation of Enemies*, p. 170.

63   Letelier, cited in Klein, *Shock Doctrine*, p. 116.

64   Constable and Valenzuela, *Nation of Enemies*, p. 186.

65   Cited in Martin Durham and Margaret Power, 'Transnational Conservatism: The New Right, Neoconservatism, and Cold War Anti-Communism', in Martin Durham and Margaret Power, eds, *New Perspectives on the Transnational Right* (New York: Palgrave Macmillan, 2010), p. 137.

66   Friedman, 'Passing Down the Chilean Recipe', p. 177.

this neoliberal recourse to the theological vocabulary of the miracle. As the conservative German jurist Carl Schmitt noted in 1922, the theistic paradigm of the miracle, in which God suspends the laws of nature and intervenes directly into the world, had long ago been displaced by the Enlightenment belief in the immanence of natural law, with deep consequences for both metaphysics and politics. In the context of outlining his infamous argument that sovereignty consists in the capacity to declare a state of exception, Schmitt argued that 'the exception in jurisprudence is analogous to the miracle in theology'.[67] While reactionary thinkers still believed in the necessity of divine and sovereign intervention, he argued, the dominant belief of his own time was that the 'machine now runs by itself'.[68] For US neoliberal economists, who supposedly believe in the immanent laws of the market, no miracles should have been needed.

In Chile, Friedman and the Chicago Boys' economic advice was underpinned by their faith in a naturally occurring equilibrium that would be achieved by an 'invisible hand' if the market was protected from collective political action and state intervention. Friedman credited Adam Smith with the insight that, while the market looks chaotic to the 'untrained eye', it is a 'finely ordered and delicately tuned system' of 'natural liberty'.[69] This conception of the market also had its theological lineage, as earlier neoliberals were well aware.[70] Yet, rather than being structurally modelled on the miraculous interventions of a transcendent God, the idea of the market as a natural order had the same systematic structure as a world ordered by an absent God who governed exclusively through natural laws. Neoliberalism was founded on the rejection of this model of the market, which the German ordoliberal Alexander Rüstow disparaged as a reflection of theological faith in the 'eternal wisdom of the natural law'.[71] Wilhelm Röpke mocked the idea that the

67   Carl Schmitt, *Political Theology: Four Chapters on the Concept of Sovereignty*, ed. George Schwab (Chicago: University of Chicago Press, 2005), p. 36. In May 1933, Schmitt joined the Nazi Party, and attempted to position himself as the crown jurist of National Socialism.

68   Ibid., p. 48.

69   Milton Friedman, 'Essay Four: Adam Smith's Relevance for 1976', in Lanny Ebenstein, ed., *The Indispensable Milton Friedman: Essays on Politics and Economics* (Washington, DC: Regnery, 2012), p. 50.

70   Peter Harrison, 'Adam Smith and the History of the Invisible Hand', *Journal of the History of Ideas* 72: 1 (2011), p. 49.

71   Alexander Rüstow, 'Appendix', in Alexander Röpke *International Economic*

competitive market was a natural order 'miraculously directed by the "invisible hand" mentioned by Adam Smith, which in reality is nothing but the "divine reason" of deistic philosophy'. The problem with such a belief, according to the neoliberals, was that it led to misplaced optimism about the self-regulating properties of the market, and neglect of the 'non-economic prerequisites' of a market economy, including its moral prerequisites.[72]

On the surface, Friedman's model seems to replicate this immanent market order that needs only to be freed from interference. He assigned the price mechanism the role of distributing the rewards and punishments that dictate where individuals and firms should direct their efforts, and he argued that this impersonal direction was disastrously impaired by the 'invisible hand in politics', as politicians seeking to promote the good instead produced ends that were 'no part of their intention'.[73] On closer examination, however, even at their most technical, the Chicago economists were deeply aware of the non-economic prerequisites for their preferred market order. If romanticism and demagoguery were the greatest barriers to 'good economics', a working market order required market subjects responsible for their own fates. The Chicago economists were also aware that the market did not create its own virtues. Röpke had argued that invocations of an invisible hand obscured the fact that the 'market economy needs a firm moral, political and institutional framework', including 'well weighed laws appropriate to the economic system'.[74] For Friedman, achieving such a market-compatible framework was the junta's political miracle.

In extolling Chile's political miracle, Friedman argued that a free market, unlike a military structure, is typified by dispersed authority – 'bargaining, not submission to orders, is the watchword'.[75] But submission remained central to his account of the market. Economic pain (like physical torture) was designed to break the political subjectivities that led people to resist the 'fate' doled out by the market. Everyone in this country was 'educated in weakness', minister of the economy Baraona

---

Disintegration (London: William Hodge, 1942), p. 270.

72　Wilhelm Röpke, *The Social Crisis of Our Time*, transl. Annette Schiffer Jacobsohn and Peter Schiffer Jacobsohn (Chicago: University of Chicago Press, 1950 [1942]), p. 52.

73　Friedman, 'Essay Four', p. 52.

74　Röpke, *Social Crisis of Our Time*, p. 52.

75　Friedman cites his earlier comments in Friedman, 'Passing Down the Chilean Recipe', p. 177.

warned; 'to educate them in strength it is necessary to pay the price of temporary unemployment, of bankruptcies'.[76] When asked about the high bankruptcy rate, junta member Admiral Merino concurred: 'Let fall those who must fall', he said. 'Such is the jungle of economic life. A jungle of savage beasts, where he who can kill the one next to him, kills him. That is reality'.[77] Such statements were a long way from the myth of the sweetness of commerce, but they were not far divorced from the tenets of the neoliberal market, for which, as Michel Foucault has stressed, the central principle was not exchange but *competition*, with its systematic production of winners and losers.[78] Weakening solidarity and creating competitive subjects was central to what Pinochet identified as the junta's ultimate goal: 'not to make Chile a nation of proletarians, but a nation of entrepreneurs'.[79]

Pinochet's Chile was not the only place where Friedman had identified a dual miracle. Two years prior to heralding Chile's miraculous transformation, he and his wife, Rose Director Friedman, declared that the 'story of the United States is the story of an economic miracle and a political miracle'.[80] The Friedmans attributed these earlier miracles to two complementary sets of ideas, both published in 1776. Alongside Smith's account of the market as a realm of voluntary social relations that requires 'no external force, no coercion, no violation of freedom', they placed the US Declaration of Independence's contention that all individuals are 'endowed by their Creator with certain unalienable Rights', among them 'Life, Liberty, and the pursuit of Happiness'. According to the Friedmans, these two ideas were mutually constitutive. 'Economic freedom', they argued, 'is an essential requisite for political

---

76   Constable and Valenzuela, *Nation of Enemies*, pp. 186–7.

77   Ibid., p. 187.

78   Michel Foucault, *The Birth of Biopolitics: Lectures at the Collège de France 1978–1979*, ed. Michel Senellart, transl. Graham Burchell (New York: Palgrave Macmillan, 2008), p. 118.

79   Michael Moffitt, 'Chicago Economics in Chile', *Challenge* 20: 4 (1977), p. 35. Depoliticising society by transforming proletarians into entrepreneurs had long been a central goal of European neoliberals. Mitigating the 'sensitivity and instability' of mass society, according to Roepke, required a policy of 'decentralization, de-proletarianization, the anchoring of men in their own resources, encouragement to small farmers and small business, increased property ownership, and the strengthening of the middle classes'. Wilhelm Röpke, *Economics of the Free Society*, transl. Patrick M. Boarman (Chicago: Henry Regnery Company, 1963), 220.

80   Milton Friedman and Rose D. Friedman, *Free to Choose: A Personal Statement* (New York: Harcourt Brace Jovanovich, 1980), pp. 1.

freedom.' The market enables individuals to pursue their own values and ends, while the guarantee that they will be unmolested in doing so fosters economic development. Both Smith and Jefferson, the Friedmans argued, saw concentrated government power as the great danger, and 'protection of the citizen against the tyranny of government as the perpetual need'.[81] The inalienable rights of the American Declaration of Independence, from this perspective, existed not to found a sovereign state, but to ensure that state power was used to foster economic initiative. It would ultimately be towards this same end that the neoliberals would mobilise individual rights in Chile.

Inflated Expectations

The reliance of the immanent laws of the market on extra-economic violence and the imposition of a moral code is clear even in relation to the most technical of areas: the Chicago Boys' remedies for inflation. From the Chicago perspective, inflation is not merely one problem among others; it is a spanner in the well-oiled market machine. For price signals and market sovereignty to replace human direction in shaping human behaviour, price stability is essential. During their Chicago studies, Pinochet's economists had been converted to the tenets of monetarism, for which inflation, in Friedman's often-repeated dogma, was 'always and everywhere a monetary phenomenon' – a product of a more rapid increase in the money supply than in output.[82] Friedman depicted Chicago's 'counter-revolution in monetary theory' – which displaced Keynesian attempts to foster economic stability through taxation and public spending – as 'a scientific development that has little ideological or political content'.[83] In his 1976 Nobel Prize lecture, he struck a technocratic tone, arguing that the 'socially destructive inflation' and 'suppression of human freedom' afflicting many countries were not results of 'evil men', nor of 'differences of values among citizens', but of erroneous judgments about the consequences of government actions.[84]

---

81   Ibid., pp. 1–4.
82   Milton Friedman, 'Essay Fifteen: The Counter-Revolution in Monetary Theory', in Ebenstein, *Indispensable Milton Friedman*, p. 184.
83   Ibid., p. 167.
84   Friedman, cited in Schliesser, 'Friedman, Positive Economics, and the Chicago Boys', pp. 186–7.

In truth, the realities underpinning inflation were deeply political, as Friedman implicitly recognised. The correlate of the monetarist conviction that inflation is always caused by an increase in the supply of money is that it occurs because governments want to 'provide "goodies" for their supporters and constituents' without increasing taxes.[85] As we saw in the previous chapter, the Mexican MPS member Gustavo Velasco attributed his country's inflation to excessive popular expectations in the context of a welfare state. The Chicago economists also saw inflation as a 'moral crisis' bound up with heightened expectations and a failure of personal and familial responsibility among the working class in a context of victorious political struggles.[86]

As early as 1958, on a panel devoted to inflation at the MPS conference in Princeton, Friedman argued that inflation damaged free societies by strengthening unions, which were more able to win pay rises in inflationary conditions, and by generating pressure for government subsidies and price controls to protect people from rising prices.[87] Friedman's fellow panellist, the French philosopher Jacques Reuff, gave an even starker account of the problem: 'Inflation is a far greater threat to liberty throughout the world today than Marxism', he told his fellow liberals.[88] Reuff argued that inflation weakened the regulatory role of the price mechanism and discouraged submission to its dictates. In Friedman's view, the only solution to inflation was *restraint*, both on the part of the people, who should avoid demanding government intervention in the face of a downturn, and on the part of government, which should refuse to bow to such demands. 'The crucial problem', which in 1958 remained largely unresolved, was 'how to get such "restraint"'.[89]

The problem of restraint was all the more difficult because, as Friedman later recognised, some benefited from inflation while others

---

85   Milton Friedman, *Money Mischief: Episodes in Monetary History* (New York: Harcourt Brace, 1994), p. 236; Adam J. Tooze, 'Who Is Afraid of Inflation? The Long-Shadow of the 1970s', *Journal of Modern European History* 12: 1 (2014), p. 58.

86   In a similar vein, Melinda Cooper uses the term 'the moral crisis of inflation' to describe the ways in which Chicago School economists and neoconservatives in the United States united in opposition to social welfare, and especially welfare to single mothers. Melinda Cooper, *Family Values: Between Neoliberalism and the New Social Conservatism* (New York: Zone, 2017), p. 30.

87   Milton Friedman, 'Inflation' in *Mont Pèlerin Society*, 9th Mont Pèlerin Society Meeting, Princeton: Hoover Institution Archives, 1958, Box 12, Folder 6.

88   Jacques Reuff, 'Inflation and Liberty', in *Mont Pèlerin Society*, 9th Mont Pèlerin Society Meeting, Princeton: Hoover Institution Archives, 1958, 1, Box 12, Folder 5–6.

89   Ibid., p. 5.

suffered, so 'society is divided into winners and losers'; the prime winners, he argued, were debtors, as the real value of debt was diminished by increases in prices, and the prime losers were creditors and the entire 'savings and loan industry', whose returns on their lending were simultaneously diminished.[90] If inflation had distributional consequences, including transferring money from creditors to debtors, then the decision to treat combatting inflation as the primary economic goal could not be value-free. This was clear in Chile, where Allende's government broke with a long tradition of responding to inflation by cutting social services, especially for the poor. When the opposition blocked new taxes that would have financed social programmes, the UP government accepted inflation as a 'lesser evil' than failing to fulfil its election commitments to Chile's poorest citizens.[91]

The consequent price rises are generally represented, even by sympathetic commentators, as evidence of the government's economic incompetence.[92] It is true that the government was unable to fulfill its earlier Keynesian hopes that higher wages and public spending would stimulate demand without serious inflation. In 1973, a government member of the Central Bank laid out the following options: 'reduce the speed of societal change; detain the redistribution of income; lower the level of employment; reduce the growth rate; decrease the level of capital accumulation – or increase inflation'. By 1972, he noted, the Allende government, 'with much regret, had to opt for sacrificing monetary stability'.[93] Chile's inflation was the consequence not of economic ignorance in the context of a basic unanimity of values, but of a political commitment to Chile's poorest people in dramatically constrained circumstances. The Chicago Boys would make precisely the opposite choice. Pinochet's *economic* miracle was to preserve monetary stability by sacrificing Chile's poor.

As Friedman had predicted, the junta's 'shock' approach produced 'severe difficulties' – but not for all sections of the Chilean population. As he acknowledged, the immediate effect was 'severe recession', as Chile's GDP fell by 13 per cent per annum.[94] In an open letter to

90   Friedman, *Money Mischief*, p. 496.

91   The consumer price index increased by 40 per cent in 1971 and by 163 per cent in 1972. Peter A. Goldberg, 'The Politics of the Allende Overthrow in Chile', *Political Science Quarterly* 90: 1 (1975), pp. 105–6.

92   See Valdés, *Pinochet's Economists*.

93   Goldberg, 'Politics of the Allende Overthrow', pp. 105–6.

94   Friedman and Friedman, *Two Lucky People*, p. 405.

Friedman and Harberger, Andre Gunder Frank denounced 'economic genocide' in Chile. Frank pointed out that the removal of price controls, combined with the destruction of trade union power, had drastically reduced real wages, to the extent that, by December 1975, one hour of work at the official minimum wage purchased 160 grams of bread.[95] From 1975, stark spending cuts and the 'freeing' of prices on two thousand commodities caused purchasing power to fall to 40 per cent of its 1970 level.[96] While the real incomes of the poorest plummeted, the share of national income in the hands of the upper 5 per cent of income receivers rose from 25 per cent to 50 per cent.[97]

What Friedman termed a 'temporary transitional period' and Gunder Frank called 'economic genocide as a calculated policy' was a deliberate attempt to strip Chileans of non-market social reproduction and force them to submit to the judgment of the market.[98] This was what Friedman meant when he said that 'underdeveloped' countries needed 'an atmosphere of freedom, of maximum opportunities for individuals to experiment and of incentives for them to do so in an environment in which there are objective tests of success and failure – in short, a vigorous, free, capitalistic market'.[99] In Chile, the political miracle was that a (transcendent) military regime operating under a state of emergency had secured the central condition for the (immanent) operation of the price mechanism: submission. Once this condition was met, the 'normal' order could be restored. 'The really important thing about the Chile business', Friedman said decades later, 'is that free markets did work their way in bringing about a free society'.[100] That miracle, however, cannot be attributed to the work of the free market. It was Pinochet's jurists who devised an institutional structure to lock in the junta's economic reforms and prepare for a return to a (limited) democracy.

95   Andre Gunder Frank, 'Economic Genocide in Chile: Open Letter to Milton Friedman and Arnold Harberger', *Economic and Political Weekly* 11: 24 (1976), p. 883.
96   Constable and Valenzuela, *Nation of Enemies*, p. 173.
97   Gunder Frank, 'Economic Genocide in Chile', p. 882.
98   Friedman and Friedman, 'Appendix A', p. 592; Gunder Frank, 'Economic Genocide in Chile', p. 880.
99   Valdés, *Pinochet's Economists*, p. 95.
100 Friedman, 'Commanding Heights: Milton Friedman'.

Amnesty International in Pinochet's Chile

In November of 1973, within months of Pinochet's coup, Amnesty International sent an investigative team to report on Chile's human rights situation. When the team – a law professor, a judge and an Amnesty researcher – arrived in Santiago, the atmosphere of repression was immediately clear.[101] They found Chile absolutely overwhelmed by the military. One team member recalled that there was 'no rule of law whatsoever – it was just a façade'.[102] Amnesty's subsequent reports focused on this absence of legality while avoiding contested political territory. Amnesty described its mandate as working for adequate treatment of all prisoners, fighting for the rule of law, and seeking the release of those it called 'prisoners of conscience', defined as 'any person who is physically restrained (by imprisonment or otherwise) from expressing (in any form of words or symbols) any opinion which he honestly holds and which does not advocate or condone personal violence'.[103] Dismayed by the Chilean Bar Association's indifference to the junta's crimes, one team member addressed a letter his legal colleagues, reminding them that Chile had endorsed the UDHR and ratified the two human rights covenants, and that it was 'unconscionable' that these could so quickly be discarded.[104]

The Amnesty team's mandate was strictly limited: 'the revolutionary cause, either before or after the revolution, was none of our business', one team member stressed.[105] The report itself provided an extremely detailed and balanced account of imprisonment, torture and disappearance under Pinochet's rule. It depicted the coup as the outcome of 'an atmosphere of bitter social tension, after months of increased polarization between pro-Allende and anti-Allende factions'.[106] Despite asking, 'Who are the

---

101 Along with Plant, the team comprised the Berkeley law professor Frank Newman and the Orange County judge Bruce Sumner. See Patrick William Kelly, 'The 1973 Chilean Coup and the Origins of Transnational Human Rights Activism', *Journal of Global History* 8 (2013), p. 172.

102 Roger Plant, 'Life under Pinochet', Amnesty International Canada, 14 August 2013, at amnesty.ca.

103 Edy Kaufman, 'Prisoners of Conscience: The Shaping of a New Human Rights Concept', *Human Rights Quarterly* 13: 3 (1991), p. 343.

104 Kelly, 'The 1973 Chilean Coup', p. 174.

105 Ibid., p. 173.

106 Amnesty International, *Chile: An Amnesty International Report* (London: Amnesty International Publications, 1974), p. 6.

political prisoners? Why are they detained?' the report answered neither question, instead reverting to the universalising platitude that the 'political prisoners have stemmed from all sections of the Chilean population'.[107] Amnesty's 1977 report, which claimed to provide a 'legal and historical report on the situation of disappeared prisoners', began with the lines: 'When the military took over on 11 September 1973 the Junta declared a "state of siege" throughout the country'.[108] Here, the coup appeared as the 'year zero' that began history anew – a response to a 'social tension' and 'polarization' whose causes remained unintelligible.

Despite the new centrality to which Amnesty elevated the UDHR, this taking up of human rights was distinctly partial, and emphatically did not include social and economic rights. Its 1974 report on Chile made clear that it would exclude from consideration the approximately 200,000 workers 'who lost their employment for political reasons, many of them apparently being reduced to starvation levels'.[109] Not only the 'non-political' economic consequences of the coup, but even the use of starvation as a political weapon, was relegated outside the frame of human rights, giving credence to Klein's account of human rights as 'blinders'.[110] A year later, Amnesty's 1975 report noted that the 'varying economic and social difficulties in the Third World' had hampered the organisation's attempts to 'become more culturally diverse' by recruiting members outside Europe and North America, and to 'harness the opposition to torture and sympathy for prisoners of conscience' in the non-Western world.[111] The challenge was to mobilise support 'despite the political, social, financial and other problems that exist'.[112] In striking contrast to the economic concerns that animated Allende's government, and anticolonial human rights activism of the previous decade, poverty and economic inequality were not of concern in their own right. They entered the frame only insofar as they affected advocacy against torture, and the cultivation of sympathy for its victims.

It could be argued, in response to Klein's position, that Amnesty's narrow approach provided a politically pragmatic response to the junta's

---

107   Ibid., p. 15.
108   Amnesty International, *Disappeared Prisoners in Chile*, p. 9.
109   Amnesty International, *Chile: An Amnesty International Report*, p. 6.
110   Klein, *Shock Doctrine*.
111   Amnesty International, *Amnesty International Annual Report 1974/75* (London: Amnesty International Publications, 1975), p. 10.
112   Ibid., p. 10 (my emphasis).

regime of terror, offering more to those subjected to the worst of its violence than did critiques of economic shock treatment. From this perspective, legalistic human rights activism would complement the goals of leftists, who aimed to discredit a hated regime, thereby 'promoting a new, hopefully socialist, future'.[113] My argument is different: the problem was not simply that the human rights NGOs dealt with political violence in isolation from the economic transformations it facilitated, as Klein has argued. Rather, it is that they thereby bolstered the neoliberal dichotomy between violent politics and free civil society, thus contributing to a narrowing of the political and economic margins. The assumption that Chile's key problem was unrestrained political power did not distinguish between political mobilisation to challenge arbitrary economic power and authoritarian mobilisation to entrench it. Rather, Amnesty's portrayal of politics as a field of 'tension' and 'polarisation' reinforced the neoliberal attempt to constrain politics within strictly defined bounds, shaping a distinctly non-socialist future.

Much attention has been devoted to Amnesty's founder Peter Benenson's origin myth, which traces the organisation to his own indignation at reading, as he rode the London Tube, about two Portuguese students imprisoned by Salazar's dictatorship for raising a toast to liberty.[114] Less attention has focused on the coordinates of Benenson's journey between his London law chambers and the Church of St-Martins-in-the-Fields, where he supposedly got off the train and formulated the plan for Amnesty International. Amnesty has commonly been viewed as inaugurating a new focus on what Elaine Scarry terms the 'body in pain' as the prototypical site of human rights abuse. By ignoring the political views of the accused and focusing only on the fact of their imprisonment, its goal, it is assumed, is to respond to the universal suffering of the human body. In its early days, however, Amnesty described itself as 'An International Movement for Freedom of Opinion and Religion'.[115] Its focus on the *conscience* drew on a human rights

---

113   Alfonso Salgado, 'Communism and Human Rights in Pinochet's Chile: The 1977 Hunger Strike Against Forced Disappearance', *Cold War History* 18: 2 (2017), p. 173.

114   Elements of Benenson's foundation myth, as Tom Buchanan notes, do not stand up to historical scrutiny. Tom Buchanan, '"The Truth Will Set You Free": The Making of Amnesty International', *Journal of Contemporary History* 37: 4 (2002), p. 576.

115   Tobias Kelly, 'A Divided Conscience', *Public Culture* 30: 3 (1 September 2018), p. 376.

tradition that, as we have seen, conceptualised the person as a spiritual, not a material, being. Amnesty's conscience clause was in the same lineage as Malik's contention that conscience is the most 'sacred and inviolable thing' about the person, which had informed both his opposition to social and economic rights and his attempt to protect the person from the intrusions of mass politics.[116]

Benenson, a convert to Catholicism, shared this spiritual vision of the dignity of the human person. In his initial formulation, Amnesty was to be 'an international movement to guarantee the free exchange of ideas and the free practice of religion'.[117] The category of the prisoner of conscience signalled this shift of focus from the political action of the 'political prisoner' towards her 'conscientiously held beliefs'. In the stark context of the violent anticolonial struggles still being waged in South Africa, Palestine and the Portuguese colonies, the new category of the prisoner of conscience marked a prohibition of violence and a new privileging of speech as the legitimate mode of expression. This emphasis on nonviolence, which drew on the Quaker background of important Amnesty founders, generated an attempt to protect the conscience that was often 'ambiguous and discriminatory'.[118] An early test of the prohibition on violence in Amnesty's definition of the prisoner of conscience led to the expulsion of Nelson Mandela from the list of such prisoners, after he justified the African National Congress's decision to establish an armed wing by arguing: 'If war were inevitable, we wanted the fight to be conducted on terms most favourable to our people.'[119] There was also controversy over whether communists could be prisoners of conscience at all, given that all communists, an official 1981 Amnesty document explained, 'wanted the overthrow of the capitalist state by violence'.[120]

For Benenson, as for Malik, the appropriate response to human rights violations was individual spiritual transformation, not collective

---

116 Commission on Human Rights, 'Commission on Human Rights Verbatim Record Fourteenth Meeting [Excerpt]', in Allida Black, ed., *The Eleanor Roosevelt Papers, vol. I: The Human Rights Years, 1945–1948* (Charlottesville: University of Virginia Press, 2010), pp. 506–7.

117 Buchanan, ' "The Truth Will Set You Free"', p. 591.

118 Kelly, 'Divided Conscience', p. 370.

119 Nelson Mandela, *The Historic Speech of Nelson Rolihlahla Mandela at the Rivonia Trial: As Delivered from the Dock on April 20, 1964* (Johannesburg: Learn & Teach Publications, 1988); Randall Williams, *The Divided World: Human Rights and Its Violence* (Minneapolis: University of Minnesota Press, 2010).

120 Cited in Kelly, 'Divided Conscience', p. 370.

political action. The main purpose of the new organisation, Benenson contended, was to promote cooperation amongst the world's idealists.[121] Amnesty, he wrote in a private letter, is 'geared to appeal to the young searching for an ideal, and to women past the prime of their life who have been, unfortunately, unable to expend in full their maternal impulses'.[122] If this was borne in mind, Benenson wrote, in a somewhat extraordinary admission, it 'matters more to harness the enthusiasm of the helpers than to bring people out of prison . . . the real martyrs prefer to suffer, and, as I would add, the real saints are no worse off in prison than elsewhere on this earth'.[123] Benenson's vision was explicitly anti-democratic. In another theologically charged letter, he maintained: 'When each citizen is individually on the road to the Kingdom, then I believe that there will be a just society on earth without need for the intervention of Parliament.'[124] If only a few leading citizens took this path of spiritual transformation, he wrote, 'we would be nearer the goal than if 51 per cent of the electors voted for laws designed to promote social justice'.[125]

Benenson himself came out of the Catholic NGO Pax Christi, and he took inspiration from the 'wish' of Frank Buchman's anti-communist, Christian 'Moral Re-Armament Movement' (MRA) 'to change people, and especially leading people'.[126] During his days as a graduate student, Malik was also a member of the MRA's precursor, the Oxford Group, which Buchman, its founder, described as a 'Christian revolution for remaking the world'.[127] Kwame Nkrumah, in stark contrast, cited the MRA as an agent of neocolonialism in Africa. In 1961, the liberal jour-nalist Honor Balfour wrote that Amnesty International's 'conscience clause' 'smacks of a form of political Buchmanism'.[128] The gap between Amnesty's version of human rights and Nkrumah's was wide. Amnesty's human rights had little in common with the programme of economic self-determination and violent anti-colonial struggle promoted by

---

121   In Buchanan, ' "The Truth Will Set You Free" ', p. 593.
122   Ibid.
123   Ibid.
124   Ibid., p. 582.
125   Ibid.
126   Ibid.
127   Robyn Creswell, *City of Beginnings: Poetic Modernism in Beirut* (Princeton and Oxford: Princeton University Press, 2019), note 49, p. 216. Buchman, *Remaking the World* (London: Blandford Press, 1958), p. 28.
128   Buchanan, ' "The Truth Will Set You Free" ', p. 585.

diplomats from postcolonial societies in the UN during the same period. While Amnesty was principled in its criticisms of the Chilean junta's human rights abuses, Benenson's own vision was closer to that of the Catholic jurists and politicians who had produced the new institutional order that would ensure that Chile's return to democracy would not mark a return to the mass, socialist politics of the Allende years.

Modernising Chile

Prior to the coup, a young economics student at the Catholic University wrote a critique of the dominant monetarist perspective of his economics school, whose blindness to social misery, he argued, was an affront to the university's Christian anthropology. The student stressed that 'certain economic structures' could never allow 'man . . . to live in conditions which are compatible with human dignity'.[129] His letter would seem to support the argument, made most prominently by Juan Gabriel Valdés – the son of the founder of Chile's Christian Democrats, Gabriel Valdés – that there was 'a permanent and irreconcilable struggle between the ideas promoted by Chicago and the Catholic point of view'.[130] How curious, then, that this same young student, José Piñera, went on to play a major role in Pinochet's 'modernisation' of Chilean society, and is idolised today by the neoliberal right as the architect of the world's first fully privatised national social security system.[131]

The story of the institutionalisation of neoliberalism in Chile is not only a story of economists struggling to reduce state intervention and secure price stability through massive austerity. It is also the story of an attempt to make explicit what Harberger implicitly recognised in describing Latin American romanticism as the key barrier to good economics: the market does not create its own virtues, but requires a moral, legal and institutional order to produce submissive subjects. Piñera, who continued his studies at Harvard before returning to Chile after the coup to assist in founding 'a new country devoted to liberty',

---

129   José Piñera, undated memo cited in Valdés, *Pinochet's Economists*, p. 210.
130   Valdés, *Pinochet's Economists*, p. 235.
131   There were, of course, significant leftist Catholic currents in Chile, but their project for a moderate social democratic transition to socialism 'came violently to an end in the 1970s (in Chile with Allende's murder)'. Miguel Vatter, 'Christian Human Rights', *Politics, Religion & Ideology* 17: 4 (2016), p. 451.

personally embodies the synthesis of conservative Catholicism and radically market-centred economics that defined Chile's new institutional order.[132] While the Chicago economists inspired the junta's early economic reforms, the impetus for its institutional order came from other branches of twentieth-century neoliberalism: German ordoliberalism, James Buchanan and Gordon Tullock's public choice theory, and Hayek's constitutionalism.[133] In contrast to Friedman's naive rhetoric about natural liberty, these conservative strands of neoliberalism were far more useful to those seeking to bolster the legal foundations of the competitive market. They shared an evolutionary social theory, an attention to the role of morality (and particularly Christianity) in a market order, and a commitment to using law to protect the intermediate institutions of civil society from political interference.

Piñera was central to the 'Seven Modernizations', which launched in 1979 to fundamentally recast political expectations by reconstituting social reproduction as a private responsibility.[134] This goal enabled neoliberals and conservative Catholics to form a 'defensive front against the uncontrollable "collectivization" of the economy' and its demoralisation of Chilean society.[135] Health, education and social security were privatised, and the social and economic rights agenda that Santa Cruz had struggled to realise was reversed. The (non-market-compatible) universal provision of welfare was abandoned, replaced by technical criteria that directed limited assistance to the poorest households. These reforms obscured the political relation between poverty, wealth and inequality (stressed by Marxism and dependency theory) and sought to destroy collective and class identities. Modernisation also entailed the 'improvement' and capitalisation of the land. Pinochet promulgated decrees expropriating the Mapuche nation's collective ownership of land and incorporating 'vast areas of "undeveloped" native forests in southern Chile into the global economic market'.[136] Rather than *laissez-faire*, the consolidation of land-ownership in the hands of forestry giants and

---

132   Nancy MacLean, *Democracy in Chains: The Deep History of the Radical Right's Stealth Plan for America* (New York: Penguin, 2017).

133   MacLean traces the influence of Buchanan's constitutionalism in Chile, but he was not the sole architect of Chile's 'constitution of liberty'.

134   Taylor, *From Pinochet to the 'Third Way'*, p. 86.

135   Valdés, *Pinochet's Economists*, p. 246.

136   Alejandra Gaitán-Barrera and Govand Khalid Azeez, 'Beyond Recognition: Autonomy, the State, and the Mapuche Coordinadora Arauco Malleco', *Latin American and Caribbean Ethnic Studies* 13: 2 (2018), p. 117.

large land-owners was fostered by tax incentives and subsidies to logging companies.[137] Although the means differed, the goal of this modernisation process remained the same as that embraced by the Chicago Boys: depoliticising Chilean society, destroying non-market sources of social reproduction, and producing responsible, entrepreneurial subjects.

The reconciliation of neoliberalism with Christianity that underpinned this agenda was promoted in the right-wing journal *PEC* (*Politics, Economics, Culture*), which published Röpke's essays on the topic and was responsible for introducing the term '*neo-liberalismo*' into Chile.[138] Drawing on his German colleague Walter Eucken, who remained in Germany under the Nazis, Röpke argued that the widespread politicisation of a 'totalitarian' system deprives people of 'the freedom of moral decision essential to Christianity'.[139] Röpke argued that the experience of Nazism made clear to both Catholics and Protestants that they must build an anti-totalitarian society and economy 'which would express both Christian and liberal ideas'.[140] Against both the 'doctrinaire ideology of modern democracy' and *laissez-faire*, Röpke upheld an idea of freedom that 'guarantees the rights of the person, limits the action of the State' and secures the rights of families, minorities and religious groups. A précis for liberalism, he argues, could be written drawing only on the writings of the Roman statesman Cicero and the medieval Christian theologian Thomas Aquinas, in whom we find the 'venerable patrimony of the personalist philosophy' that was crystallised in the political philosophy of the Catholic Church.[141] The social goal of the Church, Röpke argued, was to dissipate class struggle and rescue the economy from 'an omnivorous collectivism' – which was 'exactly what the representatives of neo-liberalism hold'.[142]

Hayek's own approach to religion was pragmatic; he believed 'most people need it' because religion fosters submission to the principles and

---

137   Ibid.
138   It first appeared in Wilhelm Röpke's essay 'Social-cristianismo y neo-liberalismo' in 1964. Taylor C. Boas and Jordan Gans-Morse, 'From Rallying Cry to Whipping Boy: The Concept of Neoliberalism in the Study of Development', Annual Meeting of the American Political Science Association, Philadelphia, 2006, p. 24; Wilhelm Röpke, 'Social-Cristianismo y Neo-Liberalismo', PEC 67, 68 (1964), pp. 6–8, 2–3, 6.
139   Wilhelm Röpke, 'Liberalism and Christianity', Modern Age 1: 2 (1957), p. 128.
140   Ibid., p. 128.
141   Ibid., p. 130.
142   Ibid., p. 131.

traditions on which civilisation depends.[143] This focus on securing submission provided a bridge between neoliberal defences of the market and Catholic anti-totalitarianism. While the agnostic Hayek came to see the value of religion, and particularly Christianity, in securing a market order, he also helped to convince Chilean conservatives that depoliticising civil society and protecting 'natural' hierarchies, the Church and the family required a competitive market order.

Jaime Guzmán, who drafted the junta's 1974 Declaration of Principles, had been interested in using law to depoliticise Chilean society since his early days as president of the Catholic University Law School's Student Union. As a student, Guzmán led the ultraconservative Catholic *gremialista* student group, which united with the Chicago Boys in 1967 to oppose a student revolt demanding democratic selection of the university hierarchy.[144] Guzmán – then a devotee of the fascist corporatism of Franco's Spanish dictatorship and the reactionary anti-liberal Catholic tradition of Juan Donoso Cortés and Joseph de Maistre – was never a friend of democracy. In Chile, that tradition was represented by Jaime Eyzaguirre and Osvaldo Lira, the latter of whom was an early disciple of Jacques Maritain, who contributed to the early stages of the UDHR, and who Lira described as 'one of the greatest neo-Scholastic figures'.[145] For this conservative corporatist tradition, the person was enmeshed in intermediate institutions that were threatened by the intrusions of those Lira termed the 'ignorant, uncultivated and unintelligent' masses.[146] Guzmán's Declaration of Principles reflected this tradition by defining the role of social power as 'securing the independence and depoliticisation of all intermediate societies between individuals and the state'.[147] It was this goal, and a common 'totalitarian' adversary, that facilitated Guzmán's reconciliation of conservative Catholicism with neoliberalism. The ultimate outcome was Chile's 1980 'Constitution of Liberty'. In

---

143 Cited in Erwin Dekker, 'Left Luggage: Finding the Relevant Context of Austrian Economics', *Review of Austrian Economics* 29: 2 (2016), p. 114. For a fuller account of Hayek's views on religion and submission see Jessica Whyte, 'The Invisible Hand of Friedrich Hayek: Submission and Spontaneous Order', *Political Theory*, 47: 2 (2019).

144 See Valdés, *Pinochet's Economists*.

145 Renato Cristi and Carlos Ruiz, 'Conservative Thought in Twentieth Century Chile', *Canadian Association of Latin American and Caribbean Studies* 15: 30 (1990), p. 45.

146 Ibid., p. 48.

147 Ibid., p. 50.

indicting the lawlessness of the junta, human rights NGOs missed the central place given to law and rights in its attempt to tear up the political foundations of Chilean society.

A Constitution of Liberty

In 1991, following Guzmán's assassination on the campus of the Catholic University, Piñera described him as a 'martyr of the revolution', adding that they had 'fought together many battles for liberty, democracy and human rights.'[148] If these men were struggling for human rights – and it is worth temporarily suspending disbelief – this was a distinctive notion of human rights for which preserving human dignity required protecting the person (and the market) from the political revolt of the masses. Guzmán, as his biographer Renato Cristi correctly notes, was more than Pinochet's 'crown jurist': 'When it came to constitutional matters, Guzmán wore the crown.'[149] The story of human rights and neoliberalism in Chile is not simply a story of the massive human rights violations that accompanied market reforms, or of the new human rights NGOs that contested the Junta's violence. It is also the story of the institutionalisation of the conservative vision of neoliberal human rights, whose development I have traced in the previous chapters. Chile was the testing ground for a model of individual rights that aimed to depoliticise civil society and preserve the inequalities of a market order by protecting the market from the intrusions of 'the masses'.

In June 1976, Guzmán responded to criticisms of the junta's human rights record by arguing that the 'theme of human rights is a problem of free, modern states'. Faced with terroristic, international communism, he continued, it is necessary to 'guarantee the rights of all the persons within a community', especially the 'majority who want to live in peace.'[150] Guzmán's understanding of rights gave a neoliberal twist to Schmitt's assertion that 'there exists no norm that is applicable to chaos.'[151] If a

---

148   José Piñera, 'Chile's Road to Freedom', *José Piñera* (blog), 11 March 2018, at josepinera.org.

149   Renato Cristi, 'The Metaphysics of Constituent Power: Schmitt and the Genesis of Chile's 1980 Constitution', *Cardoso Law Review* 21: 5–6 (2000), p. 1769.

150   In Silvia Borzutzky, *Human Rights Policies in Chile: The Unfinished Struggle for Truth and Justice* (New York: Palgrave Macmillan, 2017), p. 120.

151   Schmitt, *Political Theology*.

functioning competitive market is the only guarantee of social peace and human rights, Guzmán believed, then it is legitimate to suspend the rights of those who threaten the market order. Far from renouncing law and rights, Guzmán was central to the adoption of a constitution that locked in the junta's reforms by emphasising a version of freedom 'intrinsically connected to private property, free enterprise, and individual rights'.[152] Like Hayek's major work, published two decades earlier, Chile's constitution was called *The Constitution of Liberty*. Hayek's biographer Bruce Caldwell has argued that, although Hayek's books were in Guzmán's library, 'relevant testimonies doubt that Guzmán had read them'.[153] Yet, in 1987, Guzmán himself attributed his conversion to neoliberalism to his 'discovery of Hayek'.[154] In Hayek's work, Pinochet's crown jurist found proposals for a 'constitution of liberty' that would protect the market from (democratic) interference.[155]

In his late works, Hayek argued that the 'spontaneous order' of the market required an appropriate legal regime to insulate it from political intervention. While he argued that the rules governing individual conduct themselves evolve through a process of selection, he believed it was at least possible that the rules on which a spontaneous order rests may be designed.[156] Rather than a doctrine of *laissez-faire* that precludes all constructivism, Hayekian neoliberalism aimed to fine-tune rules to secure submission to the overall order.[157] When asked in 1978 whether his account of spontaneous order inherently biased outcomes 'in favour of past discriminations or past inequities', Hayek responded bluntly: 'It

---

152   Karin Fischer, 'The Influence of Neoliberals in Chile Before, During, and After Pinochet', in Philip Mirowski and Dieter Plehwe, eds, *The Road from Mont Pèlerin: The Making of the Neoliberal Thought Collective* (Cambridge, MA: Harvard University Press, 2009), pp. 327–8.

153   Caldwell and Montes, 'Friedrich Hayek and His Visits to Chile', p. 47.

154   In an interview of 22 August 1987, Guzmán told Constable and Valenzuela that 'his discovery of Hayek had significantly altered his own views since 1974, when he wrote the regime's "Declaration of Principles" with its corporatist tone'. Constable and Valenzuela, *Nation of Enemies*, p. 340.

155   Fischer, 'Influence of Neoliberals in Chile', p. 327.

156   Friedrich Hayek, *Law, Legislation and Liberty: A New Statement of the Liberal Principles of Justice and Political Economy, vol. I: Rules and Order* (London: Routledge, 1998), p. 45.

157   See Miguel Vatter, 'Neoliberalism and Republicanism: Economic Rule of Law and Law as Concrete Order (Nomos)', in Damien Cahill, Melinda Cooper, Matijn Konings and David Primrose, eds, *The SAGE Handbook of Neoliberalism* (London: Sage, 2018), pp. 370–81; Whyte, 'The Invisible Hand of Friedrich Hayek'.

accepts historical accidents.'[158] It was this conservative reverence for 'spontaneous' evolution that made Hayek's thought attractive to Catholic antitotalitarians in Pinochet's administration, and to the traditional Chilean right, who were horrified by the 'levelling' policies of Allende's government. Asked about the vigilante killings carried out on behalf of large land-owners seeking to reclaim their expropriated property in the wake of the coup, a Chilean judge showed what was at stake in such respect for 'historical accidents'. 'From time immemorial, we sat at the table and the maid didn't', he said. 'People did not want that hierarchy to change.'[159] For all his talk of spontaneity, Hayek was convinced that 'favourable accidents do not just happen. We must prepare for them.'[160] In Chile, Hayek saw the miracle of a state that was prepared to use its powers to prepare the terrain for such favourable accidents by constitutionally protecting the market.

In *The Constitution of Liberty*, Hayek identified constitutionalism ('the principle of legal limitation of power by higher principles to Parliament itself') as the key US contribution to politics.[161] This principle of constitutionally limited government, he argued, used 'inviolable individual rights' to bind temporary majorities.[162] While the United States was founded on a British tradition of liberty, he remarked elsewhere, South America was rooted in the French Revolution and 'overly influenced by the totalitarian type of ideologies' of popular sovereignty.[163] In a normal situation, Hayek believed that judicial review would be sufficient to prevent government overstepping the margin of freedom provided by the constitution – just as the US Supreme Court had done when, in 'its most spectacular decision', it had 'saved the country from an ill-conceived measure' by striking down President Roosevelt's New Deal National Recovery Administration Act.[164] In Chile, by contrast, he saw a crisis that could only be averted by a 'liberal dictator'.[165]

158   Friedrich Hayek et al., *Nobel Prize-Winning Economist Oral History Transcript*, (Los Angeles: Oral History Program, University of California, Los Angeles, 1983), p. 342, at archive.org.

159   Constable and Valenzuela, *Nation of Enemies*, p. 126.

160   Friedrich Hayek, *The Constitution of Liberty: The Definitive Edition*, ed. Ronald Hamowy (Chicago: University of Chicago Press, 2011), p. 82.

161   Ibid., p. 262.

162   Ibid., p. 270.

163   Friedrich Hayek, 'Liberty Clean of Impurities: Extracts from an Interview with Friedrich von Hayek', *El Mercurio*, 12 April 1981.

164   Hayek, *Constitution of Liberty*, p. 284.

165   Hayek, 'Liberty Clean of Impurities'.

During the first of his two visits to Chile during the junta's rule, Hayek spoke with Pinochet about the dangers of 'unlimited democracy'.[166] As Hayek recalls, the general listened carefully, and requested that he send him any materials he had written on the question.[167] While the Austrian economist might conceivably have sent a large bundle of his writings, his secretary recalls that he asked her to send the chapter 'The Model Constitution' from his three-volume work *Law, Legislation and Liberty*.[168] There, Hayek used the term 'unlimited democracy' to refer to the 'particular form of representative government that now prevails in the Western world'.[169] Doubting that a functioning market had ever arisen under such a democracy, he also suggested it was likely that such unlimited democracy would destroy an existing market order.[170] 'The Model Constitution' also forthrightly defends emergency powers; 'freedom may have to be temporarily suspended', Hayek wrote, echoing Carl Schmitt, 'when those institutions are threatened which are intended to preserve it in the long run'.[171]

Hayek expanded on these themes in a 1981 interview with the Chilean newspaper *El Mercurio*. Echoing Schmitt, he argued that, when a government is in a 'situation of rupture', it is 'practically inevitable for someone to have absolute powers'.[172] As the market is necessary to preserve freedom, when the market is threatened, society may temporarily be converted into an organisation, and government may rule by decree. He would prefer a 'liberal dictator', he told the newspaper, to a 'democratic government lacking in liberalism'.[173] This was not the first time Hayek had expressed sympathy for liberal dictators. In 1978, he

---

166 Hayek visited Chile twice during the rule of the military junta, once in 1977 and again in 1981. Cited in Caldwell and Montes, 'Friedrich Hayek and His Visits to Chile', p. 279.

167 Andrew Farrant and Edward McPhail, 'Can a Dictator Turn a Constitution into a Can-Opener? F. A. Hayek and the Alchemy of Transitional Dictatorship in Chile', *Review of Political Economy* 26: 3 (2014), p. 336.

168 Caldwell and Montes, 'Friedrich Hayek and His Visits to Chile', p. 285.

169 Hayek, *Law, Legislation and Liberty, vol. I* (London: Routledge, 1998), p. 3.

170 Ibid., p. 72.

171 Ibid., p. 111. In *The Constitution of Liberty*, Hayek writes that, when it comes to the rule of law, 'the conduct of Carl Schmitt under the Hitler regime does not alter the fact that, of the modern German writings on the subject, his are still among the most learned and perceptive'. Hayek, *Constitution of Liberty*, note 1, p. 309.

172 Hayek, 'Liberty Clean of Impurities'.

173 In Farrant, McPhail, and Berger, 'Preventing the "Abuses" of Democracy', p. 514.

singled out Pinochet and the Portuguese dictator Oliveira Salazar as leaders of 'authoritarian governments under which personal liberty was safer than under many democracies'. In 1962, he sent Salazar a copy of *The Constitution of Liberty* with a note expressing his hope that it would help the dictator 'design a constitution which is proof against the abuses of democracy'. Five years later, Hayek praised the regime of Indonesia's General Suharto – also brought to power by a CIA-backed anti-communist coup – in similar terms.[174] In each case, the threat that democracies would interfere with the 'spontaneous order' of the market led him to support brutally violent dictatorships that were prepared to take all necessary measures to preserve existing inequalities.

In Chile, Hayek praised the junta for its willingness to run the country 'without being obsessed with popular commitments or political expectations of any kind'.[175] Coercion was justified, he believed, to 'provide an effective external framework within which self-generating orders can form'.[176] The fragile 'spontaneous order' of the market required a strong state to protect it from political interference. James Buchanan struck a similar note in his paper 'Limited or Unlimited Democracy', presented at the regional Mont Pèlerin Society meeting in Viña del Mar, the Chilean seaside town where the coup was plotted. The Virginia School neoliberal criticised the 'totalitarian thrust of unlimited democracy', and stressed that any government (whether a democracy or a 'junta') must be strictly limited for the sake of 'insuring and protecting individual liberties'.[177] Contemplating the return to democracy, Baraona, twice minister for the economy during Pinochet's rule, argued that Chile's 'new democracy . . . will have to be authoritarian, in the sense that the rules needed for the system's stability cannot be subjected to political processes'. The single proactive role of the state, he contended, would be 'to enforce market discipline on society'.[178] In Chile, constitutionally enshrined rights, including human rights, became tools for enforcing such market discipline.

---

174   Cited in Farrant and McPhail, 'Can a Dictator Turn a Constitution into a Can-Opener?', pp. 336–41.

175   Cited in Caldwell and Montes, 'Friedrich Hayek and His Visits to Chile', p. 280.

176   Hayek, *Law, Legislation and Liberty, vol. I*, p. 140.

177   James M. Buchanan, 'Democracy: Limited or Unlimited?', Viña del Mar Regional Meeting of the Mont Pèlerin Society (Viña del Mar: Center for Study of Public Choice, 1981), pp. 1–14.

178   Boas and Gans-Morse, 'From Rallying Cry to Whipping Boy', p. 43.

Men Are Born Free and Equal, in Dignity and Rights

The junta's blend of conservative Catholicism and neoliberalism found its definitive expression in the country's 1980 constitution, which combined a Catholic stress on dignity, freedom of conscience, the protected status of the Church and the centrality of the family as 'the basic core of society', with commitments to private enterprise, 'choice', market competition and human rights. Incongruously for a constitution introduced by a torturous dictatorship, its first article was: 'Men are born free and equal, in dignity and rights.'[179] Approved in a plebiscite that was officially described as 'free, secret and informed', but which was held in a climate of intense repression in which no electoral rolls existed and a blank vote was counted as 'yes', the constitution provided the blueprint for the junta's 'protected democracy'. Americas Watch – formed as an off-shoot of what became Human Rights Watch to head off claims that the organisation was a US Cold War front – concluded it was 'not in a position to determine' what the result would have been under fair voting procedures. Even 'Pinochet's critics', it suggested, 'have acknowledged that in 1980 the government had an unusually high degree of support in part because the economy was doing very well'. Americas Watch recounted that many had pointed to 'the trauma of the 1970–73 period as having helped General Pinochet secure approval for the constitution.'[180]

The claim that the economy was 'doing very well' at the time of the plebiscite tells us more about the class politics of this US-based human rights organisation than about Chile's economy. Gallup polls prior to the plebiscite showed very high levels of satisfaction with Pinochet's regime among the upper class, 58.8 per cent of whom (as against only 33.2 per cent of the middle class) described the worst possible outcome of a no vote as a 'return to the year 1973'.[181] In 1980, real wages were still only 88.5 per cent of their 1970 level, and unemployment and inequality had both spiralled. Those for whom the economy was 'doing very well' were

---

179   Hon. Government Junta et al., 'Constitution of the Republic of Chile', Pub. L. No. 1150 (1980), pdf at confinder.richmond.edu.

180   Americas Watch Committee, *Chile: Human Rights & the Plebiscite* (New York: Americas Watch Committee, 1988), pp. 27–8.

181   The answer of Allende's constituents, the working-class and urban and rural poor, were not cited.

a small, wealthy minority.[182] In tracing support for the plebiscite to the 'trauma' of Allende's rule, Americas Watch echoed the views of this minority and of the major producers' organisations, which published manifestos in *El Mercurio* warning of a return to Allende's chaos if the plebiscite failed.

If, in 2016, Chile still shared with Mexico the dubious honour of being the most unequal country in the world, this was in no small part a product of the success of the Pinochet regime in consolidating its economic agenda through constitutional means.[183] It is through this lens that we should view debates about the status of the human rights defined in the constitution. Defenders of the constitution note that it enshrined more rights than the constitution it replaced, while critics have tended to dismiss these rights as window-dressing that entrenched the arbitrary power of Pinochet and the military.[184] For Americas Watch, the move to establish a new constitution that limited sovereignty by 'respect for the essential rights originating from human nature' (Article 5) was a flawed but positive step. From the perspective this book has advanced, human rights were not mere window-dressing. Rather, the Pinochet constitution embodied the realisation, which the neoliberals had achieved as early as the 1940s, that the institutionalisation of human rights could prevent political interference with the inequalities of the competitive market, and depoliticise civil society.

This is most obviously true of Article 24, which proclaims the 'right of ownership in its diverse aspects over all classes of corporeal and incorporeal property', including 'rights of private citizens over waters'; or Article 22, which outlaws discrimination in favour of state companies. On closer inspection, even what first appear to be social and economic rights (to health, education and social security) are actually rights of private enterprise to compete in offering relevant services on the same terms as the state. The right to education, for instance, gives parents the 'preferential right and duty to educate their children', and private companies free rein in establishing education providers. The result of these education rights, as their architect Piñera celebrates on his website today, has been the 'prevalence of private education' in Chile.[185] Such rights were based on a

---

182   Taylor, *From Pinochet to the 'Third Way'*, p. 60.

183   Organisation for Economic Co-operation and Development, 'Income Inequality Update', November 2016, pdf at oecd.org.

184   Caldwell and Montes, 'Friedrich Hayek and His Visits to Chile', p. 288.

185   Piñera, 'Chile's Road to Freedom'.

blend of neoliberal market ideology with the Catholic principle of 'subsidiarity', which entailed that the state would fulfil only those functions that could not be fulfilled by intermediate institutions or the private sector.[186] Consequently, the constitution stipulated that educational and other intermediate institutions should be free of politics, and introduced penalties for those who violated this stricture. Going further, it declared it unconstitutional to use or incite political violence or 'advocate the establishment of a totalitarian system'.

It was in this context that many on the left began using the language of human rights. Those who remained committed to Marxism found that, while they were more likely to escape repression by framing their claims in the language of human rights, making themselves heard in this discursive space required them to adopt a depoliticised, legalistic language. At great personal risk, communist militants protested for the release of their relatives and comrades, notably holding a ten-day hunger strike inside the ECLA office in Santiago in 1977. As the regime depicted 'international communism' as a threat to the country's wellbeing, and subjected active communists and labour organisers to torture and disappearance, these militants obscured their political affiliations and presented their demands in neutral, humanitarian terms. While they did not initially use the language of human rights, when their protest was portrayed as a human rights campaign by UN figures and the foreign press, they adopted this language, appealing to the UDHR in a letter to the UN secretary-general, Kurt Waldheim.[187]

While key figures in Pinochet's regime described Marxism as a cancer, human rights, stripped of all relation to political violence, redistribution and revolutionary aspiration, became part of the Christian 'Western' heritage within which they wished to position Chile – thus the repeated references in the 1980 constitution to dignity, 'freedom of conscience' and human rights. There is no doubt that regime figures were aggravated by the attentions of organisations like Amnesty International, which they believed would be better directed at the Soviet Union or Vietnam.[188] Nonetheless, while the attentions of human rights organisations were focused on the regime's violent means, they did not challenge

---

186   Renato Cristi, 'The Genealogy of Jaime Guzmán's Subsidiary State', in Robert Leeson, ed., *Hayek: A Collaborative Biography, Part IX: The Divine Right of the 'Free' Market* (London: Palgrave Macmillan, 2017), p. 256.

187   Salgado, 'Communism and Human Rights in Pinochet's Chile'.

188   Constable and Valenzuela, *Nation of Enemies*.

its ends. Today, Chile is not only a highly unequal neoliberal society. It is also a society in which the judiciary has been rehabilitated, as human rights NGOs have promoted a 'new constitutionalism' that limits legislative power in the name of human rights.[189]

The shift from armed anticolonial struggle to Amnesty's brand of human rights activism was stark. In Chile, Amnesty's impartiality and refusal of violence gave it a legitimacy that enabled it to travel the country and speak out against torture and disappearance. But it simultaneously contributed to normalising a closure of the political imagination and delegitimising other emancipatory visions.[190] As one sociologist writes, in the face of the depoliticisation of Chilean society in the wake of the coup, human rights is now 'the sole base on which a better future can be constructed'.[191] Just as Harberger and his neoliberal colleagues once hoped, Chile has been transformed from a 'society in which political mobilisation was the characteristic route to recognition into one where individual access to the market is the preferred means of advancement' – a development fostered by the extension of credit, which has made consumption available to the poor at the cost of entwining them in a disciplinary relation of indebtedness.[192] In the wake of the junta, torture and disappearance have been largely replaced by ongoing human rights trials. Even so, key aspects of the junta's programme remain, along with two of its most significant commitments: the subjection of politics to law, and a conservative Catholic suspicion of mass politics.

One might have expected that the end of the junta and the election of a democratic government coalition, La Concertación de Partidos por la Democracia, would mark a break with the 'limited' or 'protected' democracy instituted by Guzmán and supported by his neoliberal allies. Quite the opposite is true. As Fernando Atria notes: 'Democratic politics is no longer seen as the best insurance against human rights violations, but as

---

189   Javier Couso, 'Models of Democracy and Models of Constitutionalism: The Case of Chile's Constitutional Court, 1970–2010', *Texas Law Review* 89: 7 (2011), pp. 1517–36.

190   Benenson presented Amnesty International's brand of anti-political human rights activism as a more credible alternative to the CPGP-sponsored 'Appeal for Amnesty in Spain'. Buchanan, 'The Truth Will Set You Free', p. 580-81.

191   Jorge Larrain, 'Changes in Chilean Identity: Thirty Years after the Military Coup', *Nations and Nationalism* 12: 2 (2006), p. 337.

192   Ibid., p. 334.

the primary danger.'[193] As Atria suggests, while in some contexts it may be reasonable to assume that judges should protect individual rights and the constitution from democratic politics, in Chile, whose key problem has been authoritarian anti-democratic tendencies, including in the judiciary, this focus is difficult to justify. It was Pinochet's 1980 constitution that first gave judges a substantial role in adjudicating matters which, prior to the coup, belonged to the political process. But 2005 amendments to the constitution, after the 'return to democracy', dramatically *expanded* the powers of the constitutional court to determine the constitutionality of legislation, in the name of protecting human rights.

The consequence has been what one Chilean scholar calls an 'unprecedented willingness by the Constitutional Court to strike down legislation deemed contrary to the constitution' or to international human rights law.[194] Today, the courts are increasingly involved in adjudicating matters of healthcare, tax policy and sexuality rights. Simultaneously, 'helped logistically by a dense network of international nongovernmental organisations', marginalised groups have been encouraged to channel their struggles through the courts on the assumption that, given its 'rights-oriented' ethos, the judiciary will be better able to support the marginalised and subaltern than the political process.[195] In reality, the results of this process have been 'very frustrating' for the most marginalised groups, notably prisoners and indigenous people, as the courts have been unwilling to challenge widespread abuse in the prison system or the continued use of Pinochet-era counterterror laws against the Mapuche.[196] Today, the neoliberal programme remains in place, while, in the name of human rights, Chile's constitutional order restrains democracy and closes down the margin of freedom in ways that Guzmán could not have imagined.

---

193   Fernando Atria, 'The Time of Law: Human Rights Between Law and Politics', *Law and Critique* 16: 2 (2005), p. 150.

194   Couso, 'Models of Democracy', p. 1535.

195   Javier Couso, 'The Limits of Law for Emancipation (in the South)', *Griffith Law Review* 16: 2 (2007), p. 350.

196   Ibid., p. 350; Gaitán-Barrera and Azeez, 'Beyond Recognition', p. 117; Human Rights Watch, 'World Report 2018' (New York: Human Rights Watch, 2017), p. 136.

5

Powerless Companions or Fellow Travellers? Human Rights and the Neoliberal Assault on Post-Colonial Economic Justice

The aim must be to reduce inequality in every area where it is found. To do this therefore we must refashion, or 'revolutionise', the laws which lead to the reproduction of the relations of domination and exploitation.

Mohammed Bedjaoui

Attempts to enforce the [New International Economic Order] would lead to a Hobbesian war of all against all, to a spread of totalitarian government, and to further erosion of the West.

Peter Bauer and Basil Yamey

In early 1985, the development economist Peter Bauer used a speaking opportunity at a Paris colloquium to reiterate the central tenets of the neoliberal development discourse he had done so much to shape. Bauer, aptly described by the *Economist* magazine as being to foreign aid what Friedrich Hayek was to socialism, told his audience that the so-called 'Third World' comprised 130 countries with nothing in common other than requesting and receiving help from 'the West'.[1] In a period of neoliberal ascendancy, criticisms of aid and of demands for postcolonial redistribution of wealth were increasingly common. What made this particular speech different was the fact that Bauer was speaking at the

---

1 Peter Bauer, 'L'Aide Au Développement: Pour Ou Contre?', in Rony Brauman, ed., *Le Tiers-Mondisme En Question* (Paris: Olivier Orban, 1986), p. 188.

inaugural colloquium of a new political foundation, Liberté sans Frontières (LSF), established by the French leadership of the respected humanitarian organisation Médecins sans Frontières.[2] What was the key neoliberal development theorist doing at such an event? And what can answering this question tell us about the relation between human rights and neoliberalism in that period – and our own?

Although LSF was billed, innocuously, as a research centre devoted to the problems of development and human rights, its first organised event, a colloquium titled 'Le Tiers-Mondisme en question' ('Third Worldism in Question'), revealed its political bent. The foundation was established to challenge the affirmations of postcolonial sovereignty and economic self-determination that defined *tiers-mondisme* – the movement that insisted (as Alfred Sauvy stressed when, in 1952, he coined the term 'Tiers Monde' through analogy with Emmanuel Sieyès's account of France's revolutionary Third Estate) that those colonised or recently decolonised peoples who had been ignored, exploited and reduced to nothing now 'wanted to be something'.[3] LSF's introductory materials criticised *tiers-mondisme* for promoting 'simplistic' theses that blamed underdevelopment on the looting of the Third World by the West, the deterioration of the terms of trade, the power of multinationals, and the development of cash crops at the expense of food crops.[4]

An examination of Liberté sans Frontières directs attention to the economic questions that the human rights NGOs in Latin America largely disregarded. Far from vacating the economic field and confining itself to criticising violations of civil and political rights, as Amnesty International had done in Chile, LSF mobilised the language of human

2　I thank Rony Brauman for confirming that Bauer, whose essay is included in the published proceedings of the colloquium, did present in person.

3　Alfred Sauvy, 'Trois Mondes, Une Planète', *Vingtième Siècle, Revue d'histoire*, October 1986, p. 83; Emmanuel Sieyès, 'What Is the Third Estate?', in Michael Sonenscher, ed., *Political Writings* (Indianapolis: Hackett, 2003), p. 94. Sauvy's concept of the 'Tiers Monde', as Sundhya Pahuja notes, 'designated a political relation, not a set demographic'. Sundhya Pahuja, *Decolonising International Law: Development, Economic Growth, and the Politics of Universality* (Cambridge: Cambridge University Press, 2011), p. 261. It is to designate this antagonistic political relation, at a specific historical juncture, that I use the term 'Third World' in this chapter. The 'Third World', in Vijay Prashad's oft-cited phrase, 'was not a place. It was a project.' Vijay Prashad, *The Poorer Nations: A Possible History of the Global South* (London: Verso, 2013), p. xv.

4　Liberté Sans Frontières, 'Fondation Liberté Sans Frontières pour l'information sur les Droits de l'homme et le Développement, Document de Présentation' (Paris: Médecins Sans Frontières, January 1985), p. 4, at speakingout.msf.org.

rights explicitly against Third Worldist demands for postcolonial economic redistribution. Rony Brauman, a former member of the Maoist Gauche Prolétarienne, who was president of MSF and director of LSF, later reflected that he was interested in contesting the idea that 'poverty, misery in the Global South was the by-product of our prosperity in the Global North'. This idea placed the 'blame' for postcolonial poverty on the 'shoulders of the Global North', rather than on those postcolonial leaders he believed bore responsibility for their peoples' plights.[5] LSF went beyond merely criticising the violation of human rights to contest what it depicted as a Western guilt complex over colonialism.

A particular target of LSF's campaign was the demand for postcolonial economic restructuring that found its most important expression in the Non-Aligned Movement–sponsored proposal for a 'New International Economic Order' (NIEO). Adopted by the United Nations General Assembly in 1974, the NIEO declaration aimed at an international economic order 'which shall correct inequalities and redress existing injustices'.[6] The NIEO consolidated the postcolonial demand for a right to economic self-determination, examined in Chapter 3. Its ambitious programme for reorganising the postcolonial international economic order amounted to a neoliberal nightmare defined by effective control over natural resources, regulation of the activities of multinational corporations, just commodity prices, technology transfers, debt forgiveness and monetary reform. In 1997, Brauman reflected that when he had founded LSF he was 'ferociously anti-Third Worldist', because he felt that Third Worldist claims about Northern responsibility in the economic and social disaster of the South, and the need for 'a New Economic Order', reflected 'at best derisory sentimentalism and at worst complicity with the bloodiest regimes'.[7] Far from merely criticising postcolonial violence, LSF challenged the entire anticolonial economic agenda.

The vision of human rights promoted by figures associated with LSF was far from being what Samuel Moyn calls a 'powerless companion' of

5   Author interview with Rony Brauman, MSF Office, Rue Saint-Sabin, Paris, 7 October 2015.

6   United Nations General Assembly, 'Declaration on the Establishment of a New International Economic Order' (United Nations Documents, 1 May 1974), at un-documents.net. No vote was requested on this resolution.

7   Stany Grelet and Mathieu Potte-Bonneville, 'Qu'est-Ce Qu'on Fait Là ? Entretien Avec Rony Brauman', *Vacarme*, 2 September 1997.

ascendant neoliberalism.[8] Rather, LSF's leadership drew on the rejection of structuralist economic analyses and redistribution pioneered by rising neoliberal thinkers, and used the language of human rights to shift responsibility for poverty from international economic arrangements onto Third World states. LSF offers a particularly stark example of a more general phenomenon – the uptake of neoliberal ideas by human rights NGOs in the period of their simultaneous rise. Like the dominant strand of human rights politics in Europe and the United States at the time, LSF embraced a dichotomy promoted by neoliberal thinkers between politics as violent, coercive and ultimately 'totalitarian', on the one hand, and the market or 'civil society', on the other, as a realm of free, mutually beneficial, voluntary relations. LSF went further than most, however, in directly entering the economic fray to prosecute an argument against postcolonial economic equality and in favour of a liberal economy. In doing so, it lent its moral prestige to the neoliberal counterattack on the struggle for postcolonial economic justice, and became complicit in the dramatic deepening of inequality that has been its consequence. Moreover, it helped to shape a distinctively neoliberal human rights discourse, in which civil and political rights are essential aspects of the institutional structure necessary to facilitate a liberal market order.

Liberté sans Frontières and the Question of Human Rights

The inaugural LSF colloquium, 'Le tiers-mondisme en question', was held in January 1985 in the voluptuous surrounds of the Palais de Luxembourg. A central theme of the colloquium was the need for a shift from political ideology to human rights.[9] But the version of human rights LSF promoted was not ideologically neutral. LSF's board largely comprised MSF officials and intellectuals of the 'liberal conservative right'.[10] It drew many of its personnel from the anti-communist Comité des intellectuels pour l'Europe des libertés (CIEL),

---

8 Samuel Moyn, 'A Powerless Companion: Human Rights in the Age of Neoliberalism', *Law and Contemporary Problems* 77 (2015).

9 Eleanor Davey, 'Famine, Aid, and Ideology: The Political Activism of Médecins sans Frontières in the 1980s', *French Historical Studies* 34: 3 (2011), p. 543.

10 The description is Brauman's. Grelet and Potte-Bonneville, 'Qu'est-Ce Qu'on Fait Là ?'

(Jean-Claude Casanova and Jean-François Revel) and the Reaganite anti-communist organisation Resistance International (Jacques Broyelle, François Furet, Alain Besançon).[11] Brauman recalls that when he and Claude Malhuret first approached the latter about joining LSF's board, Besançon, an anti-communist historian of the Soviet Union, outlined five conditions: the foundation must be 'pro-European, pro-American, anti-communist, anti-Soviet and pro-Israeli.'[12] 'We said fine, it's perfect', Brauman recalls. 'This is what we think.'[13] It was this bundle of commitments that were central to LSF's understanding of human rights. In defending human rights, participants at the colloquium stressed that 'the ravages of authoritarian planning were greater than those of capitalism', Brauman reflected, and that 'liberal, free enterprise societies were the most efficacious in preventing political and economic catastrophe.'[14]

The influence of Marxism on the French left, as the anti-totalitarian political philosopher Claude Lefort had noted five years earlier, had generated a 'vehement, ironic or "scientific" condemnation of the bourgeois notion of human rights.'[15] Throughout the 1970s, however, this condemnation had increasingly been replaced with a new human rights ideology, spurred in part by the publication of Solzhenitsyn's *The Gulag Archipelago*. As has been well noted, the growing influence of Soviet dissidents helped to discredit revolutionary Marxism, clearing away a major barrier to the widespread acceptance of human rights as a progressive cause.[16] In France, increasingly fervent attacks on Marxism coincided with the rise of what the French 'New Philosopher' André Glucksmann termed a 'humanism of bad news', which aimed to

---

11   Alain Gresh, 'Une Fondation Au-Dessus de Tout Soupçon', *Le Monde Diplomatique*, May 1985.

12   Author interview with Rony Brauman, MSF Office, Rue Saint-Sabin, Paris, 7 October 2015.

13   Ibid. Brauman described the last of these conditions as 'the fifth, but not the last, not the least!'

14   Brauman, cited in Renée C. Fox, *Doctors Without Borders: Humanitarian Quests, Impossible Dreams of Médecins Sans Frontières* (Baltimore: John Hopkins University Press, 2014), p. 53.

15   Claude Lefort, *The Political Forms of Modern Society: Bureaucracy, Democracy, Totalitarianism*, ed. John B. Thompson (Cambridge: Polity, 1986), p. 900.

16   Robert Horvath, ' "The Solzhenitsyn Effect": East European Dissidents and the Demise of the Revolutionary Privilege', *Human Rights Quarterly* 29: 4 (2007), pp. 879–907; Samuel Moyn, *Not Enough: Human Rights in an Unequal World* (Harvard, MA: Harvard University Press, 2018).

ameliorate the status quo while recasting the promise of emancipatory social transformation as totalitarian.[17]

At the time of the LSF Colloquium, Brauman situated LSF's 'ideology of *droits de l'homme*' in the context of the demise of political messianism, and within a new morality of urgency for which 'man' becomes the ultimate end.[18] This moralised human rights discourse, expressed in the claim to be concerned with 'man' and 'human realities' rather than messianic, utopian ideologies, was shared by many human rights activists at the time. But LSF's human rights campaign differed from the moral 'anti-politics' of human rights epitomised by Amnesty International. While the latter NGO shared both LSF's antipathy to politics and its focus on civil and political rights, it attempted to avoid Cold War polarisation by focusing on the 'suffering simply because they are suffering', and adopting prisoners of conscience on either side of the Iron Curtain.[19] LSF fiercely rejected such even-handedness; its leadership joined the Cold War fray, prosecuting an argument for the superiority of liberalism and campaigning against both neutralism and pacifism, which its introductory materials depicted as attempts to 'disarm the democracies and prevent them from defending themselves'.[20]

Just as they rejected neutrality, participants at the LSF colloquium stressed that not all human rights were created equal. Brauman turned to the history of French political thought to distinguish LSF's liberal conception of rights from a vision that presupposed a robust account of popular sovereignty. He rejected the 'maximalist conception inherited from Rousseau' for making democracy a means to the common good, and the state the guarantor of collective welfare.[21] Instead, he upheld a model of rights predicated on the erasure of status divisions, which he attributed to the nineteenth-century liberal Alexis de Tocqueville. By contrasting Rousseau with Tocqueville, Brauman situated LSF's conception of human rights on one side of a debate that pitted the affirmation

---

17   Paul Berman, *Power and the Idealists: Or, the Passion of Joschka Fischer and Its Aftermath* (New York: W. W. Norton, 2007), p. 235.

18   Rony Brauman, 'Ni Tiers-Mondisme, Ni Cartiérisme', in Brauman, *Le Tiers-Mondisme En Question*, p. 12.

19   Tom Buchanan, '"The Truth Will Set You Free": The Making of Amnesty International', *Journal of Contemporary History* 37: 4 (2002), p. 579.

20   Liberté Sans Frontières and Claude Malhuret, 'Invitation de Liberté sans Frontières au Colloque des 23 et 24 Janvier 1985' (Médecins Sans Frontières, 11 January 1985), at speakingout.msf.org.

21   Brauman, 'Ni Tiers-Mondisme, Ni Cartiérisme', p. 13.

of 'the will of the people', which had informed national liberation movements, against a deep, aristocratic–liberal suspicion of 'the masses', and
support for France's colonial mission.[22] In doing so, he positioned his
own human rights politics in a lineage that, as we have seen, the neoliberals also claimed. Hayek's original name for the Mont Pèlerin Society
was the 'Acton-Tocqueville Society', and, as we have seen, the neoliberals
praised Tocqueville's criticisms of mass democracy as a necessary antidote to the totalitarianism of Rousseauian popular sovereignty.[23] This
contrast between Rousseau and Tocqueville enabled Brauman to uphold
a narrow, non-revolutionary conception of human rights, defined by
civil and political rights and equality before the law, both against a
conception of rights as expressions of popular sovereignty, and against
state guarantees of social welfare.

Participants at the LSF colloquium depicted civil and political rights
as 'categorical imperatives', while making clear that social and economic
rights were 'less fundamental, universal, and timelessly important'.[24]
This distinction was borrowed from Raymond Aron, whose influence
on the men who established LSF was such that the foundation came
close to being named the Fondation Raymond Aron pour le Tiers
Monde.[25] Malhuret also placed the foundation in a liberal tradition
stretching from Tocqueville to Aron. 'We were Aronian', he reflected
decades later, 'which means Tocquevillian and Aronian'.[26] The figure
Allan Bloom called 'the last of the liberals' was a distinctly French liberal,
but Aron was also an Atlanticist who played an important role in transatlantic and European liberal networks. He was present at the 1938
Walter Lippmann Colloquium, and at the founding meeting of the Mont
Pèlerin Society just under a decade later.[27]

22   Jennifer Pitts, *A Turn to Empire: The Rise of Imperial Liberalism in Britain and
France* (Princeton: Princeton University Press, 2005), p. 205; Peter Hallward, 'The Will
of the People: Notes Towards a Dialectical Voluntarism', *Radical Philosophy* 155 (June
2009), pp. 17–29.

23   Friedrich Hayek, 'Memorandum on the Proposed Foundation of an International
Academy of Political Philosophy Tentatively Called the "Acton-Tocqueville Society"'
(Albert Hunold Papers, 1 August 1945).

24   Fox, *Doctors Without Borders*, p. 54.

25   See Davey, 'Famine, Aid, and Ideology', p. 543.

26   Author interview with Claude Malhuret, Sénat – Palais du Luxembourg, Paris,
October 7, 2015.

27   Philip Mirowski and Dieter Plehwe, eds, *The Road from Mont Pèlerin: The
Making of the Neoliberal Thought Collective* (Cambridge: Harvard University Press,
2009).

Aron and Hayek were friends, and, despite their differences over the possibility of a 'third way' between the free market and economic planning, which ultimately led to Aron's resignation from the MPS in 1955, the two had strikingly similar views about human rights.[28] Both men criticised the drafters of the UDHR for having 'confused incompatible ideas', in Aron's words, by failing to distinguish rights, which constrained the state in the interests of individual freedom, from social and economic objectives that relied on the extension of state power.[29] In terms that were later taken up by participants at the LSF colloquium, Aron distinguished civil and political rights, which he depicted as what Immanuel Kant had termed 'categorical imperatives', or fundamental moral principles, from social objectives that may be 'theoretically desirable' but do not amount to rights.[30] Just as Hayek had criticised the UDHR by arguing that to speak of rights in a socioeconomic context 'debases the word "right"', Aron argued that, when compared to the 1789 Declaration of the Rights of Man and of the Citizen, the UDHR reflected 'the decline of all rights, of the very notion of the rights of man'.[31] The eighteenth-century authors 'did not entrust the state the goal of promoting what we today call "social and economic rights"', he wrote, but were concerned to *limit* state power. In contrast, the twentieth-century drafters downgraded the right to private property and expanded the powers of the state to provide for the welfare of its population. In this transition, he argued, 'the state is the victor', since rights no longer restrict or condemn it.[32]

Looking back, Brauman reflected that this distinction between 'the categorical imperative, like not to torture people and free speech' and 'wishable social objectives', such as social security, was 'at the core of Liberté sans Frontières'.[33] LSF, like both Aron and Hayek, focused on violations of civil and political rights, and warned that the state mobilisation necessary for social and economic welfare in former colonies

28   Nicholas Gane, 'In and Out of Neoliberalism: Reconsidering the Sociology of Raymond Aron', *Journal of Classical Sociology* 16: 3 (2016), pp. 261–79.

29   Raymond Aron, 'Sociology and the Philosophy of Human Rights', in Dominique Schnapper and Milton Karl Munitz, eds, *Power, Modernity and Sociology: Selected Sociological Writings* (Aldershot: Edward Elgar, 1988), pp. 194–210.

30   Ibid., p. 122.

31   Ibid., p. 129.

32   Ibid., p. 136.

33   Author interview with Rony Brauman, MSF Office, Rue Saint-Sabin, Paris, 7 October 2015. Brauman stressed that he no longer subscribed to this view.

would threaten economic and political freedom. Aron did not share Hayek's contention that wealthy democracies would set forth along the 'road to serfdom' if they attempted to provide for material welfare, but he worried that 'under-developed countries' could not 'make the passage from the formal to the material without recourse to violence.'[34]

The French humanitarians positioned themselves in opposition to both Marxist critiques of the formalism of rights and anticolonial affirmations of self-determination as the foundational human right.[35] This shift in priorities was reflected in the composition of the colloquium: while Third Worldism had stressed the political agency of national liberation movements, no nationals of the countries under discussion spoke at the LSF colloquium.[36] In this respect, LSF emblematised what Kristin Ross suggests is a key legacy of French opposition to Third Worldism: the transformation of the 'colonial or third-world other' from militant and articulate fighter and thinker to passive object of sympathy.[37] Making this shift required a concerted attack on Third Worldist critiques of postcolonial economic exploitation.

Contesting 'Western Guilt'

The invitation to the 'Third Worldism in Question' colloquium was sent by MSF's head, Malhuret, who would soon complete a spectacular transition from medical doctor to secretary of state for human rights in Jacques Chirac's right-wing government. Third Worldism, Malhuret wrote, promotes a few simple ideas: 'the West has looted the resources of the third world, terms of trade have deteriorated, the actions of multinational corporations are harmful.'[38] The invitation framed the colloquium as a challenge to publicly accepted notions like 'the rich world's cows eat the soybeans of the poor', or ' "a new international economic

---

34   Aron, 'Sociology and the Philosophy of Human Rights', p. 136.

35   See Roland Burke, *Decolonization and the Evolution of International Human Rights* (Philadelphia: University of Pennsylvania Press, 2010), p. 35; Joseph R. Slaughter, *Human Rights, Inc.: The World Novel, Narrative Form, and International Law* (New York: Fordham University Press, 2007).

36   Davey, 'Famine, Aid, and Ideology', p. 542.

37   Kristin Ross, *May '68 and Its Afterlives* (Chicago: University of Chicago Press, 2002), p. 167.

38   Liberté Sans Frontières and Malhuret, 'Invitation de Liberté sans Frontières au Colloque''Invitation de Liberté sans Frontières au Colloque'.

order" is the only solution to under-development'.[39] LSF was established, as an article in the *Guardian* noted, to counter Third Worldism, 'which it accuses of feeding on a European guilt complex that blames all the problems of the Third World on Western economic dominance'.[40] Such an analysis, LSF figures argued, serves to excuse those who should bear responsibility for the problems of former colonies: postcolonial states.

In contesting Western responsibility for Third World poverty, the men of LSF set themselves against an analysis of colonial exploitation that had played a central role in anticolonialism, dependency theory and French *tiers-mondisme* in the previous decades. Frantz Fanon's *The Wretched of the Earth* epitomised this argument, powerfully insisting that Europe was, quite literally, a product of the Third World. 'The wealth which smothers her was stolen from the underdeveloped peoples'.[41] This indictment was reiterated by Jean-Paul Sartre in his infamous 1961 preface to Fanon's book. Addressing himself to his French compatriots, Sartre wrote: 'You know well enough that we are exploiters. You know too that we have laid hands on first the gold and metals, then the petroleum of the "new continents", and that we have brought them back to the old countries'.[42] By the time LSF was founded, Sartre's influence had waned, along with the Third Worldism he championed.

By the time of the LSF colloquium, earlier critiques of the complicity of wealthy nations in postcolonial poverty were being usurped by new concerns with human rights abuses in the post-colony.[43] LSF argued that the Asian 'miracle' economies of South Korea, Singapore and Taiwan had been condemned for failing to conform to Third Worldist tenets, while disastrous programmes – in Mao's China, Ho Chi Minh's Vietnam, Julius Nyerere's Tanzania, Kwame Nkrumah's Ghana, Fidel Castro's Cuba, and the Nicaraguan Sandinistas – had been presented as models.[44] In stark contrast to the arguments of Fanon and Sartre, this new anti-totalitarian

---

39   Ibid.

40   Laurence Binet, 'Famine and Forced Relocations in Ethiopia 1984–1986', MSF Speaking Out (Geneva: Médecins Sans Frontières, 2013), p. 100, at speakingout.msf.org.

41   Frantz Fanon, *The Wretched of the Earth* (London: Penguin, 1978), p. 81.

42   Fanon Frantz, 'Preface', in ibid., p. 21.

43   Paige Arthur, *Unfinished Projects: Decolonization and the Philosophy of Jean-Paul Sartre* (London: Verso, 2010).

44   Liberté Sans Frontières, 'Fondation Liberté Sans Frontières Pour l'information Sur Les Droits de l'homme et Le Développement, Document de Présentation', January 1985, p. 3.

human rights organisation focused on left-wing 'totalitarian' regimes, largely ignoring the lamentable human rights records of both the right-wing authoritarian regimes then terrorising much of Latin America and those dictatorial Asian regimes it celebrated.

LSF played a central role in delegitimising Third Worldist accounts of economic exploitation. Its mission, Brauman explained at the time, was 'to challenge a perception of the problem in which their poverty is a reflection of our wealth, and our liberties are based on the absence of theirs'.[45] In his introduction to the published proceedings of the inaugural LSF colloquium, Brauman situated LSF within a new morality of urgency and an ideology of *les droits de l'homme*, which makes 'man' the highest value. Nonetheless, his speech overwhelmingly addressed economic matters, and challenged a series of Third Worldist theses: that Europe had trampled its own values in colonial plunder; that this plunder was the source of Europe's opulence; that the world economic system was a neocolonial system that made the rich richer and the poor poorer; that the Third World was the victim of a blind and cynical West; and that its bread basket was held hostage to the economic powers of Western countries. Such structuralist theses, Brauman argued, were a 'game of mirrors' in which Europe only ever saw itself.[46]

MSF's leading figures, a news article of the time noted, 'are disgusted by the fashionable current wisdom holding the west responsible for the Third World's destitution and that seeks to make us feel guilty about our standard of living'.[47] This theme of guilt and responsibility was taken up most ferociously by Pascal Bruckner, the French essayist and 'New Philosopher' who today is best known for his vehement attacks on multiculturalism and Islam.[48] Bruckner delivered a key speech, 'Third World, Guilt, Self-Hate', at the inaugural LSF colloquium.[49] In *Le Sanglot*

45   Cited in Claude Julien, 'Une Bête à Abattre: Le "Tiers-Mondisme"', *Le Monde Diplomatique*, May 1985.

46   Brauman, 'Ni Tiers-Mondisme, Ni Cartiérisme', p. 16.

47   Laurence Binet, ed., 'Médecins Sans Frontières' Officials Issue an Indictment, Calling Tiers-Mondisme a Sham, Patrick Forestier Interviews Rony Brauman, President of MSF France', *Paris-Match* (France), 23 January 1985 (in French)', in MSF Speaks Out, *Famine and Forced Relocations in Ethiopia 1984–1986* (Geneva: Médecins Sans Frontières, 2013), pp. 24–5, pdf at speakingout.msf.org.

48   Most recently, Bruckner has reprised this theme of Western guilt in Pascal Bruckner, *An Imaginary Racism: Islamophobia and Guilt*, (Cambridge: Polity, 2018).

49   Eyal Weizman, *The Least of All Possible Evils: Humanitarian Violence from Arendt to Gaza* (London: Verso, 2012), p. 40.

de l'homme blanc ('Tears of the White Man'), published just before the colloquium, Bruckner had launched an excoriating attack on what he depicted as the Third Worldist guilt complex about colonialism. 'How long will the peoples of Europe continue to be blamed for the atrocities committed by their ancestors?' he asked – just two decades after France's withdrawal from Algeria.[50] For Bruckner and the founders of LSF, Third Worldism was a product of masochism and guilt, which generated a willingness to tolerate Third World repression. Despite these accusations, the LSF figures implicitly recognised that Third Worldism was what Kristin Ross has termed 'an aggressive new way of accusing the capitalist system' and the neo-imperialist relations that had succeeded formal colonialism.[51] LSF constituted a similarly aggressive counterattack. Its disparate group of liberals, humanitarians, Atlanticists and Reaganites found unity in the rejection of 'Western guilt' over colonialism and opposition to Third Worldist demands for restructuring the international economic order. In doing so, they drew on themes developed by the neoliberals over the previous decades.

The Neoliberal Precedent: The Mont Pèlerin Society and Colonial Guilt

The arguments rehearsed by the humanitarians in the 1980s have more recently become staples of a newer, revisionist 'case for colonialism', but they also have a much older ancestry.[52] Much of their logic can be traced to an earlier stage of neoliberal thinking; the need to challenge what Röpke termed 'the ill-timed Christian emphasis on Western guilt' over colonialism had shaped MPS discussions of development since the early 1950s.[53] The theme of colonial guilt emerged in the context of the controversy over Rüstow's criticisms of the colonial powers for

50 Pascal Bruckner, *The Tears of the White Man: Compassion as Contempt* (New York: Palgrave Macmillan, 1987), p. 119.

51 Ross, *May '68 and Its Afterlives*, p. 163.

52 Bruce Gilley, 'The Case for Colonialism', *Third World Quarterly*, 2017. This article was recently withdrawn by the editor after significant protest and the resignation of many members of the journal's editorial board. See 'Open Letter to *Third World Quarterly* on the Publication of "The Case for Colonialism"', openDemocracy, 20 September 2017, at opendemocracy.net.

53 Dieter Plehwe, 'The Origins of the Neoliberal Economic Development Discourse', in Mirowski and Plehwe, *Road from Mont Pèlerin*, p. 256.

trampling on the 'human dignity of the colonial peoples', which I examined in Chapter 3.[54] Rüstow's argument at the 1957 MPS meeting in Saint Moritz that 'we' still lack guilt and a sense of penitence towards the victims of colonialism reflected his Christian faith. While he also argued that, without European intervention, former colonies would be more 'backward' than they are today, his fellow panellists, Edmond Giscard d'Estaing, Peter Bauer, Karl Brandt and Arthur Shenfield, reacted vehemently to this concern for colonial crimes and to his suggestion that Europeans had something to be guilty about.[55]

Against the backdrop of the Algerian war, Giscard d'Estaing rejected the 'simplification grossière' of depicting colonialism as the domination of one people by another. Colonialism, he suggested, enabled nomadic desert peoples (for instance) to benefit from oil they would otherwise waste. Shenfield and Brandt praised the developmental accomplishments of colonialism, and the latter rejected Rüstow's attribution of guilt: 'one can leave the hypocritical assault on colonialism to those who practice it now with the plain intent to enslave peoples', he contended, referring to the anti-colonialism of the Soviet Union.[56]

At this stage, the MPS discourse on colonialism was classically liberal, and it drew heavily on John Locke's justification of colonialism as 'improvement'. God meant for the earth to be cultivated, Locke had contended, and thus he gave it to the 'industrious and rational'.[57] Those who 'fail' to improve the land – d'Estaing's nomadic desert people who wasted the oil beneath their feet, for instance – had no grounds for complaint if it was appropriated by others. The rise of anticolonialism made the neoliberals starkly aware of the difficulties of maintaining colonial rule, and, more importantly, of securing the continued exploitation of the colonies in its wake. 'I need hardly tell liberals that it is not easy for them to advocate the rule of others for their own good', Shenfield told the panel.[58] Although Shenfield attributed this point to John Stuart Mill, we have seen that Mill believed despotism was legitimate in

54   Alexander Rüstow, *Freedom and Domination: A Historical Critique of Civilization*, ed. Dankwart A. Rüstow, transl. Salvador Attanasio (Princeton, NJ: Princeton University Press, 1978), pp. 662–3.

55   Plehwe, 'Origins of the Neoliberal Economic Development Discourse', p. 254.

56   Karl Brandt, 'Liberal Alternatives in Western Policies Toward Colonial Areas', 8th MPS Meeting, St Moritz: Hoover Institution Archives, 1957, Box 11, Folder 3.

57   John Locke, *Two Treatises of Government and a Letter Concerning Toleration*, ed. Ian Shapiro (New Haven: Yale University Press, 2003), p. 114.

58   Arthur Shenfield, 'Liberalism and Colonialism', *Foreign Policy Perspectives* 4 (1986).

governing 'barbarians' – 'provided the end be their improvement'.[59] Writing in the context of rising anticolonial struggles, Shenfield feared that the repression necessary to maintain colonialism would be 'bitter enough to poison the West itself and sap its own liberalism'.[60] Justice may be with the French in Algeria, he warned, but the attempt to maintain French rule may ruin France herself.

The reaction to Rüstow's book elevated the rejection of Western guilt into a formative tenet of neoliberal development discourse. Yet, rather than a backward-looking attempt to secure the colonial order, this rejection was forward-looking, orientated towards forestalling Third Worldist demands for restitution. This is clearest in the work of Bauer, who had stressed since the early 1970s that 'it is untrue that the west has caused the poverty of the underdeveloped world, whether through colonialism or otherwise'.[61] Bauer, a Hungarian-born British development economist and MPS member, was a vehement opponent of state-directed development and Cold War modernisation theories. In 1981, several years before the LSF Colloquium, Bauer published a book that attributed accounts of Western responsibility for Third World poverty to colonial guilt.[62] In his presentation to the LSF Colloquium he reiterated this argument and forcefully criticised the idea that foreign aid was compensation for Western errors; no restitution was necessary, he contended, as former colonies had benefited from colonialism.[63]

Bauer's response to postcolonial demands of the 1970s was largely consistent with the earlier MPS members' Lockean defence of European colonialism. Referring to an English student pamphlet that accused the British of taking 'the rubber from Malaya, the tea from India, raw materials from all over the world', Bauer – who had begun his career working for a trading company with rubber interests in Malaya – retorted that this was the opposite of the truth; 'the British took the rubber *to* Malaya and the tea *to* India', he wrote.[64] Far from the West causing the poverty

59 John Stuart Mill, *On Liberty* (Indianapolis: Hackett, 1978), p. 10.
60 Ibid., p. 3.
61 Bauer (1971), cited in Plehwe, 'Origins of the Neoliberal Economic Development Discourse', 260.
62 Peter Bauer, *Equality, the Third World, and Economic Delusion*, pp. 66–85.
63 Peter Bauer, 'L'Aide au Développement: Pour ou Contre?', in Rony Brauman, ed., *Le Tiers-Mondisme en Question* (Paris: Olivier Orban, 1986), p. 187.
64 Bauer, *Equality, the Third World, and Economic Delusion*, p. 86; Paul Lewis, 'Peter Bauer, British Economist, Is Dead at 86', *New York Times*, Business Day section, 14 May 2002.

of the Third World, Bauer argued that (what he euphemistically called) 'contacts with the West' had been the central agents of material progress.[65] At the LSF colloquium, Bauer argued that the world's poorest peoples were indigenous communities and 'Amazonian Indians', precisely because they enjoyed the fewest 'external contacts'. Taiwan, Hong Kong, Malaysia and Singapore, in contrast, offered proof of the economic benefits such 'contacts' brought.[66] Elsewhere, Bauer claimed that not even the transatlantic slave trade could be claimed as a cause of 'African backwardness', as slavery had been endemic in Africa prior to the slave trade and was only ended by the West. 'Whatever one thinks of colonialism it can't be held responsible for Third World poverty', he concluded.[67]

Bauer reserved his most strenuous criticism for those who spoke of 'economic colonialism' or 'neo-colonialism', to define the situation of post-independence states. Such terminology, he argued, 'confuses poverty with colonial status, a concept which has normally meant lack of political sovereignty'.[68] Bauer took direct aim at the analysis of neo-colonialism developed by Kwame Nkrumah that we examined in Chapter Three. Bauer challenged this politicisation of economic relations, and rejected Nkrumah's charge that neo-colonialism was keeping the African continent 'artificially poor'.[69] A nation can be subjected to political colonialism, he argued, but it makes no sense to speak of colonisation or domination in the economy as economic relations are not the product of the imposition of a single will. On the contrary, he argued that the market impersonally coordinated the free, voluntary interactions of numerous individuals, and must be protected (by the state and law) from political interference.

Drawing on the theorisation of the market as information processor that enabled people to draw on dispersed, tacit knowledge, developed by his MPS colleague Hayek, Bauer depicted the market as a system of disseminated knowledge and mutually beneficial free exchange that produces order without the need for conscious and deliberate planning. Prices for raw materials were set by the market and not determined by

65   Bauer, *Equality, the Third World, and Economic Delusion*, p. 87.
66   Bauer, 'L'Aide Au Développement', p. 187.
67   Bauer, *Equality, the Third World, and Economic Delusion*, p. 89.
68   Ibid., p. 90.
69   Kwame Nkrumah, *Neo-Colonialism: The Last Stage of Imperialism* (New York: International, 1966), p. xx.

the West, he argued – they were the products of numerous individual decisions, and not of the actions of a single decision-maker or of collective collusion.[70] For the neoliberals, any intervention that altered the results achieved by the subtle mechanism of the price system would prevent its feedback loops from operating. This neoliberal position provided the humanitarians with a weapon in their struggle against Third Worldism. Price fluctuations were 'not dependent on international speculators but on the market', Malhuret contended. And the 'tendency of international trade is that all parties to an exchange benefit.'[71] But the neoliberals' argument was not simply economic; rather, they followed Montesquieu in arguing that, as commercial relations were founded on mutual need, the 'natural effect of commerce is to lead to peace'.[72] Neoliberal thinkers depicted the market as a realm of peaceful and mutually beneficial relations, and portrayed politics as a Schmittian field of friend/enemy distinctions and violent coercion.[73] 'Peter was resolutely against the politicization of life', Bauer's friend Anthony Daniels reflected at a 2004 dinner held in his honour at Princeton University. 'Such politicization, in his view, not only was inimical to development, but destructive of civilization – another value for which Peter cared deeply'.[74]

'Difference' Against Equality

Bauer concluded his speech at the LSF Colloquium by rejecting the premise of discussions about Third World poverty: 'There is no problem in the Third World', he argued; 'there are only differences of income' – differences which are 'neither surprising nor reprehensible'.[75] Along with his neoliberal colleagues, Bauer replaced the language of 'inequality' (which implied unjust structural relations) with that of 'difference' (which was

---

70   Peter Bauer and Basil Yamey, *The Economics of Under-Developed Countries* (Cambridge: Cambridge University Press, 1972), p. 155.

71   Malhuret, cited in Gresh, 'Une Fondation Au-Dessus de Tout Soupçon'.

72   Baron de Montesquieu, *The Spirit of the Laws* (Cambridge: Cambridge University Press), p. 338.

73   Carl Schmitt, *The Concept of the Political*, transl. George Schwab (Chicago: University of Chicago Press, 1996).

74   Anthony Daniels, 'Peter Bauer and the Third World', *Cato Journal* 25: 3 (2005), p. 488.

75   Bauer, 'L'Aide Au Développement', p. 190.

merely the necessary condition of a competitive economy). There was nothing emancipatory about this stress on difference. For the neoliberals, 'difference' was the apolitical condition of a competitive economy, which, as Foucault notes, is defined not by the exchange of equivalents but by a 'game of differentiations' in which some have large incomes and others do not.[76] The neoliberal rhetoric of 'difference' naturalised and justified deep and racialised inequalities, and obscured the history of colonial exploitation. Differences between countries, Bauer argued, do not stem from the 'pillaging of one by another'.[77] Repeatedly, he took aim at the contention articulated most succinctly by Tanzania's President Julius Nyerere: 'In one world, as in one state, when I am rich because you are poor, and I am poor because you are rich, the transfer of wealth from rich to poor is a matter of right; it is not an appropriate matter for charity'.[78]

All Bauer's writings aimed to demolish the premise that the wealth of the colonial powers was a consequence of the poverty of the colonised – and vice versa. The prosperity of the United States and Japan, he insisted, has nothing to do with the poverty of Chad, Mali and Nepal.[79] The development economist therefore rejected the very category of the 'Third World', arguing that it conflated 'a vast and diverse collection of societies differing widely in religion, culture, social institutions, personal characteristics and motivations'. It was a travesty to 'lump together Chinese merchants of Southeast Asia, Indian villagers, tribal societies of Africa, oil-rich Arabs of the Middle East, aborigines and desert peoples, inhabitants of huge cities in India, Africa and Latin America', Bauer wrote, and envisage them all as 'a low-level uniform mass'.[80] Along the same lines, the founders of LSF rejected the 'notion of a (non-existent) unified third world', and the political indictment of the global capitalist economy that it implied.

Responding to the prevalence of such arguments in our own time, Vijay Prashad has argued that complaints about the homogenisation of distinct histories and regions embodied in the term 'Third World' miss the point

---

76   Michel Foucault, *The Birth of Biopolitics: Lectures at the Collège de France 1978–1979*, ed. Michel Senellart, transl. Graham Burchell (New York: Palgrave Macmillan, 2008), p. 142.

77   Bauer, 'L'Aide Au Développement', p. 191.

78   Cited in Peter Bauer and John O'Sullivan, 'Ordering the World About: The New International Economic Order', *Policy Review*, Summer 1977, p. 56.

79   Bauer, 'L'Aide Au Développement', p. 190.

80   P. T. Bauer, 'Western Guilt and Third World Poverty', *Commentary Magazine*, January 1976.

that the term itself was an 'act of artifice for a global social movement'.[81] The unity of the 'Third World', such as it was, was premised neither on a shared culture nor on a racialised nationalism but on the difficult attempt to build a form of political solidarity capable of challenging the unequal arrangement of the international economy.[82] The insistence on heterogeneity may be motivated by a critical urge. But, as Arif Dirlik suggests, 'unaccompanied by a sense of structural context, it culminates in a radical empiricism that undercuts its own call for critical understanding'.[83] In affirming difference against the abstractions of Third Worldism, the neoliberals, and their humanitarian allies, drew on a tradition of anti-rationalist anti-egalitarianism that stems back at least to Edmund Burke's conservative critique of the French Revolution. They joined a lineage of liberal and cosmopolitan opponents of revolution who have long 'depicted the levelling abstractions of egalitarian fanaticisms as violent denials of the empirical complexities that only the joint work of representative institutions and market transactions is capable of coordinating'.[84]

Consistent with this lineage, Bauer criticised proposals for redistribution, which he argued rest on the belief that, as we are all 'basically the same', wealth differentials must reflect 'some perversion of the natural and just course of events by some malevolent force, in particular, the power of the rich to impoverish the rest'.[85] The rejection of what Jacques Rancière and Alain Badiou term the 'axiom of equality' played a key role in neoliberal thought.[86] Bauer, like Mises much earlier,

81   Vijay Prashad, *The Darker Nations: A People's History of the Third World* (New York: New Press, 2007), p. 13.

82   For an excellent critical account of the attempt to develop solidarity in a context of deep *political* differences, see Umut Özsu, ' "Let Us First of All Have Unity among Us": Bandung, International Law, and the Empty Politics of Solidarity', in *Bandung, Global History, and International Law: Critical Pasts and Pending Futures*, ed. Michael Fakhri, Vasuki Nesiah, and Luis Eslava (New York: Cambridge University Press, 2017).

83   Arif Dirlik, 'Spectres of the Third World: Global Modernity and the End of the Three Worlds', *Third World Quarterly* 25: 1 (February 2004), pp. 131–48.

84   Alberto Toscano, *Fanaticism: On the Uses of an Idea* (London: Verso, 2010), p. 240.

85   Peter Bauer and Basil Yamey, 'World Wealth Redistribution: Anatomy of the New Order', in Karl Brunner, ed., *The First World & the Third World: Essays on the New International Economic Order* (Rochester: University of Rochester Policy Center Publications, 1978), p. 198.

86   Equality, for Rancière, is 'not an end to attain, but a point of departure, a supposition to maintain in every circumstance'. Jacques Rancière, 'The Ignorant Schoolmaster: Five Lessons in Intellectual Emancipation' (Stanford: Stanford University Press, 1991), p. 138.

stressed the basic inequality of people, and of peoples, arguing that economic achievement depends primarily on 'aptitudes, motivations, mores and modes of thought and on social institutions and political arrangements'. Those who benefit from a market economy are those who are most adaptable, entrepreneurial, industrious, ingenious, thrifty, ambitious and resourceful, he claimed, while the 'less adaptable may go to the wall'.[87]

The Morals of Development

Bauer depicted generalised poverty as a result of the absence of an institutional structure capable of promoting the subjective qualities the competitive market required. His remedies were not as brutal as those used by the Chicago Boys in Chile, but the aim was the same: to eradicate non-market sources of social reproduction in order to enforce submission to the market and cultivate entrepreneurial subjects. Far from advancing *laissez-faire*, Bauer advocated a legal and institutional structure that would foster individualism by replacing communal land tenure with individual property rights, freeing individuals from the 'hand of custom' and the extended family system ('with its drain on resources and its stifling of personal initiative').[88]

While neoliberals in the US, the UK and Europe bolstered their challenge to the welfare state by bemoaning its weakening of family responsibility, as we saw in Chapter 2, the neoliberal development theorists faced precisely the opposite problem: in the Global South, they believed that the extended family structure was too effective in its welfare function; in cushioning individuals from the imperatives of wage labour, the extended family was a barrier to a competitive market order, and its redistributive moral economy diminished the rewards of individual entrepreneurialism. Outside any West African bank, the South African economist and Oxford chair in colonial economics, S. Herbert Frankel, told the 1958 MPS meeting, one sees people waiting for their relatives to draw money 'ready to pounce on them like vultures, because they believe they have the "right" to be supported or assisted by

---

87   Bauer and Yamey, *Economics of Under-Developed Countries*, p. 68.
88   Ibid., p. 68.

a relative who has some wealth'.[89] The problems of development were not strictly economic. The challenge for the neoliberals was to overcome the egalitarianism of communal cultures and the assumption that basic welfare was a right, and to instil the morals of the market and a culture of individual rights.

For Bauer, what was required was not state passivity or *laissez-faire*, but the conscious and appropriate reshaping of institutional structures and subjectivities. Institutions, he believed, should ensure political stability, the enforcement of law and order, and a rule of law to prevent discrimination against more productive groups (minorities or foreigners whose economic successes were resented by majorities). While the state should not compensate the losers of this market game, it should 'make them aware of their opportunities and rights'.[90] In Bauer's works, stretching back to the 1950s, we find the central tenets of a neoliberal human rights discourse, for which human rights were legal and moral technologies inseparable from, and necessary for the promotion of, a liberal, competitive market order. This human rights discourse would increasingly be adopted by human rights NGOs from the 1970s, most explicitly by LSF.

Reflecting on his motivations in founding LSF from a distance of more than three decades, Malhuret acknowledged: 'Bauer was for me extremely important'. It was in Bauer's books that it was possible to read that everything thinkers on the left were saying about economic development and redistribution was wrong, 'and the only way to develop a country is the way that the Western countries, and Australia and America, have taken during the nineteenth and twentieth centuries'.[91] Following Bauer in obscuring the role of colonial development in the 'normal development' of the colonial powers, Malhuret argued that the French in 1777 or 1778 were in exactly the same economic situation as people in the Third World now, with the same life expectancy, the same famines, the same agricultural problems. 'And what did they do?' he asked. 'They did not write a charter about economic and social rights, they wrote a charter that would allow them, from that

---

89 S. Herbert Frankel, '"Undeveloped Countries": Discussion on Two Papers Submitted by Peter Bauer to the 9th Meeting of the Mont Pèlerin Society, Princeton, September 1958', in Albert Hunold ed. Mont Pèlerin Quarterly, 1:1 (April 1959), p. 17.

90 Bauer and Yamey, *Economics of Under-Developed Countries*, p. 217.

91 Author interview with Claude Malhuret, Sénat – Palais du Luxembourg, Paris, 7 October 2015, p. 1.

point on, to build a political system which would, little by little, take them out of poverty'.[92] In disparaging demands for redistribution, the humanitarians of LSF committed themselves to an (anti)-political vision that combined human rights with 'renewed faith in the efficicacy of the market economy'.[93] Liberté sans Frontières proposed that 'respect for natural rights may be the condition sine qua non of real economic and social development'.[94] In doing so, they joined the battle alongside the neoliberal ideologues against the clearest competing vision of international order and economic relations: the New International Economic Order.

Competing Utopias: Human Rights and the New International Economic Order

At the 1973 Algiers meeting of the Non-Aligned Movement (NAM), Algeria's President Houari Boumediène stressed the 'vital need for the producing countries to operate the levers of price control'.[95] The success of the 1973 oil embargo by the Organisation of Arab Petroleum Exporting Countries (OPEC) had bolstered confidence that similar collective action on the part of producers of raw materials could alter the terms of trade and transform an international economic system that was perpetuating exploitation, racial discrimination and the impoverishment of the Third World. The Algiers meeting saw NAM turn towards economic questions, rejecting the understanding of the market as a free space of mutually beneficial exchanges and challenging the economic order inherited from colonialism. The following year, 1974, the UN General Assembly passed the 'Declaration on the Establishment of a New International Economic Order', which proclaimed the 'right of all States, territories and peoples under foreign occupation, alien and colonial domination or apartheid to restitution and full compensation for

---

92   Ibid.
93   John Davenport, ' "Undeveloped Countries": Discussion on Two Papers Submitted by Peter Bauer to the 9th Meeting of the Mont Pèlerin Society, Princeton, September 1958', in Albert Hunold ed. Mont Pèlerin Quarterly, 1:1 (April 1959), p. 7.
94   Cited in Gresh, 'Une Fondation Au-Dessus de Tout Soupçon'.
95   Jennifer Bair, 'Taking Aim at the New International Economic Order', in Mirowski and Plehwe, Road from Mont Pèlerin, p. 350.

the exploitation and depletion' of their natural resources by colonial powers.[96]

If the NIEO declaration used the language of rights, its vision differed starkly from the human rights agenda pursued by major human rights NGOs such as Amnesty International or Human Rights Watch, which depicted Third World suffering as an internal problem caused by the failure of postcolonial states to comply with human rights norms. It was this latter vision of individual human rights that Moyn dubbed the 'last utopia'[97] But throughout the 1970s, as Antony Anghie notes, much of the world was still struggling for the 'utopia of development', and saw the NIEO as the best chance of achieving it.[98] While Bauer and his fellow neoliberals depicted the market as a realm of free and mutually beneficial exchange, advocates of the NIEO argued that an economic framework developed to govern trade between equals could not resolve the colonial inheritance of unequal economic relations. They directly contested the view that the market should be governed only by a framework that did not interfere with the setting of prices, like that enshrined in the General Agreement on Tariffs and Trades – which, like the UDHR, came into force in 1948, while much of the world's population still lived under colonial rule.

Following earlier physiocrat and classical liberal opposition to industrial combinations, opponents of the NIEO depicted the attempt by producers of raw materials to influence prices as a coercive intervention into the free and voluntary relations of market exchange and a threat to the rights of buyers. In accruing to themselves the powerful language of freedom, they gave a progressive gloss to their campaign against Third Worldism that appealed to those who had become increasingly uneasy about violence in the Third World, especially in the wake of the Nigerian civil war (1967–70), the exodus of asylum seekers from Vietnam in the wake of the US war, and the genocide in Cambodia.[99]

Such evocations of market freedom obscured the coercion and political intervention that upheld existing 'free' market relations. No market

96   United Nations General Assembly, 'Declaration on the Establishment of a New International Economic Order'.

97   Samuel Moyn, *The Last Utopia: Human Rights in History* (Cambridge: Belknap, 2010).

98   Antony Anghie, 'Whose Utopia? Human Rights, Development, and the Third World', *Qui Parle* 22: 1 (2013), p. 73.

99   On French humanitarianism, see Eleanor Davey, *Idealism Beyond Borders: The French Revolutionary Left and the Rise of Humanitarianism, 1954–1988* (Cambridge: Cambridge University Press, 2015).

is unregulated, and there is no realm (as the neoliberals themselves insisted) of natural equilibrium. All economic relations are subjected to rules and regulations, which distribute wealth in various ways. The relevant question is therefore not whether a market is 'free' or regulated, but who benefits from the distributional outcomes entailed by various modes of regulation – and how just those benefits are.[100] Rather than aiming to replace free-market relations with coercive price control, as their opponents claimed, defenders of the NIEO challenged the order of 'freedom' and 'equality' that benefited colonial powers and their corporations at the expense of former colonies, and they called for ' "substantive equality" to compensate for inequality'.[101] Here, they followed Marx, who argued in his *Critique of the Gotha Program* that 'equal right', which measures unequal individuals by a single standard, ignores their different abilities and needs, and can only result in inequality. 'To avoid all these defects', Marx wrote, 'right, instead of being equal, would have to be unequal'.[102]

The neoliberals, in contrast, celebrated equal right precisely for its role in perpetuating existing inequalities. Hayek and his neoliberal colleagues were fervent defenders of the rule of law because they believed that, given that people are unequal, the 'only way to place them in an equal position would be to treat them differently'.[103] They saw a stress on formal equality before the law as a means to prevent redistribution for the purpose of greater substantive or socioeconomic equality, and to rule out demands for foreign aid, support for industries of former colonies, or reparations to transform the legacies of past injustice.[104]

Bedjaoui was the strongest critic of this order of equal right. The Algerian lawyer disparaged the 'froth and veneer of decolonisation', and highlighted the persistence of 'universal exploitation, and the dichotomy between poverty and affluence' in the wake of formal independence.[105] The very neutrality and formalism of international law had

100   Bernard E. Harcourt, *The Illusion of Free Markets: Punishment and the Myth of Natural Order* (Cambridge, MA: Harvard University Press, 2010), p. 190.

101   United Nations, 'Towards the New International Economic Order', p. 4.

102   Karl Marx, 'Critique of the Gotha Program', in Lawrence H. Simon, ed., *Selected Writings* (Indianapolis: Hackett, 1984), p. 321.

103   Friedrich Hayek, *The Constitution of Liberty: The Definitive Edition*, ed. Ronald Hamowy (Chicago: University of Chicago Press, 2011), p. 150.

104   Ibid.

105   Mohammed Bedjaoui, *Towards a New International Economic Order* (New York: Holmes & Meier, 1979), p. 78.

permitted colonisation, exploitation and racial discrimination, Bedjaoui argued, and facilitated the enrichment of the wealthy countries at the expense of impoverished ones.[106] Just as Marxist critics of human rights have argued that abstract equality and freedom mask substantive inequality and domination, Bedjaoui rejected the 'phantom sovereignty' that masked relations of domination under the cover of formal equality.[107] Instead, he invoked a new international law that would facilitate 'corrective or compensatory inequality' to promote the development of the Third World.[108]

What role did human rights play in this new international law? Although critics have noted Bedjaoui's universalism, they tend to depict him, and the NIEO agenda, as 'generally unsympathetic' to the rhetoric of human rights.[109] Bedjaoui's strident defence of the sovereignty of newly independent states did put him firmly at odds with the new human rights movement of the time, and the NIEO has been depicted as a programme of 'state rights against private capital', for which the freedom and rights of individual citizens was an 'ancillary product' of national independence.[110] In reality, however, Bedjaoui was not indifferent to individual rights, and nor did he subordinate the individual to the state. The Algerian lawyer celebrated the fact that the 'State, that Moloch or Kronos that devours its own people, or rather, devours itself, is in process of being de-hallowed', and stressed that the equitable sharing of the world's resources required attending to the problem of 'human rights'. 'What would be the use of exploiting for man's benefit the immense riches of the sea-bed, within the framework of the new 'law of mankind', he asked, 'if man's dignity or integrity is threatened'?[111] While Bedjaoui mobilised the language of human dignity and rights, his horizon, and his universalism, extended far beyond the liberal individualism of the major human rights NGOs of his time. Like his anticolonial

---

106   Ibid., p. 63; Umut Özsu, '"In the Interests of Mankind as a Whole": Mohammed Bedjaoui's New International Economic Order', *Humanity: An International Journal of Human Rights, Humanitarianism, and Development* 6: 1 (2015), pp. 129–43.

107   Bedjaoui, *Towards a New International Economic Order*, p. 81.

108   Ibid., p. 249.

109   Özsu, '"In the Interests of Mankind as a Whole"', p. 142.

110   Vanessa Ogle, 'State Rights against Private Capital: The "New International Economic Order" and the Struggle over Aid, Trade, and Foreign Investment, 1962–1981', *Humanity: An International Journal of Human Rights, Humanitarianism, and Development* 5: 2 (2014), p. 212.

111   Bedjaoui, *Towards a New International Economic Order*, p. 239.

predecessors who had successfully fought for the recognition of national self-determination as a human right, Bedjaoui sought to challenge the postcolonial persistence of economic exploitation and political domination.[112]

Bedjaoui drew on the history of the rights of man to contest those who criticised the NIEO as futile utopianism. 'When in 1788 and 1789 the French people presented their 'books of grievances' (*cahiers de doléances*), he wrote, 'there were, as there are today, knowledgeable souls who considered them to be pure rhetoric, far removed from reality'. Like Alfred Sauvy before him, Bedjaoui compared the Third World to the Third Estate; for the former, too, he predicted optimistically: 'Today's rhetoric will be tomorrow's reality'.[113] Whatever its rhetorical force, this analogy broke down as the Third World project came under sustained assault from the world's most powerful economic interests. The Third Estate, Sieyès famously argued, resembled a 'strong, robust man with one arm in chains'.[114] It sought only to break this bondage, and end the privileges that gave the nobility exclusive rights.[115] However revolutionary it was in its (rather limited) time and place, Sieyès's defence of 'free competition' and legal equality did not serve well those people whose experience of colonial bondage had sapped their strength and economic resources, leaving them less robust than Sieyès's rising bourgeoisie.[116] Instead, the languages of free competition and equality before the law became central to a neoliberal counterattack, to which the NIEO would ultimately succumb.

Contesting the New International Economic Order

In 1981, with neoliberalism in the ascendancy, US President Ronald Reagan used his speech at the Cancún summit on development to exhort Third World leaders to embrace 'the magic of the market'. Cancún has been described as the 'death-knell of the NIEO', the moment when it

---

112   See Burke, *Decolonization and the Evolution of International Human Rights*; Slaughter, *Human Rights, Inc.*

113   Bedjaoui, *Towards a New International Economic Order*, p. 184.

114   Sieyès, 'What Is the Third Estate?', p. 96.

115   Emmanuel Sieyès, 'An Essay on Privileges', in Michael Sonenscher, ed., *Political Writings* (Indianapolis: Hackett, 2003), p. 69.

116   Sieyès, 'What Is the Third Estate?', p. 95.

was finally displaced by the neoliberal counter-revolution in develop-ment theory.[117] The early success of the Third Worldist economic agenda provided a strong impetus for the consolidation of what Mark Mazower has termed 'the real new economic order'.[118] By the early 1980s, Third World states were struggling under the weight of spiralling foreign debt, and the NIEO agenda had been largely displaced by the US-led global project of trade liberalisation, deregulation and privatisation, which made the former's proposals for economic decolonisation look utopian indeed. At the same time, the human rights–based 'critique of the atroc-ity, misrule and despotism of the state' was wielded by both human rights advocates and neoliberals against the utopia envisaged by Third Worldists.[119]

From its inception, Liberté sans Frontières sought to contest the argument that a 'new international economic order' was the solution to underdevelopment.[120] In his introduction to the proceedings of the LSF Colloquium, Brauman argued that the absurd and dangerous NIEO would result in inflation and a transfer of wealth from the poorest to the most favoured individuals and nations.[121] He contended that the NIEO was built on the false premise that the terms of trade between rich and poor countries were deteriorating and that, if implemented, it would lead away from the successful path pursued by Asian countries like South Korea.[122] Looking back more recently, Malhuret reflected that LSF's founders believed 'the path taken by the New [International] Economic Order was leading to a dead end', while countries with liberal economies – the so called 'Asian Tigers' – were developing rapidly.[123] The real stake in this attack on the NIEO was defending the efficacy of a

---

117 Jennifer Bair, 'Taking Aim at the New International Economic Order', in Mirowski and Plehwe, *Road from Mont Pèlerin*, p. 355.

118 Mark Mazower, *Governing the World: The History of an Idea, 1815 to the Present* (London: Penguin, 2012).

119 The quote is from Moyn, 'A Powerless Companion', p. 156. For an astute account of the neoliberal attack on the NIEO, see Umut Özsu, 'Neoliberalism and the New International Economic Order: A History of "Contemporary Legal Thought"', in Christopher Tomlins and Justin Desautels-Stein, eds, *Searching for Contemporary Legal Thought* (Cambridge: Cambridge University Press, 2017), pp. 330–47.

120 Liberté Sans Frontières and Malhuret, 'Invitation de Liberté sans Frontières au Colloque'.

121 Brauman, 'Ni Tiers-Mondisme, Ni Cartiérisme', p. 16.

122 Rony Brauman, 'Tiers-Mondisme: Les Intentions et Les Résultats', *Le Monde Diplomatique*, November 1985.

123 Author interview with Claude Malhuret.

liberal economic order against demands for redistribution and state planning. The 'burden of human error and bad local political decisions, rather than external elements, is the determining factor in a number of tragic situations', Brauman stressed.[124]

Despite the stated aims of LSF to provide a forum 'free of ideological presuppositions', its attacks on Third Worldism and the NIEO intersected with the agenda of Reaganite neoliberals, who had become increasingly concerned that the new nations were vilifying 'the West' and the free enterprise system.[125] Philippe Laurent, then Executive Director of MSF Belgium, recalls a meeting in which Malhuret explained his proposed organisation as a 'war machine' that would combat Third Worldism and 'fight for neoliberal ideas'. Malhuret's model, Laurent recalls, was the Reaganite US think tank the Heritage Foundation. Both Malhuret and Brauman visited the Heritage Foundation, and while they both later reflected that it was too far to their right, there was nonetheless a disconcerting similarity in the two groups' responses to the NIEO.[126] The same year that LSF held its first colloquium, the Heritage Foundation declared that, in the name of a New International Economic Order, the General Assembly had attacked 'the very essence and philosophy of the free enterprise system'. The undeveloped world, it charged, seemingly without irony, 'prefers to strive to get a share of the West's wealth as a kind of wealth transfer payment rather than work at creating its own wealth'.[127]

By the early 1980s, such views were becoming mainstream. By that time, the United States had overcome what the US diplomat Daniel Patrick Moynihan called the 'massive failure of American diplomacy' in the face of Third World claims, and was forcefully challenging the Third World agenda.[128] In a 1975 article that resulted in his appointment as US ambassador to the UN, Moynihan had warned that the Third World was advancing a vision of the future that came 'ominously close to looting'. Moynihan argued that the spontaneous ideology of Third Worldism was an inheritance of Fabianism. He laid out an oppositional strategy with

---

124   Brauman, cited in Binet, 'Famine and Forced Relocations in Ethiopia', p. 63.

125   Roger A. Brooks, 'The United Nations at 40: Myth and Reality', Heritage Foundation, 9 August 1985, at heritage.org.

126   Author interview with Rony Brauman; author interview with Claude Malhuret.

127   Burton Yale Pines, 'The UN and the Free Enterprise System', in *The UN Under Scrutiny* (Washington, DC: Heritage Foundation, 1982), p. 2.

128   Burke, *Decolonization and the Evolution of International Human Rights*, p. 10.

three key 'points of systematic attack': defending liberal institutions, including 'the most creative international institution of the twentieth century', the multinational corporation; challenging the idea of a crisis in the Third World, pointing out that 'these economies do less well than they ought: that the difference is of their own making and no one else's, and no claim on anyone else arises in consequence'; and, following the lead of organisations like Amnesty International, 'speaking for political and civil liberty' with 'enthusiasm and zeal'.[129]

These lines of attack are echoed in the LSF founding document almost a decade later. That document stridently advances the superiority of liberal democracy, and defends multinational corporations from 'simplistic' attacks on their power. It rejects an economic 'diagnosis marked by catastrophism' (which it attributes to critical development scholars René Dumont, Susan George and Frances Moore Lappé), and shifts responsibility for postcolonial poverty onto the 'suicidal' policies of Third World states. Finally, it proposes a global campaign to highlight the abuses of political liberties and human rights in the Third World.[130] The human rights vision outlined by LSF was not simply an alternative to the structural analysis embodied in the NIEO – rather, it was part of a concerted attempt to shift attention from the global economy to the Third World state. Despite these similarities, however, much had changed in the decade that separated Moynihan's article, written at the peak of the OPEC oil blockade, from the LSF colloquium.

The success of the NIEO, as Berger has noted, would have required the capacity to redistribute resources on a global scale.[131] By the time the NIEO was calling for the extension of redistributive welfare policies to the global arena, these policies were in crisis.[132] Anghie has argued that, given that the human rights movement of the 1970s shifted attention away from the structure of the global economy, it is 'surely not a coincidence' that this movement flourished alongside the imposition of neoliberal policies by the international financial institutions. I have suggested

---

129   Daniel P. Moynihan, 'The United States in Opposition', *Commentary*, 1 March 1975.

130   Liberté Sans Frontières, 'Fondation Liberté Sans Frontières'.

131   Mark T. Berger, 'After the Third World: History, Destiny and the Fate of Third Worldism', *Third World Quarterly* 25: 1 (2004), p. 24. Nils Gilman describes it as 'a call for *socialism among states*'. Nils Gilman, 'The New International Economic Order: A Reintroduction', *Humanity: An International Journal of Human Rights, Humanitarianism, and Development* 6: 1 (2015), p. 4.

132   Berger, 'After the Third World', p. 24.

that there is more at stake in this 'non-coincidence' than a shift of optics. The activist humanitarians of MSF did not merely divert attention from global economic structures to individual rights violations on the part of states. Rather, their focus on human rights violations by postcolonial states was only one aspect of a concerted campaign against Third Worldism and the utopia embodied in the NIEO. The NIEO was not without limitations of its own, foremost among which was the relative neglect of inequalities *within* countries, but its failure was not simply a product of these internal limitations. Rather, its failure, as Umut Özsu notes, 'was at root an affirmation of the weakness of public authority in the face of private power, the Global South in the face of the Global North, the developmental state in the face of the state legitimated market'.[133] In 1979, Hayek warned that the 'strongest support of the trend towards socialism comes today from those who claim they want neither capitalism nor socialism but a 'middle way' or a 'third world'.[134] To follow them, he argued, was a sure path to socialism, and 'socialism as much as fascism or communism inevitably leads into the totalitarian state'.[135] Increasingly, the Third World vision of economic redistribution was viewed not only as economically suicidal but also as 'totalitarian'.

Neoliberal Human Rights

While the human rights advocates of LSF mobilised neoliberal economic analyses to challenge Third Worldism and the NIEO, the neoliberal economists embraced the language of human rights. They soon saw that this new language, and the organisations that mobilised it to curtail the range of feasible political options and to license interventions into postcolonial societies, could bolster their own agenda of imposing market discipline on former colonies. Neoliberal human rights dispensed with the project of guaranteeing broad popular rights to basic welfare, but not with 'economic rights' per se. Rather, they saw in human rights the possibility of securing the rights of investors and the wealthy in the face of challenges

---

133   Özsu, '"In the Interests of Mankind as a Whole"', p. 137.

134   Friedrich Hayek, *Law, Legislation and Liberty: A New Statement of the Liberal Principles of Justice and Political Economy, vol. III: The Political Order of a Free People* (London: Routledge, 1998), p. 151.

135   Ibid.

to their property and power.[136] The human rights discourse they developed was not confined to property rights; it aimed to bolster the institutional and moral foundations of a competitive market economy and to shape entrepreneurial subjects. In contrast to those anticolonialists who had fought to establish the right to self-determination, the neoliberals saw the promise of human rights in constraining sovereign power, especially in the post-colony, and in restraining the politicisation of the economy.

In an article written with John O'Sullivan in 1977 – Moyn's human rights 'breakthrough' year – Bauer explicitly mobilised the language of human rights to contest the NIEO. Under the heading 'Human Rights in the Third World', Bauer and Sullivan contended: 'Western liberal opinion has been strangely and culpably blind to the extent of the persecution of economically productive, perhaps relatively well-off but politically unpopular, minorities'.[137] This account of the human rights abuses carried out by postcolonial states merges cases of assault on classical civil and political liberties with violations of economic (or market) freedoms. Third World governments, they argued, had persecuted minorities, discriminated against them in employment, and conducted expulsions and 'even massacre'. They had suppressed freedom of the press, engaged in forced collectivisation of agriculture, restricted the inflow of foreign capital, established state monopolies and restrictive licensing of economic activities, and suppressed private firms. It was these human rights abuses, Bauer and O'Sullivan argued, that had resulted in the 'poverty and economic backwardness' of Third World societies.[138]

The treatment of abuses of civil rights on the same plane as the licensing of economic activity or the establishment of state monopolies reflected the refusal of the neoliberals to view the economy as a separate sphere, distinct from the political. Rather than an economy inhabited by egoistic 'man' and a political sphere inhabited by abstract citizens, the neoliberals argued that economic control was 'not merely control of a sector of human life which can be separated from the rest, it is the control of the means for all our ends'.[139] Securing freedom therefore

---

136   For an account of the economic aspects of this, see Quinn Slobodian, *Globalists: The End of Empire and the Birth of Neoliberalism* (Cambridge, MA: Harvard University Press, 2018), p. 123.

137   Bauer and O'Sullivan, 'Ordering the World About', p. 59.

138   Ibid.

139   Friedrich Hayek, *The Road to Serfdom: Text and Documents*, ed. Bruce Caldwell (Chicago: University of Chicago Press, 2007), p. 127.

required the shaping of a competitive market and the use of rights to protect the sphere of individual's means from political intervention. In contrast to the common argument that the entrenchment of neoliberalism saw the decline of 'social and economic rights', neoliberals had their own distinctive account of 'economic rights'. These were not the rights to food, clothing, housing and education enshrined in the UDHR, which sought to offer some protection from market forces. On the contrary, neoliberal 'economic rights' sought to protect the market freedom of private capital.

The neoliberal rejection of politics did not entail a rejection of government intervention or an advocacy of *laissez-faire*; on the contrary, it implied what Bauer termed 'state action on a wide scale'.[140] Rewriting Adam Smith's invisible hand, Bauer stressed the necessity to devise suitable institutions to harness selfish interests to the general interest. The premise of *neo*liberal thought was that the institutional structure profoundly influences the operation of the economic system, and 'does not arise from the operation of the system itself'.[141] Neoliberalism countenanced a significant role for state action in relation to the market, as Foucault noted; but this action served to secure the conditions for the market, not to compensate for its effects.[142] What Foucault missed, as he prepared his lectures on neoliberalism, was the extent to which the new interventionist politics of human rights, which fascinated him at the time, shared in the dominant 'state phobia' (which conflated state welfarism with totalitarianism) that he portrayed as his time's inheritance from a previous generation of neoliberals.[143]

Foucault's designation of neoliberalism as a form of state phobia is thus misleading; the neoliberals were not phobic of the state per se, but only of its role in reducing differentials in income, which Bauer warned could only be achieved by 'a quasi-totalitarian power'.[144] Like Moynihan, Bauer criticised the failure of Western delegates to oppose the NIEO – but he went much further, protesting that Moynihan's 'conciliatory

140   Bauer and Yamey, *Economics of Under-Developed Countries*, p. 150.
141   Ibid., p. 156.
142   Foucault, *The Birth of Biopolitics*, p. 138.
143   Ibid., p. 76. On Foucault and the interventionist human rights NGOs, see Jessica Whyte, 'Human Rights: Confronting Governments? Michel Foucault and the Right to Intervene', in Costas Douzinas, Matthew Stone and Illan Rua Wall, eds, *New Critical Legal Thinking: Law and the Political* (London: Routledge, 2012).
144   Bauer, 'L'Aide Au Développement', p. 189.

remarks towards the Third World on the alleged damage to it by Western exploitation and ethnic discrimination are inappropriate'.[145] Allegations of exploitation were not only untrue, but positively harmful to the Third World, he argued, as they diverted attention from the personal and social causes of material progress and encouraged the view that incomes were extracted rather than earned. In his own version of Hayek's famous 'road to serfdom', Bauer argued that any concession to a belief in Western exploitation of former colonies legitimised severe maltreatment, including expropriation and massacre.

The politicisation of economic life was the central feature of Bauer's account of totalitarianism, just as it was the central problem of the neoliberals in Chile. In his letter to *Commentary*, Bauer protested the 'fanciful' contention of 'The United States in Opposition' that Third Worldism was a variant of Fabian Socialism.[146] Moynihan's vision of the Third World as 'a brotherhood of gradually evolving Fabians', he argued, obscured the blatant reality that it was in fact characterised by virulent antagonism to the West and the market system, and severe maltreatment, including expropriation and massacre, of millions of people. Despite rejecting this account of Third Worldism as a form of Fabianism, he nonetheless held late British colonial policy responsible for the politicisation of economic life in the former colonies. At the end of the British Empire, he argued, updating earlier neoliberal criticisms of Britain's Fabian-inspired post-war colonial policy, limited government had been replaced by economic controls and 'the ready-made framework of a *dirigiste* or even totalitarian state was handed over by the British to the incoming independent governments'.[147] Bauer's commitment to a form of Hayek's 'Road to Serfdom' thesis meant he saw little meaningful distinction between reformist socialism and totalitarianism: J. A. Hobson's *Imperialism* (1902) led directly to Lenin's *Imperialism: The Highest Stage of Capitalism* (1916), he argued, then on to the

---

145 Peter Bauer, 'Letter to Commentary on Moynihan Article', in Karl Brunner, ed., *The First World and the Third World* (Rochester: University of Rochester Policy Center Publications, 1978), p. 142.

146 Ibid., p. 139.

147 Peter Bauer, 'Hostility to the Market in Less Developed Countries', in Karl Brunner, ed., *The First World and the Third World: Essays on the New International Economic Order* (Rochester: University of Rochester Policy Center Publications, 1978), p. 174.

denunciation of neocolonialism penned by Nkrumah, and ultimately to the totalitarian state.

While the lines of influence that pass from Hobson to Lenin to Nkrumah are real enough, the point of Bauer's genealogy was to characterise capitalism as peaceful and nonviolent, and any politicisation of the economy in the name of equality as requiring 'world government with totalitarian powers'.[148] In this, Bauer joined the long lineage of neoliberal attacks on Marxist theories of imperialism that stretch back to the 1930s (see Chapter 3). Against Lenin's claim that imperialism was a phenomenon of capitalism in its monopoly stage, the neoliberals argued that imperialism was a *distortion* of the peaceful economic relations of capitalism caused by the politicisation of the economy. The real cause of inter-state conflict and colonialism, they argued, was the erosion of the liberal distinction between sovereignty and property, which had made territorial control the necessary precondition for the utilisation of the natural resources of a country. Following in the lineage of Lionel Robbins's claim that finance capital was a pacifying influence, Bauer sought to shift the blame for the pervasive violence of postcolonial societies from the economic system onto politics.[149]

From this perspective, political intervention that sought to restrain or compensate for the results of the market would lead to coercion and conflict. Echoing this perspective, Bauer argued that, if successful, Third World demands for 'wealth transfers' would result in 'the spread of totalitarian government and a further erosion of the position of the West'.[150] These results would be greatly exacerbated if international redistribution was combined with egalitarian domestic measures, as equality could only be achieved through 'an immense extension of the use of the coercive power of governments over individuals' in order to homogenise the diversity of existing nations and individuals.[151] Underpinning the NIEO, Bauer identified a fundamental and unjustified 'belief in the natural equality of man as an economic performer'.[152] Rejecting this premise, he argued that political action to equalise living

---

148   Bauer, *Equality, the Third World, and Economic Delusion*, p. 8.
149   Lionel Robbins, *The Economic Causes of War* (New York: Howard Fertig, 1968), p. 99.
150   Bauer and Yamey, 'World Wealth Redistribution', p. 219.
151   Ibid.
152   Ibid., p. 198.

standards 'implies extensive forcible remodelling of peoples and socie-ties, far-reaching coercion, and wholesale politicisation of life'.[153]

For the human rights advocates, who situated themselves within the broader anti-totalitarian movement, such an argument tied the defence of human rights to the active rejection of economic equality. Brauman attributed his own discovery of the problem of totalitarianism to Hannah Arendt's *Eichmann in Jerusalem*, which he read in the period in which he founded LSF.[154] By then, anti-totalitarianism was already pervasive among French intellectuals who were breaking with communism and with their previous anticolonial commitments. As early as 1978, Jacques Julliard had launched the media polemic against *tiers-mondisme* with an article that prophesied that, in Africa, there would be 'no socialism except a totalitarian socialism'.[155] As critics noted at the time, the terms of this *anti-tiers-mondiste* condemnation of the postcolonial state repli-cated colonialist predictions about what would eventuate in the colonies if independence were achieved, depicting them as places of barbarism and oppression.[156] The anti-totalitarianism of LSF had less in common with Arendt's work on totalitarianism, which she depicted as a phenom-enon of imperialism, than with that of the neoliberals, for whom social-ism led straight to totalitarianism.[157] Increasingly, the Third World vision of economic redistribution appeared to be not only economically suicidal, but also a 'totalitarian' threat to human rights.

We cannot understand the neoliberal victory if we view it only in economic terms. The success of neoliberalism was not predicated merely on its arguments for the superior efficiency of markets, or its challenges to the economics of socialist planning. Rather, neoliberals pioneered a series of political arguments about the dangers of wealth redistribution, interference with the market and mass participation in politics, espe-cially in the post-colony, that helped to legitimise austerity and the crushing of Third Worldist demands for global wealth redistribution. These arguments were taken up enthusiastically by the humanitarians of LSF. The power of a small humanitarian NGO cannot be compared to

---

153   Ibid., p. 212.
154   Brauman, cited in Weizman, *Least of All Possible Evils*, p. 29.
155   See Ross, *May '68 and Its Afterlives*, p. 161.
156   Sitbon, cited in Ross, *May '68*, p. 161.
157   Hayek, *Law, Legislation and Liberty, vol. III*, p. 151. On Arendt's influence on Brauman, see Weizman, *Least of All Possible Evils*.

the combined weight of the G7 countries and the Bretton Woods institutions, who also took aim at the NIEO in this period. The humanitarians nonetheless played an important role in shifting responsibility for
Third World poverty away from the legacy of colonialism and the
neocolonial framework of the global economy, and onto the leaders of
individual Third World states.

It is true, as Brauman reflected decades later, that, in attacking resid-
ual Third Worldism in the mid 1980s, LSF 'attacked a very weak
adversary'.[158] But the central LSF contribution was the one its introductory materials laid out clearly: humanitarians could provide a moral
argument that would make international liberalism acceptable to First
World 'progressives' who, in the wake of the wars in Vietnam, Algeria,
Kenya and elsewhere, generally remained critical of direct imperialist
intervention and accepted Third Worldist critiques of the world economy. LSF's introductory materials warned that, by focusing their attention on the superior economic efficiency of liberalism, its advocates had
ceded the ground of justice and generosity to their left-wing opponents,
and raised the suspicion that they were merely defending selfish (class)
interests. Humanitarians, LSF wagered, were better equipped than 'the
specialists of the economy, politics or business' to win an argument that
liberalism is not simply conducive to economic growth, but in fact the
only system capable of securing justice and liberty.[159] The humanitarians
lent their moral prestige to what the Heritage Foundation called the 'free
enterprise ideological counter-attack' on Third Worldism and the NIEO.
Their key impact was on the terrain of political idealism, as they helped
long-cherished right-wing themes cross over to the political left, and
re-signified state-led redistribution as a totalitarian threat to liberty and
human rights.

Looking back on the history of LSF, a decade after it was dissolved in
1989, Brauman reflected: 'We realised that our ideas no longer shocked
anyone. They had become commonplace. Third-Worldism was dead.'[160]
Almost twenty years later, in a context of rising concern for the economic
equality brought about by decades of neoliberal reforms, Brauman
reflected in 2015: 'I see myself and the small group that I brought

---

158   Author interview with Rony Brauman', p. 1.
159   Liberté Sans Frontières, 'Fondation Liberté Sans Frontières Pour l'information
Sur Les Droits de l'homme et Le Développement, Document de Présentation', January
1985, p. 7.
160   Binet, 'Famine and Forced Relocations in Ethiopia', p. 111.

together as a kind of symptom of the rise of neoliberalism . . . We had the conviction that we were a kind of intellectual vanguard, but no', he laughed, 'we were just following the rising tendency'.[161] I have suggested that this assessment is, if anything, too modest: rather than being a symptom, the humanitarians who founded LSF explicitly mobilised the language of human rights in order to contest the vision of substantive equality that defined the Third Worldist project and the NIEO. They were not powerless companions of the rising neoliberals, but active, enthusiastic and influential fellow-travellers. Their special contribution was to pioneer a distinctly neoliberal human rights discourse, for which a competitive market order accompanied by a liberal institutional structure was truly the last utopia.[162]

161   Author interview with Rony Brauman, MSF Office, Rue Saint-Sabin, Paris, 7 October 2015.

162   Moyn, *The Last Utopia*.

Afterword: Human Rights, Neoliberalism and Economic Inequality Today

The mere want of fortune, mere poverty, excites little compassion.

Adam Smith

Can all 842 million people who do not have access to nutritionally adequate food be victims of human rights violations?

Amnesty International

In 2015, the human rights lawyer Philip Alston used his new position as the UN special rapporteur for extreme poverty and human rights to issue a 'clarion call' to human rights defenders. Extreme economic inequality should be seen as 'a cause of shame on the part of the international human rights movement', Alston argued. Moreover, he charged that major human rights organisations, including Amnesty International and Human Rights Watch, had been deeply reluctant to factor questions of distribution and resources into their advocacy, and consequently the deep structures that perpetuate such inequalities have been left untouched. While reprimanding the human rights NGOs for their failure to address social and economic rights, Alston also argued against conflating these 'lop-sided and counter-productive institutional choices' with the structure of human rights law. Economic and social rights are a key part of that structure, he contended, even if they are often treated as 'minor league discussions' by human rights NGOs, and the United States has spent several decades trying to undermine them.[1]

---

1 Philip Alston, 'Extreme Inequality as the Antithesis of Human Rights', OpenGlobalRights, 27 August 2015, at openglobalrights.org.

Today, Alston is not alone in advocating that human rights organisations shift their attention to social and economic rights and economic inequality. Since the Global Financial Crisis of 2007–08, the UN Human Rights Council, which Alston reports to, has commissioned multiple reports on debt, economic inequality and social and economic rights. Even those human rights NGOs Alston criticises have slowly changed their practices in the decades since their inceptions. As early as 2001, Amnesty International expanded its mandate to include all human rights, and has subsequently focused increasing attention on social, economic and cultural rights. Human Rights Watch, while remaining more reluctant to shift its focus from civil and political rights, has recently paid more attention to 'arbitrary or discriminatory government policies that result in the violation of economic, social, or cultural rights'.[2] Newer organisations, such as the Center for Economic and Social Rights, founded in 1993, have emerged to fight 'for social justice through human rights'.[3] And grassroots movements across the globe often use the language of human rights to challenge austerity, the expropriation of land for mining, and the privatisation of public resources.[4]

And yet there is more at stake in Alston's intervention than a concern for poverty and inequality in their own right. This long-time human rights lawyer is also concerned to salvage the 'legitimacy of the overall human rights enterprise'.[5] If the human rights movement is currently facing powerful contestation globally, he writes, this is largely due to the perception that its preoccupations 'do little or nothing to address the most abiding and pressing challenges confronted by a large part of humanity'.[6] Although Alston's attention to social and economic rights, poverty and economic equality is salutary, the interests of the 'human rights enterprise' are not necessarily identical with those of that 'large part of humanity' whose most pressing concerns it has so far failed to address.[7] It is therefore not obvious that bolstering the threatened

2   Human Rights Watch, 'Frequently Asked Questions', at hrw.org.

3   Centre for Economic and Social Rights, 'Home', at cesr.org.

4   Paul O'Connell, 'On the Human Rights Question', *Human Rights Quarterly* 40: 4 (2018); Radha D'Souza, *What's Wrong with Rights? Social Movements, Law and Liberal Imaginations* (London: Pluto, 2018).

5   Philip Alston, 'Phantom Rights: The Systemic Marginalization of Economic and Social Rights', OpenGlobalRights, 4 August 2016, at openglobalrights.org.

6   Ibid.

7   Philip Alston, '"Report of the Special Rapporteur on Extreme Poverty and Human Rights"', 27 May 2015, p. 8.

legitimacy of that 'enterprise' is the surest way to address humanity's most pressing challenges. Despite their claim to work in the interests of all human beings, the strength of official human rights organisations and institutions is not necessarily an index of the state of humanity itself.

Today, Alston's warnings about the fate of the human rights movement are increasingly amplified by those who claim that human rights are in crisis. Scholars declare that we are living through the 'twilight of human rights law' and have reached the 'endtimes of human rights'.[8] Meanwhile, a rising parade of authoritarian leaders frame civil rights and anti-discrimination law as the exclusive concern of 'cosmopolitan', 'globalist' elites, and introduce new laws restricting the activities of human rights NGOs. Organisations that campaign for the human rights of immigrants have faced particularly severe repression; in Hungary, for instance, the right-wing government has introduced a suite of laws that criminalise any support activities that can be construed as 'facilitating illegal immigration'. Today rhetoric about national sovereignty and control over borders is resurgent, while the disastrous consequences of recent humanitarian interventions, notably in Libya, have weakened the consolidation of new norms that would enable intervention in the face of gross violations of human rights. As I finalised this book, in June 2018, the United States announced its withdrawal from the United Nations Human Rights Council, which US ambassador to the UN Nikki Haley described as a 'cesspool of political bias'.[9] The following words read as a neat description of this mood of crisis:

> Human rights is now common currency in the languages of many nations and in the languages of relations between nations . . . Few would say, however, that human rights are alive and well in all or most countries. Few would insist that the international effort has brought a substantial improvement in the welfare of many human beings. Even its staunch supporters have noted that international protection has faltered, perhaps even relapsed; that there is in fact a 'crisis' in human rights.[10]

---

8   Eric Posner, *The Twilight of Human Rights Law* (Oxford University Press, 2014); Stephen Hopgood, *The Endtimes of Human Rights* (Cornell University Press, 2015).

9   BBC News, 'US Envoy Nikki Haley Berates Human Rights Groups – BBC News', 21 June 2018, at bbc.com.

10   Louis Henkin, 'The United States and the Crisis in Human Rights Symposium: Human Rights and United States Foreign Policy', *Virginia Journal of International Law* 14 (1974), pp. 653–72.

Despite their contemporary ring, those words were written in 1974, by Louis Henkin – the founder of contemporary human rights law. Henkin's explanation for that crisis has lost little of its currency. While the language of *human* rights suggested universal acceptance, he pointed out that no such consensus on a list of rights existed, or could be expected to exist. The Universal Declaration of Human Rights was 'a product of the days when the UN was much smaller and dominated by Western states and Western ideas', he argued, and even its fragile compromise between civil and political rights and social and economic rights unravelled in the transition from an aspirational document to legally binding covenants.[11] The belief in the universal defence of human rights had foundered, he argued, on the unwillingness of states to accept interference in their internal affairs. Meanwhile, the United States perceived human rights as export commodities, 'a kind of white man's burden' that it was only prepared to take up when there were no costs to offset its national interest in doing so.[12]

Up to this point, Henkin's diagnosis sounds like a snapshot of our own time. But, writing at a time of Cold War conflict and ascendant Third Worldism, he also complained that 'the human rights lexicon and movement are used to support other values', namely economic self-determination and sovereignty equality; this 'politicization', he argued, was the ultimate cause of the crisis of human rights.[13] Although he saw little chance of overcoming this situation in the short term, Henkin laid out a series of proposals for responding to it, including a new focus on ad hoc monitoring of state practice and the founding of new organisations more able to intervene across borders. Most importantly, he stressed the need to 'depoliticize human rights', and to convince African states that what he dismissively referred to as 'their particular struggle against racial repression' could be served only by ' "neutral" human rights principles' and 'impartial machinery operating universally'.[14] Henkin believed this would reassure the United States that leadership on human rights would not jeopardise her relations with white supremacist states such as Rhodesia and South Africa, and would enable her to embrace the cause of human rights as a means to further both her values

---

11   Ibid., p. 655.
12   Ibid., p. 664.
13   Ibid., p. 663.
14   Ibid., p. 669.

and her interests. 'Then', he predicted, 'the fundamental revolution in principle that made human rights everywhere everyone's business might be realized without jeopardy to other international business.'[15]

In response to the human rights 'crisis' of his time, this dean of human rights law laid out a programme for what Joseph Slaughter calls 'the hi-jacking of human rights' – that is, he sought to win the language away from anticolonialists, who used it to defend self-determination and anti-racism, and reinvent human rights as an (apolitical) adjunct to US power.[16] The central premise of this programme was that there was no necessary conflict between the particular interests of the United States and the universal values of 'humanity'. Within less than three years of Henkin's 'crisis', US President Jimmy Carter would embrace this premise, arguing that US foreign policy was strongest when it emphasised 'morality and a commitment to freedom and democracy'.[17] But it was only later, with the end of the Cold War, that it really became possible to maintain that linking human rights to the global promotion of competitive markets represented the 'depoliticisation' of human rights. Perhaps the last prominent believer in this strategy is Hillary Clinton, who used a 2015 speech to urge that 'great democracies' like the United States and Canada should combat the rise of extremism by showing the world that 'free people and free markets, human rights and human dignity, respect for our fellow men and women is our core strength'.[18]

As we have seen, this same belief in the complementarity of interests and values, free markets and human rights, was central to neoliberal attempts to develop a universal morality to support the global extension of a competitive market. For the neoliberals, unless individuals are free to pursue their own interests on the market, all talk of human rights is meaningless. For them, this was the lesson of the United States' 'constitution of liberty'. And, at the same time, they argued that the competitive market would not survive without a robust system of individual rights and a conducive moral atmosphere. By the time major states and

---

15   In a context of politicisation, Henkin believed it was 'not surprising that the United States is prepared to sacrifice only a little to bring pressure against Rhodesia and South Africa.' Henkin, 'United States and the Crisis in Human Rights Symposium'.

16   Joseph R. Slaughter, 'Hijacking Human Rights: Neoliberalism, the New Historiography, and the End of the Third World'. *Human Rights Quarterly* 40: 4 (2018).

17   Morris Morley and Chris McGillion, *Reagan and Pinochet* (Cambridge: Cambridge University Press, 2015), pp. 7–8.

18   Justin Giovannetti, 'World Leaders Need to Tackle Rise of Extremism, Hillary Clinton Says', *Globe and Mail*, 21 January 2015.

international financial institutions had embraced the belief that only free markets could secure free people, and that human dignity was intimately tied to a market order that freed individuals from dependence, these had been neoliberal articles of faith for decades. Since the end of World War II, organised neoliberalism had been focused on promoting a world order in which morals and interests would reinforce each other. In human rights standards, they too saw a means to 'depoliticise' international economic relations, protecting the right to trade and securing the space in which individuals and corporations could pursue their interests unhindered.

As a recipe for combating the rise of extremism, this combination of free markets and human rights has not been a great success. Instead, right wing movements, overtly racist parties and authoritarian leaders have come to power by publicly disparaging the 'globalist' agenda, even as many of them have embraced the austerity politics and attacks on welfare (and racialised welfare recipients) that have defined the neoliberal consensus for decades.[19] While neoliberalism survived the Global Financial Crisis largely 'unscathed', as Philip Mirowsi notes, it has not survived entirely unchanged.[20] Today, the explicit appeals to 'Western civilisation' and the racialised fear of 'the masses' that defined early neoliberalism are resurgent, and appeals to humanitarianism are increasingly replaced by xenophobic and exclusionary attempts 'to beat people into submission' in order to protect the 'smooth operation of the market economy'.[21]

That neoliberalism tends to produce authoritarianism was a lesson learnt in the Global South long before the recent rise of right-wing authoritarianism in Europe and the United States. As the imposition of neoliberal reforms by international financial institutions eroded states' 'political capacity to govern', these same states often relied more heavily on repression in order to implement unpopular economic policies.[22] In the postcolony, the 'crumbling' of the independence and sovereignty for

---

19   Quinn Slobodian, 'Neoliberalism's Populist Bastards', *Public Seminar* (blog), 15 Februry 2018, at publicseminar.org.

20   Philip Mirowski, *Never Let a Serious Crisis Go to Waste: How Neoliberalism Survived the Financial Meltdown* (Verso Books, 2013), 8.

21   Ludwig von Mises, *Human Action: A Treatise on Economics* (San Francisco: Fox & Wilkes, 1996), p. 257.

22   Bonny Ibhawoh, 'Structural Adjustment, Authoritarianism and Human Rights in Africa', *Comparative Studies of South Asia, Africa and the Middle East* xix: 1 (1999), p. 158.

which anticolonialists had fought subjected these states to the 'tutelage of international creditors', severing the ties between citizenship and rights to public services.[23] In the Global North, renewed demands for sovereignty and control have eschewed the internationalism and egalitarianism that animated earlier postcolonial attempts to challenge the dependence that structured the international economy, and have instead valorised nativism and exclusion.

The belief in the elective affinities between the economic interests and human rights of the world's people has led to the sacrificing of these rights in cases where the two have turned out to clash. For the neoliberals, this was explicit and clear. Compatibility with the competitive market was the criterion by which all rights and institutions were to be judged. Others have fought sincerely for human rights, and seen their embrace by major states and corporations as the best means towards their protection. In either case, for all the utopianism of mid-century neoliberalism, dreams of freedom, rights and perpetual peace have given way to ongoing wars, mass displacement and the weakening of the very civil liberties neoliberals claimed to defend.

Alston's 2018 report on extreme poverty and human rights in the United States offers a stark snapshot of the impact of decades of neoliberalism in one of its key heartlands.[24] Despite the great wealth of the United States, he reported that around 40 million of its citizens lived in poverty, 18.5 million in extreme poverty, and 5.3 million in 'Third-World conditions of poverty'. Meanwhile, in the period since 1980, annual income earnings of the top 0.001 per cent of the population had risen by 636 per cent, while the average annual wage for the bottom 50 per cent had stagnated.[25] Largely for the pragmatic reason that the US has still not ratified the Covenant on Economic, Social and Cultural Rights, Alston's report highlights the extent to which poverty deprives the poor of civil and political rights: people in poverty often lack access to impartial justice, he showed, and economic inequality deprives them of political rights by allowing wealthy elites to capture the political process. In contrast to the neoliberal trade-off, which promised (a

---

23   Achille Mbembe, *On the Postcolony*, Studies on the History of Society and Culture 41 (Berkeley: University of California Press, 2001), p. 74.

24   OHCHR, 'Statement on Visit to the USA, by Professor Philip Alston, United Nations Special Rapporteur on Extreme Poverty and Human Rights', 15 December 2017, at ohcr.org.

25   Ibid.

margin of) freedom at the expense of equality, his report points towards the horizon of what Étienne Balibar calls *égaliberté* – that is, the recognition that 'equality is *practically* identical with freedom', as the deprivation of one always damages the other.[26]

Can major human rights bodies and NGOs move towards that horizon and break with the neoliberal human rights heritage? Much depends on how freedom and equality are understood. From that perspective, Alston's appeals to Hayek to argue for an emphasis on equality of opportunity, as 'perfect equality is not achievable and arguably not desirable', suggests caution about the belief that the human rights enterprise is likely to pose a serious challenge to a 'resilient' and 'adaptable' neoliberal order.[27] Not only does Alston seek to define equality in a way that would be acceptable to a figure like Hayek, who was 'known for his aversion to government intervention to achieve more equality'.[28] He also campaigns for the international financial institutions, the World Bank and the International Monetary Fund, to 'promote respect for human rights' in order to minimise their own 'reputational costs'.[29]

It is no doubt true that the Bank's reluctance to embrace human rights is based on a 'double standard', given its willingness to intervene on issues as diverse (and as political) as counterterrorism, corruption and the rule of law. Nevertheless, in counselling it to overcome what he casts as an anachronistic norm of non-intervention, motivated by cultural relativism, and become a force for the dissemination of human rights norms, Alston allows the Bank to evade responsibility for its own role in the poverty and inequality he then calls upon it to rectify. In advocating social and economic rights to rectify the inequality and economic insecurity that has 'laid the groundwork for popular revolt', and in calling on the international financial institutions to forestall such revolt, Alston's new agenda for human rights ultimately remains consistent with previous attempts to moralise capitalism and pacify the 'revolt of the masses', which was the central concern of neoliberalism in the middle of the twentieth century.

The rise of right-wing, racist movements and parties, including those that aim to entrench rather than ameliorate the inequalities of the

26 Étienne Balibar, *Masses, Classes, Ideas: Studies on Politics and Philosophy Before and After Marx*, transl. James Swenson (New York: Routledge, 1994), p. 48.
27 Alston, '"Report of the Special Rapporteur on Extreme Poverty and Human Rights"', p. 6.
28 Ibid., p. 6.
29 Ibid., p. 15.

neoliberal period, suggests that the project of subordinating politics to human rights norms and transferring governance to international financial bodies has failed to create more inclusive and equal polities. The insistence that freedom requires submission to the market, and the acceptance of the inequalities it produces, has led neither to equality nor to freedom. The rise of the right calls for a break with the neoliberal dichotomy between peaceful (civilised) markets and violent (savage) politics. For human rights, this means recognising that the absence of global consensus on a list of human rights cannot be resolved by 'depoliticisation'. Rather than seeking to transcend politics by recourse to morality, markets or law, the inequalities of our time call for the reinvigoration of political contestation over ends. Only a political struggle against those institutions, governments and corporations that have promoted and benefited from the inequality and 'economic powerlessness' of the neoliberal age can open a horizon of freedom for all.[30] A break with neoliberalism requires a break with the morals of the market.

---

30   Makau Mutua, 'Human Rights and Powerlessness: Pathologies of Choice and Substance Essay Collection: Classcrits: Part I: Thinking through Law's Questions of Class, Economics, and Inequality', *Buffalo Law Review* 56 (2008).

Acknowledgements

This book is the product of many years spent thinking about the stakes of political appeals to humanity. Much of that thinking has been done with others, in seminars and reading groups, and over coffees or long dinners with friends.

I owe special debts to all those who read draft chapters: Jon Piccini, Liz Humphrys, Glenda Sluga, Umut Özsu, Julia Dehm, Nick Heron, Jon Symons, Peter Hallward, Anna Yeatman, Dimitris Vardoulakis and Ihab Shalbak.

I am very fortunate to be part of a number of intellectual communities that have provided spaces for thinking through difficult questions, refining clunky prose, and much else in between. For astute feedback on early drafts, I am grateful to the fabulous women of my Sydney research group – Clare Monagle, Zora Simic, Kate Fullager, Avril Alba, Francis Flanagan, Amanda Third, Amanda Kearney and Baylee Britts. In the later stages, my colleagues on the editorial collective of the journal *Humanity* have been stimulating and generous companions in the quest to understand the politics of 'humanity', and provided incisive feedback on a late draft of Chapter 3; my sincere thanks to Toby Kelly, Ayça Çubukçu, Vasuki Nesiah, Angela Naimou and Timothy Nunan.

The writing of this book coincided almost entirely with my time at Western Sydney University, and numerous colleagues helped to provide the stimulating environment in which it was written. Special thanks to Mark Kelly, Ben Etherington, George Morgan, Cristina Rocha, Alana

Lentin, Penny Rossiter, Anna Pertierra, David Burchell, Dimitris Vardoulakis, Margarite Poulos, John Hadley, Paul Alberts and Alex Ling for discussions that have shaped my thinking in numerous ways. Two people must be singled out: this book owes an enormous amount to an ongoing conversation with Anna Yeatman and Charles Barbour, and to the very different ways in which they each embody all that a politically engaged intellectual should be.

My students at Western Sydney University also profoundly influenced the thinking that went into this book. The multiple opportunities I had to teach the course 'Human Rights and Culture' to diverse groups of students, many of whom had migrated from countries that had experienced the harder edge of 'humanitarian interventions', made an enormous difference to my attempts to think through the complex politics of universalism and intervention. I also learnt much from those who taught with me on this course as we grappled with these questions together: many thanks to Michael Karadjis, Omid Tofighian and Hermann Ruiz-Salgado.

Many other friends and colleagues helped me to think more clearly about the questions at stake in this book – or gave me welcome respite from thinking about it. As well as those already mentioned above, my thanks are due to Ben Golder, Daniel McLoughlin, Ian Hunter, Ben Graham, Danielle Celermajer, Dirk Moses, Natasha Wheatley, Simon Lumsden, Jo Faulkner, Kiran Grewal, Dieter Plewhe, James Martel, Jeannie Morefield, Illan Wall, Joey Slaughter, Ntina Tzouvala, Allison Weir, Nick Kompridis, Sam Moyn, Justin Clemens, Adam Bartlett, Bryan Cooke, Sonja van Wichelen, Ellen Roberts, Alison Ross, Amir Ahmadi, Bruce Buchan, Dave Trudinger, John Cleary, Knox Peden, Andrea Maksimovic, Damien Lawson, Sarah Roberts and Craig McGregor.

Over many years, I have learnt much from exchanging both writing and ideas with five women who, as well as having sharp minds, have also been wonderful and supportive friends. Love and thanks to Vicki Sentas, Eve Vincent, Tanya Serisier, Liz Humphrys, and Charlotte Epstein.

I am very grateful to Petro Alexiou and Eleni Pitsilioni-Alexiou, both for their friendship and for providing a temporary home and writing retreat while I finalised the manuscript.

Late in the drafting, I benefited immensely from the superb research assistance of Alejandra Gaitán Barrera. Alejandra read the manuscript with a sharp eye, an extraordinary attention to detail and a courageous political sensibility. This book is significantly better for her efforts.

My thanks to Sebastian Budgen at Verso, to the anonymous reader for helpful critical suggestions, to Charles Peyton and Duncan Ranslem for their excellent work on the manuscript, and to Melissa Weiss for her fabulous work on the cover.

I would also like to thank Rony Brauman and Claude Malhuret for generously agreeing to meet with me and share their reflections on Liberté sans Frontières and French humanitarianism in the 1980s.

An earlier version of Chapter 5 was previously published in *Radical Philosophy* 2.02 as 'Powerless Companions or Fellow Travellers? Human Rights and the Neoliberal Assault on Post-Colonial Economic Justice'. Research for this book was supported by the award of an Australian Research Council DECRA award (DE160100473).

My family have been enduring sources of love and care. My brothers, Joe and Nick Whyte, continue to inspire me, and I am grateful to Brian Derum and Anne Johnson for all their support over the years. I am also very grateful to the Shalbaks for welcoming me into their family, and for their extraordinary hospitality and grace. Conversations with Areej and Naya have also helped me consider the way that human rights travel, and given me new perspectives on what we hold in common.

I owe the greatest debt to Ihab Shalbak. Ihab read numerous drafts, and his intellectual generosity and deep appreciation for the politics of scholarship made each chapter better than it would otherwise have been. He did far more to make this book possible than I can express here, and each page has been profoundly enriched by years of conversations with him. So too has my life.

Bibliography

Commission on Human Rights

'Summary Record of the Fourteenth Meeting of the Commission on Human Rights', 4 February 1947, in William A. Schabas, ed., *The Universal Declaration of Human Rights: The Travaux Préparatoires, Universal Declaration of Human Rights* (Cambridge: Cambridge University Press, 2013), vol. 1.

'Commission on Human Rights Verbatim Record Fourteenth Meeting [Excerpt]', in *The Eleanor Roosevelt Papers, I: The Human Rights Years, 1945–1948*, Charlottesville: The University of Virginia Press, 2010.

'Summary Record of the Seventy-First Meeting of the Commission on Human Rights', 14 June 1948, in Schabas, *Universal Declaration of Human Rights*, vol. 2.

'Summary Record of the Seventy-Seventh Meeting of the Commission on Human Rights' in Schabas, Universal Declaration of Human Rights, vol. 2.

'Summary Record of the One Hundred and Twenty Ninth Meeting of the Commission on Human Rights' (Lake Success: United Nations Economic and Social Council, 27 June 1949), at uvallsc.s3.amazonaws.com.

Commission on Human Rights Drafting Committee

'Summary Record of the Third Meeting of the Drafting Committee of the Commission on Human Rights', 11 June 1947, in Schabas, ed., *The Universal Declaration of Human Rights*, Vol. 1

United Nations General Assembly Third Committee

'Summary Record of the Ninety-First Meeting of the Third Committee', 2 October 1948, in Schabas, *The Universal Declaration of Human Rights*, vol. 3.

'Summary Record of the Hundred and Twenty-Seventh Meeting of the Third Committee', 9 November 1948, in Schabas, *The Universal Declaration of Human Rights*, vol. 3.

'Summary Record of the Hundred and Thirty- Eighth Meeting of the Third Committee', 15 November 1948, in Schabas, *Universal Declaration of Human Rights*, vol. 3.

'Summary Record of the Two Hundred and Ninety Fourth Meeting of the Third Committee', 26 October 1950, at hr-travaux.law.virginia.edu
'Summary Record of the Two Hundred and Ninety Fifth Meeting of the Third Committee of the United Nations General Assembly', 27 October 1950), at hr-travaux.law.virginia.edu/document/iccpr/ac3sr295/nid-1845.
'Summary Record of the Two Hundred and Ninety Sixth Meeting of the Third Committee of the United Nations General Assembly', (27 October 1950), at hr-travaux.law.virginia.edu.

United Nations General Assembly
'Verbatim Record of the Hundred and Eightieth Plenary Meeting of the General Assembly', 9 December 1948, in Schabas, *Universal Declaration of Human Rights*, vol.3.
'Verbatim Record of the Hundred and Eighty-Second Plenary Meeting of the United Nations General Assembly', 10 December 1948, in Schabas, *Universal Declaration of Human Rights*, vol. 3.
'Verbatim Record of the Hundred and Eighty-Third Plenary Meeting of the United Nations General Assembly', 10 December 1948, in Schabas, *Universal Declaration of Human Rights*, vol. 3.
'Official Record of the 1496th Plenary Meeting of the United Nations General Assembly', 16 December 1966, p. 11, at undocs.org.

Division of Human Rights
Division of Human Rights, 'Textual Comparison of the Draft International Bill of Human Rights submitted by the Delegation of the United Kingdom to the Drafting Committee of the Commission on Human Rights, and the Draft Outline of an International Bill of Rights' in Schabas, *The Universal Declaration of Human Rights*, vol.1.
'United States Proposals Regarding an International Bill of Rights', 28 January 1947, in Schabas, *Universal Declaration of Human Rights*, vol. 1.

United Nations Documents
United Nations General Assembly, 'International Bill of Human Rights: A Universal Declaration of Human Rights' (10 December 1948), in Schabas, *Universal Declaration of Human Rights*, vol. 3.
United Nations General Assembly, 'International Covenant on Economic, Social and Cultural Rights' (United Nations Human Rights Office of the High Commissioner, 16 December 1966), at ohchr.org.
United Nations General Assembly, 'Permanent Sovereignty over Natural Resources, General Assembly Resolution 1803 (XVII)', 14 December 1962, at legal.un.org.
United Nations General Assembly, 'Declaration on the Establishment of a New International Economic Order' (United Nations Documents, 1 May 1974), at un-documents.net.

General Bibliography
Acton, H. B. *The Morals of Markets: An Ethical Exploration*. Longman and the Institute of Economic Affairs, 1971.

'After the Coup in Cairo'. *The Wall Street Journal*, 7 July 2013, sec. Review & Outlook.

Allawi, Ali A. *The Crisis of Islamic Civilization*. New Haven: Yale University Press, 2009.

Allende, Salvador. 'First Speech to the Chilean Parliament'. Marxists Internet Archive, 1970.

———. 'Address to the Third UN Conference on Trade and Development (UNCTAD)'. In *Salvador Allende Reader*, edited by James D. Cockcroft. Brighton: Ocean Press, 2000.

Alston, Philip. 'U.S. Ratification of the Covenant on Economic, Social and Cultural Rights: The Need for an Entirely New Strategy'. *American Journal of International Law* 84, no. 2 (April 1990): 365–93.

———. ' "Report of the Special Rapporteur on Extreme Poverty and Human Rights" ', 27 May 2015.

———. 'Phantom Rights: The Systemic Marginalization of Economic and Social Rights'. OpenGlobalRights, 2016, at <openglobalrights.org/phantom-rights-systemic-marginalization-of-economic-and-social-rights>.

———. 'Extreme Inequality as the Antithesis of Human Rights; OpenGlobalRights'. Accessed 2 July 2018, at <openglobalrights.org/extremeinequality-as-the-antithesis-of-human-rights>.

Americas Watch Committee. *Chile: Human Rights & the Plebiscite*. New York: Americas Watch Committee, 1988.

Amnesty International. *Chile: An Amnesty International Report*. London: Amnesty International Publications, 1974.

———. *Amnesty International Annual Report 1974/75*. London: Amnesty International Publications, 1975.

———. *Disappeared Prisoners in Chile*. London: Amnesty International Publications, 1977.

———. 'Human Rights and Human Dignity: A Primer on Social and Economic Rights'. Accessed 2 July 2018, at <amnesty.org>.

Anderson, Carol, and Carol Elaine Anderson. *Eyes Off the Prize: The United Nations and the African American Struggle for Human Rights, 1944–1955*. Cambridge University Press, 2003.

Anghie, Antony. 'Civilization and Commerce: The Concept of Governance in Historical Perspective'. *Villanova Law Review* 45, no. 5 (2000): 887–912.

———. *Imperialism, Sovereignty and the Making of International Law*. Cambridge: Cambridge University Press, 2004.

———. 'Whose Utopia? Human Rights, Development, and the Third World'. *Qui Parle* 22, no. 1 (2013): 63–80.

Arendt, Hannah. *The Origins of Totalitarianism*. San Diego: Harcourt Brace and Co., 1976.

———. *On Revolution*. London: Penguin Books, 1990.

———. *The Human Condition*. Chicago: The University of Chicago Press, 1998.

Aron, Raymond. 'Sociology and the Philosophy of Human Rights'. In *Power, Modernity and Sociology: Selected Sociological Writings*, edited by Dominique Schnapper and Milton Karl Munitz, 194–210. Aldershot: Edward Elgar, 1988.

Arthur, Paige. *Unfinished Projects: Decolonization and the Philosophy of Jean-Paul Sartre*. London: Verso, 2010.

Asad, Talal. 'What Do Human Rights Do? An Anthropological Enquiry'. *Theory and Event* 4, no. 4 (2000).

———. *On Suicide Bombing*. New York: Columbia University Press, 2007.

Asian-African Conference. 'Final Communiqué of the Asian-African Conference of Bandung'. Djakarta: Centre Virtuel de la Connaissance sur l'Europe, 24 April 1955.

Atria, Fernando. 'The Time of Law: Human Rights Between Law and Politics'. *Law and Critique* 16, no. 2 (2005): 137–59.

Bair, Jennifer. 'Taking Aim at the New International Economic Order'. In *The Road from Mont Pèlerin: The Making of the Neoliberal Thought Collective*, edited by Philip Mirowski and Dieter Plehwe, 347–85. Cambridge: Harvard University Press, 2009.

Balibar, Étienne. *Masses, Classes, Ideas: Studies on Politics and Philosophy Before and After Marx*. Translated by James Swenson. New York: Routledge, 1994.

———. ' "Rights of Man" and "Rights of the Citizen" '. In *Masses, Classes, Ideas: Studies on Philosophy and Politics Before and After Marx*. London: Routledge, 1994.

Bankovsky, Miriam. 'Alfred Marshall's Household Economics: The Role of the Family in Cultivating an Ethical Capitalism'. *Cambridge Journal of Economics*. Accessed 27 December 2018, <doi.org/10.1093/cje/bey003>.

Baroody, Jamil M. 'Economic Problems of the Arab East'. In *Problems of the Middle East*, 1–3. New York, 1947.

Bauer, Peter, 'Western Guilt & Third World Poverty'. *Commentary Magazine* (blog). Accessed 27 June 2018, at <commentarymagazine.com/articles/western-guilt-third-world-poverty>.

———. 'Hostility to the Market in Less Developed Countries'. In *The First World and the Third World: Essays on the New International Economic Order*, edited by Karl Brunner. Rochester: University of Rochester Policy Center Publications, 1978.

———. 'Letter to Commentary on Moynihan Article'. In *The First World and the Third World*, edited by Karl Brunner, 139–47. Rochester: University of Rochester Policy Center Publications, 1978.

———. *Equality, the Third World, and Economic Delusion*. London: Methuen, 1981.

———. 'L'Aide Au Développement: Pour Ou Contre?' In *Le Tiers-Mondisme En Question*, edited by Rony Brauman. Paris: Olivier Orban, 1986.

———. *From Subsistence to Exchange and Other Essays*. Princeton: Princeton University Press, 2000.

Bauer, Peter, and John O'Sullivan. 'Ordering the World About: The New International Economic Order'. *Policy Review*, Summer 1977, 55–70.

Bauer, Peter, and Basil Yamey. *The Economics of Under-Developed Countries*. Cambridge: Cambridge University Press, 1972.

———. 'World Wealth Redistribution: Anatomy of the New Order'. In *The First World & the Third World: Essays on the New International Economic Order*, edited by Karl Brunner, 191–219. Rochester: University of Rochester Policy Center Publications, 1978.

———. 'Black Africa: The Living Legacy of Dying Colonialism'. *North & South*, 1984.

Baxi, Upendra. *The Future of Human Rights*. Oxford: Oxford University Press, 2008.

Becker, Gary S. *A Treatise on the Family*. Cambridge: Harvard University Press, 1991.

Bedjaoui, Mohammed. *Towards a New International Economic Order*. New York: Holmes & Meier Publishers, 1979.

Beitz, Charles R. *The Idea of Human Rights*. Oxford: Oxford University Press, 2011.

Berger, Mark T. 'After the Third World: History, Destiny and the Fate of Third Worldism'. *Third World Quarterly* 25, no. 1 (2004): 9–39.

Berman, Paul. *Power and the Idealists: Or, the Passion of Joschka Fischer and Its Aftermath*. New York: W. W. Norton & Company, 2007.

Beveridge, William. 'Social Insurance and Allied Services'. Inter-departmental Committee on Social Insurance and Allied Services, 1942.

Binet, Laurence. 'Famine and Forced Relocations in Ethiopia 1984–1986'. MSF Speaks Out. Geneva: Médecins Sans Frontières, 2013, at <speakingout.msf.org/en/famine-and-forced-relocations-in-ethiopia>.

———, ed. 'Médecins Sans Frontières Officials Issue an Indictment, Calling Tiers-Mondisme a Sham, Patrick Forestier Interviews Rony Brauman, President of MSF France, Paris-Match (France), 23 January 1985 (in French)'. In *Famine and Forced Relocations in Ethiopia 1984-1986*, 24–25. MSF Speaks Out. Geneva: Médecins Sans Frontières, 2013.

Black, Allida, ed. 'Memorandum of Conversation: Eleanor Roosevelt Marjorie Whiteman to Ernest Gross and Jack Tate'. In *The Eleanor Roosevelt Papers*, I: The Human Rights Years, 1945–1948: 709–11. Charlottesville: The University of Virginia Press, 2010.

———, ed. 'On Lovett and Social and Economic Rights: Memorandum of Conversation with Eleanor Roosevelt'. In *The Eleanor Roosevelt Papers*, I: The Human Rights Years, 1945–1948: 754–56. Charlottesville: The University of Virginia Press, 2010.

Blaue, Judith, and Alberto Moncado. *Human Rights: A Primer*. Paradigm Publishers, 2009.

Boas, Taylor C., and Jordan Gans-Morse. 'From Rallying Cry to Whipping Boy: The Concept of Neoliberalism in the Study of Development', 1–48. Philadelphia, 2006.

Bobbio, Norberto. *Liberalism and Democracy*. London: Verso, 2005.

Booth, Robert, and Owen Bowcott. 'Where Do We Stand a Year after the Grenfell Tower Fire?' *The Guardian*, 14 June 2018, sec. UK news.

Borzutzky, Silvia. *Human Rights Policies in Chile: The Unfinished Struggle for Truth and Justice*. New York: Palgrave Macmillan, 2017.

Bowden, Brett, and Leonard Seabrooke. 'Introduction'. In *Global Standards of Market Civilization*, 1–16. London: Routledge, 2006.

Brandt, Karl. 'Liberal Alternatives in Western Policies Toward Colonial Areas', 1–13. St. Moritz: Hoover Institution Archives, 1957.

Brauman, Rony. 'Tiers-Mondisme: Les Intentions et Les Résultats'. *Le Monde Diplomatique*, November 1985.

———. 'Ni Tiers-Mondisme, Ni Cartiérisme'. In *Le Tiers-Mondisme En Question*, 11–19. Paris: Olivier Orban, 1986.

Brooks, Roger A. 'The United Nations at 40: Myth and Reality'. The Heritage Foundation, 9 August 1985, at <heritage.org/report/the-united-nations-40-myth -and-reality>.

Brown, Wendy. '"The Most We Can Hope For . . .": Human Rights and the Politics of Fatalism'. *The South Atlantic Quarterly* 103, no. 2 (10 June 2004): 451–63.

———. 'American Nightmare: Neoliberalism, Neoconservatism, and De-Democratization'. *Political Theory* 34, no. 6 (2006): 690–714.

———. *Undoing the Demos: Neoliberalism's Stealth Revolution*. MIT Press, 2015.

Bruckner, Pascal. *The Tears of the White Man: Compassion as Contempt*. New York: Palgrave Macmillan, 1987.

———. *An Imaginary Racism: Islamophobia and Guilt*. Cambridge: Polity, 2018.

Bryson, Valerie. 'Feminism Between the Wars'. In *Contemporary Political Ideologies*, edited by Roger Eatwell and Anthony Wright, 211–28. London: Continuum, 1999.

Buchanan, James M. 'Democracy: Limited or Unlimited?', 1–14. Viña del Mar: Center for Study of Public Choice, 1981.

Buchanan, Tom. '"The Truth Will Set You Free": The Making of Amnesty International'. *Journal of Contemporary History* 37, no. 4 (2002): 575–97.

Buchman, Frank N. D. *Remaking the World*. London: Blandford Press, 1958.

Burgin, Angus. *The Great Persuasion: Reinventing Free Markets since the Depression*. Cambridge: Harvard University Press, 2012.

Burke, Edmund. *The Writings and Speeches of Edmund Burke, Vol. 5: India: Madras and Bengal: 1774–1785: 1774–1785*, edited by P. J. Marshall and William B. Todd. Oxford University Press, 1981.

———. 'Miscellaneous Writings'. In *Select Works of Edmund Burke*, edited by E.J. Payne, Vol. 4. Indianapolis: Liberty Fund.

Burke, Roland. *Decolonization and the Evolution of International Human Rights*. Philadelphia: University of Pennsylvania Press, 2010.

Caldwell, Bruce, and Leonidas Montes. 'Friedrich Hayek and His Visits to Chile'. *The Review of Austrian Economics* 28, no. 3 (2015): 261–309.

'Cecil Rhodes's Great Speech'. *The Examiner*. 13 November 1900.

Centre for Economic and Social Rights. 'Home'. Accessed 31 December 2018, at <www.cesr.org>.

Césaire, Aimé. *Discourse on Colonialism*. Translated by Joan Pinkham. New York: Monthly Review Press, 1972.

Chen, Yifeng. 'The International Labour Organisation and Labour Governance in China 1919-1949'. In *China and ILO Fundamental Principles and Rights at Work*, edited by Roger Blanpain, 19–54. Alphen aan den Rijn: Kluwer Law International, 2014.

Chimni, B. S. 'Anti-Imperialism'. In *Bandung, Global History, and International Law: Critical Pasts and Pending Futures*, edited by Luis Eslava, Michael Fakhri, and Vasuki Nesiah, 35–48. Cambridge: Cambridge University Press, 2017.

Clavin, Patricia. *Securing the World Economy: The Reinvention of the League of Nations, 1920–1946*. Oxford: Oxford University Press, 2013.

———. 'What's in a Living Standard? Bringing Society and Economy Together in the ILO and the League of Nations Depression Delegation, 1938-1945'. In *Globalizing Social Rights: The International Labour Organization and Beyond*, edited by Sandrine Kott and Joëlle Droux, 233–48. New York: Palgrave Macmillan, 2013.

Constable, Pamela, and Arturo Valenzuela. *A Nation of Enemies: Chile under Pinochet*. New York: W. W. Norton & Company, 1993.

Cooper, Frederick. 'Modernizing Bureaucrats, Backward Africans, and the Development Concept'. In *International Development and the Social Sciences: Essays on the History and Politics of Knowledge*, edited by Randall M. Packard, 64–92. Berkeley: University of California Press, 1997.

———. *Decolonization and African Society: The Labor Question in French and British Africa*. Cambridge: Cambridge University Press, 2010.

Cooper, Melinda. *Family Values: Between Neoliberalism and the New Social Conservatism*. New York: Zone Books, 2017.

Couso, Javier. 'The Limits of Law for Emancipation (in the South)'. *Griffith Law Review* 16, no. 2 (2007): 330–52.

———. 'Models of Democracy and Models of Constitutionalism: The Case of Chile's Constitutional Court, 1970-2010'. *Texas Law Review* 89, no. 7 (2011): 1517–36.

Creswell, Robyn. 'Tradition and Translation: Poetic Modernism in Beirut'. Doctor of Philosophy, Department of Comparative Literature, New York University, 2012.

———. *City of Beginnings: Poetic Modernism in Beirut*. Princeton and Oxford: Princeton University Press, 2019.

Cristi, Renato. 'The Metaphysics of Constituent Power: Schmitt and the Genesis of Chile's 1980 Constitution'. *Cardoso Law Review* 21, no. 5-6 (2000): 1749–76.

———. 'The Genealogy of Jaime Guzmán's Subsidiary State'. In *Hayek: A Collaborative Biography, Part IX: The Divine Right of the 'Free' Market*, edited by Robert Leeson, 249–62. London: Palgrave Macmillan, 2017.

Cristi, Renato, and Carlos Ruiz. 'Conservative Thought in Twentieth Century Chile'. *Canadian Association of Latin American and Caribbean Studies* 15, no. 30 (1990): 27–66.

Daniels, Anthony. 'Peter Bauer and the Third World'. *Cato Journal* 25, no. 3 (2005): 483–88.

Davey, Eleanor. 'Famine, Aid, and Ideology: The Political Activism of Médecins sans Frontières in the 1980s'. *French Historical Studies* 34, no. 3 (2011): 529–58.

———. *Idealism Beyond Borders: The French Revolutionary Left and the Rise of Humanitarianism, 1954-1988*. Cambridge: Cambridge University Press, 2015.

Davis, Mike. *Late Victorian Holocausts: El Niño Famines and the Making of the Third World*. London: Verso, 2001.

De Grazia, Victoria. *Irresistible Empire: America's Advance through Twentieth-Century Europe*. Cambridge: The Belknap Press of Harvard University Press, 2005.

Dean, Mitchell. 'Rethinking Neoliberalism'. *Journal of Sociology* 50, no. 2 (2012): 150–63.

———. 'Michel Foucault's "Apology" for Neoliberalism'. *Journal of Political Power* 7, no. 3 (2 September 2014): 433–42.

DeGooyer, Stephanie, Alastair Hunt, Lida Maxwell, Samuel Moyn, and Astra Taylor. *The Right to Have Rights*. London: Verso, 2018.

Dekker, Erwin. 'Left Luggage: Finding the Relevant Context of Austrian Economics'. *The Review of Austrian Economics* 29, no. 2 (2016): 103–19.

Díaz, Ramón P. 'Capitalism and Freedom in Latin America'. In *Freedom, Democracy and Economic Welfare: Proceedings of an International Symposium*, edited by Michael A. Walker, 245–69. Vancouver: The Fraser Institute, 1988.

Dirlik, Arif. 'Spectres of the Third World: Global Modernity and the End of the Three Worlds'. *Third World Quarterly* 25, no. 1 (February 2004): 131–48.

Donnelly, Jack. 'Human Rights: A New Standard of Civilization?' *International Affairs* 74, no. 1 (January 1998): 1–23.

Douzinas, Costas. 'Seven Theses on Human Rights: (3) Neoliberal Capitalism & Voluntary Imperialism'. *Critical Legal Thinking* (blog), 23 May 2013, at <critical-legalthinking.com>.

Durham, Martin, and Margaret Power. 'Transnational Conservatism: The New Right, Neoconservatism, and Cold War Anti-Communism'. In *New Perspectives on the Transnational Right*, edited by Martin Durham and Margaret Power, 133–48. New York: Palgrave Macmillan, 2010.

Ebeling, Richard M. 'Introduction'. In *Monetary and Economic Policy Problems Before, During, and After the Great War*, xv–lxix. Indianapolis: Liberty Fund, 2012.

———. 'Mises the Man and His Monetary Policy Ideas Based on His "Lost Papers"'. *Mises Wire*, 7 April 2018.

Ebenstein, Alan. *Hayek's Journey: The Mind of Friedrich Hayek*. New York: Palgrave Macmillan, 2003.

Eckel, Jan. 'Under a Magnifying Glass'. In *Human Rights in History*, edited by Stefan-Ludwig Hoffman, 321–42. Cambridge: Cambridge University Press, 2010.

Estaing, Edmond Giscard d'. 'Libéralisme et Colonialisme', 1–4. St. Moritz: Hoover Institution Archives, 1957.

Eucken, Walter. *The Foundations of Economics: History and Theory in the Analysis of Economic Reality*. Translated by T.W. Hutchison. Berlin: Springer-Verlag, 1992.

Farrant, Andrew, and Edward McPhail. 'Can a Dictator Turn a Constitution into a Can-Opener? F. A. Hayek and the Alchemy of Transitional Dictatorship in Chile'. *Review of Political Economy* 26, no. 3 (2014): 331–48.

Farrant, Andrew, Edward McPhail, and Sebastian Berger. 'Preventing the "Abuses" of Democracy: Hayek, the "Military Usurper" and Transitional Dictatorship in Chile?' *American Journal of Economics and Sociology* 71, no. 3 (2012): 513–38.

Ferguson, Adam. *An Essay on the History of Civil Society*. Edited by Fania Oz-Salzberger. Cambridge: Cambridge University Press, 2001.

Finkelstein, Daniel. 'Tories Should Embrace the Human Rights Act'. The Times. Accessed 2 July 2018, at <thetimes.co.uk>.

Fischer, Karin. 'The Influence of Neoliberals in Chile before, during, and after Pinochet'. In *The Road from Mont Pèlerin: The Making of the Neoliberal Thought Collective*, edited by Philip Mirowski and Dieter Plehwe, 305–46. Cambridge: Harvard University Press, 2009.

Foucault, Michel. *The History of Sexuality Vol.1*. New York: Pantheon Books, 1990.

———. *The Birth of Biopolitics: Lectures at the Collège de France 1978–1979*. Edited by Michel Senellart. Translated by Graham Burchell. New York: Palgrave Macmillan, 2008.

Fox, Renée C. *Doctors Without Borders: Humanitarian Quests, Impossible Dreams of Médecins Sans Frontières*. Baltimore: John Hopkins University Press, 2014.

Frantz, Fanon. 'First Truths on the Colonial Problem'. In *Toward the African Revolution*, translated by Haakon Chevalier, 120–26. New York: Grove Press, 1967.

——. *The Wretched of the Earth*. London: Penguin, 1978.

Fraser, Nancy, and Linda Gordon. ' "Dependency" Demystified: Inscriptions of Power in a Keyword of the Welfare State'. *Social Politics* 1, no. 1 (1994): 4–31.

Freud, Sigmund. *Civilization and Its Discontents*. New York: W. W. Norton & Company, 2017.

Friedman, Milton. 'Neo-Liberalism and Its Prospects'. *Farmand*, 17 February 1951.

——. 'Inflation'. 9th Mont Pèlerin Society Meeting, Princeton: Hoover Institution Archives, 1958, Box 12, Folder 6.

——. 'A Statistical Note on the Gastil-Wright Survey of Freedom: Discussion'. In *Freedom, Democracy and Economic Welfare: Proceedings of an International Symposium*, edited by Michael A. Walker, 126–48. Vancouver: The Fraser Institute, 1988.

——. Commanding Heights: Milton Friedman. Public Broadcasting Service, 1 October 2000.

——. *Capitalism and Freedom*. Chicago: The University of Chicago Press, 2002.

——. 'Essay Fifteen: The Counter-Revolution in Monetary Theory'. In *The Indispensable Milton Friedman: Essays on Politics and Economics*, edited by Lanny Ebenstein, 167–89. Washington D.C.: Regnery Publishing, 2012.

——. 'Essay Four: Adam Smith's Relevance for 1976'. In *The Indispensable Milton Friedman: Essays on Politics and Economics*, edited by Lanny Ebenstein, 37–52. Washington, DC: Regnery Publishing, 2012.

——. *Money Mischief: Episodes in Monetary History*. New York: Harcourt Brace & Company, 1994.

——. 'Passing down the Chilean Recipe'. *Foreign Affairs* 73, no. 1 (1994): 177–78.

Friedman, Milton, and Rose D. Friedman. *Free to Choose: A Personal Statement*. New York: Harcourt Brace Jovanovich, 1980.

——. *Two Lucky People: Memoirs*. Chicago: The University of Chicago Press, 1998.

——. 'Appendix A, Chapter 24 (Chile): Documents'. In *Two Lucky People: Memoirs*, 591–602. Chicago: The University of Chicago Press, 1998.

——. 'Appendix B, Chapter 28 (Free to Choose): Documents'. In *Two Lucky People: Memoirs*, edited by Milton Friedman and Rose D. Friedman, 603–6. Chicago: The University of Chicago Press, 1998.

Gaitán-Barrera, Alejandra, and Govand Khalid Azeez. 'Beyond Recognition: Autonomy, the State, and the Mapuche Coordinadora Arauco Malleco'. *Latin American and Caribbean Ethnic Studies* 13, no. 2 (2018): 113–34.

Gane, Nicholas. 'In and Out of Neoliberalism: Reconsidering the Sociology of Raymond Aron'. *Journal of Classical Sociology* 16, no. 3 (2016): 261–79.

Gasset, José Ortega y. *The Revolt of the Masses*. London: Unwin Books, 1969.

Gerig, Benjamin. *The Open Door and the Mandates System: A Study of Economic Equality before and since the Establishment of the Mandates System*. London: George Allen & Unwin Ltd., 1930.

Gilley, Bruce. 'The Case for Colonialism'. *Third World Quarterly*, 2017.

Gilman, Nils. 'The New International Economic Order: A Reintroduction'. *Humanity: An International Journal of Human Rights, Humanitarianism, and Development* 6, no. 1 (2015): 1–16.

Giovannetti, Justin. 'World Leaders Need to Tackle Rise of Extremism, Hillary Clinton Says -'. *The Globe and Mail*, 21 January 2015.

Glendon, Mary Ann. 'The Influence of Catholic Social Doctrine on Human Rights'. In *15th Plenary Session*, 67–82. Vatican City: The Pontifical Academy of Social Sciences, 2010.

Glucksmann, Andre. 'The 2004 TIME 100 – Bernard Kouchner'. *Time Magazine*, April 26, 2014.

Goldberg, Peter A. 'The Politics of the Allende Overthrow in Chile'. *Political Science Quarterly* 90, no. 1 (1975): 93–116.

Golder, Ben. *Foucault and the Politics of Rights*. Stanford University Press, 2015.

Goldschmidt, Nils. 'Walter Eucken's Place in the History of Ideas'. *The Review of Austrian Economics* 26, no. 2 (2013): 127–47.

Gong, Gerrit W. *The Standard of 'Civilization' in International Society*. Oxford: Clarendon Press, 1984.

Goodhart, Michael E., ed. *Human Rights: Politics and Practice*. Third edition. Oxford and New York: Oxford University Press, 2016.

Grede, William. J. 'Moral Effects of the Welfare State'. 9th Mont Pèlerin Society Meeting, Princeton: Hoover Institution Archives, 1958, Box 12, Folder 6.

Grelet, Stany, and Mathieu Potte-Bonneville. 'Qu'est-Ce Qu'on Fait Là ? Entretien Avec Rony Brauman'. *Vacarme*, 2 September 1997.

Gresh, Alain. 'Une Fondation Au-Dessus de Tout Soupçon'. *Le Monde Diplomatique*, May 1985.

Grewal, Kiran Kaur. *The Socio-Political Practice of Human Rights: Between the Universal and the Particular*, Abingdon: Routledge, 2017.

Gunder Frank, Andre. 'Economic Genocide in Chile: Open Letter to Milton Friedman and Arnold Harberger'. *Economic and Political Weekly* 11, no. 24 (1976): 880–88.

Gupta, Partha Sarathi. *Imperialism and the British Labour Movement, 1914–1964*. London: The Macmillan Press Ltd., 1975.

Hacking, Ian. *The Taming of Chance*. Cambridge: Cambridge University Press, 2010.

Hagenbuch, Walter. 'The Welfare State and Social Policy'. 9th Mont Pèlerin Society meeting, Princeton: Hoover Institution Archives, 1958, Box 12, Folder 5.

Hallward, Peter. 'The Will of the People: Notes towards a Dialectical Voluntarism'. *Radical Philosophy*, no. 155 (June 2009): 17–29.

———. 'Fanon and Political Will'. *Cosmos and History: The Journal of Natural and Social Philosophy* 7, no. 1 (2011): 104–27.

Hans-Hermann, Hoppe. 'Why Mises (and Not Hayek)?' *The Mises Daily*, 4 October 2011.

Harberger, Arnold. 'Capitalism and Freedom in Latin America: Discussion'. In *Freedom, Democracy and Economic Welfare: Proceedings of an International Symposium*, edited by Michael A. Walker, 271–74. Vancouver: The Fraser Institute, 1988.

———. 'Secrets of Success: A Handful of Heroes'. *The American Economic Review* 83, no. 2: Papers and Proceedings of the Hundred and Fifth Annual Meeting of the American Economic Association (1993): 343–50.

———. 'Good Economics Comes to Latin America, 1955–95'. *History of Political Economy* 28, no. supplement (1996): 301–11.

———. Commanding Heights: Arnold 'Al' Harberger. Public Broadcasting Service, 3 October 2000.

Harcourt, Bernard E. *The Illusion of Free Markets: Punishment and the Myth of Natural Order*. Cambridge: Harvard University Press, 2010.

Harmer, Tanya. *Allende's Chile and the Inter-American Cold War*. Chapel Hill: The University of North Carolina Press, 2011.

Harrison, Peter. 'Adam Smith and the History of the Invisible Hand'. *Journal of the History of Ideas* 72, no. 1 (2011): 29–49.

Hartman, Saidiya V. *Scenes of Subjection: Terror, Slavery, and Self-Making in Nineteenth-Century America*. Oxford: Oxford University Press, 1997.

Hayek, Friedrich. 'Memorandum on the Proposed Foundation of an International Academy of Political Philosophy Tentatively Called the "Acton-Tocqueville Society"'. Albert Hunold Papers, 1 August 1945.

——. 'The Use of Knowledge in Society'. *The American Economic Review* 35, no. 4 (1945): 519–30.

——. 'Individualism: True and False'. In *Individualism and Economic Order*, 1–32. Chicago: The University of Chicago Press, 1958.

——. 'The Moral Element in Free Enterprise', *The Freeman*, July 1962.

——. 'Opening Address to a Conference at Mont Pèlerin'. In *Studies in Philosophy, Politics and Economics*, 148–59. Chicago: The University of Chicago Press, 1967.

——. *Studies in Philosophy, Politics and Economics*. Chicago: The University of Chicago Press, 1967.

——. 'The Confusion of Language in Political Thought'. *Institute of Economic Affairs*, Occasional Papers, no. 20 (1968): 9–36.

——. Noble Prize-Winning Economist Interviewed by Thomas Hazlett, 12 November 1978. Oral History Program, UCLA.

——. 'Liberty Clean of Impurities Extracts from an Interview with Friedrich von Hayek'. *El Mercurio*. 12 April 1981.

——. 'Cosmos and Taxis'. In *Law, Legislation and Liberty: A New Statement of the Liberal Principles of Justice and Political Economy*, I: Rules and Order: n35–54. London: Routledge, 1998.

———. 'Epilogue: The Three Sources of Human Values'. In *Law, Legislation and Liberty: A New Statement of the Liberal Principles of Justice and Political Economy*, 3: The Political Order of a Free People: 196–208. London: Routledge, 1998.

——. 'Justice and Individual Rights: Appendix to Chapter Nine'. In *Law, Legislation and Liberty: A New Statement of the Liberal Principles of Justice and Political Economy*, 2: The Mirage of Social Justice: 101–6. London: Routledge, 1998.

——. *Law, Legislation and Liberty: A New Statement of the Liberal Principles of Justice and Political Economy*. Vol. I: Rules and Order. London: Routledge, 1998.

——, ed. *Law, Legislation and Liberty: A New Statement of the Liberal Principles of Justice and Political Economy*. Vol. II: The Mirage of Social Justice. London: Routledge, 1998.

——. *Law, Legislation and Liberty: A New Statement of the Liberal Principles of Justice and Political Economy*. Vol. III: The Political Order of a Free People. London: Routledge, 1998.

——. 'Notes: Chapter Ten: The Market Order or Catallaxy'. In *Law, Legislation and Liberty: A New Statement of the Liberal Principles of Justice and Political Economy*, 2: The Mirage of Social Justice: 184–89. London: Routledge, 1998.

------. 'The Discipline of Abstract Rules and the Emotions of the Tribal Society'. In *Law, Legislation and Liberty: A New Statement of the Liberal Principles of Justice and Political Economy*, 133–52. London: Routledge, 1998.

------. 'Foreword to the 1956 American Paperback Edition'. In *The Road to Serfdom: Texts and Documents*, edited by Bruce Caldwell, II: 39–52. The Collected Works of F. A. Hayek. Chicago: The University of Chicago Press, 2007.

------. *The Road to Serfdom: Text and Documents*. Edited by Bruce Caldwell. The Collected Works of F. A. Hayek. Chicago: The University of Chicago Press, 2007.

------. '"Conscious" Direction and the Growth of Reason'. In *The Collected Works of F. A. Hayek: Studies on the Abuse and Decline of Reason*, 13: 149–55. Chicago: The University of Chicago Press, 2010.

------. *The Constitution of Liberty: The Definitive Edition*. Edited by Ronald Hamowy. Chicago: The University of Chicago Press, 2011.

Hayek, Friedrich, Earlene Craver, Pacific Academy of Advanced Studies, and Los Angeles Oral History Program University of California. *Nobel Prize-Winning Economist Oral History Transcript*. Los Angeles: Oral History Program, University of California, Los Angeles, 1983.

Henkin, Louis. 'The United States and the Crisis in Human Rights Symposium: Human Rights and United States Foreign Policy'. *Virginia Journal of International Law* 14 (1973–4): 653–72.

Hill, Mike, and Warren Montag. *The Other Adam Smith*. Stanford University Press, 2014.

Hirschman, Albert O. *The Essential Hirschman*. Edited by Jeremy Adelman. Princeton: Princeton University Press, 2013.

------. *The Passions and the Interests: Political Arguments for Capitalism before Its Triumph*. Princeton: Princeton University Press, 2013.

Hobson, J. A. 'The Ethics of Internationalism (1906-7)'. In *Writings on Imperialism and Internationalism (Routledge Revivals)*, edited by Peter Cain. Abingdon: Routledge, 2013.

------. *Imperialism: A Study*. New York: Cosimo Classics, 2005.

Holbik, Karel. 'The Tasks and Problems of Marxism in Chile's Economy'. *Journal of Institutional and Theoretical Economics* 129, no. 2 (1973): 333–46.

Hon. Government Junta, Augusto Pinochet Ugarte, Sergio Fernández Fernández, and Mónica Gutierrez Madariaga. Constitution of the Republic of Chile, Pub. L. No. 1150 (1980), at <confinder.richmond.edu/admin/docs/Chile.pdf>.

Hopgood, Stephen. *The Endtimes of Human Rights*. Cornell University Press, 2015.

Horne, Alistair. *A Savage War of Peace: Algeria 1954-1962*. New York Review of Books, 2011.

Horvath, Robert. '"The Solzhenitsyn Effect": East European Dissidents and the Demise of the Revolutionary Privilege'. *Human Rights Quarterly* 29, no. 4 (2007): 879–907.

Howson, Susan. *Lionel Robbins*. Cambridge: Cambridge University Press, 2011.

Hülsmann, Jörg Guido. *Mises: The Last Knight of Liberalism*. Auburn: Ludwig von Mises Institute, 2007.

Human Rights Watch. 'Frequently Asked Questions'. Human Rights Watch, 24 September 2008, at <hrw.org/frequently-asked-questions>.

------. 'About Us'. Human Rights Watch, 21 April 2015, at <hrw.org/about>.

------. 'World Report 2018'. New York: Human Rights Watch, 2017.

Hunold, Albert. 'Preface'. In *Freedom and Serfdom: An Anthology of Western Thought*, edited by Albert Hunold, 7–9. Dordrecht: D. Reidel Publishing Company, 1961.

Hunt, Lynn. *Inventing Human Rights: A History*. New York: W. W. Norton & Company, 2007.

Hunter, Ian. 'Spatialisations of Justice in the Law of Nature and Nations: Pufendorf, Vattel and Kant'. Unpublished Draft Paper, n.d.

Ibhawoh, Bonny. 'Structural Adjustment, Authoritarianism and Human Rights in Africa'. *Comparative Studies of South Asia, Africa and the Middle East* xix, no. 1 (1999): 158–67.

Inter-American Juridical Committee. 'Draft Declaration of the International Rights and Duties of Man'. Rio de Janeiro: United Nations Economic and Social Council, 8 January 1947.

International Commission on Intervention and State Sovereignty. 'The Responsibility to Protect: Research, Bibliography, Background. Supplementary Volume to the Report of the International Commission on Intervention and State Sovereignty'. Ottawa: International Development Research Centre, 2001.

International Labour Organization. Constitution of the International Labour Organization (ILO) (1919).

——. 'Family Allowances: The Remuneration of Labour According to Need'. Series D (Wages and Hours). Geneva, 1924.

'Interview with Milton Friedman; Federal Reserve Bank of Minneapolis'. Accessed 2 July 2018, at <minneapolisfed.org/publications/the-region/interview-with-milton-friedman>.

'J. A. Hobson: Imperialism (Introductory)'. Accessed 28 December 2018, at <marxists.org/archive/hobson/1902/imperialism/intro.htm>.

James M. Buchanan. *Theory of Public Choice: Political Applications of Economics*. Ann Arbor: University of Michigan Press, 1972.

Jensen, Steven L. B. *The Making of International Human Rights: The 1960s, Decolonization, and the Reconstruction of Global Values*. Cambridge: Cambridge University Press, 2016.

Jouvenel, Bertrand de. 'Broodings on the Welfare State'. 9th Mont Pèlerin Society Meeting, Princeton: Hoover Institution Archives, 1958, Box 12, Folder 5.

Jouvenel, Bertrand de. *On Power: Its Nature and the History of Its Growth*. Boston: Beacon Press, 1962.

Judson, Pieter M. *The Habsburg Empire*. Harvard: Harvard University Press, 2016.

Julien, Claude. 'Une Bête à Abattre : Le "Tiers-Mondisme"'. *Le Monde Diplomatique*, May 1985.

Kaufman, Edy. 'Prisoners of Conscience: The Shaping of a New Human Rights Concept'. *Human Rights Quarterly* 13, no. 3 (1991): 339–67.

Kelly, Patrick William. 'The 1973 Chilean Coup and the Origins of Transnational Human Rights Activism'. *Journal of Global History* 8 (2013): 165–86.

Kelly, Tobias. 'A Divided Conscience'. *Public Culture* 30, no. 3 (1 September 2018): 367–92.

Kinley, David. *Civilising Globalisation: Human Rights and the Global Economy*. Cambridge and New York: Cambridge University Press, 2009.

Klein, Naomi. *The Shock Doctrine: The Rise of Disaster Capitalism*. New York: Picador, 2008.

Knight, Sam. 'The Year the Grenfell Tower Fire Revealed the Lie That Londoners Tell Themselves'. *The New Yorker*, 27 December 2017.

Knox, Robert. 'Valuing Race? Stretched Marxism and the Logic of Imperialism'. *London Review of International Law* 4, no. 1 (2016): 81–126.

Kobrin, Stephen J. 'Expropriation as an Attempt to Control Foreign Firms in LDCs: Trends from 1960 to 1979'. *International Studies Quarterly* 28, no. 3 (1984): 329–48.

Kollontai, Alexandra. 'Communism and the Family'. *The Worker*, 1920.

Koskenniemi, Martti. *The Gentle Civilizer of Nations: The Rise and Fall of International Law 1870-1960.* Hersch Lauterpacht Memorial Lectures. Cambridge: Cambridge University Press, 2004.

———. 'Race, Hierarchy and International Law: Lorimer's Legal Science'. *The European Journal of International Law* 27, no. 2 (2016): 415–29.

Lamy, Pascal. 'Lamy Calls for Mindset Change to Align Trade and Human Rights'. Accessed 31 December 2018, at <wto.org/english/news_e/sppl_e/sppl146_e. htm>.

Larrain, Jorge. 'Changes in Chilean Identity: Thirty Years after the Military Coup'. *Nations and Nationalism* 12, no. 2 (2006): 321–38.

Laski, Harold J. *The Rise of European Liberalism (Works of Harold J. Laski): An Essay in Interpretation.* Abingdon: Routledge, 2015.

Lauren, Paul Gordon. *The Evolution of International Human Rights: Visions Seen.* Philadelphia: University of Pennsylvania Press, 2011.

League of Nations. 'The Covenant of the League of Nations (Including Amendments Adopted to December, 1924)'. The Avalon Project, Yale Law School, 1924.

Lefebvre, Alexandre. *Human Rights and the Care of the Self.* London: Duke University Press, 2018.

Lefort, Claude. *The Political Forms of Modern Society: Bureaucracy, Democracy, Totalitarianism.* Edited by John B. Thompson. Cambridge: Polity Press, 1986.

Lenin, Vladimir I. 'Preface to the French and German Editions'. In *Imperialism, the Highest Stage of Capitalism*, 7–14. Rough Draft Printing, 2014.

Lenin, Vladimir Ilich. 'Imperialism: The Highest Stage of Capitalism'. In *Revolution, Democracy, Socialism: Selected Writings*, edited by Paul Le Blanc. Pluto, 2008.

Letelier, Orlando. 'Economic "Freedom's" Awful Toll; The "Chicago Boys" in Chile'. *Review of Radical Political Economics* 8, no. 3 (1976): 44–52.

Lewis, Paul. 'Peter Bauer, British Economist, Is Dead at 86'. *The New York Times.* 14 May 2002, sec. Business Day.

Liberal International. 'Oxford Manifesto', 1947.

Liberté Sans Frontières. 'Fondation Liberté Sans Frontières Pour l'information Sur Les Droits de l'homme et Le Développement, Document de Présentation'. Paris: Médecins Sans Frontières, January 1985.

Liberté Sans Frontières, and Claude Malhuret. 'Invitation de Liberté sans Frontières Au Colloque Des 23 et 24 Janvier 1985'. Médecins Sans Frontières, 11 January 1985.

Lindkvist, Linde. *Religious Freedom and the Universal Declaration of Human Rights.* Cambridge University Press, 2017.

Lippmann, Walter. *The Good Society.* London: Billing and Sons Ltd., 1943.

Liu, Lydia He. *The Clash of Empires.* Harvard University Press, 2004.

Locke, John. *Two Treatises of Government and A Letter Concerning Toleration.* Edited by Ian Shapiro. New Haven: Yale University Press, 2003.

Lorimer, James. *The Institutes of Law: A Treatise of the Principles of Jurisprudence as Determined by Nature.* Edinburgh: T. & T. Law Publishers, 1872.

Losurdo, Domenico. *Liberalism: A Counter-History.* London: Verso, 2011.

MacLean, Nancy. *Democracy in Chains: The Deep History of the Radical Right's Stealth Plan for America.* New York: Penguin Books, 2017.

Malik, Charles. 'Human Rights and Religious Liberty'. *The Ecumenical Review* 1, no. 4 (1949): 404–9.

———. 'Human Rights in the United Nations'. *International Journal* 6, no. 4 (1951): 275–80.

———. 'The Near East: The Search for Truth'. *Foreign Affairs* 30, no. 2 (1952): 231–64.

———. 'The Relations of East and West'. *Proceedings of the American Philosophical Society* 97, no. 1 (1953): 1–7.

———. 'Some Reflections on Technical and Economic Assistance'. *Bulletin of the Atomic Scientists* X, no. 3 (1954): 93–96.

———. 'Call to Action in the Near East', *Foreign Affairs,* 34:4 (1956).

Mandela, Nelson. *The Historic Speech of Nelson Rolihlahla Mandela at the Rivonia Trial: As Delivered from the Dock on April 20, 1964.* Learn & Teach Publications, 1988.

Mantena, Karuna. *Alibis of Empire: Henry Maine and the Ends of Liberal Imperialism.* Princeton: Princeton University Press, 2010.

Marks, Susan. 'False Contingency'. *Current Legal Problems* 62, no. 1 (1 January 2009): 1–21.

———. 'Human Rights and Root Causes: Human Rights and Root Causes'. *The Modern Law Review* 74, no. 1 (January 2011): 57–78.

Marx, Karl. *Capital: A Critique of Political Economy.* Translated by Ben Fowkes. V. 1: Penguin Classics. London ; New York, N.Y: Penguin Books in association with *New Left Review*, 1981.

———. 'Critique of the Gotha Program'. In *Selected Writings*, edited by Lawrence H. Simon. Indianapolis: Hackett Publishing, 1984.

———. 'On the Jewish Question'. In *Early Writings*, New Ed edition. London: Penguin, 2000.

Marx, Karl, and Friedrich Engels. *The Communist Manifesto.* London: Pluto Press, 2008.

Masala, Antonio. 'Wilhelm Röpke and Alexander Rüstow in Turkey: A Missed Legacy?' Yildiz Technical University, 2016.

Mazower, Mark. 'The End of Civilization and the Rise of Human Rights'. In *Human Rights in the Twentieth Century*, edited by Stefan-Ludwig Hoffman, 29–44. Cambridge: Cambridge University Press, 2010.

———. *Governing the World: The History of an Idea, 1815 to the Present.* London: Penguin, 2012.

Mbembe, Achille. *On the Postcolony.* Studies on the History of Society and Culture 41. Berkeley: University of California Press, 2001.

McCloskey, Deirdre. *The Bourgeois Virtues: Ethics for an Age of Commerce.* Chicago: The University of Chicago Press, 2006.

Meyer, Justus. 'The Concept of Colonialism'. Stanford: Hoover Institution Archives, 1957, 15, Box 11, Folder 2.

Michael. Ignatieff. *Human Rights as Politics and Idolatry*. University Center for Human Values Series. Princeton, N.J.: Princeton University Press, 2001.

Mill, John Stuart. 'Considerations on Representative Government'. In *Essays on Politics and Society*, edited by J.M. Robson, 371–578. Toronto: University of Toronto Press, 1977.

———. *On Liberty*. Indianapolis: Hackett Publishing, 1978.

Mills, Charles W. *White Ignorance*. Oxford: Oxford University Press, 2017.

Mirowski, Philip, and Dieter Plehwe, eds. *The Road from Mont Pèlerin: The Making of the Neoliberal Thought Collective*. Cambridge: Harvard University Press, 2009.

Mises, Ludwig von. *Socialism: An Economic and Sociological Analysis*. Translated by J. Kahane. New Haven: Yale University Press, 1962.

———. *Human Action: A Treatise on Economics*. San Francisco: Fox & Wilkes, 1996.

———. *Liberalism: The Classical Tradition*. Edited by Bettina Bien Greaves. Translated by Ralph Raico. Indianapolis: Liberty Fund, 2005.

———. *Marxism Unmasked: From Delusion to Destruction*. Irvington: Foundation for Economic Education, 2006.

———. 'On the History of German Democracy'. In *Nation, State, and Economy*, edited by Bettina Bien Greaves, translated by Leland B. Yeager, 80–109. Indianapolis: Liberty Fund, 2006.

———. *Theory and History: An Interpretation of Social and Economic Evolution*. Auburn: Ludwig von Mises Institute, 2007.

———. *The Anti-Capitalistic Mentality*. Auburn: Ludwig von Mises Institute, 2008.

———. 'Observations on Professor Hayek's Plan'. *Libertarian Papers* 1, no. 2 (2009): 1–3.

———. *Omnipotent Government: The Rise of the Total State & Total War*. Auburn: Ludwig von Mises Institute, 2010.

———. *Economic Calculation in the Socialist Commonwealth*. Translated by S. Adler. Auburn: Ludwig von Mises Institute, 2012.

Mitchell, Timothy. *Colonising Egypt*. Berkeley: University of California Press, 1991.

Mitoma, Glenn. 'Charles H. Malik and Human Rights: Notes on a Biography'. *Biography* 33, no. 1 (12 June 2010): 222–41.

Moffitt, Michael. 'Chicago Economics in Chile'. *Challenge* 20, no. 4 (1977): 34–43.

Montecinos, Verónica. 'Economics: The Chilean Story'. In *Economists in the Americas*, edited by Verónica Montecinos and John Markoff, 142–94. Cheltenham: Edward Elgar, 2009.

Montesquieu, Baron de. *The Spirit of the Laws*. Cambridge: Cambridge University Press, 1989.

Morefield, Jeanne. *Empires Without Imperialism: Anglo-American Decline and the Politics of Deflection*. Oxford: Oxford University Press, 2014.

Morley, Morris, and Chris McGillion. *Reagan and Pinochet*. Cambridge University Press, 2015.

Morsink, Johannes. *The Universal Declaration of Human Rights: Origins, Drafting, and Intent*. Pennsylvania Studies in Human Rights. Philadelphia: University of Pennsylvania Press, 1999.

———. *The Universal Declaration of Human Rights: Origins, Drafting, and Intent*. Philadelphia: University of Pennsylvania Press, 1999.

Moyn, Samuel. *The Last Utopia: Human Rights in History*. Cambridge: The Belknap Press of Harvard University Press, 2010.

——. 'A Powerless Companion: Human Rights in the Age of Neoliberalism'. *Law and Contemporary Problems* 77 (2015): 147–69.

——. *Christian Human Rights*. Philadelphia: University of Pennsylvania Press, 2015.

——. *Not Enough: Human Rights in an Unequal World*. Cambridge: Harvard University Press, 2018.

Moynihan, Daniel P. 'The United States in Opposition'. *Commentary*, 1 March 1975.

Mutua, Makau. *Human Rights: A Political and Cultural Critique*. Philadelphia: University of Pennsylvania Press, 2002.

——. 'Human Rights and Powerlessness: Pathologies of Choice and Substance Essay Collection: Classcrits: Part I: Thinking through Law's Questions of Class, Economics, and Inequality'. *Buffalo Law Review* 56 (2008): 1027–34.

Myrdal, Gunnar. *An International Economy: Problems and Prospects*. New York: Harper & Brothers, 1956.

——. *The Political Element in the Development of Economic Theory*. Translated by Paul Streeten. London: Routledge, 2002.

Nasser, Gamal Abdul. 'Speech Announcing the Nationalization of the Suez Canal Company', 26 July 1956.

Neier, Aryeh. 'Social and Economic Rights: A Critique'. *Human Rights Brief* 13, no. 2 (2006): 1–3.

——. *The International Human Rights Movement: A History*. Princeton: Princeton University Press, 2012.

Nkrumah, Kwame. *Neo-Colonialism: The Last Stage of Imperialism*. New York: International Publishers, 1966.

O'Connell, Paul. 'On Reconciling Irreconcilables: Neo-Liberal Globalisation and Human Rights'. *Human Rights Law Review* 7, no. 3 (1 January 2007): 483–509.

——. 'On the Human Rights Question'. *Human Rights Quarterly* 40, no. 4 (2018): 962–88.

Ogle, Vanessa. 'State Rights against Private Capital: The "New International Economic Order" and the Struggle over Aid, Trade, and Foreign Investment, 1962–1981'. *Humanity: An International Journal of Human Rights, Humanitarianism, and Development* 5, no. 2 (2014): 211–34.

'OHCHR; Statement on Visit to the USA, by Professor Philip Alston, United Nations Special Rapporteur on Extreme Poverty and Human Rights'. Accessed 2 July 2018, at <ohchr.org>.

Okafor, Obiora Chinedu. 'The Bandung Ethic and International Human Rights Praxis: Yesterday, Today, and Tomorrow'. In *Bandung, Global History, and International Law: Critical Pasts and Pending Futures*, edited by Michael Fakhri, Vasuki Nesiah, and Luis Eslava. New York: Cambridge University Press, 2017, 518–19.

'Open Letter to Third World Quarterly on the Publication of "The Case for Colonialism"'. openDemocracy, 20 September 2017, at <opendemocracy.net>.

Orford, Anne. *International Authority and the Responsibility to Protect*. Cambridge University Press, 2011.

Organisation for Economic Co-operation and Development. 'Income Inequality Update', November 2016, at <oecd.org/social/OECD2016-Income-Inequality-Update.pdf>.

Ortega y Gasset, José. *The Revolt of the Masses*, London: Unwin Books, 1969.

Owens, Patricia. *Economy of Force: Counterinsurgency and the Historical Rise of the Social.* Cambridge: Cambridge University Press, 2015.

Özsu, Umut. '"In the Interests of Mankind as a Whole": Mohammed Bedjaoui's New International Economic Order'. *Humanity: An International Journal of Human Rights, Humanitarianism, and Development* 6, no. 1 (2015): 129–43.

———. 'Neoliberalism and the New International Economic Order: A History of "Contemporary Legal Thought"'. In *Searching for Contemporary Legal Thought*, edited by Christopher Tomlins and Justin Desautels-Stein, 330–47. Cambridge: Cambridge University Press, 2017.

———. '"Let Us First of All Have Unity among Us": Bandung, International Law, and the Empty Politics of Solidarity'. In *Bandung, Global History, and International Law: Critical Pasts and Pending Futures*, edited by Michael Fakhri, Vasuki Nesiah, and Luis Eslava. New York: Cambridge University Press, 2017.

Pahuja, Sundhya. *Decolonising International Law: Development, Economic Growth, and the Politics of Universality.* Cambridge: Cambridge University Press, 2011.

Pedersen, Susan. *Family, Dependence, and the Origins of the Welfare State: Britain and France, 1914–1945.* New York: Cambridge University Press, 1993.

———. *The Guardians: The League of Nations and the Crisis of Empire.* Oxford University Press, 2015.

Pernet, Corinne A. 'Developing Nutritional Standards and Food Policy: Latin American Reformers between the ILO, the League of Nations Health Organization, and the Pan-American Sanitary Bureau'. In *Globalizing Social Rights: The International Labour Organization and Beyond*, edited by Sandrine Kott and Joëlle Droux, 249–61. New York: Palgrave Macmillan, 2013.

Perugini, Nicola, and Neve Gordon. *The Human Right to Dominate.* Oxford Studies in Culture and Politics. Oxford, New York: Oxford University Press, 2015.

Petersmann, Ernst-Ulrich. 'Time for a United Nations "Global Compact" for Integrating Human Rights into the Law of Worldwide Organizations: Lessons from European Integration'. *European Journal of International Law* 13, no. 3 (1 April 2002): 621–50.

Piñera, José. 'Chile's Road to Freedom'. *José Piñera* (blog), 11 March 2018, at <josepinera.org>.

Pipes, Daniel. 'The Rise of Western Civilisationism'. *The Australian*, 14 April 2018.

Pitts, Jennifer. *A Turn to Empire: The Rise of Imperial Liberalism in Britain and France.* Princeton: Princeton University Press, 2005.

Plant, Roger. 'Life under Pinochet'. Amnesty International Canada, 14 August 2013, at <amnesty.ca/blog/life-under-pinochet-roger-plant-remembers>.

Plehwe, Dieter. 'Introduction'. In *The Road from Mont Pèlerin: The Making of the Neoliberal Thought Collective*, edited by Philip Mirowski and Dieter Plehwe, 1–42. Cambridge: Harvard University Press, 2009.

———. 'The Origins of the Neoliberal Economic Development Discourse'. In *The Road from Mont Pèlerin: The Making of the Neoliberal Thought Collective*, edited by Philip Mirowski and Dieter Plehwe, 238–79. Cambridge: Harvard University Press, 2009.

Pollis, Adamantia and Peter Schwab. 'Human Rights: A Western Construct with Limited Applicability'. In *Human Rights: Cultural and Ideological Perspectives*, edited by Adamantia Pollis and Peter Schwab, 1–18. New York; London: Praeger, 1980.

Posner, Eric. *The Twilight of Human Rights Law*. Oxford University Press, 2014.

Prasad, Monica. *The Politics of Free Markets*. Chicago: University of Chicago Press, 2006.

Prashad, Vijay. *The Darker Nations: A People's History of the Third World*. New York: The New Press, 2007.

———. *The Poorer Nations: A Possible History of the Global South*. London: Verso, 2013.

Radha D'Souza. *What's Wrong with Rights?: Social Movements, Law and Liberal Imaginations*. London, Pluto Press, 2018.

Rancière, Jacques. *On the Shores of Politics*. London: Verso, 2006.

Rappard, William. 'The Practical Working of the Mandates System'. *Journal of the British Institute of International Affairs* 4, no. 5 (1925): 205–26.

———. 'Foreword'. In *The Open Door and the Mandates System: A Study of Economic Equality before and since the Establishment of the Mandates System*, edited by Benjamin Gerig, 10–14. London: George Allen & Unwin Ltd., 1930.

———. 'Human Rights in Mandated Territories'. *The Annals of the American Academy of Political and Social Science* 243, no. 1 (1946): 118–23.

———. 'The Mandates and the International Trusteeship Systems'. *Political Science Quarterly* 61, no. 3 (1946): 408–19.

———. 'Opening Address to the Mont Pèlerin Society'. Mont Pèlerin: Hoover Institution Archives, 1947.

———. 'On Reading von Mises'. In *On Freedom and Free Enterprise: Essays in Honor of Ludwig von Mises*, edited by Mary Sennholz, 17–33. Auburn: Ludwig von Mises Institute, 2008.

Rappard, William. 'The Relation of the Individual to the State'. *The Annals of the American Academy of Political and Social Science* 189, no. 1 (1937): 215–18.

Read, Leonard E. 'Leonard E. Read Journal – August 1957'. Foundation for Economic Education, 1957, at <history.fee.org/leonard-read-journal/1957/leonard-e-read-journal-august-1957>.

Reagan, Ronald. 'President Reagan's 1986 State of the Union Address'. U.S. House of Representatives, 4 February 1986.

Reed, Adolph Jr. 'Marx, Race, and Neoliberalism'. *New Labor Forum* 22, no. 1 (2013): 49–57.

Reinhoudt, Jurgen, and Serge Audier, eds. *The Walter Lippmann Colloquium: The Birth of Neo-Liberalism*. London: Palgrave Macmillan, 2018.

Reuff, Jacques. 'Inflation and Liberty'. 9th Mont Pèlerin Society Meeting, Princeton: Hoover Institution Archives, 1958, 1, Box 12, Folder 5–6.

Robbins, Lionel. *The Economic Causes of War*. New York: Howard Fertig, 1968.

Robertson, H. M. *Aspects of the Rise of Economic Individualism: A Criticism of Max Weber and his School*. New York: Kelly and Milliman, 1959.

Rodrigues, João. 'The Political and Moral Economies of Neoliberalism: Mises and Hayek'. *Cambridge Journal of Economics* 37, no. 5 (1 September 2013): 1001–17.

Roediger, David R. *The Wages of Whiteness: Race and the Making of the American Working Class*. London: Verso, 2007.

Roosevelt, Eleanor. *On My Own*. New York: Harper, 1958.

Roosevelt, Franklin D. 'Campaign Address at Detroit, Michigan'. Edited by Gerhard Peters and John T. Woolley. The American Presidency Project, 1932.

Röpke, Wilhelm. *International Economic Disintegration*. London: William Hodge and Company, Limited, 1942.

———. *The Social Crisis of Our Time*. Translated by Annette Schiffer Jacobsohn and Peter Schiffer Jacobsohn. Chicago: The University of Chicago Press, 1950.

———. 'Economic Order and International Law'. *Receueil Des Cours*, 1954.

———. 'Liberalism and Christianity'. *Modern Age* 1, no. 2 (1957): 128–34.

———. 'Discussion on the Welfare State'. 9th Mont Pèlerin Society Meeting, Princeton: Hoover Institution Archives, 1958, Box 12, Folder 6.

———. *International Order and Economic Integration*. Dordrecht: D. Reidel Publishing Company, 1959.

———. *A Humane Economy: The Social Framework of the Free Market*. Translated by Elizabeth Henderson. Chicago: The Institute for Philosophical and Historical Studies, 1961.

———. *Economics of the Free Society*. Translated by Patrick M. Boarman. Chicago: Henry Regnery Company, 1963.

———. 'Social-Cristianismo y Neo-Liberalismo'. *PEC*, no. 67, 68 (1964): 6–8, 2–3, 6.

———. *Against the Tide*. Auburn: Ludwig von Mises Institute, 1969.

———. *The Moral Foundations of Civil Society*. New Brunswick: Transaction Publishers, 2002.

Ross, Kristin. *May '68 and Its Afterlives*. Chicago: The University of Chicago Press, 2002.

Roth, Kenneth. 'Defending Social and Economic Rights'. In *International Human Rights*. Oxford: Oxford University Press, 2013.

Rougier, Louis. 'Address by Professor Louis Rougier'. In *The Walter Lippmann Colloquium: The Birth of Neo-Liberalism*, edited by Jurgen Reinhoudt and Serge Audier, 96–102. London: Palgrave Macmillan, 2018.

Ruskola, Teemu. *Legal Orientalism: China, the United States, and Modern Law*. Cambridge: Harvard University Press, 2013.

Rüstow, Alexander. 'Appendix'. In *International Economic Disintegration*, by Wilhelm Röpke, 267–83. London: William Hodge and Company, Limited, 1942.

———. 'Crossword Puzzle Moscow'. 7th MPS Meeting, Berlin: Hoover, Institution Archives, 1956, Box 7, Folder 12.

———. 'Human Rights or Human Duties?', 1–11. Kassel: Hoover Institution Archives, 1960.

———. 'Organic Policy (Vitalpolitik) versus Mass Regimentation'. In *Freedom and Serfdom: An Anthology of Western Thought*, edited by Albert Hunold, 171–90. Dordrecht: D. Reidel Publishing Company, 1961.

———. *Freedom and Domination: A Historical Critique of Civilization*. Edited by Dankwart A. Rüstow. Translated by Salvador Attanasio. Princeton: Princeton University Press, 1978.

Said, Edward W. *Out of Place: A Memoir*. New York: Alfred A. Knopf, 1999.

Salgado, Alfonso. 'Communism and Human Rights in Pinochet's Chile: The 1977 Hunger Strike Against Forced Disappearance'. *Cold War History* 18, no. 2 (2017): 169–86.

'Saudi Arabia's Engagement in, and Interaction with, the UN Human Rights System: An Analytical Review'. *The International Journal of Human Rights* 14, no 7.

Sauvy, Alfred. 'Trois Mondes, Une Planète'. *Vingtième Siècle, Revue d'histoire*, October 1986.

Schabas, William A., ed. *The Universal Declaration of Human Rights: The Travaux Préparatoires*. Cambridge: Cambridge University Press, 2013.

Schliesser, Eric. 'Friedman, Positive Economics, and the Chicago Boys'. In *The Elgar Companion to the Chicago School of Economics*, edited by Ross B. Emmett, 175–95. Cheltenham: Edward Elgar, 2010.

Schmitt, Carl. *The Concept of the Political*. Translated by George Schwab. Chicago: The University of Chicago Press, 1996.

———. *Political Theology: Four Chapters on the Concept of Sovereignty*. Edited by George Schwab. Chicago: The University of Chicago Press, 2005.

Schulak, Eugen Maria, and Herbert Unterköfler. *The Austrian School of Economics: A History of Its Ideas, Ambassadors, and Institutions*. Translated by Arlene Oost-Zinner. Auburn: Ludwig von Mises Institute, 2011.

Schumpeter, Joseph. *Imperialism and Social Classes*. Translated by Heinz Norden. New York: Meridian Books, 1966.

Shaw, Bernard, ed. *Fabianism and the Empire: A Manifesto by the Fabian Society*. London: Grant Richards, 1900.

Shenfield, Arthur. 'Liberalism and Colonialism'. *Foreign Policy Perspectives*, 1986.

Sieyès, Emmanuel. 'An Essay on Privileges'. In *Political Writings*, edited by Michael Sonenscher, 68–91. Indianapolis: Hackett Publishing, 2003.

———. 'What Is the Third Estate?' In *Political Writings*, edited by Michael Sonenscher, 92–162. Indianapolis: Hackett Publishing, 2003.

Sikkink, Kathryn. *Evidence for Hope: Making Human Rights Work in the 21st Century*. Princeton University Press, 2017.

Simpson, Brian A. W. *Human Rights and the End of Empire: Britain and the Genesis of the European Convention*. Oxford: Oxford University Press, 2004.

Simpson, Gerry. 'James Lorimer and the Character of Sovereigns: The Institutes as 21st Century Treatise'. *The European Journal of International Law* 27, no. 2 (2016): 431–46.

Slaughter, Joseph R. *Human Rights, Inc.: The World Novel, Narrative Form, and International Law*. New York: Fordham University Press, 2007.

———. 'Hijacking Human Rights: Neoliberalism, the New Historiography, and the End of the Third World'. *Human Rights Quarterly* 40, no. 4 (2018): 735–75.

Slobodian, Quinn. *Globalists: The End of Empire and the Birth of Neoliberalism*. Cambridge: Harvard University Press, 2018.

———. 'Neoliberalism's Populist Bastards'. *Public Seminar* (blog). Accessed 31 December 2018, at <publicseminar.org/2018/02/neoliberalisms-populist-bastards>.

Sluga, Glenda. 'René Cassin: Les Droits de l'homme and the Universality of Human Rights, 1945–1966'. In *Human Rights in the Twentieth Century*, edited by Stefan-Ludwig Hoffman, 107–24. Cambridge: Cambridge University Press, 2011.

———. *Internationalism in the Age of Nationalism*. Pennsylvania: University of Pennsylvania Press, 2013.

Smith, Mark B. 'Social Rights in the Soviet Dictatorship: The Constitutional Right to Welfare from Stalin to Brezhnev'. *Humanity: An International Journal of Human Rights, Humanitarianism, and Development* 3, no. 3 (2012): 385–406.

Soss, Joe, Richard C. Fording, and Sanford F. Schram. *Disciplining the Poor: Neoliberal Paternalism and the Persistent Power of Race*. Chicago: The University of Chicago Press, 2011.

Stahn, Carsten. *The Law and Practice of International Territorial Administration: Versailles to Iraq and Beyond*. Cambridge: Cambridge University Press, 2008.

Stanley, Brian. '"Commerce and Christianity": Providence Theory, the Missionary Movement, and the Imperialism of Free Trade, 1842–1860'. *The Historical Journal* 26, no. 1 (1983): 71–94.

Taylor, Marcus. *From Pinochet to the 'Third Way': Neoliberalism and Social Transformation in Chile*. London: Pluto Press, 2006.

The Mont Pèlerin Society. 'The Mont Pèlerin Quarterly'. *The Journal of the Mont Pèlerin Society* I, no. 1 (April 1959): 1–36.

Tilley, Lisa and Robbie Shilliam, 'Raced Markets: An Introduction', *New Political Economy* 23: 5 (2017), 534–43.

Tompkins Bates, Beth. *The Making of Black Detroit in the Age of Henry Ford*. Chapel Hill: University of North Carolina Press, 2013.

Tooze, Adam J. 'Who Is Afraid of Inflation? The Long-Shadow of the 1970s'. *Journal of Modern European History* 12, no. 1 (2014): 53–60.

Toscano, Alberto. *Fanaticism: On the Uses of an Idea*. Verso, 2010.

Traboulsi, Fawwaz. *A History of Modern Lebanon*. Pluto Press, 2007.

Trotsky, Leon. 'The Fabian "Theory" of Socialism'. In *Chapter IV: Trotsky's Writings on Britain*. London: New Park Publications, 1974.

Tzouvala, Ntina. 'Civilisation'. In *Concepts for International Law: Contributions to Disciplinary Thought*, edited by Jean d'Aspremont and Sahib Singh. Cheltenham: Edward Elgar, 2018.

'"Undeveloped Countries". Discussion on Two Papers Submitted by Peter Bauer to the 9th Meeting of the Mont Pèlerin Society, Princeton, September 1958'. In Albert Hunold ed., *Mont Pèlerin Quarterly*, 1:1 (April 1959), 5–26.

'US Envoy Nikki Haley Berates Human Rights Groups – BBC News'. Accessed 2 July 2018.

Valdés, Juan Gabriel. *Pinochet's Economists: The Chicago School in Chile*. Cambridge: Cambridge University Press, 1995.

Varouxakis, Georgios. 'The Godfather of "Occidentality": Auguste Comte and the Idea of "The West"'. *Modern Intellectual History*, October 2017, 1–31.

Vatter, Miguel. 'Christian Human Rights'. *Politics, Religion & Ideology* 17, no. 4 (2016): 447–53.

———. 'Neoliberalism and Republicanism: Economic Rule of Law and Law as Concrete Order (Nomos)'. In *The SAGE Handbook of Neoliberalism*, edited by Damien Cahill, Melinda Cooper, Martijn Konings, and David Primrose, 370–81. London: Sage Publications, 2018.

Vitalis, Robert. *America's Kingdom: Mythmaking on the Saudi Oil Frontier*. Stanford University Press, 2007.

Walker, Michael A. 'Preface'. In *Freedom, Democracy and Economic Welfare: Proceedings of an International Symposium*, edited by Michael A. Walker, ix–xvi. Vancouver: The Fraser Institute, 1988.

Weizman, Eyal. *The Least of All Possible Evils: Humanitarian Violence from Arendt to Gaza*. London: Verso, 2012.

Whately, Richard. 'Introductory Lectures on Political Economy'. Online Library of Liberty, 1831.

Wheaton, Henry. *Elements of International Law: With a Sketch of the History of the Science*. Philadelphia: Carey, Lea & Blanchard, 1836.

Whelan, Daniel J. ' "Under the Aegis of Man": The Right to Development and the Origins of the New International Economic Order'. *Humanity: An International Journal of Human Rights, Humanitarianism, and Development* 6, no. 1 (2015): 93–108.

Whiteside, Noel. 'The Beveridge Report and Its Implementation: A Revolutionary Project'. *Histoire@Politique* 3, no. 24 (2014): 24–37.

Whyte, Jessica. 'Human Rights: Confronting Governments? Michel Foucault and the Right to Intervene'. In *New Critical Legal Thinking: Law and the Political*, edited by Costas Douzinas, Matthew Stone, and Illan Rua Wall, 11–31. London: Routledge, 2012.

———. 'Is Revolution Desirable?: Michel Foucault on Revolution, Neoliberalism and Rights'. In *Re-Reading Foucault: On Law, Power and Rights*, edited by Ben Golder, 2012.

———. Interview with Rony Brauman, Rue Saint-Sabin, Paris 7 October 2015.

———. Interview with Claude Malhuret, Sénat, Palais du Luxembourg, Paris, 7 October, 2015.

———. 'The Invisible Hand of Friedrich Hayek: Submission and Spontaneous Order', *Political Theory* 47, no. 2 (2019), 194–202.

Williams, Randall. *The Divided World: Human Rights and Its Violence*. Minneapolis: University of Minnesota Press, 2010.

Yale Pines, Burton. 'The U.N. and the Free Enterprise System'. In *The U.N. Under Scrutiny*, 1–8. Washington D.C.: The Heritage Foundation, 1982.

Yeatman, Anna. 'Gender, Social Policy and the Idea of the Welfare State'. In *Gender and Social Policy*, edited by Sheila Shaver. Cheltenham: Edward Elgar, 2018.

Zhao, Jun. 'China and the Uneasy Case for Universal Human Rights'. *Human Rights Quarterly* 37, no. 1 (2015): 29–52.

Zivi, Karen. *Making Rights Claims: A Practice of Democratic Citizenship*. Oxford University Press, 2012.

Zweiniger-Bargielowska, Ina. 'Rationing, Austerity and the Conservative Party Recovery after 1945'. *The Historical Journal* 37, no. 1 (1994): 173–97.

Index